Francis Lieber and the Nineteenth-Century Copyright Debate

Law & Literature

Edited by

Daniela Carpi and Klaus Stierstorfer

VOLUME 27

Francis Lieber and the Nineteenth-Century Copyright Debate

Literature as Transnational Property in the USA

By

Fenja Rebecca Heisig

DE GRUYTER

Wissenschaftspreis 2026 der Osnabrücker Wissenschaftlichen Gesellschaft
Dissertation am Fachbereich Sprach- und Literaturwissenschaft der Universität Osnabrück

ISSN 2191-8457
ISBN 978-3-11-223939-1
ISBN 978-3-11-223940-7 (PDF)
ISBN 978-3-11-223941-4 (E-PUB)
DOI https://doi.org/10.1515/9783112239407

Library of Congress Control Number: 2026936130

Bibliographic information published by the Deutsche Nationalbibliothek
The Deutsche Nationalbibliothek lists this publication in the Deutsche Nationalbibliografie; detailed bibliographic data are available on the Internet at http://dnb.dnb.de.

De Gruyter and Walter de Gruyter GmbH are part of De Gruyter Brill.
www.degruyterbrill.com

Questions about General Product Safety Regulation: productsafety@degruyterbrill.com

Printing: CPI books GmbH, Leck

MIX
Papier | Fördert gute Waldnutzung
FSC® C083411

Contents

Acknowledgements

When I applied for a position as a doctoral candidate and research assistant at Osnabrück University back in 2020, I had no idea that I would spend the first years of my PhD mostly at home, working at my desk. It was a challenging time for research that thrives on exchange and discussion – and certainly not the ideal time to be writing a thesis. Given these circumstances, I am all the more grateful for the support I received throughout the writing process and for all the people who made it possible for me to bring this work to publication.

Firstly, I would like to thank my thesis advisor, Peter Schneck, without whom this work would not exist. He shared my nerdy fascination with all things Lieber – no matter how obscure the source – and gave me the opportunity to research, teach, and travel. Thank you to my *Osna Crew*, Cedric and Debora, for making Osnabrück feel like a second home and for all the advice and laughter – both of which were needed at times. I am also deeply grateful to my second thesis advisor, Nora Slonimsky, for engaging in discussions about the fine nuances of early copyright history, for generously sharing her insights and feedback, and most of all, for always believing in this project.

My heartfelt thanks go to Claudia Schnurmann, who recognized my potential before I did and offered me my very first position at a university ten years ago. She once told me that no nineteenth-century historian could escape Francis Lieber – and she was right. I am profoundly grateful for her ongoing support throughout the writing process and for all the Lieber anecdotes along the way. I would also like to thank Jan Kucharzewski, whose literary studies seminars were so engaging that they made me want to become a researcher myself. Many thanks as well to Nicole Waller for her valuable advice during my final year of writing and for offering me so many insights into academia.

I am grateful to the Deutsche Forschungsgesellschaft for funding my research, which allowed me to work alongside so many like-minded researchers and doctoral candidates at the Collaborative Research Center "Law and Literature," as well as to travel to the Huntington Library for archival research. Special thanks to Klaus Stierstorfer for making it possible for me to publish this thesis with De Gruyter Brill, and to both him and Daniela Carpi for giving me the opportunity to contribute to the *Law & Literature* series. I would also like to sincerely thank the Osnabrücker Wissenschaftliche Gesellschaft for honoring my dissertation with their Wissenschaftspreis 2026.

I owe special thanks to the archivists and library staff at the South Caroliniana Library and The Sheridan Libraries Special Collections for digitizing source materials and enabling me to conduct archival research from my desk

 | HTTPS://DOI.ORG/10.1515/9783112239407-203

during lockdowns. My gratitude also goes to the library staff at The Huntington, who helped me scan hundreds of sources in just three weeks – this work would not be the same without their support.

To my friends and family: Thank you for standing by me over these five years. I could not have done this without you. Thank you to Cynthia, Nathy, Öykü, and Nicole for listening to my endless PhD ramblings, for always believing in me, and for your encouraging words on the tough days. Many thanks to Nicole, Oliver, Bettina, Katja, Guido, and Noah for letting me escape into another world during weekend pen-and-paper sessions – I needed those breaks away from my desk. Thank you to Alan and Noah for showing me that finishing a thesis really is possible. I am also grateful to the Ü35 lunch crew – you made me believe I could actually write a thesis. A very special thanks goes to Julia, who spent countless hours co-working with me online, reading my drafts, and chatting about everything and nothing when we simply couldn't write another word. Our Thursday co-working sessions kept me going, and I'm not sure I would have finished without them.

Thank you to my mother-in-law, who believed in me fiercely from the moment we met, and to both my parents and my brother, who always had my back and never doubted that I would complete my doctorate – even when I did. I am forever grateful for your unwavering support. A special thank you to my mother, who was the very first person to read this entire work – more than once, in fact. And finally, thank you to Philipp – for everything. You are my rock.

CHAPTER 1

Introduction

When the research organization *OpenAI* first launched *ChatGPT* on November 30, 2022, the chatbot's ability to generate fully-formed original texts in response to user prompts sent shockwaves through numerous industries and ushered in the current artificial intelligence boom.[1] We encounter predictive artificial intelligence (AI) models in various different contexts today, such as transportation, finance, marketing, human resources, and telecommunication, and *ChatGPT* is merely the most prominent example. As a generative pre-trained transformer, *ChatGPT* is trained on massive data sets of myriad texts, taken from books, articles, and the web in general. Through these example texts, *ChatGPT* learns to predict the next morpheme in a word and the next word in a sentence. As a result of this process, the transformer gains the ability to generate complex texts in response to external prompts. Put simply, *ChatGPT* goes beyond copying and reassembling text blocks – it generates entirely new texts but does so on the basis of texts written by others. While *ChatGPT* learns and adapts, it does not create new knowledge. It can merely be trained to predict the most probable response on the basis of the data it has access to.

While artificial intelligence promises opportunities for many, such as improved medical services, scientific and technological progress, and the completion of tedious and time-consuming tasks, its ability to generate complex texts also raises many questions: How can such a powerful tool be used in a responsible manner? How can it be implemented in educational settings, the medical field, and the legal system? What do its abilities imply for innovation and research in science and the humanities? How can misuse such as cybercrime or election interference be prevented? How will "deepfakes" of photos, videos, and audio influence society's brittle relation to "the truth" in digital spaces? No easy answers exist, but one thing becomes abundantly clear: Artificial intelligence will revolutionize most industries and pose fundamental opportunities but also challenges to society at large. One area that is notably

1 ChatGPT stands for "Chat Generative Pre-trained Transformer" and refers to a chatbot that generates text based on a large language model and in response to user prompts. *OpenAI* developed *ChatGPT* with funding from Microsoft. After releasing a free-to-use version to the public in 2022, a premium service with additional features followed in 2023.

 | HTTPS://DOI.ORG/10.1515/9783112239407-001

affected by the changes large language models (LLM) like *ChatGPT* give rise to are the humanities, especially literary studies.

The ability of LLMs like *ChatGPT* to generate entirely new texts rather than simply copying and combining elements from other texts poses questions about the very foundations of the discipline: Is this process a form of writing, which implies the original creation of text? Is it plagiarism, since LLms assemble new texts without citing references? Is it stealing when the software uses texts available on the web, written by others – or is this the normal process of inspiration and creation? Who is the author of the texts LLMs create, and is the author also the owner of the text? Can a software be an author and what is the role of the person writing the prompt? Are the programmers of *ChatGPT* authors, or is *OpenAI*? Or are the authors of all the texts LLMs are trained on the actual authors of the resulting texts? Is it unethical that *OpenAI* profits financially from texts generated by using immense data sets the company does not own and has not created – and does this fall under fair use for educational purposes? Is it plagiarism if one claims authorship of a text an LLM wrote in response to a prompt? If it was, would the LLM be recognized as an author and a legal person – or is this an entirely new kind of offense? And who can be held responsible for the content of generated texts if they are hateful and discriminatory, spread misinformation or incite violence? As is becoming evident, LLMs challenge both existing legal norms and literary assumptions surrounding authorship, ownership, and copyright. It also reveals discrepancies between different legal systems globally in how they approach the regulation of copyright and AI content. This technological innovation touches on axioms already disputed between the fields of law and literature, questions of creativity and originality, of inspiration and innovation, and of infringement and ownership. As the influence of AI grows, it might fundamentally change the status of authorship in law and in society and, as Jessica Silbey points out, intellectual property law becomes "vital terrain over which fundamental values are being contested in light of twenty-first-century technological progress."[2]

1.1 Copyright in the Context of Cultural and Legal Adaptation Processes

Technological progress and its challenges to societal values, literary theory, and copyright law may appear to be new features of the rapidly developing

2 Jessica Silbey, *Against Progress. Intellectual Property and Fundamental Values in the Internet Age* (Stanford: Stanford UP, 2022), 4.

digital age, but arguably upheavals of a similar magnitude have occurred before: When the introduction of the printing press during the fifteenth century ushered in print as the first mass media, it slowly but surely revolutionized access to knowledge and innovation all over the globe. Books could be printed quickly and in large numbers and distributed both domestically and internationally. Since booksellers and authors could generate income through the sale of books, authorship was professionalized in the course of the following centuries. Consequently, an entirely new form of property gradually developed: The property in written works, today referred to more broadly as intellectual property. Whether and how to protect written works posed similar challenges to the law in subsequent centuries as the availability of texts in digital form via the web or the rapid generation of texts through predictive AI does today. Printing, like the digital revolution, constituted a legal caesura with long-term and wide-ranging implications for the law, which each jurisdiction approached differently.[3]

Continental-European jurisdictions gravitated towards protecting print literature by granting comprehensive authors' rights (*droit d'auteur*), while Great Britain and the US introduced copyright as a temporary monopoly on printing rights, offering an incentive for authors to publish their works for the benefit of society (see chapter 4). The question of protecting the interests of both authors and publishers became the central issue in the nineteenth century. Not only the method, but also the scope of protection differed between jurisdictions and the unauthorized reprinting of books – often called literary "piracy" by its opponents – became an issue for authors in England and Europe once the newly-founded US government refused to extend copyright protection to works by foreign authors. Instead of drafting international copyright legislation, the US government even encouraged the import and reprint of foreign works to encourage the progress of science and useful arts, to provide access to knowledge and information, and to further education. This contentious issue sparked lively transatlantic debates between countries in Europe,

3 For an overview of how print culture emerged in Europe following the invention of the printing press, see Elizabeth Eisenstein, *The Printing Revolution in Early Modern Europe* (Cambridge: Cambridge UP, 2005); Colin Clair, *A History of European Printing* (London/New York: Academic Press, 1976); and Lucien Febvre and Henri-Jean Martin, *The Coming of the Book. The Impact of Printing 1450– 1800* (London/New York: Verso, 1997). For an examination of early printing privileges in Venice, a printing hub during the Renaissance, see Christopher Witcombe, *Copyright in the Renaissance: Prints and the Privilegio in Sixteenth-Century Venice and Rome* (Leiden: Brill, 2004).

especially England, France and the German states, and the US.[4] While the discussion centered on the legal question of literary property and international copyright protection, it was actually about differences in fundamental values: The purpose and significance of literature, science and knowledge, the contribution of authors to education, democracy and nation-building, the importance of international knowledge exchange and cooperation, the nature of property and authorship, and the capacity and right of the law to protect intellectual creation.[5]

1.2 Research Niche

Scholarly research often juxtaposes Anglo-American copyright, a temporary monopoly that allows authors to generate revenue through the publication of their writing, with continental-European morality-based authors' rights to protect the integrity and control the distribution of their work. As Alain Strowel points out,

---

4 The historical and legal situation in Germany is relevant to this work and Francis Lieber discusses Germany frequently. The terminology used in this context is complicated by the political changes in Germany during the nineteenth century and needs further examination: Lieber was born in the Kingdom of Prussia, which was part of the Holy Roman Empire of the German Nation until its dissolution in 1806. During the Napoleonic Wars (1803–1815) France fought against Prussia, Russia and Austria, until the German Confederation was founded during the Congress of Vienna in 1815. Thirty-nine German states were part of the German Confederation and the Lieber family resided in the sovereign state of Prussia. A movement for pan-German unity was soon born from discontent with the political status quo and during the German revolutions of 1848 to 1849 attempts were made to unify all German states into a "Greater Germany." These attempts ultimately failed and the German states remained divided until the founding of the German Empire in 1871. In the bulk of his diary entries and publications, Lieber calls "Germany" his home but focuses on Prussia as a sovereign state, mostly discussing Prussian state legislation. Throughout this work, the term "German states" will be used to refer to the thirty-nine states of the German Confederation, but the term "Germany" appears in many quotes from original sources and usually refers to a cultural concept or geographical territory, rather than a political and legal reality.

5 The United States effectively became a constitutional republic in 1789. The authors of many nineteenth-century sources, including Francis Lieber, often speak of the US as a nation in their works – they use this term to invoke the idea of a uniform population with a collective identity and a shared language, culture, and history. This work refers to the US as a country, a republic, and a jurisdiction but also includes references to the nation-building efforts at the time. The idea of inter*national* copyright as a copyright regime between different nations also prominently features in this work and primary sources frequently speak of nations, not of the US as a republic and the German states as a confederation specifically. These incongruencies in terminology characterize the discourse at the time, especially Lieber's contributions, and will therefore appear frequently throughout this work.

> Droit d'auteur and copyright – that is, the civil law and common law approaches to the protection of intellectual works – are frequently set back-to-back. On the one hand, droit d'auteur, often invested with a sacred character, is tied into natural law; on the other, copyright is traditionally considered as a positive right, created by the legislator. In parallel fashion, droit d'auteur is often associated with (natural) property, whereas copyright is generally associated with the idea of a (legal) monopoly.[6]

He argues that these systems actually have a lot in common; what distinguishes them is the interpretive framework through which they are approached. Other researchers, most prominently Peter Baldwin, perpetuate this juxtaposition.[7] Baldwin goes so far as to present both positions as diametrically opposed in his recent work *The Copyright Wars. Three Centuries of Transatlantic Battle*, stating that "the battle between these views has also been what the Germans call a *Kulturkampf*, a clash of ideologies and fundamental assumptions, that has stretched back well over two centuries."[8] He writes that

> [i]nherent in the clash between copyright and authors' rights are strikingly divergent attitudes toward the creation and dissemination of culture, the reciprocal obligations and interests of creators and society, and the nature and social function of art, literature, and music.[9]

The contrast Baldwin delineates here results in the conceptualization of two inherently different positions on the legal protection of literary works, but arguably the distinction between Anglo-American copyright and continental-European authors' rights were not as distinct during the nineteenth century as is often indicated. Rather, these positions were more permeable: The existence and influence of continental-European authors' rights tendencies in the US can be discerned when opinion pieces and political demands published and distributed by participants of the copyright debate are included in the analysis.

The nineteenth-century debate on international copyright crystallized these tendencies, because the justification of or opposition to an international copyright in the US was discussed in relation to the foundations of

6 Strowel, "Droit D'auteur," 235.

7 Peter Baldwin, *The Copyright Wars. Three Centuries of Trans-Atlantic Battle* (Princeton: Princeton UP, 2014).

8 Baldwin, *Copyright Wars*, 14.

9 Baldwin, *Copyright Wars*, 19.

copyright law. All actors involved legitimized their positions either through appeals to or criticisms of existing copyright law and its purpose – or through references to other existing systems, such as the copyright regimes in German states or France. Transatlantic mediators conveyed and translated European legal understandings of *Urheberrecht* and authors' rights to the US, and vice versa.[10] One of the most prominent voices in the nineteenth-century debate on copyright and literary property was Francis Lieber (1798–1872), whose works on the issue unite American and European perspectives and exemplify the presence of authors' rights tendencies in the US.

As a Prussian migrant, Lieber moved to the US in 1827 where he became a naturalized citizen in 1835. As an immigrant who was both a US citizen and passionately loved his "Heimat" (homeland) Germany, Lieber truly was a "citizen of two worlds."[11] He authored comprehensive treatises on political and legal issues, as well as a manual for the training of law students, and texts on international law and cooperation. Steven Samson claims that Lieber was on a scientific and pedagogical "cultural nation-building mission."[12] As a language tutor, swim instructor, editor and publicist, author and professor, and as both a doctor of mathematics and an honorary doctor of law, Francis Lieber became active in different fields throughout his life. Researchers have represented him, as Wilson Smith wrote in 1955,

> as a liberal, a nineteenth-century conservative, a nationalist, an internationalist, a preacher, a reformer, an idealist, a man of practical bent, a middle-class apologist, and a zealous European revolutionist; then there has been readier agreement that at one time or another he was a scholar, political scientist, sociologist, author, publicist, political economist, teacher, historian, philologist, penologist, encyclopedist, international lawyer, military expert, and athlete.[13]

---

10 Urheberrecht is a German concept that comprises the creator's (*Urheber*) absolute and exclusive right (*Recht*) of protection for their intellectual property, especially with regard to books.

11 See Hugo Preuß, *Franz Lieber. Ein Bürger zweier Welten* (Berlin: Carl Habel, 1886). The phrase "citizen of two worlds" originally referred to Marie-Joseph-Paul-Yves-Roch-Gilbert du Motier, Marquis de La Fayette, who was born and raised in France but travelled to North America to aid colonists in the American Revolutionary War.

12 Steven Alan Samson, "Francis Lieber: Transatlantic Cultural Missionary" in *Francis Lieber and the Culture of the Mind*, ed. Charles R. Mack and Henry H. Lesesne (Columbia: University of South Carolina Press, 2005), 129–142, 129.

13 Wilson Smith, "Francis Lieber's Moral Philosophy," *Huntington Library Quarterly* 18.4 (1955): 395–408, 395.

During his lifetime, Lieber was well-known in the US and in the German states. His popularity was due to his activities as editor, author, scholar, and outspoken proponent of free trade, democracy, and international cooperation, as well as to his far-reaching network of private and professional contacts. As Claudia Schnurmann points out, his acclaim was also due to his extensive self-portrayal and his desire to be known, read, and quoted.[14]

Lieber was an extraordinarily active thinker and writer and, with his numerous publications, he contributed significantly to the field of law as well as to the establishment of the political and social sciences in the US. He worked as a professor of history, political philosophy and economy at South Carolina College,[15] and later as a professor of history and political sciences at Columbia College in New York City (today Columbia University). Harvard University awarded him an honorary doctorate in 1850,[16] and he was accepted as a member of the *American Academy of Arts and Science* and of the *Academie Française*.[17] Most notable, along with his publications, is Lieber's extensive private and professional literary network. While many of his contemporaries appreciated his independence in thinking, his boldness, his industry, and his liberal politics, historians today admire Lieber's wide circle of friends and correspondents, which included influential jurists, statesmen, historians, and politicians.[18] In 1873, *The Atlantic Monthly* even stated that "[o]f the thousands of Germans who have come to our shores, the late Dr. Lieber is, perhaps, the only political writer of any prominence [the Germans] have given us."[19]

Of great significance is Lieber's continued interest in copyright, literature as property, the social and political function of authorship, and the creation of an international copyright act in the US. Lieber significantly contributed to the

14 Claudia Schnurmann, *Brücken aus Papier. Atlantischer Wissenstransfer in dem Briefnetzwerk des deutsch-amerikanischen Ehepaars Francis und Mathilde Lieber, 1827–1872* (Berlin: LIT, 2014), 12.

15 Catalogue of the Trustees, Faculty and Students, of the South Carolina College. January 1847. Francis Lieber papers. mssLI. Box 88, no. 7. No LI number. The Huntington. San Marino, CA.

16 Jared Sparks, president of Harvard College from 1849 to 1853, sent Lieber a "Diploma of the honorary Degree of Doctor of Law, conferred upon you by the Corporation and Overseers of this University, which you will be pleased to accept as a token of the high respect entertained by them for your character, learning, and eminent success in the cultivation of letters." Sparks, Jared. Letter to Francis Lieber. October 4, 1850. Francis Lieber papers. OCLC 713642823. MS 0324. Manuscripts Division, South Caroliniana Library. Columbia, SC.

17 Schnurmann, *Brücken*, 13.

18 Gilman, "Francis Lieber," 272.

19 J. J. Lalor, "The Germans in the West." *The Atlantic Monthly*, Oct. 1873: 459–470.

copyright debate in the US – not because he was especially vocal or substantially influenced the resulting international copyright legislation, but because his unique transnational perspective brought value to the debate. As a mediator between two cultural contexts, Lieber offered a different view by synthesizing influences from two cultural-legal contexts into a cross-cultural framework which positions literature as a transnational form of property. At home in Prussia and the US, Lieber acted as a mediator between the US and the German states – a translator of political and legal ideas and concepts between two different cultural spheres. In this context, a mediator is a person who goes beyond linguistic translation. In *The Mediating Person: Bridges between Cultures* Stephen Bochner defines a mediator as

> an individual who serves as a link between two or more cultures and social systems. The essence of the mediating function is to shape the exchanges between the participating societies so that the contact will benefit both cultures, on terms that are consistent with their respective value systems.[20]

Not every bi-cultural person is a mediator. Rather, a mediator is someone familiar with two or more cultural-legal-political contexts, who actively bridges the gap between cultural, legal, political, and linguistic spheres by transporting sources between contexts, translating them, and explaining them along with their connotations and implications.

Francis Lieber contributed to the copyright debate as a mediator during the most active period of the debate. As Thorvald Solberg, first register of copyrights in the US copyright office, summarized, the eventual passage of an international copyright law in the US in 1891 was preceded by a

> period of considerably more than a century of Federal legislation, twenty-five public acts relating wholly or in part to copyright [...] together with nine private copyright acts. In addition to the bills introduced which thus became laws, a great many copyright measures have been presented to Congress which were never enacted [...] Altogether more than two hundred copyright bills have been laid before Congress for its consideration. Some of these bills have received no attention, others have been given some regard, while a few have secured considerable attention and discussion. Public interest in these proposed measures is shown and has been made known to Congress by numerous petitions and memorials relating to copyright from private individuals, business and labor

20 Stephen Bochner, "Introduction" in *The Mediating Person: Bridges between Cultures*, ed. Stephen Bochner (Cambridge: Schenkman Publishing Company, 1981), 3–5, 3.

> organizations, teachers, college professors, librarians, and representatives of the press.[21]

Throughout the nineteenth century actors with varying interests raised concerns regarding copyright legislation.[22] The US had an active public sphere and the debate about international copyright was part of the larger struggle for a shared national identity. Criticisms of the state of copyright law in the US were manifold but directed at two main issues: Firstly, the question whether copyright as a temporary monopoly was an adequate measure to protect authors' works, or whether written works should be recognized as literary property and protected through property rights. Secondly, the question whether copyright protection should be extended to include foreign works by authors who were not citizens or residents of the US, and whether such an international copyright would impede domestic literary production and trade. Naturally, those working in the book industry – authors, printers, typesetters, publishers, and booksellers – were involved in the ensuing copyright debate and lawyers, jurists, and politicians also took an interest. Associations were founded, signatures collected, pamphlets published, and politicians petitioned as the copyright debate turned into a public pamphlet war. While authors tended to demand comprehensive protection for written works, conceptualizing them as a literary form of property that deserved unlimited domestic and international protection, publishers leaned towards copyright limited in scope and duration. Exceptions existed: Some publishers argued that the flourishing reprinting industry in the US harmed domestic authors' sales, impeded domestic literary production in favor of the import of British works, and interfered with the cultivation of independent national literature. But the discussions

21 Thorvald Solberg, *Copyright in Congress 1789– 1904* (Washington: Government Printing, 1905), 5.

22 The constitutional copyright clause endowed Congress with the power to "promote the Progress of Science and useful Arts, by securing for limited Times to Authors and Inventors the exclusive Right to their respective Writings and Discoveries" (US Constitution, Article I, Section 8, Clause 8). The consequent *Copyright Act of 1790* granted authors the exclusive right to publish their works for fourteen years, with the possibility of a fourteen-year renewal, for the explicit purpose of encouraging learning. It thereby followed the British copyright act, the *Statute of Anne* of 1710, in form and content. But additionally, the US-American act also specifically permitted the import, reprint and sale of works from outside the US, denying copyright to authors who were not citizens or residents of the US. In 1831 Congress revised the act, extending the copyright term to twenty-eight years with the possibility of a fourteen-year extension. In 1834 the Supreme Court decided in the case *Wheaton v Peters* that authors had a common law right to control the initial publication of their work but once published, common law rights to the work were superseded by statutory law.

went beyond questions of economic gain and addressed republican values instead, such as public access to information in the form of cheap books, the status of the author as an agent of democratic nation-building efforts, national identity, and honor, pride, and proper conduct in international contact.

Impassioned calls were published by both sides: In 1838, an anonymous author published *A Plea for Authors, and the Rights of Literary Property*, in which they praised authors as key figures in the developing nation, who contributed to democracy, education, and national prosperity through their works. Authors deserved adequate remuneration for their work and positive influence but even though the government was responsible for the education of the people, it failed to protect the authors who contributed to it.[23] The author advocated for perpetual copyright protection for literature, which he considered a form of property. Literary property must be protected like corporeal forms of property. The author alone was entitled to all honor, profit, and responsibility for the work, they wrote, even if they are not citizens or residents of the US (*Plea*, 10, 12). The work called for both legal change and a shift in perspective for publishers, who also stood to benefit from international copyright, as the work claimed (*Plea*, 31).

George Ticknor Curtis, a lawyer and politician from Massachusetts, published *A Treatise on the Law of Copyright in Books, Dramatic and Musical Compositions, Letters and other Manuscripts, Engravings and Sculpture, as Enacted and Administered in England and America; with some Notices of the History of Literary Property* in 1847.[24] In this comprehensive work he assessed whether the law of copyright could be framed and understood in terms of literary property and whether the general law that constituted all other kinds of property also applied to literary property (*Treatise*, 2). Curtis argued in favor of broadening the scope of copyright law to secure the rights of authors in the United States. He framed copyright as a property and as a natural right and investigated how this understanding of copyright as literary property could be reconciled with the limited copyright codified in law. As Oren Bracha points out, readers applauded Curtis's support for the cause of international copyright and the extended duration of protection, "the two common causes of

23 *A Plea for Authors, and the Rights of Literary Property. By an American* (New York: Adlard and Saunders, 1838), 5–6. Hereafter abbreviated as *Plea*.

24 George Ticknor Curtis, *A Treatise on the Law of Copyright in Books, Dramatic and Musical Compositions, Letters and Other Manuscripts, Engravings and Sculpture, as Enacted and Administered in England and America; with Some Notices of the History of Literary Property* (Boston: Charles C. Little and James Brown, 1847). Hereafter abbreviated as *Treatise*.

non-jurists who took interest in copyright from the perspective of supporters of literature."[25]

In the same year, E. P. Hurlbut published *Essays on Human Rights and Their Political Guarantees* and examined intellectual property in the context of human rights.[26] He took a firm stance on the protection of authors' rights and the introduction of international copyright. While he examined the legal foundation of copyright and gave an overview of cases concerned with common law copyright in England and in the US, Hurlbut was "not so much concerned with the actual condition of the law, as with what it ought to be" (*Essays*, 77). He argued that all authors everywhere were entitled to the protection of their written works, even across national borders, and framed this as a question of right, "which the enlightened conscience of mankind cannot fail to perceive" (*Essays*, 77). It was a matter of justice and fairness to prevent "piracy" and to protect domestic authors and national literature against the import or reprint of foreign works, according to Hurlbut. This was especially true in a young republic without a fully developed national literature, since "the moral tone and the intellectual character of a nation are judged by her literature" (*Essays*, 77).

With *On International Copyright, In a Letter to the Hon. William C. Preston*, Francis Lieber published his own passionate call for the introduction of international copyright protection in 1840. He framed literature as the purest form of property and called for immediate legal change in the US. While his position was not uncommon in the US, he nevertheless contributed to the debate in a unique way: He was inspired by his transnational background to combine Anglo-American and continental-European understandings of copyright law in his demands. Like the anonymous author of *A Plea for Authors, and the Rights of Literary Property*, Lieber substantiated his calls for international copyright protection with appeals to natural law, justice, and respect for authors, and framed literature as a form of property which requires perpetual protection. His work preceded Curtis's *Treatise on the Law of Copyright in Books* by several years and while Curtis presented similar arguments in favor of literary property and international copyright, he also highlighted the importance of protecting the market value of a work through copyright.[27] Lieber, on the other hand, took a more comprehensive stance based on moral claims,

25 Oren Bracha, "Commentary on George Ticknor Curtis's Treatise on the Law of Copyright (1847)" in *Primary Sources on Copyright (1450– 1900)*, ed. Lionel Bently and Martin Kretschmer (Copyrighthistory.org, 2008).

26 Hurlbut, E. P., *Essays on Human Rights and Their Political Guaranties* (Edinburgh: MacLachlan, Stewart, & Co., 1847). Hereafter abbrieviated as *Essays*.

27 Bracha, "Commentary on George Ticknor Curtis."

resulting in a call for perpetual copyright protection going further than Curtis's demands. Curtis also acknowledged the necessity for a compromise between natural rights justifications and "the imperfections of the actual positive regime," as Bracha writes.[28] In his initial statements on literary property, Lieber did not accept such a compromise. Many arguments presented by Lieber in 1840 are echoed by Hurlbut and others later on, including appeals to justice, fairness, morality and integrity.

Henry Charles Carey (1793–1879), an economist, politician, and publisher at Carey & Lea publishing house, was a firm opponent of international copyright. He published his arguments in the collection *Letters on International Copyright* in 1853 and became the most influential opponent of international copyright in the US at the time.[29] Carey's stance on international copyright is informed by his criticism of centralization in the US. He considered access to knowledge an important aspect of a nation, but favored decentralizing and the protection it afforded to literature. He rejected any attempts to structure the book trade through federal measures or to centralize it in the big cities (*Letters*, 71). He also did not understand copyright as a form of property because authors, as he claimed, "did nothing but reproduce ideas that were common property" and therefore could not claim a right of property to them (*Letters*, 11). In many ways, Carey's public appeal mirrored the form and title of Lieber's *On International Copyright* and though Carey does not mention Lieber, his work appears to be a response to Lieber's earlier pamphlet.

Evidently, a lively debate on copyright took place between many different actors during the nineteenth century, a written exchange of blows and counter-blows. As an advocate of literary property and international copyright, Francis Lieber was an active contributor to this debate with a solid position, which invites further study: As a Prussian migrant he was raised in a different legal context and when he moved to the US, he brought with him a separate set of legal norms. Therefore, Lieber adopted a different perspective on the law from those raised in the US, influenced by a different array of ideas and expectations. He used these insights to carve out a niche for himself as an expert on US politics and law, but also as a reformer. He employed copyright law as a way to discuss authorship and the social and political function of literature, and even addressed notions of citizenship, political participation, and international relations. He questioned prevalent legal norms, challenged legislation, and with his works and activism he aimed for fundamen-

---

28 Bracha, "Commentary on George Ticknor Curtis."

29 Henry Charles Carey, *Letters on International Copyright* (Philadelphia: Hart, Carey and Hart, 1853). Hereafter abbreviated as *Letters*.

tal legal change. His written demands for international copyright legislation highlighted the mutually constitutive relationship between legal and literary discourses and advanced the cultural and legal emergence and differentiation of the concept of literature as a form of property.

While robust research exists on copyright reforms in the US during the nineteenth century, scholars usually focus either on US-American authors, lawyers, and politicians, or on British activists, such as Charles Dickens.[30] They emphasize the influence of British legislation on US-American copyright law, while continental-European understandings of Urheberrecht and authors' rights are often considered in comparison with or opposition to Anglo-American copyright law.[31] Examinations of copyright law during the nineteenth century are often conducted by legal scholars, who focus on the legal sphere and tend to limit themselves to legal texts and comments by those directly involved in the drafting process.[32] Such a perspective usually privileges the "winning side" by disregarding alternative ideas and claims that were not incorporated into the final legislation. However, challenges to legal norms and subsequent conceptual changes to the understanding of copyright and property often originated in public debates, long before legal change took place to reflect normative changes. Therefore, the literary and cultural study of

30 See for example central works such as: Saunders, David. *Authorship and Copyright* (London: Routledge, 1992); Barnes, James J., *Authors, Publishers, and Politicians. The Quest for an Anglo-American Copyright Agreement 1815– 1854* (Columbus: Ohio State UP, 1974); Meredith L. McGill, *American Literature and the Culture of Reprinting, 1834–1853* (Philadelphia: University of Pennsylvania Press, 2003); Melissa J. Homestead, *American Women Authors and Literary Property* (Cambridge: Cambridge UP, 2005); Martin Buinicki, *Negotiating Copyright: Authorship and the Discourse of Literary Property Rights in Nineteenth-Century America* (London: Routledge, 2006); Oren Bracha, *Owning Ideas. Intellectual Origins of American Intellectual Property, 1790–1909* (Cambridge: Cambridge UP, 2016). For the British context see: Mark Rose, *Authors and Owners. The Invention of Copyright* (Cambridge: Harvard UP, 1993); Paul K. Saint-Amour, *The Copywrights. Intellectual Property and the Literary Imagination.* (Ithaca, NY: Cornell UP, 2003).

31 See for example Peter Baldwin's *The Copyright Wars.* Alain Strowel challenged this juxtaposition in "Droit D'auteur and Copyright. Between History and Nature" in *Of Authors and Origins. Essays on Copyright Law*, ed. Brad Sherman and Alain Strowel (Oxford: Clarendon Press, 1994), 235–254, and Jane C. Ginsburg also offers a comparative perspective in: Jane C. Ginsburg, "A Tale of Two Copyrights. Literary Property in Revolutionary France and America," *Tulane Law Review*, 64.5 (1990): 991–1031, and in: Jane C. Ginsburggh "The Concept of Authorship in Comparative Copyright Law," *SSRN Electronic Journal* 3 (2005): 1–29. Ronan Deazley and others examined different histories of printing privileges and copyright recently in: Ronan Deazley et al., *Privilege and Property: Essays on the History of Copyright* (Cambridge: Open Book Publishers, 2010).

32 See for example: Lyman Ray Patterson, *Copyright in Historical Perspective* (Nashville: Vanderbilt UP, 1968).

the law can shed light on the origins of normative legal change. Due to Francis Lieber's unique position as a mediator between continental-European and US-American schools of thought, as someone who built bridges between Europe and the US, a systematic and comprehensive analysis of his contribution to the copyright debate of the nineteenth century within the context of his oeuvre expands the current historico-cultural perspective on historical debates on copyright and literary property in the US.

1.3 Research Questions

Through an examination of the works of Francis Lieber, this thesis takes into focus the literary property debate in the US during the nineteenth century in connection with the movement for international copyright as a transnational protective measure for authors and literature. This historic movement advanced a transnational debate in which writers from both sides of the Atlantic participated – mainly because the lack of international copyright affected authors in other countries as well. Participants attempted to integrate different legal understandings, such as Anglo-American common law and continental-European notions of natural law. Lieber's work is a pertinent example of this integrative legal discourse. An in-depth analysis of his work carves out another relevant perspective on the nineteenth-century copyright debate, which allows for a more comprehensive understanding of the prevalence of transatlantic influences on the legal and literary discourse surrounding copyright and literature as a form of property. His works are especially valuable because Lieber consistently worked from a comparative perspective, went beyond national boundaries, and considered copyright and literary property within a larger contrastive framework.

In existing scholarship on Lieber's writing, his most prominent work on copyright and literary property, *On International Copyright,* has often been singled out and discussed individually rather than within the context of his body of work.[33] Through this reductive approach the important correlations between Lieber's ideas on literary property and his other writings on politics, law and international relations remained unexamined. Similarly, historical assessments of Anglo-American copyright law and the international copyright

---

33 See for example Frank Freidel's article "Lieber's Contribution to the International Copyright Movement," *Huntington Library Quarterly* 8.2 (1945): 200–206. While Freidel also addresses Lieber's correspondence, he largely focuses on the creation of this one source and does not place it within the context of Lieber's other works.

debate of the nineteenth century usually neglect to comment on Lieber's arguments. Placing *On International Copyright* within the framework of Lieber's other published works makes it possible to discern connections between the works, to follow the development of his thought processes over time, and to identify correspondences between his understanding of copyright and other prominent issues, such as political ethics, hermeneutics, civil liberty, and self-government. Especially when including additional sources, such as Lieber's correspondence and his private notes, the origins of his transnational perspective can be deduced. While Lieber's motivation to participate in the debate could be seen as opportunistic and rooted in his financial benefits as an author, when considered against the background of his other works a different picture emerges: Lieber's understanding of literature as property and thus as a central feature of the state is reflected in his other works as well. By means of his position as mediator, Lieber contributed to the negotiation of authorship and literary property as a means for cultural and political participation of subjects in the state. This also opens up an opportunity to interrogate the connections between political, economic, and cultural conceptions of property and literary property in Lieber's works. He also positioned literature as a transnational form of property, the protection of which must necessarily cross national and legal boundaries.

This leads to the following research questions: When and why did Lieber begin conceptualizing literature as a transnational form of property, and how did this conceptualization change throughout his life and evolve in tandem with his understanding of authorship, literature, and property? How can an author claim ownership of literature and what is the relation between literary property and other forms of property presented in his work? Which domestic and international influences shaped this understanding and which impact did Prussian, continental-European, and Anglo-American notions have on his writing and activism, and how did he integrate these different cultural and legal ideas and norms? How is his understanding of literature as a form of property shaped by his broader understanding of the significance of authorship and the act of writing, of the role of the government in protecting it, the privileges and duties of citizens, and the relationship between countries and across national boundaries? And how did he communicate his positions and demands to legal experts, politicians, and the public? How did he engage in education and activism by utilizing his written works and his transnational literary network? How did his understanding of literature as property and his demands for international copyright protection permeate his works and how did he ultimately contribute to the US-American copyright debate?

1.4 Research Objective and Relevance

The goal of this work is to trace the beginnings of a decidedly transnational conceptualization of intellectual property throughout Lieber's works. More broadly speaking, answering the research questions will help to carve out the influence of continental-European notions of literature as property on the US-American copyright debate and to highlight its transnational dimension. It will also help to demonstrate that the US-American understanding of copyright did not develop entirely detached from continental-European understandings of authors' rights and natural law. Examining the origins and evolution of US copyright, including influences less prominent or obvious in contemporary legislation, can help provide important input for current discussions. This is especially valuable in a time when political, social, and cultural disputes about intellectual property and closely-related subject areas, such as copyright in the digital sphere, plagiarism, open access, corporate property, work-for-hire, artificial intelligence, and cultural appropriation, have become more polarized, controversial, and pressing than ever.

Questions and concerns related to intellectual property can no longer be addressed by the law alone. Rather, an interdisciplinary approach is necessary to consider such issues within the cultural and historical context and to understand their genesis and wider implications through a dialogical analysis of and reflection on the legal *and* literary histories of literary property as a paradigmatic form of intellectual property. At all times intellectual property exists within an area of tension between law and culture; legal and cultural conceptions of intellectual property counterbalance each other. By emphasizing the fundamental questions raised concerning the cultural, legal, and political functions of property – and specifically literary or intellectual property – during the copyright debate, this work calls attention to the ways in which the copyright debate of the nineteenth century and the normative and legal changes it brought about can serve as an example for contemporary disputes regarding intellectual property in today's globalized and digitized world.

The existing body of research on Francis Lieber positions him as a historical figure of lasting relevance because he contributed to US and European science and culture by conveying thoughts and ideas from one continent to the other (see chapter 2). He not only passed ideas forward – he engaged with them and implemented them in a different cultural, legal, and political context through discussion, publication, and teaching. In the process, Lieber transformed and adapted these ideas and both the US and Europe profited from his activities. What made Lieber remarkable was his ability to synthesize rather than just convey ideas. He acted not just as a transmitter but as a pivot who transformed, cultivated, and adapted ideas to a new context. In his publications Lieber engaged in interdisciplinary work. He brought together and amalgamated ideas and methods from different disciplines and molded them into a new work, from which more than one discipline and more than one country could profit. Francis Lieber earned his place in interdisciplinary research, especially in the field of politics and international law, as a synthesizer *and* as an original thinker, whose ideas are still examined in research today. While his additions to the laws of war and the law of nations are well-researched, his contribution to the international copyright debate of the nineteenth century, a subject closely related to international law, remains understudied. This work will fill that gap in the research by means of a thorough and methodical examination of Lieber's entire oeuvre.

1.5 Method

In order to properly analyze Lieber's understanding of literature as a transnational form of property, as well as his role in and contribution to the US-American international copyright debate of the nineteenth century, it is necessary to adopt an interdisciplinary perspective on Lieber's work. One goal of this work is to trace throughout Lieber's works the beginnings of a decidedly transnational conceptualization of intellectual property, which plays a central role in contemporary notions of intellectual property in a globalized world, defined by easy digital access and constant international exchange. The question of what is intellectual property, what qualifies for protection, and how protection of intellectual property should be implemented is culturally contingent. Various cultures define intellectual property differently, depending on historical, economic, and political circumstances. While European and North American countries, as well as other former British colonies, consider individual acts of creation original, other countries value shared knowledge and creation. Not all jurisdictions agree on whether intellectual property should be unequivocally protected, or whether public welfare demands for intellectual resources to be shared. Different narrative theories and concepts of authorship lead to different decisions concerning the protection of texts. Intellectual property regulations are embedded within a cultural context and to carve out the nuances in property thought, they have to be analyzed from an interdisciplinary perspective. Therefore, an interdisciplinary approach to the study of intellectual property is essential. Differences between intellectual property regimes cannot be explored in detail if cultural circumstances are neglected. Concerning copyright, only an interdisciplinary approach that combines legal, literary, cultural, and historical studies allows for a nuanced analysis of this legal phenomenon, since notions of authorship and originality are deeply intertwined with intellectual property law and protection.

The concept of "literary property" is not an established term within legal or literary studies but it serves as an essential category to correlate theoretical and methodological legal and literary discourses and practices.[34] It is therefore a theoretical construct which did not originate exclusively within either discipline. Rather, it is characterized by its ability to transfer ideas between both fields. As Robin Wharton points out,

> [c]opyright is a legal construct, but literary property is a strange hybrid, part law, part applied literary scholarship. A copyright has an owner. Literary property has an author, which is itself yet another legal/literary hybrid. As an object of study and regulation, literary property yokes, or sutures, or interpenetrates two discursive communities – law on the one hand, and literary studies on the other [...] When I ask whether we can read an aesthetics of literary property from copyright law, I am looking to identify the features of an object of scrutiny that is shared between legal and literary study, and to understand how that object functions as a kind of discursive conduit through which these two modes of cultural production inform one another.[35]

Consequently, this work is necessarily interdisciplinary in nature. It combines areas of research pertaining to literary and cultural studies as well as to history and law. On the fundamental level, this thesis is located within the field of literary studies. It analyzes literary sources using techniques such as close reading and the examination of intertextuality, and investigates the concept of authorship and its relation to copyright, as well as literature as a form of property. By adopting a cultural-studies lens, this thesis locates the place and function of literary property within a culture, traces the origins and continuities of related concepts and ideas, and explores intercultural influences, connections, and divergences. It touches on questions about the fundamental

34 For an examination of the mutually constitutive relationship between literary narratives about property and legal narratives about property, as well as an analysis of how literature's status as literary property influences literature's engagement with the law, see Peter Schneck, "Narrative Claims: Literary Ownership and the Question of Property" in *Narrative and Law*, ed. Monika Fludernik and Frank L. Schäfer (Würzburg: Ergon Verlag, 2022), 71–92, 73.

35 Robin Wharton, "The Regulation of Authorship: Literary Property and the Aesthetics of Resistance" in *Law and Literature*, ed. Kieran Dolin (Cambridge: Cambridge UP, 2018), 291–307, 293.

nature of literature and its function within society and culture. It also analyzes primary sources within their respective historical context and places them within a larger historical framework to answer the research questions posed here. An approach shaped by the techniques of historical studies is necessary to establish a larger historical framework that informs the analysis. The respective research questions cannot be discussed without also considering the function of law in delineating what is or is not recognized as literature within a culture, who can own literature, and whether and how something intangible such as literature can even be a form of property. Questions of copyright regulation, on the other hand, always necessitate an analysis of the concept of authorship and literature as property, referring back to the field of literary studies and prompting an interdisciplinary approach to literature informed by the legal context. The constitutive relationship between law and literature is therefore at the center of the following analysis.

The methodological approach of this work must allow for an analysis of Lieber's ideas and understanding of literature as property in general and of its political and cultural functions. To approach the complex historical process of the introduction of an international copyright in the US during the nineteenth century, as well as Lieber's role within this process, this work adopts a modified version of the model of issue emergence presented by R. Charli Carpenter in her article "Setting the Advocacy Agenda: Theorizing Issue Emergence and Nonemergence in Transnational Advocacy Networks,"[36] and adapted by Lindsey M. Kingston in her work *Fully Human. Personhood, Citizenship, and Rights*.[37] Carpenter's model originates from political science and human rights research. It maps out how transnational advocacy networks mobilize around specific issues to transform them into issues of national and international relevance and to impact global policy making. Using this model allows for an analysis of the contributions of both individual actors and larger networks of advocates to norm change and – consequently – legal change. Legal change reflects a previous change in norms and a shift in public opinion. It usually follows a complex process of normative change and constitutes the final step in this process: Legal codification of normative change. Carpenter develops a framework to assess the differences and variations in issue emergence and to analyze why some problems emerge as relevant issues and bring about legal change, while other problems do not.

36 R. Charli Carpenter, "Setting the Advocacy Agenda: Theorizing Issue Emergence and Nonemergence in Transnational Advocacy Networks," *International Studies Quarterly*, 51.1, (2007): 99–120.

37 Lindsey M. Kingston, *Fully Human. Personhood, Citizenship, and Rights* (Oxford: Oxford UP, 2019).

1.6 The Model of Issue Emergence

Carpenter's model is based in large parts on a previous work on norm change, norm dynamics, and political change by Martha Finnemore and Kathryn Sikkink.[38] Carpenter adopts their work on normative change and expands it by applying it to broader so-called issues that may concern more than one norm. As Carpenter points out, advocacy for a problem is only possible once it has been defined by entrepreneurs as an issue and adopted by gatekeepers of the national or international "advocacy arena."[39] For an issue to emerge it takes permissive conditions, such as available and interested political entrepreneurs and preexisting "favorable norm pools" which the issue may align with.[40] Political entrepreneurs are usually organized in advocacy networks, defined by Margaret Keck and Kathryn Sikkink as "voluntary, reciprocal, and horizontal patterns of communication and exchange."[41] These advocacy networks are often organized beyond national borders and consist of activists "motivated by shared, principled discourse and aiming to affect political behavior through moral argument," as Carpenter writes.[42]

Within transnational advocacy networks, the twin steps of transnational network politics take place: The construction of a problem as an issue (issue definition) and the acceptance of this issue onto the international agenda

38 Martha Finnemore and Kathryn Sikkink, "International Norm Dynamics and Political Change," *International Organization* 52.4 (1998): 887–917. Finnemore and Sikkink summarize the norm life cycle, consisting of norm emergence, norm cascade, and internalization, and the actors involved in each stage of the process. Norm entrepreneurs "create" issues by framing them: They provide the necessary language to name and interpret the issues. If successful, as Finnemore and Sikkink point out, "the new frames resonate with broader public understandings and are adopted as new ways of talking about and understanding issues" (897). Norm entrepreneurs are often motivated by ideological concerns, but they also work in favor of their own interests. During norm emergence, norm entrepreneurs construct new norms and operate from organizational platforms to convince a critical mass of norm leaders and gatekeepers to embrace a new norm. New norms either reach a tipping point or they dissipate: New norms must compete with other new and existing norms, and they do not inevitably reach a tipping point. If they do, a norm cascade follows in the form of broad norm acceptance. Norm leaders convince others to adhere to the new norm, usually through measures of socialization, such as emulation, praise for norm adherence, and ridicule for norm deviation. Once norms "acquire a taken-for-granted quality and are no longer a matter of broad public debate," they reach the stage of internalization (895–902).

39 Carpenter, "Advocacy Agenda," 100.

40 Carpenter, "Advocacy Agenda," 100.

41 Margaret Keck and Kathryn Sikkink, *Activists Beyond Borders. Advocacy Networks in International Politics* (Ithaca: Cornell UP, 1998), 8.

42 Carpenter, "Advocacy Agenda," 101.

(issue adoption).[43] During issue definition issue entrepreneurs demonstrate that "a given state of affairs is neither natural nor accidental, identif[y] the responsible party or parties, and propos[e] credible solutions."[44] An issue can only emerge after it has been defined by norm entrepreneurs and accepted by a critical mass of gatekeepers and other activists.[45] Issue emergence is indispensable to effecting political activism and legal change through campaigns, concerted efforts by advocates who lobby for a specific result.[46] Once an issue is championed by bigger players within the broader network, such as politicians or prominent spokespersons, the issue has been adopted and emerges onto the international agenda.[47] Emergence is easier if issue entrepreneurs can link the issue to preexisting moral standards, a strategy of consciously and strategically grafting new issues onto preexisting issues.[48] Emergence can also be accelerated by the presence of favorable issue attributes, such as clear casual chains or perceived innocence of the victims of a problem, and by influential political actors and norm leaders who utilize their own networks to rally support for the cause.[49]

Lindsey M. Kingston adapts the work by Finnemore, Sikkink, and Carpenter by focusing on the narrative framing of issue emergence, "the supporting processes of providing […] narratives and issue framing [that] require us to acknowledge that representation matters significantly," and by highlighting "how we construct problems and tell stories."[50] During issue emergence a problem becomes an issue through a process of mobilization.[51] While external events such as shifting political alliances or current events cannot be controlled and might derail an issue's successful emergence or survival, issue

43 Carpenter, "Advocacy Agenda," 101.
44 Keck and Sikkink, *Activists*, 19.
45 Carpenter, "Advocacy Agenda," 102.
46 Carpenter, "Advocacy Agenda," 102.
47 Carpenter, "Advocacy Agenda," 103.
48 Carpenter, "Advocacy Agenda," 104.
49 Finnemore and Sikkink, "International Norm," 895; Carpenter, "Advocacy Agenda," 102.
50 Kingston, *Fully Human*, 201.
51 This process is characterized by four key themes: Firstly, the issue characteristics determine whether an issue can fit into existing discussions and moral standards within the international community. Secondly, the organizational characteristics demonstrate whether an issue can be connected to an organization's preexisting culture, ethics, and strategy, and whether enough issue entrepreneurs are available to promote the issue. Thirdly, strategic characteristics determine the framing and marketing of an issue to attract support. Lastly, environmental characteristics are external factors, such as political alignments and current events, which influence the emergence of a particular issue (*Fully Human*, 202). All key elements determine an issue's chances of successfully emerging and surviving in the competitive international issue market.

entrepreneurs can determine strategy and framing. They need to frame an issue in "understandable and relatable ways" that speak to potential supporters and policy makers. They can also emphasize aspects of an issue that connect well with preexisting norms, other current issues, and the concerns of influential organizations or advocacy networks. Through a "targeted advocacy strategy", issue entrepreneurs frame the issue as a structural and transnational problem, raise awareness, promote funding for research, garner resources and political support, and involve the press.[52]

Issues need to be presented in the form of a compelling story line, which makes sense to the public and political agents. Through the form of a narrative, issue entrepreneurs need to demonstrate relevance to national interests, political concerns, and cultural issues. To engage supporters they often resort to classical elements of story-telling, such as presenting clearly identifiable villains, victims, and heroes.[53] Building links between different but related issues, a process called frame bridging, can help mobilize support from different communities.[54] At the same time, issue frames may also oversimplify an issue or neglect core objectives in an attempt to provide an understandable and compelling narrative. The process of framing an issue in a compelling value-based narrative is referred to as "issue conveyance."[55] Only if an issue is conveyed successfully can it survive the intensity of issue competition for limited public attention and resources.[56] Often opponents of an issue offer counterframes, alternative ways of framing an issue, to prevent successful issue emergence and inhibit social change.[57] Issue entrepreneurs therefore play an essential role in identifying problems, framing them as issues relevant to a culture, conveying them through compelling narratives, and ensuring their survival in the competition for attention and resources and against counternarratives distributed by issue opponents.

1.7 Adaptation of the Model

The model of issue emergence makes it possible to summarize and evaluate the entire life cycle of an issue, from the initial identification of a problem as an issue to the final codification of normative change in the law. Therefore, it

52 Kingston, *Fully Human*, 204–205.
53 Kingston, *Fully Human*, 206.
54 Kingston, *Fully Human*, 212.
55 Kingston, *Fully Human*, 219.
56 Kingston, *Fully Human*, 206.
57 Kingston, *Fully Human*, 214.

offers a methodological approach well-suited to the analysis of Francis Lieber's contribution to the copyright debate of the nineteenth century. By understanding Lieber as an entrepreneur for the issue of international copyright, the model provides the tools to map out Lieber's framing of the issue and to analyze the narrative he provided to convey the issue. It also makes it possible to identify the ways in which Lieber utilized his advocacy network to raise support for the issue and initiate normative change, and to assess how Lieber connected the issue to other relevant political and legal concerns to address policy makers.

The model of issue emergence usually describes the emergence of an issue on the international agenda and emphasizes the support of well-organized transnational advocacy workers and large actors, such as global non-governmental organizations able to exert pressure on governments rather than just individual politicians. Early on, the issue of international copyright during the nineteenth century was identified as a structural and transnational problem by issue advocates such as Lieber. At the time, transnational advocacy networks and international non-governmental organizations did not have the infrastructure, resources, and global influence available to them today. Rather, networks were often initiated by individual actors through their private correspondence with other supporters and with politicians. They addressed the public in newspaper articles and pamphlets, at times through speeches and lectures. Interest groups were founded, such as the *Copyright Association*, but they were much smaller than national and international interest groups and associations today. To bring an issue not just on the domestic political stage, but to put it on the international agenda required significant and long-term sustained efforts, as countries were nowhere near as connected as they are today in times of globalization, mass media, and the internet. A "global community" did not exist in the form it does today. Consequently, the model needs to be adapted to the nineteenth-century context of Lieber's time, with more emphasis on individual actors and national advocacy. With these specific restrictions in mind, the model offers a clear approach to analyzing Francis Lieber's contribution, his narrative framing, his private advocacy through his transnational network, his public advocacy through his publications, and his political lobbying efforts.

1.8 Organization

The overarching aim of this work is to carve out Lieber's ideas and standpoints concerning literature as property as well as national and international copyright through a systematic integrative analysis of his literary oeuvre. This serves the purpose of mapping out Lieber's role as an issue entrepreneur for the cause of international copyright and to determine his contribution to the international copyright debate of the nineteenth century. It becomes possible to take Lieber as an example of an influential issue entrepreneur with a decidedly transnational background, thus highlighting the influence of continental-European notions of literature as property on the US-American copyright debate as well as its transnational dimension. An emphasis on the advocacy networks that issue entrepreneurs such as the one that Lieber built and maintained across the Atlantic demonstrates that the US-American understanding of copyright did not develop entirely detached from continental-European understandings of authors' rights and natural law. Evaluating the narrative framing of the issue as well the entire process towards legal change helps to denaturalize established narratives about national and international copyright in the US and globally. It also underlines the interconnectedness of moral values, normative ideas and economic, political, and legal conditions.[58]

To achieve this goal, Lieber's notions of literary property and international copyright will be examined along with their underlying concepts. The reception, translation, and synthesis of transnational influences in Lieber's works, notes, and correspondence will be analyzed, and Lieber's ideas and concepts will be considered against the background of the nineteenth-century international copyright debate in the US and in Europe. His works concerning the thematic field of literary property and copyright will be assessed in conjunction with his other publications to deduce correspondences, deviations, and connections between the texts, and to shed light on the systematic organization and inner coherence of his body of work. By comparing his standpoints with preceding and concurrent works from other cultural regions, such as Prussia and France, his texts will be placed within a transnational framework. This allows for the discernment of translation, reception, synthesis, and adaptation of foreign ideas and viewpoints within Lieber's own works, generating a deeper understanding of the transatlantic influences and convergences that shaped the literary and legal discourse of the time. Subsequently, it will be discussed whether any of Lieber's notions concerning literary property and international copyright were incorporated into the US-American cultural and political discourse of the time. By interpreting Lieber's works as an example of a viewpoint influenced by transnational notions and widely received in the US, nuance can be added to the assumption that the US pursued a unique

58 Simone Knewitz, *The Politics of Private Property. Contested Claims to Ownership in U.-S. Cultural Discourse* (Lanham: Lexington Books, 2021), 8.

path regarding international copyright during most of the nineteenth century. The scope of this project serves to ascertain the origins of a decidedly transnational conceptualization of literary property in the US, and offers a fresh perspective on the prevalence of natural rights and author's rights tendencies in the US at the time. The research questions examined here are of relevance to current debates surrounding questions of copyright and literary and intellectual property, both nationally and transnationally. The developments discussed transcend the US-American context of the nineteenth century and offer perspectives for and compatibility with other treatises on topics related to literary and intellectual property and copyright.

Archival sources help map out Lieber's understanding of literary property and copyright. They highlight the evolution of his thought processes throughout his life and make it possible to pinpoint aspects he intertwines with the subject area of literary property and copyright in his framing of these issues and his appeals for normative and legal change. The source catalogue for this work consists of Lieber's diary entries to examine his thought processes, his correspondence within his transnational network to analyze his exchange of ideas, the content of his published works to highlight the dissemination of his ideas, the reception of his publications, and his public speeches and letters to policy makers to outline his lobbying activities. For this survey of Lieber's unpublished documents archival sources from the Lieber papers at The Huntington Library, at the South Caroliniana Library and at the Sheridan Libraries Special Collections are considered.[59] These sources encompass extensive correspondence, diary entries, handwritten notes and drafts, tran-

59 Working with the sources included in this work poses significant challenges: The transcriptions of Lieber's letters and works presented in *The Miscellaneous Writings of Francis Lieber* by Daniel C. Gilman and in *The Life and Letters of Francis Lieber* by Thomas Perry are heavily edited. Lieber's documents were selected, compiled, transcribed and shortened by Mathilde Lieber before they were included in these publications. Many letters and even diary entries are therefore not the originals. Many of the documents in The Huntington Library are also mere transcripts in Mathilde Lieber's handwriting. Some of Lieber's original documents are edited in pencil by Mathilde Lieber; especially in letters sentences are crossed out and the wording is changed. Even Lieber himself changed the wording in many of the letters he received from others and he misquoted them publicly or to other correspondents, likely to present himself in a better light. It is certain that Lieber periodically changed his own wording retroactively, as some original letters with editing notes are preserved alongside the transcripts (Schnurmann, *Brücken*, 29, footnote 110). Many of Lieber's notes and letters are in German and were translated by Mathilde Lieber; the original is not always available. Gilman and Perry included many of these translations in their edited volumes without clarifying their status as translations. Consequently, earlier researchers such as Freidel and Charles B. Robson often refer to Mathilde Lieber's translations rather than the German originals. Whenever

scribed speeches and lectures, and a collection of newspaper articles. Many of these sources offer novel insights into Lieber's working methods as well as his sources and inspirations. The analysis of this comprehensive catalogue of documents serves to deepen the understanding of Lieber's property theory and the cultural and legal framework he operated within. The insights garnered from his handwritten notes and collection of books and articles supplement the analysis of his published works. In his personal correspondence, Lieber elaborated on his thought processes and opinions and engaged in activism and lobbying. His letters highlight the role Lieber played as a mediator focused on transnational knowledge exchange. Analyzing these personal documents makes it possible to narrow down the impact Lieber had on jurists and politicians, as well as his influence on political debates and the larger cultural discourse at the time. Thus, his influence as a transnational mediator, knowledge broker,[60] and legal and political thinker will be demonstrated.

On a larger scale, the analysis of Lieber's works and the assessment of the role he played in the discourse surrounding (international) copyright during the nineteenth century serve to carve out the transnational dimension of this very debate. The reception of Lieber's standpoints within the US emphasizes the presence of international cultural and legal notions of copyright, literature as property, and authorship. Lieber's positions thus highlight the impact of international – and specifically German – influences, as well as the cultivation of hybrid perspectives on copyright and literature as property, which broadened the US-American discourse at the time. Finally, the analysis of Lieber's literary oeuvre maps out the origins of his avid interest in questions of literary property and copyright. While many of the archival documents have been examined by scholars such as Charles B. Robson, Frank Freidel, and Claudia Schnurmann, some have not been part of any scholarly publications and are examined for the first time in this work.

1.9 Structure

The work begins with a detailed examination of the state of research on Francis Lieber as a historical figure. Since the bulk of the work consists of the analysis and contextualization of Lieber's literary oeuvre, the work then fol-

---

possible, the German originals rather than translations will be used, and transcripts or translations that are not in Lieber's own words or handwriting are indicated.

60 According to Claudia Schnurmann's conceptualization of Lieber as a broker of knowledge in *Brücken aus Papier* (20).

lows a structure which corresponds to the chronology of Lieber's life. This allows for the identification of important strands of argument, for the examination of their continuous development over time, and for the integration of Lieber's arguments into the historical context. To lay the groundwork for this sequential analysis, chapter 3 offers a broad overview of the historical context of the international copyright debate. This overview begins with the development of copyright notions in Great Britain, traces their transmission to the colonial context in North America, including an analysis of early states' copyright statutes, and maps out the implementation of a copyright regime in the US. The discourse surrounding the introduction of an international copyright during the nineteenth century is examined to contextualize Lieber's standpoint within this debate, as well as his contributions. Since Lieber migrated to the US from Europe and transported European and especially German notions of Urheberrecht and authors' rights to the US, an overview of the situation in Europe follows, with an emphasis on the conditions in France and the German states. Chapter 4 then introduces Lieber's earliest writings on copyright and literary property, consisting of the entries on copyright (1830) and literary property (1831) in the first edition of the *Encyclopædia Americana*, which Lieber authored soon after his arrival in the US.[61] In these entries, he first identified the problem of literary property and international copyright and began framing it as an issue. Chapter 5 analyzes Lieber's first two monographs, *Manual of Political Ethics* (1839) and *Legal and Political Hermeneutics* (1839) and traces the integration of his thoughts on copyright and literary property.[62] Chapter 6 focuses on Lieber's most productive period as an issue entrepreneur, the 1840s. The chapter consists of a detailed analysis of Lieber's framing of the issue in his works dedicated to international copyright and literary property, namely *On International Copyright, in a Letter to the*

61 Francis Lieber, "Copyright" in *Encyclopædia Americana. A Popular Dictionary of Arts, Sciences, Literature, History, Politics and Biography. Vol. III.*, ed. Francis Lieber et al. (Cornhill: B. B. Mussey & Co., 1830), 527–529. Hereafter abbreviated as "Copyright." Francis Lieber, "Literary Property" in *Encyclopædia Americana. A Popular Dictionary of Arts, Sciences, Literature, History, Politics and Biography. Vol. VIII.*, ed. Francis Lieber et al. (Philadelphia: Carey and Lea, 1831), 14–16. Hereafter abbreviated as "Literary Property."

62 Francis Lieber, *Manual of Political Ethics, Designed Chiefly for the Use of Colleges and Students at Law. Part I* (Boston: Charles C. Little and James Brown, 1838). Hereafter abbreviated as *Political Ethics I.* Francis Lieber, *Manual of Political Ethics, Designed Chiefly for the Use of Colleges and Students at Law. Part II* (Boston: Charles C. Little and James Brown, 1839). Herafter abbreviated as *Political Ethics II.* Francis Lieber, *Legal and Political Hermeneutics, Or of Principles of Interpretation and Construction in Law and Politics, with Remarks on Precedents and Authorities* (Boston: Charles C. Little and James Brown, 1839). Hereafter abbreviated as *Hermeneutics.*

Honorable William C. Preston (1840) and *Essays on Property and Labor* (1841).[63] The continuation and development of Lieber's arguments is traced through his correspondence and private notes, including a draft he drew up for a new international copyright, and through his activities as an issue entrepreneur, who framed the issue in understandable and compelling terms for policy makers and the public. Chapter 7 maps out the continued development of Lieber's framing of international copyright and literary property throughout the last decades of his life. This chapter also offers a detailed analysis of how Lieber connected these issues with other concerns, such as slavery, book tariffs, free trade, and international law, in his dynamic narrative framing. Chapter 8 concludes the analysis, highlights continuations in Lieber's framing, restates his importance as a transnational negotiator who introduced European notions into the US discourse, and finally assesses his effectiveness as an issue entrepreneur for the cause of international copyright in the US during the nineteenth century.

63 Francis Lieber, *On International Copyright, In a Letter to the Hon. William C. Preston, Senator of the United States.* (New York: Wiley and Putnam, 1840). Hereafter abbreviated as *International Copyright.* Francis Lieber, *Essays on Property and Labor as Connected with Natural Law and the Constitution of Society* (New York: Harper & Brothers, 1841). Hereafter abbreviated as *Essays.*

CHAPTER 2

State of Research

Francis Lieber was a well-known intellectual in the US during his lifetime – not least because he frequently initiated correspondence with influential politicians and judges to share his opinions and concerns with them. As a professor at South Carolina College and at Columbia College in New York City he influenced generations of students and many of his publications were printed in second editions. After he died in 1872, several biographical works focused on Lieber were published. Martin Russell Thayer (1819–1906), a Republican politician and Lieber's friend, delivered the speech "The Life, Character, and Writings of Francis Lieber" to the *Historical Society of Pennsylvania* a year after his death; the speech was later printed and published.[1] Thayer also wrote the biographical note included in *The Miscellaneous Writings of Francis Lieber*, a collection of Lieber's hitherto unpublished essays, manuscripts, and selected letters.[2] Daniel C. Gilman (1831–1908), president of John Hopkins University, assembled the collection at the request of Mathilde Lieber and published it in 1881.[3] That same year he also published a second volume with Lieber's contributions to political science in the form of lectures, articles, and essays.[4] Johann Caspar Bluntschli (1808–1881), a Swiss jurist who worked with Lieber on codes of international law, penned the introduction.[5] Only one year later, Thomas Sergeant Perry (1845–1928), a lecturer at Harvard, edited and published *The Life and Letters of Francis Lieber*.[6] During the editing process,

1 Martin Russel Thayer, *The Life, Character, and Writings of Francis Lieber. A Discourse Delivered before the Historical Society of Pennsylvania, January 13, 1873* (Philadelphia: Collins, 1873).

2 M. R. Thayer, "Biographical Discourse by Hon. M. R. Thayer" in *The Miscellaneous Writings of Francis Lieber. I. Reminiscences, Addresses, and Essays*, edited by Daniel C. Gilman (Philadelphia: J. B. Lippincott & Co., 1881), 13–44.

3 Francis Lieber, *The Miscellaneous Writings of Francis Lieber. I. Reminiscences, Addresses, and Essays*, ed. Daniel C. Gilman (Philadelphia: J. B. Lippincott & Co., 1881). Hereafter abbreviated as *Miscellaneous Writings I.*

4 Francis Lieber, *The Miscellaneous Writings of Francis Lieber. II. Contributions to Political Science, Including Lectures on the Constitution of the United States and Other Papers*, ed. Daniel C. Gilman (Philadelphia: J. B. Lippincott & Co., 1881). Hereafter abbreviated as *Miscellaneous Writings II.*

5 Bluntschli, Johann Casper, "Lieber's Service to Political Science and International Law" in *The Miscellaneous Writings of Francis Lieber. II. Contributions to Political Science*, ed. Daniel C. Gilman (Philadelphia: J. B. Lippincott & Co., 1881), 7–14.

6 Francis Lieber, *The Life and Letters of Francis Lieber*, ed. Thomas Sergeant Perry (Boston: James R. Osgood and Company, 1882). Hereafter abbreviated as *Life and Letters.*

Perry cooperated with Mathilde Lieber, who influenced the selection and presentation of Lieber's works in the collection. Franz von Holtzendorff (1829–1889), a German jurist and professor, published a German biography of Lieber's life on the basis of Perry's edited collection in 1885.[7] Soon after, German jurist Hugo Preuß (1860–1925) published a biographical sketch of Lieber's life within its historical and political context, along with an assessment of Lieber's published works and his influence in the US and in the German states.[8] Preuß was no known acquaintance of Francis or Mathilde Lieber and this work marks the transition from biographical works to scientific discourse on Lieber. Preuß described Lieber as a "citizen of two worlds" ("Bürger zweier Welten"), at home both in Prussia and in the US. He focused on Lieber's mutual interrelationships ("Wechselbeziehungen"), which spanned like threads across the Atlantic, forming an indestructible net ("ein unzerreißbares Netz") between Europe and America.[9] Preuß was the first to highlight Lieber's transnational relationships and his transatlantic network, aspects of Lieber's life and legacy which are still paramount in contemporary research on Lieber.

In 1899, Lewis R. Harley undertook the project of writing a comprehensive Lieber biography. He came into contact with Lieber's writing on political philosophy during a seminar at the University of Pennsylvania and decided to present "the story of [Lieber's] life and an exposition of his political writings" within a single volume.[10] In *Francis Lieber. His Life and Political Philosophy* Harley intertwines Lieber's ideas and philosophy with his personality, his life, and the historical context.[11] While his work follows the chronology of Lieber's life, it goes beyond the scope of a biography and instead examines Lieber's political philosophy, his stance on education and religion, his identity as an American, and his methodology as professor and researcher. In 1901, the fourth edition of Lieber's *On Civil Liberty and Self-Government* was published posthumously, and Daniel C. Gilman took that opportunity to assess the importance of Lieber's works in an article in *The Yale Law Journal*.[12] Ten years later, Ernest Nys reassessed Lieber's life and works in a two-part article in *The American Journal of International Law*. He demonstrates Lieber's importance to the study of law in the US and especially his contributions to the

7 Franz von Holtzendorff, *Franz Lieber. Aus den Denkwürdigkeiten eines Deutsch-Amerikaners (1800–1872)* (Stuttgart: W. Spemann, 1885).

8 Hugo Preuß, *Franz Lieber. Ein Bürger zweier Welten* (Berlin: Verlag von Carl Habel, 1886).

9 Preuß, *Bürger*, 3–4.

10 Harley, *Francis Lieber*, vii.

11 Lewis Harley, *Francis Lieber. His Life and Political Philosophy* (New York: Columbia UP, 1899).

12 Gilman, Daniel C. "Francis Lieber," *The Yale Law Journal* 10.7 (1901): 271–274.

emerging field of international law. Nys identifies Lieber's *Code 100* as his central work because it "has exercised an influence not generally realized on the laws of war, and has to a great extent contributed to render [war] more humane throughout the entire world."[13] In 1918, Chester Squire Phinney published his PhD thesis focused on Francis Lieber.[14] He gives a short biographical overview and evaluates Lieber's influence on American thought. Phinney brought attention to German-American cultural relations and emphasized the influence of German immigrants in the US by taking Lieber as an example.[15] He identifies "political writings [...] education, military affairs, international law and penology" as Lieber's major areas of influence and argues that it was "under the incentive of [American] highly liberal institutions" that Lieber developed his thought on these subjects, underlining the transcultural nature of Lieber's thought.[16]

Interest in Lieber's works declined over the next decade until Charles B. Robson examined the collection of Lieber's papers that Mathilde Lieber had sold to *The Huntington Library*. Robson published an overview of the source material in *The Huntington Library Bulletin* in 1933, assessing Lieber's correspondence, manuscripts, notes, drafts, and university lectures, and printed materials. He also compiled a list of Lieber's correspondents. Robson names Lieber as a central influence on "the development of civilization in the United States" and positions him as an authority on political economy, constitutional history, and international law, as well as on education and sociology.[17] He argues that Lieber pioneered methodology in some of these fields and collected and preserved data and accounts concerning all.[18] Lieber collected resources such as newspaper articles, asked acquaintances to send him government documents, and circulated questionnaires on different topics among experts. Any information Lieber acquired, he collected in scrapbooks filled with notes, newspaper clippings, statistical information, and case records.[19] These findings in his personal documents illustrate the way Lieber approached topics of interest, highlight the scope of his investigations, and

13 Ernest Nys, "Francis Lieber – His Life and His Work: Part I," *The American Journal of International Law* 5.1 (1911): 84–117, 86.

14 Chester Squire Phinney, *Francis Lieber's Influence on American Thought and Some of His Unpublished Letters* (Philadelphia: International Printing Co., 1918).

15 Phinney, *Influence*, 8.

16 Phinney, *Influence*, 55–56.

17 Charles B. Robson, "Papers of Francis Lieber," *The Huntington Library Bulletin* 3 (1933): 135–155, 135, 138–139.

18 Robson, "Papers,“ 138–139.

19 Charles B. Robson, "Francis Lieber's Theories of Society, Government, and Liberty," *The Journal of Politics* 4.2 (1942): 227–249, 232.

suggest that he engaged in original research. He developed his own methodology and made use of his extensive literary network to acquire information and data, which he then published in articles or books. Lieber combined knowledge from Europe and from the US, consulted experts, and adapted his transnational experiences to US academia.

Alongside Robson, Frank Freidel became an avid Lieber scholar. Initially, he examined Lieber's relationship with Charles Sumner and his stance on slavery.[20] His second article focuses on Lieber's contribution to the international copyright movement in the US and constitutes the only detailed examination of Lieber's stance on copyright that precedes this work.[21] Freidel examines Lieber's contribution to the early stages of the movement by analyzing his correspondence between 1839 and the late 1840s, focusing on Lieber's most active period of copyright advocacy. He identifies the years 1836 and 1837 as moments when international copyright protection became a prominent topic in politics and the media, prompted by public protests of British publishers, US-American authors, and the petition introduced to Congress by Henry Clay in 1837 (see chapter 3.1.4 and 6). Freidel claims that Lieber's involvement in the debate started in 1839, when he contacted Clay and urged him to continue his efforts. This work contextualizes that claim by demonstrating that Lieber took an earlier interest in the subject matter, visible in his early publications from the late 1820s. Freidel also demonstrates Lieber's continued involvement by presenting his letters to William Hickling Prescott, Washington Irving, and Daniel Webster, and through reference to Lieber's central work *On International Copyright* (1840). This work elaborates on Freidel's research by focusing on a longer time span, expanding it from 1827 until 1868. It also examines more sources, going beyond correspondence to include diary entries, drafts, and printed material. It contextualizes Freidel's observations to show that copyright advocacy was not merely a brief phase in Lieber's life but constituted a lifelong commitment to the issue.

Based on the archival material in *The Huntington Library*, Frank Freidel published a comprehensive Lieber biography in 1948.[22] Freidel's and Robson's works sparked renewed interest in Lieber's oeuvre: Several articles examining specific aspects of Lieber's life and work were published during the 1930s, 1940s, and 1950s. Brainerd Dyer analyzes Lieber's perspective on the American

---

20 Frank Freidel, "Francis Lieber, Charles Sumner, and Slavery," *The Journal of Southern History* 9.1 (1943): 75–93.

21 Frank Freidel, "Lieber's Contribution to the International Copyright Movement," *Huntington Library Quarterly* 8.2 (1945): 200–206.

22 Frank Freidel, *Francis Lieber. Nineteenth-Century Liberal* (Baton Rouge: Louisiana State UP, 1948).

Civil War, Merle Curti and Charles B. Robson outline Lieber's nationalism.[23] Robson also details Lieber's theory on society, government, and liberty, and Carl L. Lokke focuses on Lieber's handling of confederate records.[24] When Frank Freidel published "Francis Lieber: Transmitter of European Ideas to America" in 1956, he emphasized the aspect of transnational relationships that Hugo Preuß and Chester Squire Phinney had focused on earlier and his interest shifted towards cultural exchange. While Freidel maps out Lieber's contribution to the transfer of knowledge and ideas across the Atlantic, he mostly does not focus on reciprocal exchange of ideas between cultures. Rather, he outlines how Lieber transported European concepts to his new home country and portrays him as "a gatherer of European seeds for American planting."[25] He argues that Lieber was the most active "transmitter of European ideas to America" of his time, eager to ensure that German ideas flourished in the US.[26] Freidel names Lieber's *Encyclopædia Americana* as an example of an active transfer of ideas from one cultural context to the other and outlines Lieber's strategy "to interpret phenomena of the new world in the ideological terms of the old – to explain, identify, and label" in his *Manual of Political Ethics*.[27] Freidel summarizes Lieber's impact by stating that he was not "a great and original thinker" but merely "a conveyor and synthesizer" of ideas, who only turned "one-way traffic [into] an interchange" late in his life.[28]

More recently, other scholars have also examined Lieber's role as a transmitter of ideas from Europe to the US and vice versa. In *Brücken aus Papier*, Claudia Schnurmann supports the idea that his contemporaries perceived Lieber as a conveyor and mediator of ideas, as someone who brought ideas from the centers of academic and institutional knowledge, such as Berlin and London, to the periphery of scientific activity, Boston, Columbia, SC, and New York City.[29] He collected not just scientific knowledge but also other types of knowledge in the widest sense, such as "Beziehungswissen" (rela-

23 Brainerd Dyer, "Francis Lieber and the American Civil War," *Huntington Library Quarterly*, 2.4 (1939): 449–465; Merle Curti, "Francis Lieber and Nationalism," Huntington Library Quarterly, 4.3 (1941): 263–292; Charles B. Robson, "Francis Lieber's Nationalism," *The Journal of Politics* 8.1 (1946): 57–73.

24 Robson, "Theories," 227–249; Carl L. Lokke, "The Captured Confederate Records under Francis Lieber," *The American Archivist*, 9.4 (1946): 277–319.

25 Frank Freidel, "Francis Lieber: Transmitter of European Ideas to America," *Bulletin of the John Rylands Library* 38.2 (1956): 342–359, 353.

26 Freidel, "Transmitter,“ 343.

27 Freidel, "Transmitter,“ 347–353.

28 Freidel, "Transmitter,“ 359.

29 "Nach zeitgenössischer Einschätzung hatte sich Lieber aus den Zentren des akademischen Wissenschaffens nach Boston, Columbia/SC und New York begeben, um von dort

tional knowledge).[30] Schnurmann considers Francis Lieber an "Atlantic broker,"[31] whose intellectual and publicist activities were enabled through a vast network of not just professional and scholarly but also mundane everyday contacts, such as friends and relatives. He processed and digested knowledge from different scientific as well as practical areas in his own work, conveyed it through public and private channels, and collected works of authors from other disciplinary, temporal, and linguistic spheres.[32]

Kurt Mueller-Vollmer states that the impact of German culture on the US in the areas of philosophy, theology, political thought, literature, and education was never as significant as in the Jacksonian age in the 1820s and 1830s, the period during which Lieber migrated to the US. Mueller-Vollmer sees Lieber as an "embodiment of the close relationship" between the development of US nationalism and the reception of German culture in the US.[33] Paul D. Carrington focuses specifically on Lieber's teaching and his lasting influence on US law.[34] Michael H. Hoeflich also examines German influences on the development of US-American law while criticizing that scholars often merely focus on the stream of ideas *towards* the German states.[35] He uses the correspondence between Lieber, Joseph Story, and C. J. A. Mittermaier to demonstrate that US jurists were interested in German law and in acquaintances with German jurists. An intermediary like Lieber, who could establish contact, facilitate

die Gebiete in einem atlantischen System von Wissen in dessen sämtlichen Spielarten zusammenzufügen" (Schnurmann, *Brücken,* 21–22).

30 Schnurmann, *Brücken,* 21–22.

31 "Atlantic" here refers to spatial as well as abstract spheres, it means knowledge transported via letter across the Atlantic, but also knowledge that is produced by those working and living in the Atlantic greater area (Schnurmann, *Brücken,* 35).

32 "Lieber verarbeitete nicht nur Wissen aus unterschiedlichen akademischen und praktischen Bereichen in seinem eigenen umfangreichen Werk, vermittelte es über unterschiedliche öffentliche und private Medien und sammelte und hortete in seiner Bibliothek einen umfangreichen Fundus an Wissen anderer Autoren unterschiedlicher fachlicher, zeitlicher und sprachlicher Provenienz" (Schnurmann, *Brücken,* 21).

33 Kurt Mueller-Vollmer, "German-American Cultural Interaction in the Jacksonian Era: Six Unpublished Letters by Francis Lieber and John Pickering to Wilhelm von Humboldt," *Die Unterrichtspraxis/Teaching German* 31.1 (1998): 1–11, 1.

34 Paul D. Carrington, "The Theme of Early American Law Teaching: The Political Ethics of Francis Lieber," *Journal of Legal Education,* 42.3 (1992): 339–398, 397.

35 M. H. Hoeflich, "Transatlantic Friendships & the German Influence on American Law in the First Half of the Nineteenth Century," *The American Journal of Comparative Law* 35.3 (1987): 599–611, 599.

cross-cultural exchange of written resources, and even translate texts, carried forward the field of US-American as well as German law.[36]

Lieber's transcultural influence also remained of central interest to more recent research: Peter Schäfer and Karl Schmitt dedicate an entire anthology to Lieber's impact on German-American relationships.[37] It includes an article on Lieber's scientific achievements in the US by Peter Becker, in which he identifies Lieber as one of the first interpreters of the US, someone who explained the US to Germans.[38] George Haimbaugh expands on Becker's claim that Lieber's publications, especially his *Legal and Political Hermeneutics* and his *Code 100,* significantly influenced US law by assessing Lieber's contribution to legal studies and the law in the US today.[39] He presents Lieber's *Code 100* as the first codification of the laws of war and claims that with it Lieber laid the groundwork for the codification of martial law not only in the US, but internationally. The articles of his *Code 100* influenced the content of many different articles and conventions during the following century, including the Hague Conventions of 1899 and 1907 and the Geneva Conventions of 1949.[40] In 2005, Charles Mack and Henry Lesense published another anthology dedicated to Lieber's cultural influence, including an article by Steven Samson, which positions Lieber as a "transatlantic cultural missionary."[41]

Articles on Lieber's *Legal and Political Hermeneutics* constitute another pillar of current Lieber research, with a rise in interest sparked by James Farr's

---

36 Story urged Lieber to "study law formally so as to make himself employable in the United States as a law professor and to enable him to write for American lawyers" (Hoeflich, "Transatlantic Friendships," 603). Story wanted Lieber to "act as a go-between and translator between American lawyers and German lawyers." Since he could not read the German language himself, Story needed translators that would enable him to read German law texts (Hoeflich, "Transatlantic Friendships," 604).

37 Schäfer, Peter, and Karl Schmitt, editors. *Franz Lieber Und Die Deutsch-Amerikanischen Beziehungen Im 19. Jahrhundert* (Weimar/Cologne: Böhlau, 1993).

38 Peter Becker, "Francis Liebers wissenschaftliche Leistungen in den USA" in *Franz Lieber und die deutsch-amerikanischen Beziehungen im 19. Jahrhundert,* ed. Peter Schäfer and Karl Schmitt (Weimar/Cologne: Böhlau, 1993), 31–44, 34. In my own article I expand on this notion, see Fenja Heisig, "Travel Writing and Transnational Relations: Francis Lieber As The Stranger in America," *Current Objectives of Postgraduate American Studies,* 23.1 (2022): 24–40, doi:10.5283/copas.355.

39 George Haimbaugh, "Liebers Bedeutung für die heutige Rechtswissenschaft in den USA" in *Franz Lieber und die deutsch-amerikanischen Beziehungen im 19. Jahrhundert,* ed. Peter Schäfer and Karl Schmitt (Weimar/Cologne: Böhlau, 1993), 73–80.

40 Haimbaugh, "Bedeutung," 75.

41 Charles Mack and Henry Lesesne, eds. *Francis Lieber and the Culture of the Mind* (Columbia: University of South Carolina Press, 2005); Samson, "Cultural Missionary," 129.

research towards the end of the twentieth century.[42] A symposium entirely dedicated to *Legal and Political Hermeneutics* resulted in an anthology of articles on the subject in *Cardozo Law Review*.[43] German scholars were also interested in the work: Stephan Meder published an article on Lieber's legal hermeneutic method in 2012 and Juri Auderset focused on his political hermeneutics in 2016.[44]

Nevertheless, the *Code 100* remains Lieber's most popular work and most Lieber research focuses on his influence on international law, specifically on the laws of war and the law of nations. Elihu Root and George B. Davies reviewed the *Code 100* in *The American Journal of International Law* as early as 1907.[45] Richard Sallet assessed Lieber's contribution to the law of nations in 1964, while James Childress contextualized Lieber's understanding of the laws of war in 1976.[46] R. S. Hartigan analyzed Lieber's *Code 100* in relation to the certification of conflict in 1983 and Jordan J. Paust presented it again at the annual meeting of the *American Society of International Law* in 2001.[47] In the German states, Lieber's influence on the laws of war was examined by Betsy

---

42 James Farr, "Francis Lieber and the Interpretation of American Political Science," *The Journal of Politics*, 52.4 (1990): 1027–1049); James Farr, "The Americanization of Hermeneutics: Francis Lieber's Legal and Political Hermeneutics" in *Legal Hermeneutics: History, Theory, and Practice*, ed. Gregory Leyh (Oakland: University of California Press, 1992), 83–102.

43 Michael Herz, "Rediscovering Francis Lieber: An Afterword and Introduction," *Cardozo Law Review* 16.6 (1995): 2107–2134; Guyora Binder, "Institutions and Linguistic Conventions: The Pragmatism of Lieber's Legal Hermeneutics," *Cardozo Law Review*, 16.6 (1995): 2169–2189; William N. Jr Eskridge, "Fetch Some Soupmeat," *Cardozo Law Review* 16.6 (1995): 2209–2224; Lawrence Lessig, "The Limits of Lieber," *Cardozo Law Review*, 16.6 (1995): 2249–2272; Mike Robert Horenstein, "The Virtues of Interpretation in a Jural Sociey," *Cardozo Law Review* 16.6 (1995): 2273–2304; Aviam Soifer, "Facts, Things, and the Orphans of Girard College: Francis Lieber, Protopragmatist," *Cardozo Law Review* 16.6 (1995): 2305–2319.

44 Stephan Meder, "Interpretation und Konstruktion. Zur juristischen Hermeneutik von Francis Lieber (1800–1872)," *JuristenZeitung* 67.11 (2012): 529–538; Juri Auderset, *Transatlantischer Förderalismus* (Berlin/Boston: De Gruyter, 2016), 241–280.

45 Elihu Root and George B. Davis, "Francis Lieber," *Proceedings of the American Society of International Law at Its Annual Meeting (1907–1917)* 7 (1913): 8–30.

46 Richard Sallet, "On Francis Lieber and His Contribution to the Law of Nations Today" in *Recht im Dienste der Menschenwürde*, ed. Herbert Kraus (Würzburg: Holzner, 1964), 279–306; James Childress, "Francis Lieber's Interpretation of the Laws of War: General Orders No. 100 in the Context of His Life and Thought," *The American Journal of Jurisprudence*, 21(1976): 34–70.

47 R. S. Hartigan, *Military Rules, Regulations and the Code of War: Francis Lieber and the Certification of Conflict* (London/New York: Routledge, 1983); Jordan Paust, "Dr. Francis Lieber and the Lieber Code," *Proceedings of the Annual Meeting (American Society of International Law)* 95 (2001): 112–115.

Baker in 2003 and by Roman Schmidt-Radefeldt in 2009, who emphasized the transnational influence of Lieber's works.[48] Many articles followed during the past two decades, highlighting continued interest in Lieber's influence on the laws of war, as well as his lasting importance as an authority on international law and transnational cooperation.[49]

In 2008, Hartmut Keil published an analysis of Lieber's attitudes towards race, slavery, and abolition.[50] Keil followed up his first article with another examination of Lieber's understanding of slavery, which he examined in relation to Lieber's property theory.[51] Most recently, John Fabian Witt published an article on Lieber's theory of American emergency constitutionalism, based on one of Lieber's previously unexamined manuscripts at *The Huntington Library* and Wayne Wei-siang Hsieh focused on Lieber's contribution to the laws of war in relation to the emergence of a liberal international order for the anthology *The New Makers of Modern Strategy: From the Ancient World to the Digital Age*.[52]

48 Betsy Baker, *Johann Caspar Bluntschli, Francis Lieber Und Das Modern Völkerrecht 1861–1881* (Baden-Baden: Nomos, 2003); Roman Schmidt-Radefeldt, *Die Wurzeln des modernen Kriegsvölkerrechts als transatlantisches Erbe. Leben und Werken von Francis Lieber (1798–1872)* (Bremen: Edition Temmen, 2009).

49 See for example: Matthew J. Mancini, "Francis Lieber, Slavery, and the 'Genesis' of the Laws of War." *The Journal of Southern History*, 77.2 (2011): 325–348; Rotem Giladi, "Francis Lieber on Public War," *Goettingen Journal of International Law*, 4.2 (2012): 447–77; D. H. Dilbeck, "'The Genesis of This Little Tablet with My Name': Francis Lieber and the Wartime Origins of General Orders No. 100." *Journal of the Civil War Era*, 5.2 (2015): 231–53; Dilbeck, D. H. "The More Vigorously Wars Are Pursued, the Better It Is for Humanity: Francis Lieber and General Orders No. 100." *A More Civil War: How the Union Waged a Just War*, University of North Carolina Press, 2016, 69–96; Dilbeck, D. H. "'Responsible to One Another and to God:' Why Francis Lieber Believed the Union War Must Remain a Just War" in *New Perspectives on the Union War*, ed. Gary Gallagher and Elizabeth Varon (New York: Fordham UP, 2019), 143–159; Vöneky, Silja. "Francis Lieber and the Lieber Code – Against the Inhumanities of War." *Freiburger Informationspapiere Zum Völkerrecht Und Öffentlichen Recht*, 8 (2011): 1–7; Ringmar, Erik. "Francis Lieber, Terrorism, and the American Way of War." *Perspectives on Terrorism*, 3.4 (2009): 52–60.

50 Hartmut Keil, "Francis Lieber's Attitudes on Race, Slavery, and Abolition," *Journal of American Ethnic History* 28.1 (2008): 13–33.

51 Hartmut Keil, "'That Species of Property': Francis Lieber's Encounter with Slavery and Race" in *Paths Crossing. Essays in German-American Studies*, ed. Cora Lee Kluge (Oxford: Peter Lang, 2011), 55–83.

52 John Fabian Witt, "A Lost Theory of American Emergency Constitutionalism," *Law and History Review* 36.3 (2018): 551–591; Wayne Wei-siang Hsieh, "Francis Lieber, the Laws of War, and the Origins of the Liberal International Order" in *The New Makers of Modern Strategy: From the Ancient World to the Digital Age*, ed. Hal Brans (Princeton: Princeton UP, 2023), 391–414.

Claudia Schnurmann's German work *Brücken aus Papier* from 2014 constitutes the most comprehensive recent work on Lieber, in which she focuses on the transatlantic relationship and the lively correspondence between Lieber and his wife, Mathilde. Schnurmann includes a biography of Lieber's life, extensive reading of the voluminous correspondence between the Liebers, many transcripts of the transatlantic letters, as well as an examination of the current state of research on Francis and Mathilde Lieber. This work contributes to the exploration of transatlantic knowledge exchange and the importance of the genre of letters in historical research. Schnurmann also published the extensive letter collection *A Sea of Love* in 2018, where she contextualizes the correspondence between Francis and Mathilde Lieber and transcribes 95 selected letters exchanged between the couple from 1839 to 1845.[53]

Despite the praise offered in eulogies for Lieber's life, many of his once-popular works seem almost forgotten today. Scholars often lament that Lieber does not get the attention he deserves.[54] Yet in 1993, the Friedrich-Schiller University in Jena held a scientific colloquium in Lieber's honor that resulted in the publication of an anthology containing twelve articles dedicated to Lieber's German-American relations.[55] In 1995, *Cardozo Law Review* published an issue solely dedicated to Lieber's *Legal and Political Hermeneutics*, which contained articles from an entire symposium on *Legal and Political Hermeneutics*.[56] In 2005, *Francis Lieber and the Culture of the Mind* was published, an anthology of articles which resulted from another Lieber symposium held in Columbia, South Carolina, in 2001. Law and literature scholars also focus on Lieber's works, especially his *Legal and Political Hermeneutics*.[57] Lieber's work

53 Claudia Schnurmann, *A Sea of Love. The Atlantic Correspondence of Francis and Mathilde Lieber, 1839–1845* (Leiden: Brill, 2018).

54 These disciplines include legal studies, political sciences, and sociology. Michael Herz stated in 1995 that "Francis Lieber, once this country's most respected law professor, of whom it was written in 1873 that 'his fame will be secure in the lap of history,' [...] is forgotten despite great accomplishment. At best, one might say he is famous for being forgotten. His name comes up, but almost every modern reference to Lieber points out that few remember who he was" ("Rediscovering," 2107). An inquiry into Lieber's works from a literary studies viewpoint is rather new, Peter Schneck's article "Who Owns Uncle Tom's Cabin? Literature as Cultural Property" and his talk "The Hermeneutics of Property: Francis Lieber on Copyright, Labor, and Textual Interpretation," held at the 2019 *Forum Law as Culture*, are some of the first examples.

55 Karl Schmitt and Peter Schäfer, *Franz Lieber und die deutsch-amerikanischen Beziehungen im 19. Jahrhundert* (Weimar: Böhlau, 1994).

56 "A Symposium on Legal and Political Hermeneutics." *Cardozo Law Review*, 16.6 (1995).

57 See for example Levinson, Sanford, and Steven Mailloux, editors. *Interpreting Law and Literature. A Hermeneutic Reader.* Northwestern UP, 1988; Posner, Richard A. "Legislation and Its Interpretation: A Primer." *Nebraska Law Review*, 68.431 (1989): 431–453; Brook,

is still analyzed and cited in scholarly articles today.[58] Lieber's *General Order 100*, issued during the US Civil War on April 24, 1863, served as a template during the Hague Conventions held in 1899 and 1907, and influenced the drafting of the 1949 Geneva Convention.[59] The *Lieber Institute for Law and Warfare at West Point* researches the relationship between law and warfare and publishes *Lieber Studies*, a series of publications examining legal issues in warfare.[60] The *Lieber Correctional Institution* in Ridgeville, South Carolina, is a maximum-security state prison named after Lieber to acknowledge his contributions to prison reform and the study of penology.[61] In Lieber's honor, the University of South Carolina named the building he resided in *Lieber College*. Yearly, the *Lieber Society on the Law of Armed Conflict*, which is part of the *American Society of International Law*, awards the Francis Lieber Prize to authors of notable publications in the field of law and armed conflict.[62]

Thomas. *Cross-Examinations of Law and Literature. Cooper, Hawthorne, Stowe, and Melville*. Cambridge UP, 1990.

58 Examples of recent publications include: Stuart Streichler, *Presidential Accountability in Wartime. President Bush, the Treatment of Detainees, and the Laws of War* (Ann Arbor: University of Michigan Press, 2023); Paul H. Wise, "Saving Stones and Saving Lives: A Humanitarian Perspective on Protecting Cultural Heritage in War" in *Cultural Heritage and Mass Atrocities*, ed. James Cuno and Thomas G. Weiss (Los Angeles: Getty Publications, 2022) 309–322; Keun-Gwan Lee and The United Nations, "Recalibrating the Conception of Codification in the Changing Landscape of International Law" in *Seventy Years of the International Law Commission: Drawing a Balance for the Future* (Leiden: Brill, 2021), 300–332.

59 John Fabian Witt, *Lincoln's Code: The Laws of War in American History* (New York: Free Press, 2013), 195.

60 *Lieber Institute at West Point*, https://lieber.westpoint.edu. Accessed 24 Oct. 2023. *Lieber Studies*, https://lieber.westpoint.edu/lieber-series/. Accessed 24 Oct. 2023.

61 Gerhard Weiss, "The Americanization of Franz Lieber and the Encyclopedia Americana" in *German Culture in Nineteenth-Century America. Reception, Adaptation, Transformation*, ed. Lynne Tatlock and Matt Erlin (Rochester: Camden House, 2005), 273–288, 273.

62 Schnurmann, *Brücken*, 20–21. Lieber *Society on the Law of Armed Conflict*, https://www.asil.org/community/lieber-society-law-armed-conflict#:~:text=The%20Lieber%20Society%20serves%20as,the%20conduct%20of%20military%20operations. Accessed 24 Oct. 2023. See the call for submissions for the Francis Lieber prize 2021 at Ziegler, Andreas R. *Call for Submissions for the 2021 Lieber Prize*. 7 Nov. 2020, ilasuisse.wordpress.com/2020/11/07/call-for-submissions-for-the-2021-lieber-prize/. Accessed 11 March 2021.

CHAPTER 3

Historical Context

In *Owning Ideas*, Owen Bracha points out that while intellectual property is ever present in our daily lives today, it still seems odd: "When one thinks about it, the concept of owning an intangible product of the mind is strange and exotic," Bracha writes.[1] The product of the mind, the expression of an idea in a written work has not always been considered a form of property. The protection of literature through copyright developed along with the professionalization of authorship and the emergence of the notion of originality. For the US, the late eighteenth and the nineteenth century proved a pivotal time in the conceptualization of an American authorship-based copyright law. Economic interests, ideological narratives, and social conditions influenced the legal emergence of copyright.[2] Copyright became a democratized right rather than a printing privilege – though initially these rights were not available to parts of the population, such as married women or enslaved authors.[3] The *Copyright Act of 1790* assigned legal rights to a work to authors, rather than printers or publishers, and provided the legal and conceptual framework for the discourse on copyright. As Bracha points out,

> [w]hether they emphasized the notion of copyright as an inherent natural right or as a positivist creature of the state, based on utilitarian considerations, Americans thinking, writing and disagreeing about copyright shared a new conceptual framework. At the heart of this framework were the concepts of authors as individuals who through their mental labor create original intellectual works and of copyright as a standardized set of legal rights enjoyed by such authors owning the intellectual works they created.[4]

The physical object of property became an intangible one as "the copy" of a work became "a construct of a semi-materialist object of ownership, at once intangible and endowed with qualities equivalent to those of owned physical objects," as Bracha states.[5] The copy as "an intellectual template capable of

1 Bracha, *Owning Ideas*, 1.
2 Bracha, *Owning Ideas*, 4.
3 Bracha, *Owning Ideas*, 6.
4 Bracha, *Owning Ideas*, 45
5 Bracha, *Owning Ideas*, 6–7.

 | HTTPS://DOI.ORG/10.1515/9783112239407-003

producing an endless series of identical material embodiments" was eventually replaced by "the work," an "elusive intellectual essenc[e] capable of manifestation in numerous concrete forms."[6] Consequently, the question of how to own an intangible object arose. Ownership of a work included the power to exclude others from manufacturing and selling physical copies of the work, but gradually the market value of the work became paramount. Ownership consisted of the legal right to "internalize this market value by controlling the markets for all the concrete embodiments of the intellectual essence."[7] The ideological framework resulted from jurisprudential and economic debates and in turn shaped legal institutions. During the early nineteenth century, the mission was to fit intellectual property into the established property framework, but by the late nineteenth century intellectual property reshaped the general property framework.[8] As Bracha points out, copyright law and practices were shaped through legislation, and legislation was influenced by litigation, lobbying, and the work of interest groups.[9] As an issue entrepreneur for the cause of international copyright, Francis Lieber partook in these efforts to influence legislation and promote the recognition of an international copyright.

Through his writing and networking, Lieber contributed to the social, political, and legal discourse that shaped the ideological framework and determined the legal protection of intellectual property in the US. This chapter provides an overview of the development of the nineteenth-century US-American national and international copyright regime in order to provide the historical context within which Lieber's works and activities will be analyzed in the following chapters. Precedents of the US copyright regime trace back to the *Stationers' Company*'s printing privileges in seventeenth-century England. This chapter therefore traces US copyright back to seventeenth- and eighteenth-century copyright regimes in England and analyzes their adaptation in English colonies in North America. A closer look at copyright regulation in the newly-founded United States follows. This survey includes a brief look at the copyright clauses in the *Constitutional Provision* and the *US Constitution*. The reception and consequences of the *National Copyright Act of 1790* are outlined, followed by a summary of the situation of US authors and publishers. A detailed examination of the international copyright debate in the US during the nineteenth century is the centerpiece of this chapter and provides the nec-

6 Bracha, *Owning Ideas*, 7.
7 Bracha, *Owning Ideas*, 7.
8 Bracha, *Owning Ideas*, 7–8.
9 Bracha, *Owning Ideas*, 9–10.

essary social, legal, and political context for the discussion of Lieber's own works. An analysis of select European systems of copyright and droit d'auteur protection follows, to lay the groundwork for a comparison with Lieber's transnational understanding of copyright and literature as property. In the chapter conclusion, the different ideologies of copyright and authors' rights protection are compared and contrasted to set the stage for the examination of Lieber's publication, networking, and lobbying activities, as well as for the analysis of his transnational understanding of copyright and literary property protection.

3.1 The Copyright Debate in the US

To understand nineteenth-century copyright in the US, it is necessary to consider copyright regulations in the North American colonies during the seventeenth and eighteenth century. Prior to the American War of Independence (1775–1783), copyright in the British colonies was shaped by the British copyright regime, and consequently US copyright regulation bears traces of British influence. An overview of the development of the British copyright framework and its adaptation and alteration in the colonies and the United States lays the historical foundation for the analysis of Lieber's contribution to the US copyright discourse of the nineteenth century.

British copyright law, which would later significantly influence early US-American copyright legislation, can be traced back to the fifteenth century, when the *Worshipful Company of Stationers and Newspaper Makers* (*Stationers' Company*) was founded in London in 1403.[10] Before long, those most engaged in the London book trade became members of the *Stationers' Company* guild.[11] Initially, there were no printers in the guild as printing had not yet arrived in England, as Ian Gadd clarifies.[12] When Johannes Gutenberg (c. 1400–1468) invented the movable-type printing press in Mainz, Holy Roman Empire, around the year 1440, the sale of mass-produced printed books soon created

10 As Ian Gadd points out, the origins of the *Stationers' Company* can be traced back to 1357, but it was formally incorporated in 1403 ("Stationers' Company," 81). For a detailed account of the origins of the *Stationers' Company* and the role it played in London until the passage of the *Statute of Anne* in 1710, see Ian Gadd, "The Stationers' Company in England before 1710" in *Research Handbook on the History of Copyright Law*, ed. Isabella Alexander and H. Tomás Gómez-Arostegui (Cheltenham: Edward Elgar Publishing, 2016), 81–95.

11 Gadd, "Stationers' Company," 82.

12 Gadd, "Stationers' Company," 81.

a flourishing new market and printers and booksellers searched for new means of controlling the book trade. Writers themselves were not yet involved in the process of printing and publishing their works.[13] The publishing trade did not operate within an organized framework until the mid-sixteenth century and consequently individual printing guilds could not prevent the reprinting of works.[14] This changed when the *Stationers' Company* – its members now booksellers, printers, and binders – was granted a royal printing charter on May 4, 1557.[15] According to this royal charter, no one could operate a printing press in England without membership in the *Stationers' Company* or without a direct royal privilege. Now the *Stationers' Company* could grant its members a right akin to a perpetual copyright (a term not used until 1701), if they published and sold their works following the *Stationers' Company*'s requirements.[16] The right was designed as a publishers' right and restricted printing in England for almost 140 years. Once a printing privilege was granted, the work was registered without temporal limitations in the *Stationers' Company*'s register book.[17] Printers who were not members of the *Stationers' Company* were required to obtain a royal license and printing privilege for each individual printed work.[18] While registration with the *Stationers' Company* did not stop unlicensed reprinting entirely, it provided legal recourse in the case of "piracy."[19] Patterson argues that granting the royal printing charter to the *Stationers' Company* also aided governmental censorship and control of the press: He claims that the *Stationers' Company* licensed and censored works and thereby served as "policemen of the press" in exchange for a monopoly on printing rights.[20] Gadd, on the other hand, points out that the system of

13 Ludwig Gieseke, *Vom Privileg zum Urheberrecht: Die Entwicklung des Urheberrechts in Deutschland bis 1845* (Baden-Baden: Nomos, 1995), 138; Patterson, *Copyright*, 4–5.

14 Gadd, "Stationers' Company," 86.

15 In England, the printing press was introduced in 1476, eighty-one years before the *Stationers' Company* received its royal printing charter, demonstrating that other forms of book trade regulation had existed prior to the *Stationers' Company*'s grants. As Lyman Ray Patterson and Ian Gadd point out, individual royal grants preceded the *Stationers'* copyright. Gadd argues that "the Crown had no special or exclusive right to bestow grants relating to printing;" other institutions, such as Oxford University, also bestowed such grants (Gadd, "Stationers' Company," 83). Once more works were published during the seventeenth century, the *Stationers'* printing right crowded out other regulation because the *Stationers' Company* granted an unlimited right to print and publish a work (Patterson, *Copyright*, 6).

16 Gadd, "Stationers' Company," 82; Patterson, *Copyright*, 4–5.

17 Patterson, *Copyright*, 9.

18 Gieseke, *Privileg*, 137.

19 Gadd, "Stationers' Company," 89.

20 Patterson, *Copyright*, 6.

printing privileges was not part of royal censorship mechanisms. The *Stationers' Company* merely regulated the printing of a work. Its content was regulated through a pre-publication licensing system.[21]

This amalgamation of licensing, censorship practices, and monopolies was furthered by the *Licensing Act of 1662*, which required the *Stationers'* copyright along with a censor's license for any published work, making at-will printing illegal.[22] This censorship and licensing regime was in effect until it was abolished in 1694, causing a lapse in regulation until the *Statute of Anne* was passed in 1710.[23] Patterson understands the *Stationers'* printing privilege as "a perpetual lease of personal property, a manuscript or a copy [...] for one specific purpose, that of publishing," with the rights of the author being unclear and absent from the equation.[24] John Feather also claims that the "copies" registered with the *Stationers' Company* during the seventeenth century "were, logically enough, being treated as pieces of property," though belonging to the publisher, not the writer.[25] However, in *Authors and Owners,* Mark Rose proposes that the concepts of the individual author and the concept of literary property as cultural formations emerged hand-in-hand with the commodification of literature during the seventeenth and eighteenth centuries. In the period between the incorporation of the *Stationers' Company* and the passage of the *Statute of Anne,* the notion of the author as the originator developed. As the autonomous creator of "the work," the author came to be seen as the rightful owner of the work and slowly, copyright developed as the "institutional embodiment of the author-work relation [...] which not only makes possible the profitable manufacture and distribution of books [...] but also, by endowing it with legal reality, helps to produce and affirm the very identity of the author as author."[26] Within the environment of royal licensing and *Stationers'* printing privileges, the concept of the author as owner became the competitor of exclusive publishing rights and eventually replaced them.[27]

The *Statute of Anne,* the legislation that would legally inscribe copyright and replace the licensing system of the *Stationers' Company* in Great Britain,

21 Gadd, "Stationers' Company,“ 84.
22 Patterson, *Copyright,* 6.
23 Patterson, *Copyright,* 7.
24 Patterson, *Copyright,* 10–12.
25 John Feather, *Publishing, Piracy, and Politics: An Historical Study of Copyright in Britain* (London: Mansell, 1994), 18.
26 Rose, *Authors and Owners,* 1.
27 Rose, *Authors and Owners,* 35.

reflected this process.[28] As John Hughes points out, the drafting process of the *Statute of Anne* balanced "elements reflecting both the property concept's emergence and arguable pushback against the concept."[29] The original draft of the *Statute of Anne* was brought before the British House of Commons on January 11, 1710, as *A Bill for Encouragement of Learning, and for Securing the Property of Copies of Books to the Rightful Owners thereof*.[30] The bill was drafted in response to a petition introduced by a group of influential stationers, who complained that

> divers [sic] Persons have of late invaded the Properties of others, by reprinting several Books, without the Consent, and to the great Injury, of the Proprietors, even to their utter Ruin, and the Discouragement of all Writers in any useful Part of Learning."[31]

The "proprietors" mentioned in this complaint are doubtlessly the stationers themselves. With their complaint they sought to protect their exclusive printing rights, not an author's right to a work. Consequently, a bill was drafted and presented before the House of Commons. The preamble of the draft bill states:

> Whereas the Liberty which Printers, Booksellers and other Persons have of late frequently taken, in Printing, Reprinting, and Publishing, or causing to be Printed, Reprinted, and Published Books, and other Writings, without the Consent of the Authors thereof, in whom the undoubted Property of such Books and Writings, as the Product of their Learning and Labour, remains; or of such Persons, to whom such Authors, for good Considerations, have lawfully transferred their Right and Title therein, is not only a great Discouragement to Learning in general, which in all Civilized Nations ought to receive the greatest Countenance and Encouragement, but is also a Notorious Invasion of the Prop-

---

28 For detailed studies of the emergence of copyright legislation in Great Britain, see Mark Rose's *Authors and Owners. The Invention of Copyright* and John Feather's *Publishing, Piracy and Politics. An Historical Study of Copyright in Britain*. Catherine Seville maps out the continuing development of copyright in Great Britain in *Literary Copyright Reform in Early Victorian England. The Framing of the 1842 Copyright Act* (Cambridge: Cambridge UP, 1999).

29 Justin Hughes, "Copyright and Incomplete Historiographies: Of Piracy, Propertization, and Thomas Jefferson," *Southern California Law Review*, 79.5 (2006): 993–1084, 1012.

30 A Bill for Encouragement of Learning, London (1710), Primary Sources on Copyright (1450–1900), ed. L. Bently and M. Kretschmer, http://www.copyrighthistory.org/. Accessed 23 November 2022.

31 Ronan Deazley, "Commentary on the Statute of Anne," *Primary Sources on Copyright (1450–1900)*, ed. Lionel Bently and Martin Kretschmer (www.copyrighthistory.org, 2008).

> erty of the rightful Proprietors of such Books and Writings, to their very great Detriment, and too often to the Ruin of them and their Families.[32]

The British bill proclaimed a property in the "Product of [an author's] Learning and Labour" and introduced a perpetual protection against reprinting for these works. Interestingly, the drafters of the bill focused more on the rights of the authors than those of the stationers, positioning the author as the obvious proprietor of their own writing. As Ronan Deazley writes, "[t]he whole emphasis of the Bill as initially drafted lay behind the presumption that the 'Copy of a Book' was a clearly recognizable form of property, equal in stature as with any other chattel or estate."[33] As it passed through the British House of Commons, the bill underwent great changes; especially the preamble was considerably amended. It was shortened and the line proclaiming "the undoubted Property of such Books and Writings" eliminated. The new preamble does not speak of a property in literature and the title of the statute has been changed to omit the phrase "Securing the Property of Copies of Books to the rightful Owners thereof." The House of Commons also amended the bill by introducing a limited term of protection, namely twenty-one years. When the amended bill was finally passed by the Parliament of Great Britain, it became the *Statute of Anne*.

When the *Statute of Anne* passed in 1710 it was the first copyright act by Parliament and the world's first copyright legislation.[34] The monopoly position of the *Stationers' Company* had been legally protected by the Star Cham-

32 A Bill for Encouragement of Learning, London (1710), Primary Sources on Copyright (1450–1900), ed. L. Bently and M. Kretschmer, http://www.copyrighthistory.org. Accessed 23 November 2022.

33 Deazley, "Statute of Anne."

34 Craig Joyce, "Intellectual Property in the United States," *Oxford International Encyclopedia of Legal History* 265 (2009): 1–17, 2. *An Act for the Encouragement of Learning, by Vesting the Copies of Printed Books in the Authors or Purchasers of such Copies, during the Times therein mentioned*, passed in 1710 during the reign of Queen Anne, Queen of Great Britain and Ireland (1707–1714) and named in her honor. Initially, London booksellers petitioned for a title which vested the "property of copies of books" in them. The original title of the statute, *A Bill for the Encouragement of Learning and for Securing the Property of Copies of Books to the Rightful Owners Thereof* was later changed and the word "property" omitted over concerns regarding perpetual property claims (Hughes, "Copyright," 1012–1013). Even though the *Statute of Anne* was the world's first copyright legislation, the British book market was still comparably small next to centers of printing like Venice and Amsterdam. Britain still imported more books than it exported and was not home to any larger publishing houses. This changed in the second half of eighteenth century; by 1777 London had more booksellers than any other European city. Here, some could comfortably make a living as a writer, but most literary workmen and women continued

ber and later by parliament until 1694,[35] but the *Statute of Anne* included no censorship provisions and limited the scope of the *Stationers*' monopoly on printing rights.[36] The copyright established by the *Statute of Anne* was available to any author or assignee of the author, not just to members of the *Company*. It was limited to a fourteen-year period with a possible fourteen-year renewal term available only to the author. Nevertheless, the work still had to be entered into the *Stationers*' register book.[37] After fourteen or twenty-eight years, a work entered the public domain to "encourage learning."[38] Any existing perpetual copyrights were protected for another twenty-eight years. By making the copyright of a work available to the author, the *Statute of Anne* put into writing the concept of an author's copyright, as opposed to the publisher's copyright granted by the *Stationers' Company*. Therefore, *The Statute of Anne* was the first act that explicitly addressed and protected authors' rights; it also speaks of the "proprietor" rather than the "owner" of a work.[39] As Patterson puts it,

> The major consequence of the change of copyright from a publisher's right to an author's right, then, was this: instead of being a limited right in connection with a work for an unlimited period of time, it became an unlimited right for a limited period of time.[40]

Patterson understands the *Statute of Anne* as acting mainly in the interest of the public by preventing monopolies and in the interest of publishers by prohibiting "piracy."[41] Mark Rose argues that "[t]he Statute of Anne, then, did not settle the theoretical questions behind the notion of literary property. Still, it did represent a significant moment in a process of cultural transformation [...] The passage of the statute marked the divorce of copyright from censorship and the reestablishment of copyright under the rubric of property rather than regulation."[42]

---

to live in poverty, see Peter Burke, *A Social History of Knowledge. From Gutenberg to Diderot* (Cambridge: Polity Press, 2000), 165–166.

35 Hughes, "Copyright," 1012.

36 Patterson, *Copyright*, 12. The Star Chamber existed as a court at the *Palace of Westminster* from the fifteenth to the mid-seventeenth century, until it was abolished in 1640.

37 Gadd, "Stationers' Company," 81.

38 See for example "*The Statute of Anne*; April 10, 1710." *The Avalon Project*, Lillian Goldman Law Library, 2008. Web. 29 Sep. 2020.

39 Gieseke, *Privileg*, 138–139.

40 Patterson, *Copyright*, 18.

41 Patterson, *Copyright*, 14.

42 Rose, *Authors and Owners*, 48.

The booksellers of the *Stationers' Company* disapproved of the *Statute of Anne* because it limited their pre-existing perpetual copyrights and they engaged in a series of litigations, later known as the "Battle of the Booksellers." Booksellers appealed to an author's natural right to their work, which, they claimed, granted the author a perpetual common law copyright. The authors could in turn alienate this right to the booksellers, effectively securing the booksellers' perpetual copyright. Provincial booksellers, who were rarely granted royal printing privileges and had previously suffered due to the *Stationers' Company*'s monopoly, opposed these attempts. Authors stood united with their publishers against "pirated editions" of their works, but later used the natural rights argument to their own advantage against booksellers and demanded more rights to their own works.[43] In the court case *Millar v. Taylor* (1769) the Court of the King's Bench ruled in favor of a perpetual common-law copyright, a success for London booksellers. The verdict was promptly overturned in *Donaldson v. Becket* (1774) when the court's ruling dismissed any claims to perpetual protection by determining that copyright was merely a limited statutory grant.[44] According to this ruling, all rights to a work derive from statutory protection only and all works must enter the public domain after the expiration of the statutory copyright protection.

The time from the composition of the *Statute of Anne* in 1709 until the landmark decision in *Donaldson v. Becket* in 1774 was a decisive period in the creation of an early British copyright, a precursor of the modern Anglo-American copyright.[45] Copyright protection was determined to be a statutory grant to provide a monopoly on printing and publication for a limited amount of time to an author, enabling them to make a living by writing without depending on patronage. Since early US state regulations as well the *National Copyright Act of 1791* appear to be modeled after the *Statute of Anne*, and landmark US court cases such as *Wheaton v. Peters* (1834) refer to *Donaldson v. Becket* as precedent, US copyright can be seen to "descen[d] directly from the Stationers' copyright through the Statute of Anne," as Patterson points out.[46] It stands to reason that copyright regulation in Britain also affected copyright regulation in the colonies in North America and shaped the earliest US copyright history.

43 Baldwin, *Copyright Wars*, 58.

44 Patterson, *Copyright*, 7; Joyce, "Intellectual Property," 7. For a detailed analysis of *Donaldson v. Becket* and the significance of the decision for the understanding of the author as the proprietor of a work, see Mark Rose, "The Author as Proprietor. Donaldson v. Becket and the Genealogy of Modern Authorship," *Representations* 23 (1988): 51–85, 54.

45 Patterson, *Copyright*, 4.

46 Patterson, *Copyright*, 7.

3.1.1 Colonial Copyright Regulations

Bracha points out that developments in early US copyright history are often ignored in current copyright research. While scholars are usually aware of the rich European copyright history that precedes the *Statute of Anne*, the copyright history of the early North American colonies is neglected by many:

> the reader of standard American copyright history is likely to be left under the impression that, with the exception of an early isolated incident in Massachusetts, nothing interesting happened in that region until the late eighteenth century.[47]

Since early precursors of copyright in the US are often overlooked, the impression arises that in the US an author-based copyright emerged suddenly and with little precedent toward the end of the eighteenth century, overemphasizing the novelty of the concept.[48] Bracha himself understands American colonial printing privileges as a "somewhat crude version of its European cousin," shaped by different social and political conditions. These printing privileges gradually developed into the understanding of an author-based copyright presented in the federal *Copyright Act of 1790*,[49] where the printing privileges initially granted to publishers "were universalized and bestowed on authors."[50]

During the seventeenth century, technological progress reached the British colonies in North America with the introduction of the printing press, which was perceived as both threatening and promising by local governments. The first printing press was shipped from Britain to the Massachusetts Bay Colony in 1638 by Puritan reverend Joseph Glover (no date of birth–1638), who died during the voyage. It is uncertain who assumed responsibility for the printing press in Massachusetts Bay, but it was used by the colony's government as well as by Harvard College. The press was "treated [...] as a semi-public resource in the service of the colony" and maintained through measures of the colony's court.[51] Printing served to advance religious and civic cohesion within the colony and any use of the press was carefully controlled. From 1664 onward printing required licensing and no other printing press was to be set up in the Massachusetts Bay Colony.[52]

---

47 Bracha, "Early American," 89.
48 Bracha, "Early American," 89.
49 Bracha, "Early American," 90.
50 Bracha, *Owning Ideas*, 3–4.
51 Bracha, "Early American," 91–92.
52 Bracha, "Early American," 92–93.

When printing presses arrived in the colonies, colonial governments approached them with a mixture of worry and interest, sometimes embracing and sometimes barring them.[53] The *Statute of Anne* did not apply and printing privileges were only granted sporadically.[54] While British copyright law was created in an exchange between the government and publishers' guilds, the disorganized book trade in the colonies "could not create trade-wide regulations, enforce them, and lobby government for sustained backup and support" and the local governments in the small, rather isolated colonies did not need "an intermediary enforcing their censorship and licensing policies."[55] The first "courtesy agreements" between booksellers emerged in the colonies to regulate printing and trade, established through informal contracts or social norms and easily enforceable in the small communities.[56] Physical barriers between colonies localized the book trade and material printed in one colony was usually of limited interest to another colony.[57] Therefore, no equivalent to the *Stationers' Company* or a statutory copyright developed in the colonies. Formal legislative privileges remained rare and were granted on a case-specific basis as "sporadic, ad hoc, legislative grants" to printers or booksellers, not to authors, and acted as an economic incentive to publish a work.[58] Until the *Declaration of Independence*, no formal copyright existed in the British colonies on the North American continent, and none seemed necessary.

3.1.2 State Statutes

After the United States declared independence from the Kingdom of Great Britain in 1776, a US-American copyright regime developed but it continued to be influenced by British legislation. The *Articles of Confederation*, which were agreed upon by the thirteen existing states and approved by the *Second Continental Congress* in 1777 did not include any comment on copyright regulation. US copyright was in a transitory state "between legislative publishers' privileges and the new general regimes of author's rights," as Bracha points

---

53 Bracha, "Early American," 93.

54 Bracha, "Early American," 94–97.

55 Bracha, "Early American," 97, 98.

56 Nora Slonimsky offers an illuminating case study of Lewis and Amelia Evan's interpretation of copyright protection in eighteenth-century America, the boundaries of jurisdiction in the American continent, and related perceptions of power and authority, see Nora Slonimsky, "'To Save the Benefit of the Act of Parliament': Mapping an Early American Copyright," *Law and History Review* 40.4 (2022): 1–30.

57 Bracha, "Early American," 98.

58 Bracha, "Early American," 98–100; Bracha, "United States," 336.

out.[59] Occasionally, individual grants were allocated to authors in continuation of the colonial copyright regime. During the 1780s, all states legislated individual state copyright statutes, Delaware being the sole exception. This change was prompted by a case Andrew Law presented to the court in Connecticut in 1781,[60] lobbying efforts by authors, and a recommendation by the *Confederate Congress* in 1783 to introduce state-based copyright legislation.[61]

On January 10, 1783, Joel Barlow (1754–1812), a veteran of the American Revolution, sent a letter to Elias Boudinot (1740–1821), a delegate to the Continental Congress.[62] In his letter Barlow urged Boudinot to bring a subject of public interest before the Continental Congress, namely "the embarrassment which bears upon interests of literature & works of genius in the United States." Barlow points out that

> [t]his embarrassment is natural to every free Government; it is one of the evils of society, which requires to be removed by positive statutes securing the copyrights of Authors, & in that way protecting a species of property which is otherwise open to every invader. It is a subject which, during the more important affairs of the present revolution, we could not expect to see attended to by any

---

59 Bracha, "United States," 340.

60 For a collection of songs and tunes Andrew Law received what some consider the first author's copyright in the young republic. The copyright was granted for five years with a penalty of five hundred pounds for anyone who would reprint the songs in Connecticut. Interestingly, most of the songs were not composed but merely collected by Law and they were likely published in several works, not in one collected book. Therefore, Law did not receive a grant for one specific book but for the tunes listed in the grant and published in several different books, making this more of a publisher's than an author's grant. Law also sought to prevent any reprints of the songs in other states, despite the fact that he merely re-published many of these songs. This behavior reflects "a newly appearing possessive approach and a strong, if not always consistent or entirely good-faith, sense of entitlement toward 'his' publications," as Bracha points out, highlighting a gradual and ambiguous shift in US concepts of copyright ("Early American Printing Privileges. The Ambivalent Origins of Authors' Copyright in America" in *Privilege and Property. Essays on the History of Copyright*, ed. Ronan Deazley et al. (Cambridge: OpenBook Publishers, 2010), 89–114, 103–109).

61 Bracha, "Early American," 110; The Congress of the Federation existed between 1781 and 1789 and was superseded by the US Congress. The Congress of the Federation recommended the states pass individual copyright regulations but did not pass any legislation concerning copyright.

62 Elias Boudinot was an influential figure in copyright history. On 25 February, 1790, during the second session of the First Congress, Elias Boudinot introduced the bill to Congress which became the first federal copyright law of the United States, the *Copyright Act of 1790*, on May 31, 1790. See Benjamin W. Rudd, "Notable Dates in American Copyright 1783–1969," *The Quarterly Journal of the Library of Congress* 28.2 (1971): 137–143, 138.

> of the Legislatures, but is now much thought of by many individuals, & perhaps can not be too early proposed to the attention of Congress & the several States.[63]

He draws a comparison with other countries that already "encourage […] the exertions of genius" by securing authors' profits, echoing a romantic notion of literary genius. Barlow frames literature as the purest form of property, which originates entirely from the mind of the author. He claims that consequently "most of the civilized nations have removed the natural obstructions which lie in the way of literary emulation, & given the consequent encouragement to every species of laudable ambition." He demands that the Continental Congress pass legislation to encourage authors to produce literary works, which in turn further the "literary reputation [which] is necessary in order to complete [the US'] national character" and prevent the US from being outdone by Europe. By referring to the British *Statute of Anne,* he suggests that Congress recommend all states pass similar statutes to give "a laudable direction to that enterprising ardor of genius which is natural to our stage of society, & for which the Americans are remarkable." Should Congress not ensure the protection of literary works, Barlow claims no author would risk publication of a work just to have a shortened version rife with mistakes reprinted and sold for a cheaper price by "some ungenerous Printer."

Following Barlow's letter, Elias Boudinot brought a motion before the Continental Congress "to consider the most proper means of cherishing genius and useful arts throughout the United States by securing to the authors or publishers of new books their property in such works."[64] The members of the Continental Congress appointed a committee for this purpose, consisting of Hugh Williamson (1735–1819), Ralph Izard (1741/42–1804), and James Madison (1751–1836). The committee then received "sundry papers and memorials from different persons of the subject of literary property" and later stated that its members were persuaded that an author's intellectual productions were properly their own. "The protection and security of literary property would greatly tend to encourage genius, to promote useful discoveries and to the general extension of arts and commerce," as Hugh Williamson noted in the

---

63 Letter from Joel Barlow to the Continental Congress (1783), Primary Sources on Copyright (1450–1900), ed. L. Bently and M. Kretschmer, www.copyrighthistory.org. Accessed 18 November 2022.

64 *Journals of the Continental Congress 1774–1789* 24.180 (1922), 327.

Journals of the Continental Congress.[65] The Continental Congress followed Barlow's impetus by resolving on May 2, 1783

> [t]hat it be recommended to the several states, to secure to the authors or publishers of any new books not hitherto printed, being citizens of the United States, and to their […] executors, administrators and assigns, the copyright of such books for a certain time, not less than fourteen years from the first publication; and to secure to the said authors, if they shall survive the term first mentioned, and to their […] executors, administrators and assigns, the copyright of such books for another term of time no less than fourteen years, such copy or exclusive right of printing, publishing and vending the same, to be secured to the original authors or publishers and to their […] executors, administrators and assigns, by such laws and under restrictions as to the several states may seem proper.[66]

The members of the Continental Congress adhered to the British model when recommending that the states ensure copyright protection by granting authors or publishers the exclusive right to print, publish, and sell a work for fourteen years, followed by a possible second term of fourteen years for the author. This copyright was contingent on US citizenship. Interestingly, the earlier motion as well as the committee spoke of protecting the (literary) *property* of authors and publishers, framing an author's claim to a work as a property right. The resolution passed by Congress, on the other hand, disregards property rights and speaks of a copyright, thus framing an author's right to a work as an "exclusive right of printing, publishing and vending."[67]

Between 1783 and 1786 twelve of the thirteen United States enacted their own copyright statutes. Connecticut, Massachusetts, and Maryland passed their statutes prior to the resolution by the Continental Congress, likely modelled on the British *Statute of Anne*. New Jersey, New Hampshire, Rhode Island, Pennsylvania, South Carolina, Virginia, North Carolina, Georgia, and New York respectively passed their own copyright acts afterwards. Delaware did not pass a state copyright law.[68] Evidently, the drafters of these later copyright statutes closely adhered to the resolution presented by the Continental Congress and thus the statutes are very similar. They all resemble the *Statute of Anne* and

65 Journals, 327.

66 Continental Congress Resolution (1783), Primary Sources on Copyright (1450–1900), ed. L. Bently and M. Kretschmer, www.copyrighthistory.org. Accessed 17 November.

67 Continental Congress Resolution (1783), Primary Sources on Copyright (1450–1900), ed. L. Bently and M. Kretschmer, www.copyrighthistory.org. Accessed 17 November 2022.

68 Solberg, *Copyright Enactments*, 11–30.

address the same concerns raised earlier in the British statute. The state statutes secure an author's or publisher's copyright for a maximum of twenty-one years, but they differ in their framing of literature and copyright. Some states require authors or publishers to officially register their copyright, some even require authors or publishers to insert a copyright notice into the respective work. All acts put reprinting without consent during the twenty-one years of protection under penalty, but some states explicitly request authors and publishers to provide a sufficiently large edition of reasonably priced books.

On January 8, 1783, Connecticut passed the earliest copyright statute, even preceding the formation of the Congress committee. Passing this act was heavily promoted by lexicographer Noah Webster (1758–1843), who campaigned for the passage of copyright laws in Connecticut and other states.[69] The *Act for the Encouragement of Literature and Genius* comes equipped with a preamble stating that

> it is perfectly agreeable to the Principles of natural Equity and Justice, that every Author should be secured in receiving the Profits that may arise from the Sale of his Works, and such Security may encourage Men of Learning and Genius to publish their Writings; which may do Honour to their Country, and Service to Mankind.[70]

The act secures to

> the Author of any Book or Pamphlet not yet printed, or any Map or Chart, being an Inhabitant or Resident in these United States, and his Heirs or Assigns […] the sole Liberty of printing, publishing and vending the same within this State,

---

69 Many scholars frame Webster as "the father of copyright legislation," see for example Harry Redcay Warfel, *Noah Webster, Schoolmaster to America.* (London: The Macmillan Co., 1966), 58. Webster doubtlessly played an important role in the passage of early US-American copyright legislation but, as David Micklethwait points out, Webster was likely less influential than often claimed. Rather, Webster positioned himself as a central figure in his own writing, see David Micklethwait, *Noah Webster and the American Dictionary* (Jefferson, N. C.: McFarland, 2005), 74–81. Brian Pelanda also argues that Webster was an influential copyright activist but "he played less of a direct casual role in the passage of the various state copyright laws than he later claimed in his writings," see Brian Palanda Lee, "Declarations of Cultural Independence: The Nationalistic Imperative Behind the Passage of Early American Copyright Laws, 1783–1787." *Journal of the Copyright Society of the U.S.A.*, 58 (2011): 431–454, 448.

70 Connecticut Copyright Statute, Connecticut (1783), Primary Sources on Copyright (1450–1900), ed. L. Bently and and M. Kretschmer, www.copyrighthistory.org. Accessed 23 November 2022.

> for the Term of fourteen Years, to commence from the Day of its first Publication in this State.[71]

Persons who knowingly reprint a work thus protected within the state or import a work reprinted outside the state without consent of the author must pay to the author "double the Value of all the Copies thereof." The copyright is contingent on an author's proper registration of authorship in the Office of the Secretary of State. After fourteen years, this exclusive right can be renewed for another seven years by the author or their heirs. While authors are entitled to receive the profits of their work, at least for twenty-one years, the act also states that the inhabitants of a state need access to useful cheap books to encourage learning. Thus, if an author does not ensure that enough reasonably priced editions are printed, a complaint can be filed with the Superior Court. A judge may then summon the author and direct them to publish more affordable copies. If the author fails to comply, the court may allow the complainant to reprint more editions of the work at a reasonable price. Additionally, the act penalizes the reprinting of an unpublished manuscript without the author's consent. The drafters also clarify that the act does not protect those from punishment who print and publish "any Book [...] that may be prophane, treasonable, defamatory, or injurious to Government, Morals or Religion." Lastly, the drafters insist on reciprocal copyright, stating that the act does not extend a copyright to "any Author or Persons residing in, or Inhabitants of any other of the United States, until the State of States, in which such Person or Persons reside or dwell, shall have passed similar Laws in Favour of the Authors of new Publications."

Connecticut's *Act for the Encouragement of Literature and Genius* is a central source in early American copyright history. The act weighs authors' rights to profit from their work against the encouragement of learning – the central tension negotiated in the later *Copyright Act of 1790*, which resembles Connecticut's act in many ways. Connecticut's act does not position an author's claim to a work as a property right. Instead, the act emphasizes an author's right to financially profit from a work. Authors' financial profits should be secured by the state in order to encourage them to produce more works, which in turn "may do Honour to their Country, and Service to Mankind." The act does not recognize an author's moral right to a work; the damage done by reprinting is framed as a loss of profit, disregarding possible damage

71 Connecticut Copyright Statute, Connecticut (1783), Primary Sources on Copyright (1450–1900), ed. L. Bently and and M. Kretschmer, www.copyrighthistory.org. Accessed 23 November 2022.

to the integrity of the work and an author's reputation. The copyright acts passed by other states in the following years echo Connecticut's act, which likely served as a template. Most acts either copy passages from Connecticut's act, or reflect the content. This is not true for all state copyright acts, though: Two months later, Massachusetts passed a copyright act focused on an author's literary property.

Massachusetts' *Act for the Purpose of securing to Authors the exclusive Right and Benefit of publishing their Literary Productions, for Twenty-one Years* passed on March 17, 1783, preceding the resolution by Congress.[72] The act explicitly frames literature as a form of property in the preamble, stating as its purpose:

> Whereas the improvement of knowledge, the progress of civilization, the publick [sic] weal of the Commonwealth, and the advancement of human happiness, greatly depend on the efforts of learned and ingenious persons in the various arts and sciences: As the principal encouragement such persons can have to make great and beneficial exertions of this nature, must exist in the legal security of the fruits of their study and industry to themselves, and as such security in one of the natural rights of all men, there being no property more peculiarly man's own than that which is produced by the labour of his mind: Therefore, to encourage learned and ingenious persons to write useful books for the benefit of mankind.

These assertions are repeated in the act itself, which simply states that all works published under an author's name "shall be the sole property of the said author or authors, being subjects of the United States of *America*, their heirs and assigns, for the full and complete term of twenty-one years." Interestingly, the line of argument presented in the preamble resembles the original draft of the *Statute of Anne*, the *Bill for Encouragement of Learning, and for Securing the Property of Copies of Books to the Rightful Owners thereof* (see chapter 3.1).[73] The Massachusetts legislators made a conscious choice to adhere closely to the original draft of the British statute: In their own state statute they echo the author's property claims to the products of their learning and labor from the draft, rather than adhering to the adjusted *Statute of Anne*.

---

72 Massachusetts Copyright Statute, Massachusetts (1783), Primary Sources on Copyright (1450–1900), ed. L. Bently and M. Kretschmer, www.copyrighthistory.org. Accessed 17 November.

73 A Bill for Encouragement of Learning, London (1710), Primary Sources on Copyright (1450–1900), ed L. Bently and M. Kretschmer, www.copyrighthistory.org. Accessed 23 November 2022.

Other states followed suit and passed copyright acts in the following year, emphasizing different aspects in their preambles, such as the protection of property or the encouragement of learning. Maryland passed copyright legislation resembling the Massachusetts act on April 21, 1783, titled *An Act respecting literary property.*[74] While the Massachusetts act puts emphasis on the improvement of knowledge and the protection of civilization, the preamble of this act centers on the intent to prevent reprinting, stating:

> Whereas printers, booksellers, and other persons, may take the liberty of printing, reprinting, and publishing, or causing to be printed, reprinted, and published, books and other writings, without the consent of the authors or proprietors of such books and writings, to their great injury.

New Jersey emphasized learning and passed *An Act for the Promotion and Encouragement of Literature* on May 27, 1783. The preamble states that "Learning tends to the Embellishment of Human Nature, the Honour of the Nation, and the general Good of Mankind" and claims that "it is perfectly agreeable to the Principles of Equity, that Men of Learning who devote their Time and Talents to the preparing Treatises for Publication, should have the Profits that may arise from the Sale of their Works secured to them."[75] The preamble to New Hampshire's act, passed on November 7, 1783, again echoes the preamble of the Massachusetts act, with only a few changes in wording; the title addresses "the encouragement of literature and genius."[76] This act protects an author's work as "the sole property of said author," mirroring Massachusetts' act. Rhode Island passed an act very similar to the Massachusetts' act, bearing the same title and preamble in December 1783. This act also protects "the sole Property" of the author – but only if he is a citizen of the US.[77]

On March 15, 1784, Pennsylvania passed a copyright statute for "the Encouragement and Promotion of Learning by vesting a Right to the Copies of

74 Maryland Copyright Statute, Maryland (1783), Primary Sources on Copyright (1450–1900), ed. L. Bently and M. Kretschmer, www.copyrighthistory.org. Accessed 17 November 2022.

75 New Jersey Copyright Statute, New Jersey (1783), Primary Sources on Copyright (1450–1900), ed. L. Bently and M. Kretschmer, www.copyrighthistory.org. Accessed 17 November 2022.

76 New Hampshire Copyright Statute, New Hampshire (1783), Primary Sources on Copyright (1450–1900), ed. L. Bently and M. Kretschmer, www.copyrighthistory.org. Accessed 17 November 2022.

77 Rhode Island Copyright Statute, Rhode Island (1783), Primary Sources on Copyright (1450–1900), ed. L. Bently and M. Kretschmer, www.copyrighthistory.org. Accessed 17 November 2022.

printed Books in the Authors or Purchasers of such Copies, during the time therein mentioned."[78] While this act resembles the act passed in Maryland, it focuses on the prevention of reprinting. It frames copyright as the "exclusive right of printing, publishing and vending [a work] within this state for the term of fourteen years, to commence from the day of its first printing or publication in this state," not as property. Pennsylvania's act also clarifies that "this act shall not take place until such time as all and every of the states in the union shall have passed laws similar to the same, in conformity to the recommendation of Congress aforesaid." South Carolina's act, passed on March 26, 1784, claims to be an *Act For The Encouragement of Arts and Sciences*, rather than an act for the protection of literature specifically.[79] The act is longer than previous acts, explicitly allowing the importation and sale of works printed in "Greek, Latin, or any other foreign language, printed beyond the seas," a formulation adopted from the *Statute of Anne*. In accordance with the act, editions are to be sold in large and reasonably priced editions, otherwise a complainant may be authorized to reprint and sell a book in reasonable numbers at a reasonable price.

North Carolina passed *An Act for securing Literary Property* on December 29, 1785.[80] The preamble states that

> Nothing is more strictly a Man's own than the Fruit of his Study, and it is proper that Men should be encouraged to pursue useful Knowledge by the Hope of Reward; and as the Security of literary Property must greatly tend to encourage Genius, to promote useful Discoveries and to the general Extension of Art and Commerce.

The wording of this act is very similar to *The Copyright Act of 1790*, but precedes it. It implements a reciprocal copyright for US citizens, specifying that citizens of any state that published laws "for the Security of literary Property [...] shall be entitled to the Benefit of this Act and none others." North Carolina's act is also the first copyright statute to make explicit that the reprinting

---

78 Pennsylvania Copyright Statute, Pennsylvania (1784), Primary Sources on Copyright (1450–1900), ed. L. Bently and M. Kretschmer, www.copyrighthistory.org. Accessed 17 November 2022.

79 South Carolina Copyright Statute, South Carolina (1784), Primary Sources on Copyright (1450–1900), ed. L. Bently and M. Kretschmer, www.copyrighthistory.org. Accessed 17 November 2022.

80 North Carolina Copyright Statute, North Carolina (1785), Primary Sources on Copyright (1450–1900), eds L. Bently & M. Kretschmer, www.copyrighthistory.org. Accessed 17 November 2022.

of works already published or originally published in a different country is not prohibited. A similar provision can be found in section 5 of the *Copyright Act of 1790*. Lastly, the act emphasizes that it does not encourage or protect authors or publishers who sell books, "which may be dangerous to civil Liberty, or to the Peace or Morals of Society."

Virginia passed a copyright statute on January 7, 1786, titled *An Act for securing to the authors of literary works an exclusive property therein for a limited time.*[81] This act also ensures authors "an exclusive property" in their works, if only for twenty-one years. Also in 1786, Georgia and New York passed the last state statutes on copyright. Georgia passed an act "for the encouragement of literature and genius" on February 3, 1786, echoing New Hampshire's earlier act.[82] The preamble states that

> [w]hereas the principles of natural equity and justice, require that every author should be secured in receiving the profits that may arise from the sale of his works, and such security may encourage men of learning and genius to publish their writings, which may do honor to their country, and service to mankind.

The act is intended to promote an author's financial security and the nation's reputation but also privileges "the encouragement of learning," which requires "that the inhabitants of this State be furnished with useful books, &c. at reasonable prices." As last state, New York passed a copyright statute on April 29, 1786.[83] Preamble and content of this *Act to promote Literature* mirror Georgia's act. Delaware did not pass its own copyright statute, and in 1787 the Constitutional Convention decided to vest additional power in the Legislature of the US to "secure to literary authors their copy rights for a limited time."[84]

Until 1790 a mere forty of all books published were registered for copyright in the US in accordance with the states' statutes.[85] Copyright had not yet been

81 Virginia Copyright Statute, Virginia (1785), Primary Sources on Copyright (1450–1900), ed. L. Bently and and M. Kretschmer, www.copyrighthistory.org. Accessed 17 November 2022.

82 Georgia Copyright Statute, Georgia (1786), Primary Sources on Copyright (1450–1900), ed. L. Bently and and M. Kretschmer, www.copyrighthistory.org. Accessed 17 November 2022.

83 New York Copyright Statute, New York (1786), Primary Sources on Copyright (1450–1900), ed. L. Bently and and M. Kretschmer, www.copyrighthistory.org. Accessed 17 November 2022.

84 The Constitutional Copyright Clause, Philadelphia, Pennsylvania (1789), Primary Sources on Copyright (1450–1900), ed. L. Bently and and M. Kretschmer, www.copyrighthistory.org. Accessed 17 November 2022.

85 Bracha, "United States," 341.

commonly accepted. While the states' statutes were soon made superfluous by the federal *Copyright Act of 1790*, they nonetheless laid the foundation for a general copyright regime based on authors' natural rights and the education of the public.[86] Peter Baldwin asserts that the "Anglo-American copyright was founded in an abstract sense on natural rights ideas of an inherent relationship between the creator and his work" but these rights were restricted "to what was determined by statute" and "[l]iterary property's duration was circumscribed by the general social interest of enlarging the public domain."[87] According to Baldwin, the existing legislature was concerned with economic rights, with printing, reprinting, and selling the work, not with aesthetic rights of the author.[88] Patterson summarizes the concept of copyright emerging from the states' copyright statutes as follows:

> [C]opyright is a right to protect the author in securing his profits from the publication of his works by giving him the exclusive right of printing, publishing, and selling his works for a limited time, which right can be assigned to a publisher. It is a right which affirms and protects only those rights of the author pertaining to his economic interests. As such, it is a right to which a given work is subject, and neither confirms nor denies other rights of the author which might be appropriately recognized at common law.[89]

Since all laws in the newly-founded republic were up for discussion in the years following the initial Declaration of Independence, the states' statutes were in effect until they were superseded by the *Copyright Act of 1790*, which introduced federal copyright legislation. In 1785, James Madison (1751–1836) and others drafted a copyright bill for the Virginia House of Delegates. The bill assigned authors an "exclusive property" in their works but it was not adopted.[90] In 1787, Madison published "Vices of the Political System of the United States" in which he states that "Instances of inferior moment are the want of uniformity in the laws concerning naturalization & literary property."[91] A few months later, both James Madison and Charles Pinckney (1757–

86 Bracha, "United States," 342.
87 Baldwin, *Copyright Wars*, 72.
88 Baldwin, *Copyright Wars*, 73.
89 Patterson, *Copyright*, 191–192.
90 Hughes, "Copyright," 1023.
91 "Vices of the Political System of the United States, April 1787," *Founders Online*, National Archives, https://founders.archives.gov/documents/Madison/01-09-02-0187. Accessed 23 Aug. 2023.

1824) submitted proposals to the *Constitutional Convention*,[92] outlining Congressional powers regarding copyright: Madison argued for the power to "secure to literary authors their copy rights for a limited time" and to "encourage by proper premiums & provisions, the advancement of useful knowledge and discoveries." Pickney proposed to "secure to Authors exclusive rights for a certain time."[93] Dotan Oliar argues that Madison and Pickney were coordinated in their efforts and that both were to credit for the inclusion of Congressional rights regarding copyright and patent power in the final Constitution.[94] In his detailed examination of the origins of and influences on the *Copyright Clause* in the US Constitution, Oliar concludes that the American enactments, rather than the *Statute of Anne* (1710), were major influences on the clause. He argues that "the Founders' mindset was one of breaking away with English experience and relying on their own experience and values to erect a new intellectual property system aimed at promoting the progress of human knowledge."[95] Soon after, the US Constitution was drafted in 1787 by the *Constitutional Convention* as the first uniform federal law. It included Article I, Section 8, Clause 8, which allowed national legislature to grant authors for a limited time the exclusive rights to their works "[t]o promote the Progress of Science and useful Arts."[96] Hereafter, the first federal *Copyright Act* was legislated by Congress in 1790.

3.1.3 The *Copyright Act of 1790* and Its Consequences

The *Copyright Act of 1790* constituted the first federal copyright regulation in the US and superseded the individual states' statutes. It established a coherent copyright regime among the thirteen US states. The act was influenced both by the states' practices and legislation and by British copyright tradition in the form of the *Statute of Anne*. As Oren Bracha frames it, the act regulated "the narrow right to reproduce in print a protected text."[97] The statute grants to the author of a book, map or chart (or to their executors, administrators or

92 A convention that took place between May 25, and September 17, 1787, and resulted in a proposal for a Constitution to be ratified by the states.

93 Cited after Hughes, "Copyright," 1023.

94 Dotan Oliar, *The Origins and Meaning of the Intellectual Property Clause* (Cambridge: Berkman Klein Center for Internet and Society at Harvard University, 2005), 25.

95 Oliar, *Origins*, 33.

96 See for example: "Constitution of the United States." *United States Senate*, Secretary of the Senate, 21 Jan. 2020, www.senate.gov/civics/constitution_item/constitution.htm. Accessed 29 Sep. 2020.

97 Bracha, "United States," 335, 342.

assigns) "the sole right and liberty of printing, reprinting, publishing and vending" said book, map or chart for a term of fourteen years, following registration. Authors were eligible for a renewal of fourteen years, if they were still alive when the first term expired. This copyright was only granted to citizens or residents of the US, copyright protection was not granted to the works of foreign authors. The act explicitly states that

> nothing in this act shall be construed to extend to prohibit the importation or vending, reprinting or publishing within the United States, of any map, chart, book or books, written, printed, or published by any person not a citizen of the United States, in foreign parts or places without the jurisdiction of the United States.[98]

Lyman Ray Patterson asserts that the ideas of protecting the author and promoting learning present in the states' statutes "have become subordinated to the ideas that copyright is a government grant and a monopoly" in the *Copyright Act of 1790*.[99] Patterson points out that the copyright act identifies only a statutory right to a work while the natural rights of the author, addressed in several of the states' statutes, are not mentioned.[100]

As Peter Baldwin outlines in *The Copyright Wars. Three Centuries of Trans-Atlantic Battle*, the paths of the US and Continental-European nations regarding copyright diverged with this first US copyright act. Questions concerning the full alienation of authors' rights and the aesthetic and moral rights of the author emerged and sparked debates on both sides of the Atlantic. France and the German States put emphasis on longer terms of protection and focused on the aesthetic rights of authors. In the Anglosphere, the public domain remained the focus of protection. The full alienation of authors' rights was prioritized in discussions of copyright and property in the US.[101] The fact that copyright protection was only granted for a limited time following the *Copyright Act* was justified by Congress with the encouragement of science and learning. Protecting copyright for a period of years following publication was intended to be an incentive for the production of original work, but it was also a way to guarantee the public access to the books, maps, and charts that entered the public domain and to further arts, sciences, and education. US

98 See for example: *Copyright Act of 1790*. Edited by US Copyright Office, copyright.gov/about/1790-copyright-act.html. Accessed 30 Sep. 2020.

99 Patterson, *Copyright*, 198.

100 Patterson, *Copyright*, 200.

101 Baldwin, *Copyright Wars*, 82–85.

legislation framed the protection of an author's work as a privilege, which granted the author the exclusive right to publish, print, and redistribute the work for a limited time, instead of as the inherent right of an author to their work. US citizens could own the rights to their work temporarily; authors outside the US were denied that right altogether.

The *Copyright Act of 1790* superseded state copyright legislation and enabled writers to make a living as authors. As a federal act it facilitated interstate-trade and the distribution of books across the vast young republic. It shaped the professionalization, life, and works of US authors throughout the next decades and influenced the development of a domestic literary culture and a US national literature. Gradually, a national market for literature emerged where previously little interstate-trading was possible. Nevertheless, many publishers resorted to reprinting successful yet unprotected British works to supplement domestic literature throughout the nineteenth century.[102]

After forty years, Congress passed the *Copyright Act of 1831*, the first federal revision of copyright law in the US. The copyright term was extended to twenty-eight years, with a fourteen-year renewal period.[103] The 1834 *Wheaton v. Peters* Supreme Court case confirmed that US copyright was merely a statutory-based grant and denied the existence of an author's natural right to their published work. For a century, until Congress passed the first *International Copyright Act* in 1891, foreign works remained unprotected in the US. This affected domestic as well as foreign authors and ushered in a century of debates, petitions, and domestic and international protest.

Lara Langer Cohen and Meredith McGill describe the nineteenth century as a period of opportunity and peril for US-American authors. The "publishing conditions and emerging ideas of authorship opened up new fields of opportunity for writers," some of whom were now able to make a living for themselves as authors.[104] On the other hand, many struggled

> with the vagaries of literary property in a period before standardized author contracts and international copyright; the difficulties of carving out identities as authors in a democracy where little precedent for such role existed; and the

102 Lara Langer Cohen and Meredith L. McGill, "The Perils of Authorship, Literary Property and Nineteenth-Century American Fiction" in *Oxford History of the Novel in English, Vol 5: The American Novel to 1870*, ed. J. Gerald Kennedy and Leland S. Person (Oxford: Oxford UP, 2014), 195–212, 197.

103 See for example: *An Act to Amend the Several Acts respecting Copy Rights*. U.S. Congress. *U.S. Statutes at Large, Volume 4 1824–1835, 19th through 23rd Congress*. Library of Congress, www.loc.gov/item/llsl-v4. 23 Aug. 2023.

104 Cohen and McGill, "Perils," 195.

> pressures, as well as the possibilities, of writing at a time in which literature assumed an unparalleled cultural importance.[105]

The *Copyright Act* and its revised version enabled US authors and publishers to distribute domestic works across all US states, protected from reprinting. Soon, the interstate book trade thrived and copyright became "a source of national pride and national identity."[106] Nonetheless, authors within and outside the US criticized the *Copyright Act* heavily. The *Copyright Act* was designed to prevent "piracy," the unauthorized reprint and sale of books, maps, and charts published in the US, by granting the copyright holder the exclusive right to print, publish, and sell the work. Authors could retain their copyright by paying for the manufacturing of their work and commissioning a publisher to distribute the copies, which enabled them to retain the copyright to their works and reap most of the profits generated. Established authors could make use of this arrangement, but first-time authors could usually not afford to pay for publication themselves. Instead, they had to sell their copyright to a publisher to limit the costs and risks associated with publication.[107] Throughout the nineteenth century, this perceived injustice prompted domestic authors to advocate for more comprehensive rights to their own works.

Alice Schreyer summarizes the complaints levelled against the *Copyright Act of 1790*. She points out that many authors believed, "based on the correspondence between literary and tangible property, they had a natural, unrestricted right to the fruits of their labors."[108] The legislature and the courts, on the other hand, maintained that copyright law did not protect a natural right to a work and instead created and granted a temporary copyright after publication.[109] Copyright law also did not protect authors against derivative uses of their works, such as abbreviations, translations, and dramatizations, until

105 Cohen and McGill, "Perils," 195.

106 Cohen and McGill, "Perils," 196.

107 Other author-publisher contracts included short-term licensing of copyrights, half-cost/half-profit arrangements, and limited lease of stereotype printing plates to a publisher. These tentative arrangements were often replaced with standardized copyright clauses that usually included a set percentage of the sale profits to be paid to the author. Some contracts instead included a fee determined by a sliding scale: The more copies were sold, the higher was the percentage paid to the author (Schreyer, "Copyright," 124).

108 Alice Schreyer, "Copyright and Books in Nineteenth-Century America" in *Getting the Books Out. Papers of the Chicago Conference on the Book in 19th-Century America*, ed. Michael Hackenberg (Washington, DC: Library of Congress, 1987), 121–136, 127.

109 Schreyer, "Copyright," 127.

1870.[110] As long as "intellectual labor and judgement" was invested in a translation or an abridgement, it was considered a new work and was available for copyright.[111] In the 1853 *Stowe v. Thomas* Circuit Court case, the court touched on the distinction between idea and expression to define "literary property," determining that after publication an idea becomes common property and merely the expression, the "'combination of words' used to represent them" remains protected.[112] This also meant that while the law was somewhat effective in preventing "piracy" (copying a work but giving credit), it was less effective in preventing plagiarism (copying parts of a work without giving credit). This was only remedied with the 1909 addition of the "exclusive right to copy" to the copyright act.[113] Serial publications were also inadequately protected: An individual copyright needed to be registered for every chapter published, until composite works became eligible for copyright in 1909.[114] While authors criticized the implications of the *Copyright Act* for domestic works, its lack of protection for foreign works, which were frequently reprinted in the US without authors' consent, was also heavily criticized. Many complained that the *Copyright Act* did not achieve what it promised, namely to "promote the progress of science and useful arts" in the US. Instead, they claimed, it stunted the growth of domestic literature by causing a national dependence on cheap imported British literature and culture, rather than supporting upcoming domestic authors and their works. Domestic as well as foreign authors, publishers, lawyers, politicians, the press, and the interested public debated the issue of international copyright. These debates gave rise to a social movement of issue entrepreneurs concerned with copyright and intellectual property, as well as to the publication of many a work discussing copyright.

3.1.4 The International Copyright Debate in the US

During the nineteenth century, the US developed the largest reading audience in the world and many claimed that mass education and increasing literacy rates depended on easy access to cheap literature.[115] The demand for books increased steadily and by the late nineteenth century the US literary market

110 See for example: *An Act to Revise, Consolidate, and Amend the Statutes Relating to Patents and Copyrights, 1870*. Library of Congress, www.loc.gov/law/help/statutes-at-large/41st-congress/session-2/c41s2ch230.pdf. Accessed 30 Sep. 2020.

111 Schreyer, "Copyright," 128.

112 Schreyer, "Copyright," 128.

113 Schreyer, "Copyright," 128.

114 Schreyer, "Copyright," 129.

115 Baldwin, *Copyright Wars*, 113–114.

had become twice as large as Britain's.[116] Books sold in the US were usually only half the price of British editions, sometimes even 75 percent cheaper.[117] British editions were often more elaborate and embellished and aimed at buyers with more income. Additionally, more libraries existed in Britain, driving up the prices for individual copies. In the US, less wealthy buyers demanded access to literature, and published editions were often produced for the mass market. Libraries were rare in the vast republic and readers needed to purchase books themselves.[118] Consequently, reprinting lower-quality editions of British works in large quantities and selling them cheaply was profitable for publishers in the US. Reprinting accounted for around 25 percent of the US printing output during the nineteenth century.[119] Acquiring manuscripts or copies of successful British works and reprinting them in the US was favored by at least a quarter of publishing houses, which engaged in this practice and reaped the profits without being legally required to share them with the authors.[120] Between 1837 and 1843 a depression hit the US economy and the demand for cheap books increased further. As James J. Barnes puts it: "A mania for cheapness had descended upon the trade and things would never be the same again."[121] Not everyone agreed with these practices and protest was not limited to authors; other publishers also opposed reprinting. This "culture of reprinting," as Meredith McGill calls it in her monograph *American Literature and the Culture of Reprinting, 1834– 1853*, continued for decades despite protests, petitions, and lobbying suggesting that public support for reprinting must have existed. Reprinters apparently spoke for "broader aspects of cultural ideology," as Baldwin points out.[122] Adrian Johns identifies a "nationalism of copyright" expressed through the culture of reprinting, which in some ways furthered national literacy and education.[123]

The legislators of the *Copyright Act of 1790* emphasized the encouragement of learning. They incentivized the production of new knowledge by granting a limited monopoly on printing and publication to the author, and limited that monopoly to fourteen years to enrichen the public domain. "[E]galitarian

116 Baldwin, *Copyright Wars*, 117.
117 Baldwin, *Copyright Wars*, 119.
118 Baldwin, *Copyright Wars*, 119.
119 James J. Barnes, *Authors, Publishers, and Politicians. The Quest for an Anglo-American Copyright Agreement 1815–1854* (Columbus: Ohio State UP, 1974), 69.
120 Baldwin, *Copyright Wars*, 116
121 Barnes, *Authors*, 1.
122 Baldwin, *Copyright Wars*, 116
123 Johns offers a detailed examination of the practices of reprinting in the US during the nineteenth century and beyond, see Adrian Johns, *Piracy. The Intellectual Property Wars from Gutenberg to Gates* (Chicago: University of Chicago Press, 2009), 292.

cheap access to knowledge" was a republican value and cheap reprints allowed for quick and easy access to various kinds of literature for all citizens.[124] Especially during the early decades of the nineteenth century the US was still a developing country "highly dependent on [the] importation of cultural goods," including literature – a genuinely US-American national literature was still in its infancy.[125] The idea of a public domain with works available to anyone at little or no cost emerged and the "public good" was favored over individual authors' rights to their works. This was the case with regard to domestic authors but it became even more prevalent when nationalism entered the picture: For many, the progress and enrichment of one's own nation weighed heavier than the individual rights of foreign authors.

Meredith McGill argues that refusing copyright to foreigners was not an oversight or negligence on part of Congress, but a strategic move. Not granting copyright to foreigners recognizes copyright as a domestic issue and "underscores the statutory nature of this right while also acknowledging that the identity of the state is not founded on linguistic difference."[126] Granting copyright to foreigners did not align with the values held by Congress at the time. The denial of protection is often read retrospectively as a "failure" to pass an international copyright bill "in time" by those who advocated for copyright protection, ignoring that at the time a majority opposed the measure. Winners write history, especially if they are authors, and the source material consulted by scholars today to study copyright history has an inherent "authors'-rights bias," McGill points out, as it was mostly compiled by copyright advocates.[127] McGill claims that

124 Bracha, "United States," 369.

125 Bracha, "United States," 365. During the early nineteenth century, the US still relied on the import of British literature since few domestic works were published in the young republic. The nineteenth century, then, was characterized by aspirations to create a genuinely US-American literature that would set the US apart from Great Britain in matters of politics as well as literature. In the US, but in other European countries as well, a nationalistic sentiment arose throughout the nineteenth century, a desire to set one's nation apart from others and "clai[m] a distinctive character, given form in original works of literature and art from the common life of its people," as Robert Gross summarizes in "Building a National Literature: The United States 1800–1890" in *A Companion to the History of the Book*, ed. Simon Eliot and Jonathan Rose (Oxford: Blackwell Publishing, 2008), 315–328, 316.

126 McGill, *American Literature*, 81.

127 McGill, *American Literature*, 82.

> [l]iterary critics' bias toward the testimony of authors and the longstanding alliance of literary study with literary nationalism have combined to give international copyright advocacy undue prominence in our histories.[128]

Additionally, the question of international copyright was instrumentalized in political and partisan struggles over political principles, republican values, and the development of a market culture in the young republic.[129] By writing petitions and addressing the legislative body, direct political action was put to the test, and "debates over authors' rights turn[ed] the free circulation of print into a test case and model for the workings of state power."[130] The issue of international copyright also touched on other concerns prevalent at the time, such as the concentration of capital, governmental authority, the economy and the institution of chattel slavery, which positions slaves as personal property. These debates also

> galvanized a discussion of the dangers and advantages of the circulation of cheap print and brought into focus sharply differing positions on the relation of print to market culture, on the compatibility of the market and democracy, and on the relation of the market for print to the shape of the nation.[131]

As McGill demonstrates, international copyright was not just an economic issue and framing it as such severely limits the analytical perspective. Instead, the question of international copyright should be assessed along with its political implications.

In "Copyrighting American History," Claudia Stokes shows the politization of the debate surrounding international copyright and highlights its complexity.[132] The rejection of an international copyright was often based on the suspicion of intellectual culture and literary elitism, mistrusted by many and understood as "antidemocratic traces of European history."[133] At the same time, the international copyright movement constructed writers as laborers and used this "rhetoric of authorial labor" to counter "the widespread suspicion among Americans that literature was the realm of elite, privileged intel-

128 McGill, *American Literature*, 83.

129 McGill, *American Literature*, 79.

130 McGill, *American Literature*, 79–80.

131 McGill, *American Literature*, 83–82.

132 Claudia Stokes, "Copyrighting American History: International Copyright and the Periodization of the Nineteenth Century," in *American Literature*, ed. Susan Manning and Andrew Taylor (Durham: Duke UP, 2005), 290–317.

133 Stokes, "American History," 293.

lectuals with deeper ties to Europe than to the United States."[134] Following the Civil War the issue entrepreneurs of the copyright movement produced an outpour of literature on the subject, including pamphlets, reprints of copyright bills, and bibliographies alongside full-length literary histories of copyright, countered by a flood of publications and letters by those opposing international copyright.[135] Copyright activists and opponents even compared their struggle for or against an international copyright to the Civil War and the political divide within the country.[136] Stokes argues that literary histories were used as a vehicle by copyright advocates to "circumvent the ire of a public unsympathetic to the financial pleas of a constituency they believed to be aristocratic [...] bridging class divisions that had interfered with public support of copyright protections for so long."[137] She claims that the "quasi-academic genre of literary history" was instrumentalized by copyright advocates to lend copyright rhetoric legitimacy and credibility and to alter the public's perception of the cause and its proponents.[138] In their narrative framing, advocates also shifted focus to Britain's copyright abuses, lamenting the "piracy" of US-American books by British publishers – acts they positioned as continued tyrannical abuses by the motherland.[139] This also served to present US authors as victims of the British literary aristocracy and as defenders of US democracy, though this narrative was challenged by the open support for international copyright by popular British writers such as Charles Dickens and Matthew Arnold.[140] Copyright advocates also politicized the distribution of cheap British reprints in the US by arguing that reprints displayed British customs, aristocracy, and feudalism and encouraged their imitation, triggering "a retrogressive return of the United States to a British colony."[141] Lastly, they proposed that imitation of the more successful British novels by US writers could threaten the originality and integrity of US literary culture.[142]

---

134 Stokes, "American History," 292, 295.

135 Stokes, "American History," 295–296.

136 In his *Letters on International Copyright*, Henry Charles Carey wrote in 1868: "On the one side, there will be found a few thousand persons interested in maintaining monopolies that had been granted to authors and publishers, foreign and domestic. On the other, sixty or eighty millions, tired of taxation and determined that books shall be more cheaply furnished. War will then come [...]" (*Letters*, 14).

137 Stokes, "American History," 296–297.

138 Stokes, "American History," 299.

139 Stokes, "American History," 300–301.

140 Stokes, "American History," 301.

141 Stokes, "American History," 306.

142 Stokes, "American History," 307.

Those who favored reprinting foreign works also had political reasons: They saw reprinting as a measure to assert and maintain independence from Great Britain. By establishing a different system of publication, the US distanced itself from Great Britain and through wide dissemination of texts and knowledge, national identity and political stability would thrive.[143] Some proposed that the role of the US was not to generate new knowledge, but to make existing knowledge accessible to everyone, putting the reading public before a "foreign literary elite."[144] Manufacturers, printers, and typesetters often rejected an international copyright and advocated for the domestic manufacture and distribution of books. They understood domestic manufacture as an act of resistance against British control of the US book market. They feared that the introduction of an international copyright would return control over the printing industry to British publishers. They also asserted that the domestic manufacture of books was a cultural achievement worth defending. While the proponents of an international copyright entrusted national virtue and public education to domestic authors, opponents entrusted the same to the widest-possible dissemination of texts, a measure possible without governmental control. This also appealed to those who feared a centralization of the market through governmental intervention and were critical of the government's law making policies.[145] Other opponents of an international copyright favored the development of a culture without an "author elite," as McGill claims:

> by focusing their energies on the reproduction of foreign texts, Americans could acquire all the benefits of elite culture without encouraging the development of authors as a specially protected 'class of our own citizens'.[146]

3.1.4.1 Courtesy of Trade and Market Regulation

Factions from all parties involved in the book trade were opposed to the introduction of an international copyright, including printers, typesetters, and paper makers. While those in favor of international copyright protection often drew a picture of a lawless book market characterized by chaos, ruthlessness, greed for profit, and uncivilized behavior, the book trade developed paralegal mechanisms to regulate the market and bring order to the trade. This extralegal system of agreements and norms is usually referred to as the

143 McGill, *American Literature*, 93.
144 McGill, *American Literature*, 93.
145 McGill, *American Literature*, 99.
146 McGill, *American Literature*, 100.

"courtesy of trade." Cohen and McGill even argue that these principles constituted a de-facto copyright system that existed apart from legal measures.[147] The "courtesy of trade" agreements proposed a set of principles to be followed by all publishers engaged in reprinting. Bracha details that

> [u]nder this norm, observed by the big publishing houses, the first publisher to procure and print a text enjoyed de facto exclusivity. The informal system included dispute resolution methods and sanctions against a publisher who infringed the norm including public shaming and retaliation.[148]

A publisher often announced a claim to a foreign work in a newspaper and as Cohen and McGill assert, this "newspaper announcement of the intent to publish a foreign work informally carried the weight of a property claim."[149] Publishers often paid British authors to receive advance sheets for their books and lay claim to the publication quickly. They also paid authors a fee to obtain the right to publish authorized editions, at times complete with portraits and facsimile signatures.[150] Some even paid authors a share of the profits to establish a permanent relationship and publish future editions and additional works. Smaller publishing houses did not always adhere to the "courtesy of trade" principles, since they often proved unenforceable in reality. The structure of the market favored large publishing houses with the financial resources to pay advance sums and invest in cheap and high-volume print runs, high-speed presses, and vast distribution networks.[151] Despite intimidation and retaliation by larger publishers, a two-tier system gradually emerged: Larger publishers focused on higher-quality editions and often paid authors fees to publish their editions first; smaller publishers reprinted lower-quality editions for cheaper prices but lacked the time advantage.[152]

One does well to remember that the interests of US publishers were at no point uniform, even though the international copyright debate is often falsely boiled down to "publishers versus authors."[153] Publishers who sold books they

147 Cohen and McGill, "Perils," 199.

148 Bracha, "United States," 367.

149 Cohen and McGill, "Perils,"199.

150 Cohen and McGill, "Perils," 195.

151 McGill, *American Literature*, 105.

152 Bracha, "United States," 367.

153 Catherine Seville claims that neither Great Britain nor the United States held the moral high ground during the international copyright debate of the nineteenth century, and that showcasing "the righteous British on one side of the Atlantic, and the piratical Americans on the other" paints an inaccurate and one-sided picture, see Catherine Seville, "Nineteenth-Century Anglo-US Copyright Relations: The Language of Piracy ver-

did not produce themselves and those who mainly sold domestic works were often in favor of an international copyright, while publishers who produced the books they sold and those focused on selling British reprints were against an international copyright.[154] During the early 1840s, newspapers initiated the "cheap books war" by printing serial publications of foreign works in their daily editions, corrupting the established system of courtesies for several years.[155] Many domestic novelists also resorted to publishing in periodicals to reach a larger audience and cultivate a loyal readership, as Cohen and McGill point out. Many periodicals could actually pay contributing authors and thereby helped to professionalize authorship. This resulted in a thriving market for magazines and periodicals, while novels were published less frequently. US authors often referred to British magazines for cues for their writing and strived for positive British reviews of their work. Cohen and McGill also claim that many US authors complained less about the unauthorized publication of their own works in other countries, especially in Great Britain, as British reviews and commercial success abroad could promote their work at home as well.[156]

While opponents of an international copyright feared the centralization of governmental control and British influence on the US market, proponents of an international copyright worried that a disorderly market would have "disruptive social effects" and trigger an irresponsible handling of any form of property.[157] They assumed that cheap and easily available reprints threatened serious reading and libraries, would be wasteful, and would hold uncertainty for publishers as well as readers.[158] Many US authors felt that they could not compete with the frequent and cheap British reprints and therefore could not

sus the Moral High Ground" in *Copyright and Piracy: An Interdisciplinary Critique*, ed. Lionel Bently et al. (Cambridge: Cambridge UP, 2010), 19–43, 19. Oren Bracha asserts that while it has usually been assumed that the lack of copyright protection adversely affected foreign and US-American authors, empirical studies published recently complicate that view: According to the data examined "it is far from clear that either British or American authors were greatly prejudiced by the lack of copyright during the relevant period" ("United States Copyright, 1672–1909," in *Research Handbook on the History of Copyright Law*, ed. Isabella Alexander and H. Tomas Gomez-Arostegui (Cheltenham: Edward Elgar Publishing, 2016), 335–371, 367–368).

154 Baldwin, *Copyright Wars*, 115.

155 Schreyer, "Copyright," 126. The *Adams Steam Press* (1830–1836) as well as the introduction of the cylinder press of Robert Hoe in 1847 allowed for quicker and cheaper publication and distribution of newspapers, enabling newspaper publishers to publish books at low cost.

156 Cohen and McGill, "Perils," 201–203.

157 McGill, *American Literature*, 102.

158 McGill, *American Literature*, 103–104.

earn a living. Some feared that the dependence on the import of British literature hindered the development of a national literature and culture. Various authors published their misgivings in open letters or pamphlets, lamenting their perceived disadvantages but also elaborating on their understandings of literary property and authors' rights. British authors and publishers joined their protests, demanding changes in legislation that would enable them to publish their works in the US on their own terms and to reap the monetary benefits. Congress was petitioned many times throughout the nineteenth century to introduce an international copyright act to protect the works of foreign authors in the US and to enable domestic authors to receive reciprocal copyright protection in other countries.

3.1.4.2 Lobbying and Petitions

In the years directly following the *Copyright Act of 1790* little concern existed for questions of international copyright in the US. As Catherine Seville points out, the printing trade was fairly restricted: With experienced workers being rare, the quality and quantity of the output was limited and the production of non-fictional works – such as scientific texts, sermons, philosophical treatises, and governmental documents – was privileged, increasing the need to import fiction from Britain.[159] By the mid-1820s, the question of international copyright sparked more interest. A tariff was imposed on imported books as more copies could be manufactured within the US. Still, most were concerned with terms of domestic copyright protection and, as Barnes claims, members of Congress initially showed little interest in the question of copyright in general – they needed to be pushed towards legislative action. Private negotiations between US publishers, British publishers, and authors did not always go smoothly, but extralegal agreements were made.[160]

In 1836, British writers began petitioning Congress for international copyright protection. They were angered by the fact that their works were reprinted and published without consent or remuneration. Authors also complained that hastily printed US editions contained many misprints and without control over the prints they feared for their reputation.[161] Many mobilized acquaintances in the US to participate in the protests.[162] A Committee on International Copyright was appointed by the Senate in 1837, with senator Henry Clay as

159 Seville, "Copyright Relations," 21.

160 Barnes, *Authors*, 49–53.

161 Baldwin, *Copyright Wars*, 118.

162 Barnes, *Authors*, 60–61.

chairman and senator William C. Preston as a member (see chapter 6 for a more detailed account).[163] Steven Wilf summarizes the stance of Henry Clay in 1837 as follows:

> [g]ranting copyright privileges to foreign authors would raise the price of their books, and therefore assist American authors by leveling the playing field in the publishing industry between domestic authors and those writing abroad. Protection of non-American writers was essentially a way of raising a tariff on foreign books.[164] By shielding the domestic market from British authors, Whigs believed that a trans-regional American literary culture would flourish.[165]

The committee seemed divided on the issue of international copyright but still recommended legislative action. The corresponding international copyright bill passed in the Senate but was rejected by the House of Representatives.[166] Senator Clay reintroduced the bill and the issue was referred to the Committee on Patents. Booksellers sent written statements of protest to Washington and in 1838 the commission rejected the bill.[167] Its members argued that one of the purposes of copyright was to allow for the dissemination of knowledge to the public to advance democratic society. Granting foreign works copyright protection would work against this purpose.[168] Steven Wilf identifies the beginnings of a "turn towards the public" in Henry Clay's 1839 public appeal to mobilize and participate in the political debate.[169] For many domestic authors, participation in the movement for international copyright with its increasingly public debates shaped their sense of identity as a professional author. They also came to see themselves as part of a transatlantic community. This in turn deepened their resolve to protect the rights of their transatlantic colleagues by participating in protests.[170] By the late 1830s, the question of international copyright had reached a larger audience and, as Barnes puts it,

---

163 Barnes, *Authors*, 62.

164 That is, a tariff not easily bypassed by printing the works in the US without the consent of the author.

165 Steven Wilf, "Copyright and Social Movements in Late Nineteenth-Century America," *Theoretical Inquiries in Law* 12.123 (2011): 123–160, 133.

166 Barnes, *Authors*, 64.

167 Barnes, *Authors*, 67.

168 Wilf, "Copyright," 135.

169 Wilf, "Copyright," 133.

170 Wilf, "Copyright," 135.

> it was also apparent that the quest for an Anglo-American copyright agreement was not a purely national affair. Authors, publishers, and politicians on both sides of the Atlantic were taking an active role in its support or opposition. This interrelationship was part of a growing sense of an Atlantic community in which both Britain and America shared the same language, the same literature, and even the same economic cycles. There were times when these similarities fostered as much antagonism as co-operation, but in either case the significant areas of contact and influence increased.[171]

Senator Clay reintroduced the copyright bill again in 1838, 1840, and 1842, and each time it was assigned to the Committee on the Judiciary and rejected or dropped when large printing houses located in the bigger cities voiced protest.[172] Senator Clay criticized what he perceived as a lack of effort by US authors to support international copyright advocacy. It was around this time that Francis Lieber decided to publish his *Letter on International Copyright* in support of the cause (see chapter 6). The British publishing house Saunders presented yet another petition to Congress in 1842. Again, a committee was appointed, which then dropped the issue without resolve.[173] In 1843, the *American Copyright Club* was founded and institutionalized the existing network of issue entrepreneurs for the cause of international copyright. The club promptly published a statement in favor of international copyright, collected signatures, and sent letters to representatives. The members also directly addressed US citizens to involve them in the debate.[174] They presented a petition to Congress in 1843, which was referred to the Commission on Printing and then dropped without result.[175] While petitions remained without concrete results, international copyright advocacy was more present in public discussion in 1844 than it had been before: International copyright protection was no longer a marginal concern – issue entrepreneurs had successfully framed the issue and raised public interest. Following the end of the depression, "courtesy of trade" was revived to regulate the book trade and between 1845 and 1857 the US book market stabilized.[176] Between 1847 and 1848, the US lawyer John Jay (1817–1894) engaged in efforts to petition Congress with the support of newspapers and suggested adding a manufacturing

171 Barnes, *Authors*, 65.
172 Barnes, *Authors*, 71–73.
173 Barnes, *Authors*, 76.
174 Wilf, "Copyright," 136.
175 Barnes, *Authors*, 79.
176 Barnes, *Authors*, 79–86.

clause to the Copyright Bill.[177] Lieber himself collected signatures in support of the cause in 1848, but Jay failed to move Congress into action.[178]

Generally speaking, US authors could secure copyright for their works in Britain. British Courts tended to decide against foreigners in court cases until 1835 and in their favor afterwards, as Barnes claims. In 1838, a British international copyright act was passed.[179] By now a market for cheap books existed in Great Britain and was regulated through extralegal trade courtesies, but reprints of works by foreign authors still circulated with "dubious copyright."[180] In February 1853, Britons Edward Everett (1794–1865) and L. C. Levin designed an *Anglo-American Copyright Treaty for the Establishment of International Cooperation* and presented it to the US Senate.[181] Publishers opposed the move and the draft was leaked to the press before the Senate could decide on it.[182] Despite careful negotiations, the treaty was never passed. Eventually, Everett dropped his efforts to get the Senate to vote on the treaty.[183] In a letter to Lord Clarendon in England, Reverend J. F. T. Crampton, who had been involved in the efforts, stated that "unfortunately Americans were not yet ready for a Copyright Treaty and apparently preferred to exploit cheap foreign reprints rather than foster their own authors and literature."[184] Barnes concludes that after 1850

> the American book trade was a very different scene from what Dickens and others in Britain thought. It had become far more stable; prices of most new books had risen; cut-throat competition had given way to more gentlemanly agreements within the trade; and various amicable arrangements had been made with British authors and publishers. This new equilibrium would eventually be shattered by another major depression, but in the meantime the book trade enjoyed its image of prosperity and respectability.[185]

---

177 A manufacturing clause would require publishers to manufacture foreign works in the US, if they were to apply for copyright protection.

178 Barnes, *Authors*, 86–94.

179 Barnes, *Authors*, 153. See for example: Ronan, "Commentary on Copyright Amendment Act 1842" in *Primary Sources on Copyright (1450–1900)*, ed. Lionel Bently and Martin Kretschmer (www.copyrighthistory.org, 2008).

180 Barnes, *Authors*, 154.

181 Barnes, *Authors*, 239–242.

182 Barnes, *Authors*, 257–258.

183 Barnes, *Authors*, 258–259.

184 Cited in Barnes, *Authors*, 259.

185 Barnes, *Authors*, 29.

Regardless, as Steven Wilf claims, by 1854 every country in the world had introduced some variation of an international copyright agreement, except for the US, Russia, and the Ottoman Empire.[186]

In the Reconstruction Era following the Civil War, international copyright protection was given more attention, perhaps because granting foreign works protection was understood as "part of a larger thrust towards remaking the state regulatory apparatus in order to reflect citizenship and moral concerns."[187] There was "a growing sense that America's position was not only harming American authors, but also depriving the American people of a literature of its own," as Catherine Seville points out.[188] At the same time, the concept of citizenship was predicated on literacy, the diffusion of knowledge, and affordable access to literature. Accordingly, a tension developed between the civility of granting international copyright protection to other countries and the dependence of citizenship itself on literacy and the diffusion of knowledge via easily accessible books.[189] The "popular mobilization" Clay had demanded in 1839 finally took form following the Civil War. In 1868, authors and publishers in favor of an international copyright founded the *International Copyright Association* as a network to combine their efforts; Lieber became a member.[190] In 1870, Congress passed *An Act to Revise, Consolidate, and Amend the Statutes Relating to Patents and Copyrights* and recognized new kinds of work as copyrightable, including prints, music, drama, photographs, and fine arts. The act also established the rights to perform a work and to publish derivative works, extended the protective term to 28 years, and established the Copyright Office in the Library of Congress to centralize copyright administration.[191] It did not comment on international copyright protection.

Until 1875, Congress was petitioned over a hundred times by those opposed to and those in favor of international copyright regulation.[192] In its ruling in the 1880 *Baker v. Selden* case, the Supreme Court ruled that ideas could not be copyrighted – even though their expression could be – establishing the legal foundation for the idea/expression dichotomy that still limits the scope of

186 Wilf, "Copyright," 132.
187 Wilf, "Copyright," 137.
188 Seville, "Copyright Relations," 33–34.
189 Wilf, "Copyright," 137–138.
190 Wilf, "Copyright," 137.
191 Joyce, "Intellectual Property," 3.
192 Baldwin, *Copyright Wars*, 117.

possible copyright today.[193] Following repeated failures to establish international copyright treaties or regulations, the *American Copyright League* was founded in 1883 and mobilized authors, publishers, and journalists in favor of international copyright.[194] This movement coincided with other "citizen intellectual property political action," as Wilf claims.[195] Several new attempts to introduce an international copyright agreement in Congress failed. Wilf names the 1878 Harper Draft Treaty, the set royalty approach by Robert Pearsall Smith, and the 1884 Dorsheimer Bill as examples. These repeated failures convinced the *American Copyright League* to mobilize the broad public, rather than Congress, for their plans.[196] This, of course, did not make it easier for them to unify the wishes and demands of their diverse members, who did not always agree on the definition of copyright itself.[197]

Copyright protection laws varied significantly between European countries as well and protection of foreign works "developed in a piecemeal and uneven way" everywhere during the nineteenth century, as Sam Ricketson points out.[198] Bilateral treaties were agreed upon between different European states, such as France, the UK, and Italy, but these agreements remained largely unpredictable and unreliable for authors and publishers. Towards the second half of the nineteenth century, a trend towards multilateralism developed between Europe and North America in the wake of different international arrangements concerning communication, customs, transportation, weights and measurements, and eventually the universal exhibitions.[199] In 1886 ten

193 The idea/expression dichotomy is a fundamental legal copyright doctrine in the US to determine that an idea itself cannot be copyrighted but merely its individual expression in the form of, for example, a novel or a movie.

194 Wilf, "Copyright," 139–145.

195 Wilf, "Copyright," 140. Wilf examines the rhetoric employed by the *American Copyright League* to broaden their political base and finds that the League highlighted "the American literary figure as domestic artisan" while also employing arguments that resembled those presented by contemporary US property rights advocates (Wilf, "Copyright," 141–142). Wilf also finds that the framing of international copyright protection within the context of a "shared Anglo-American cultural milieu" reveals the xenophobic, anti-immigration beliefs that shaped the movement (Wilf, "Copyright," 143). He claims that the idea of "an Anglo-American Protestant literary culture spanning the Atlantic" shared similarities with nationalist demands for protection of domestic authors from foreign works (Wilf, "Copyright," 141–143).

196 Wilf, "Copyright," 145–146.

197 Wilf, "Copyright," 147–148.

198 Sam Ricketson, "The Public International Law of Copyright and Related Rights" in *Research Handbook on the History of Copyright Law*, ed. Isabella Alexander and H. Tomás Gómez-Arostegui (Cheltenham: Edward Elgar Publishing, 2016), 288–312, 290.

199 Ricketson, "International Law," 290.

countries, among them Great Britain, France, and the German Empire, joined the *Berne Convention* and signed an agreement to harmonize international copyright regulations.[200] The US refused to join the convention since its stance on international copyright protection was incompatible with the requirements of the *Berne Convention*.[201] That same year four public hearings were held by the Committee on Patents concerning an international copyright bill introduced by senator Jonathan Chace (1829–1917). Mark Twain (1835–1910) and others promoted the passage of the bill while publisher Roger Sherman proudly spoke in favor of "piracy"; the Committee eventually advocated for an amended version of Chace's bill which included a manufacturing clause.[202] This manufacturing clause was rejected by dogmatic interest groups, but accepted by pragmatic ones.[203] Public opinion had previously been largely opposed to international copyright but increasingly voices were raised to criticize US-American practices on the basis of morality.[204]

In 1887 publishers founded their own association in favor of international copyright, the *American Publishers' Copyright League*, which symbolized a shift towards embracing international copyright in the publishing industry.[205] Oren Bracha argues that this change was brought about through "[t]he growing size and value of the American book market, fueled by technological innovation and high literacy rates" and through "[c]hanges in the American publishing industry" which "gradually reconfigured the relevant interests."[206] Since the 1870s decreased production costs made cheaper publishing possible and newly founded publishing firms put economic pressure on the established Eastern publishing houses. Consequently, "[f]irms who had established relationships with British authors began to see the advantage in an international copyright law, which would protect them from potentially ruinous competition at home," as Seville posits.[207] Additionally, US culture gradually developed to depend less on the import of foreign cultural goods, which inspired more self-confidence within the country.[208] The courtesy of trade principle

200 "Convention for the Protection of Literary and Artistic Works." *Wikisource*, https://en.wikisource.org/wiki/Convention_for_the_Protection_of_Literary_and_Artistic_Works. 23 Aug. 2023.

201 The US did not join the agreement until 1989, when the *Berne Convention Implementation Act* took effect.

202 Seville, "Copyright Relations," 37.

203 Seville, "Copyright Relations," 37.

204 Seville, "Copyright Relations," 38–39.

205 Wilf, "Copyright," 148.

206 Bracha, "United States," 365.

207 Seville, "Copyright Relations," 36.

208 Bracha, "United States," 369.

was undermined by smaller reprinters and antitrust concerns. Republican ideology favoring "egalitarian cheap access to knowledge" was replaced by market-oriented concerns. Perhaps most importantly repeated defeats in Congress led issue entrepreneurs of international copyright to change their framing and adopt a more pragmatic approach, which allowed for compromise with large publishers and typographs.[209] Once the *American Copyright League* and the *American Publishers' Copyright League* agreed on a manufacturing clause, all interest groups cooperated and continued lobbying together, uniting behind a shared issue narrative.[210] It still took until 1891 before "this shift of interests backed by an increasingly elaborate lobbying apparatus resulted in some recognition of international copyright" in the form of the *International Copyright Act of 1891*.[211]

3.1.4.3 The International Copyright Act of 1891

In 1891, after more than six decades of lobbying efforts on all sides for the recognition of international copyright as a relevant issue, the first federal *International Copyright Act* was passed in 1891.[212] It was drafted from a bill sponsored by senator Jonathan Chace and consequently became known as the *Chace Act*. Medieval historian, book publisher, and book collector Henry Charles Lea drafted the act.[213] It focuses on "practical compromise rather than moral issues" and Lea included most interest groups in the negotiations – only foreign authors had not been consulted, and consequently British authors took issue with the manufacturing clause included.[214] The act amends the previous copyright law,[215] and removes the requirement for the author to be a resident of the United States to be eligible for copyright protection, thus offering limited copyright protection to foreign works. As Oren Bracha summarizes, protection through the act was

209 Bracha, "United States," 369.
210 Seville, "Copyright Relations," 41.
211 Bracha, "United States," 365.
212 The last copyright act was act revised, consolidated, and amended the statutes relating to copyright, see for example *International Copyright Act (The Chace Act), Washington D.C. (1891)*, ed. Oren Bracha, www.copyrighthistory.org/cam/tools/request/showRecord.php?id=record_us_1891a. Accessed 4 June.
213 Wilf, "Copyright," 149.
214 Wilf, "Copyright," 151.
215 Copyright Act, Washington D.C. (1870), Primary Sources on Copyright (1450–1900), ed. L. Bently and and M. Kretschmer, www.copyrighthistory.org. Accessed 4 June 2024.

> extended only to citizens of foreign countries that had been proclaimed by the President as offering American citizens copyright on substantially the same terms as its own citizens or as adhering to an international copyright agreement providing for reciprocity and open to the US [...] The manufacturing clause of the act conditioned the right upon the work being printed from a type set or plates made in the US and prohibited the importation of foreign copies or plates.[216]

Together with the requirement to publish the work first or simultaneously in the US these requirements "created a substantial barrier to eligibility for works not written in English that later became the subject of complaints and reform attempts."[217] As Wilf adds, the passage of the *Chace Act* only shortly appeased the stakeholders and soon dissatisfaction with US copyright law grew again.[218]

The continued rise in technology made new types of media, such as music, a copyright issue, and increased difficulties for typists and printers added to the lingering dissatisfaction.[219] The examination and discussion of literary property and the international copyright debate of the nineteenth century is often limited in scope. It usually focuses on literature in the form of printed books and disregards newspapers, magazines, schoolbooks, pamphlets, government regulations, speeches, and religious texts. These works were also reprinted without copyright and played a major part in the establishment of US literary culture.[220] As McGill points out, works deemed "obscene" were denied copyright altogether.[221]

More importantly, women writers, writers of color, writers who were enslaved or lived on reservations, and poor, working-class writers did not have equal access to copyright for their works – married women writers and enslaved writers were not even allowed to own property in the first place for much of the nineteenth century. While slaves could assert their personhood through writing and thus lay claim to their own work through authorship, they could not legally hold the copyright to their works as long as they remained

---

216 Bracha, "United States," 368.

217 Bracha, "United States," 368.

218 Wilf, "Copyright," 153.

219 Wilf, "Copyright," 152–153.

220 McGill, *American Literature*, 106.

221 Meredith L. McGill, "Copyright and Intellectual Property: The State of the Discipline," *Book History* 16 (2017): 387–427. See for example Robert Spoo's article on the suppression of James Joyce's *Ulysses* during the early twentieth century: Robert Spoo, "Copyright Protectionism and Its Discontents: The Case of James Joyce's Ulysses in America," *Yale Law Journal*, 108.3 (1998): 633–667, doi:10.2307/797499.

slaves. One example is the case of Phillis Wheatley (1753–1784), who was sold into slavery as a child and began composing poetry, declaring her personhood through writing. When a collection of her poems was published in London in 1773, she became the first published African-American poet. She was emancipated in 1775, shortly after the publication of *Poems on Various Subjects, Religious and Moral.* Other authors, such as Harriet Jacobs (1813/15–1897) and Frederick Douglass (1817/18–1895), escaped slavery and later gained recognition and influence by publishing slave narratives, among other things.[222] By writing about their experience as slaves, these authors could take control of their narratives, assert their personhood, and raise their voices publicly. However, this was only possible for those who escaped slavery; how many other slaves authored works that they could not legally lay claim to is unknown.

Melissa Homestead's study *American Women Authors and Literary Property* examines the relationship of women authors to copyright law and the debates surrounding it. As Homestead points out, demands for an international copyright were often justified "on the ground that the men laboring in the field of letters should be able to provide financially for their wives and children," begging the question of how women writers fit into that picture.[223] Women writers celebrated great successes on the literary market during the nineteenth century, but

> under broader copyright law principles, women (and especially married women) had a profoundly different relationship to property than that enjoyed by their male peers [since] the law effectively created a distance [between women authors and the market] by refusing to grant most women the legal status of proprietors.[224]

When a woman author married, her husband became the registered proprietor of her copyright.[225] Despite this impediment, women writers still published many works throughout the nineteenth century and some – such as Harriet Beecher Stowe's *Uncle Tom's Cabin* (1852) or *Ramona* by Helen Hunt Jackson (1884) – were immediate bestsellers.[226] Many women writers cri-

222 See for example: *Narrative of the Life of Frederick Douglass, an American Slave, Written by Himself* (1845) by Frederick Douglass; *Incidents in the Life of a Slave Girl* (1861), published under the pseudonym Linda Brent by Harriet Jacobs. Douglass and Jacobs were also avid abolitionists, political activists, and educators.

223 Homestead, "American Women," 2.

224 Homestead, "American Women," 2–3.

225 Homestead, "American Women," 9.

226 Homestead, "American Women," 3.

tiqued these inequalities and demanded the right to own property after marriage. The issue was elaborated on and negotiated by different women writers in their literary works. The intersection between coverture and copyright is examined by Homestead in detail, because it led to larger dispossession among women authors than male authors.[227] No property was to be owned, no contract signed, no inheritance or income received by the wife herself.[228] If a wife was abandoned but not divorced by her husband, her situation was especially precarious as she struggled to support herself while her husband received her earnings. Often husbands registered their wives' copyright under their own names.[229] This did not change until statutory reform of coverture law began in the second half of the nineteenth century, following lobbying by women and women authors.[230] By the 1880s legislative reform had enabled women to legally own property, to sign contracts, and to keep their own wages.[231] But, as Homestead points out,

> [w]ith abused and dispossessed male authors figuring so prominently in American copyright advocacy, the absence of dispossessed women (as authors rather than widows of authors) in these obsessively reiterated scenes of the miseries of authors is striking.[232]

By 1909, President Theodore Roosevelt felt that US copyright law needed a complete revision because it did not account for new technologies.[233] Many felt that other countries were far ahead of the US in their copyright regulation and that the US failed to keep pace with its own rapid development.[234] Wilf finds that a new conception of copyright had emerged in the US, namely "the

227 The doctrine of coverture dates back to late-medieval England and assigns the status of *feme sole* to unmarried women and the status of *feme covert* to married women. Once married, a husband assumed all his wife's legal rights, obligations, and privileges, including her right to own property. During the mid-nineteenth century, a women's rights movements arose and amendments of the doctrine followed in the form of *Married Women's Property Acts* in various states in the US. Still, it took until the 1960s for all women in the US to obtain the rights to own property, to inherit, and to choose a profession.

228 Homestead, "American Women," 29.

229 Homestead, "American Women," 34.

230 Homestead, "American Women," 35.

231 Homestead, "American Women," 252.

232 Homestead, "American Women," 252–253.

233 Wilf, "Copyright," 154.

234 Wilf, "Copyright," 154.

idea that it stood at the crossroads of competing interest groups."[235] Many associations took an interest in copyright and were included in the drafting of the new copyright legislation, but no one, as Wilf notes, was there to represent the public as a stakeholder.[236] In 1909, Congress passed *An Act to Amend and Consolidate the Acts Respecting Copyright* to summarize and codify existing legislation, revising and overwriting nineteenth century copyright law in the US.[237]

The gradual development of a US-American copyright during the late eighteenth and the nineteenth century along with the century-long debate on international copyright set the stage for Francis Lieber's own framing of and demands for domestic and international copyright protection. As a migrant from Prussia, Lieber brought with him his own viewpoint of copyright, literary property, and authors' rights. He combined German and continental-European understandings of Urheberrecht and droit d'auteur protection with Anglo-American understandings of copyright and public welfare in his narrative, resulting in a unique transnational perspective on the copyright debate in the US. An examination of continental-European understandings of copyright lays the groundwork for identifying and discussing the different influences on Lieber's work on copyright.

3.2 Continental-European Systems of Urheberrecht and Droit d'Auteur Protection

Francis Lieber was born in Berlin, Kingdom of Prussia, in 1798. At the time Prussia was occupied by French troops and part of Napoleon Bonaparte's Continental System. Lieber studied in the city of Jena, located in the Grand Duchy of Saxe-Weimar-Eisenach, travelled to other German states, and spent some time in Greece and Italy. Before he migrated to the US he spent a year in England. Lieber's perception of fundamental social institutions such as property is thus necessarily influenced by the circumstances he grew up in, the education he received, his close contacts, and the literature he consumed. His understanding of property theory and his definitions of literature, authorship, and authors' rights are likely an amalgamation of Prussian and continental-European influences, paired with Anglo-American notions developed dur-

235 Wilf, "Copyright," 155.
236 Wilf, "Copyright," 155.
237 See for example: *An Act to Amend and Consolidate the Acts Respecting Copyright.* Edited by U.S. Copyright Office, www.copyright.gov/history/1909act.pdf.

ing his short time in England and the decades he lived in the US. To properly examine Lieber's understanding of copyright, authors' rights, and literary property, it is worth peeling back the layers of his perception to identify the influences he incorporated in his own works. The subsequent summary lays the groundwork for the analysis of Lieber's transnational perspective in the following chapters.

During the eighteenth and nineteenth centuries, two distinct understandings of literary property and authors' rights developed in Europe: The continental-European *authors' rights* or *moral rights* system, based on the French *droit d'auteur* regime, privileges the protection of an author's moral and economic rights, while the Anglo-American *copyright system*, based on the *Statute of Anne*, centers the dissemination of works to the public and aims to prevent printing and publishing monopolies.[238] The aims of both systems differed fundamentally: As David Saunders summarizes, the objective of copyright systems was to "provide a remedy against unauthorized reproduction of a protected commodity"; the goal of droit d'auteur systems, also referred to as *droit moral* systems, was "to protect the integrity of an authorial personality."[239]

In eighteenth-century France the discussion of literary property and authors' rights was initially limited to the question of economic control over publication, sale, and distribution of a work, with little regard for questions of an author's aesthetic integrity. During the *Ancien Régime* (c. 1500–1792) royal publishing monopolies regulated the publishing industry. Booksellers – and rarely authors themselves – could apply for a privilege granting them the exclusive publication rights for a work. These privileges were granted mostly to Parisian booksellers who were members of the publishing guild. Any privileges granted to authors for their manuscripts were perpetual, but once a work was transferred to a printer for publication these rights became limited to the author's lifespan. To receive a printing privilege booksellers or authors had to meet certain formalities, such as depositing copies at the national library. A printing privilege also afforded specific remedies in case reprinting caused financial damages.[240] When lawmakers reformed royal publishing privileges in 1777, they signaled that statutes – rather than natural rights – substantiated the copyright to a work. During the French Revolution (1789–1799), the revolutionary laws of 1791 and 1793 abolished the publishing guild,

238 Moscati, Laura, "Intellectual Property in the European Legal Context: Tools and Perspectives," *European Business Law Review* 22 (2011): 79–92, 79–83.

239 Saunders, *Authorship and Copyright*, 8.

240 Ginsburg, "Tale," 997.

broke up monopolies, and granted authors fully alienable literary property to trade in negotiations with booksellers.[241] The German states did not have unified copyright legislation during the eighteenth century, resulting in fragmented and decentralized copyright regulation. Royal printing privileges still existed but were put into question by natural rights theorists, such as Immanuel Kant (1724–1804) and Johann Gottlieb Fichte (1762–1814).[242] The *Prussian Civil Code of 1794* adapted some of the French revolutionary laws but also implemented novel elements, such as the introduction of an author's publication right (*Verlagsrecht*) which enabled the author to transfer only the publication and sales rights to a publisher, while maintaining ownership of the work.[243]

Peter Baldwin argues that legislation did not differ significantly between Britain, the US, France, and the German states during the eighteenth century, but rather shared key similarities. In all countries limited property rights began to replace royal privileges; statutory rights slowly replaced natural rights claims. All countries granted copyright only temporarily as a statutory, not a natural right.[244] Consequently,

> [a]uthorial property rights were a temporary way station on the road to the public domain. The author was enshrined as bearer of rights to his own work, but only the economic claims of publishing and selling were at stake.[245]

During the nineteenth century, the continental-European system and the Anglo-American system became more pronounced in their differences as questions of the full alienation of rights and of the aesthetic claims of an author emerged. France and the German states put emphasis on longer terms of protection and focused on the aesthetic rights of the authors. In the Anglosphere the protection of the public domain became paramount and the full alienation of authors' rights a priority.[246] In this subchapter, the situation in continental-Europe will be examined in relation to France and the German states during the late eighteenth and early nineteenth centuries. This examination serves to establish the historical context of Francis Lieber's narrative

241 Baldwin, *Copyright Wars*, 73–76.

242 Baldwin, *Copyright Wars*, 76–77.

243 Baldwin, *Copyright* Wars, 76. See for example: *Allgemeines Landrecht für die Preußischen Staaten* (01.06.1794). opinioiuris.de, https://opinioiuris.de/quelle/1621. Accessed 24 Aug. 2023.

244 Baldwin, *Copyright Wars*, 80–81.

245 Baldwin, *Copyright Wars*, 58.

246 Baldwin, *Copyright Wars*, 82–85.

and helps pinpoint the influences which shaped his early understanding of literary property and copyright. By identifying continental-European influences and distinguishing them from the Anglo-American body of thought, the transnational dimension of Lieber's work on property and copyright can be carved out.

3.2.1 The Situation in France

In France the system of royal printing privileges prevailed and enabled royal censorship as well as the protection of a printer's investment in a work. Printers in Paris profited from the protection offered by the privilege system, while reprints were published frequently in cities outside of Paris, as well as in Belgium, the Netherlands, and Switzerland.[247] During the early eighteenth century, booksellers in Paris wished to protect their royal printing privileges against provincial booksellers and against state policy makers. Meanwhile, provincial booksellers felt that their Parisian counterparts received preferential treatment.[248] Frédéric Rideau identifies two opposing viewpoints, one proposing an "individualist natural property" mostly advocated by Parisian booksellers, and one proposing a "social contract" between society and authors mostly advocated by provincial booksellers.[249]

In 1725, lawyer Louis d'Héricourt, who worked for booksellers in Paris, claimed that an author was entitled to a "propriété litteraire" on account of the labor they invested in the work, but that the publisher also invested labor during the publication process. His argument introduced the concept of literary property and served to equate the work of the author with the work of the publisher.[250] While the author remained in the background during early discussions of booksellers' rights, Héricourt identified the author as the source of a natural property right. He was likely influenced by John Locke's labor theory and by the newly prevalent idea that the individual – rather than God – was responsible for the creation of a work of art.[251] This reframing transformed "temporary economic monopolies granted by virtue of a royal sovereignty against the common law [...] into automatic measures to secure

247 Gieseke, *Privileg*, 141.
248 Gieseke, *Privileg*, 141–142.
249 Frédéric Rideau, "Aspects of French Literary Property Developments in the Eighteenth (and Nineteenth) Centuries" in *Research Handbook on the History of Copyright Law*, ed. Isabella Alexander and H. Tomás Gómez-Arostegui (Cheltenham: Edward Elgar Publishing, 2016), 391–422, 402.
250 Rideau, "Aspects,“ 393–394.
251 Rideau, "Aspects," 395; Gieseke, *Privileg*, 142.

a pre-existing right [...] an act of 'justice'," as Frédéric Rideau claims.[252] Other lawyers, such as Joseph-Félicité Cochu (1739–1821) and Simon Nicolas Henri Linguet (1736–1794),[253] argued that the bond between author and book was unique and thus not to be regulated by a political authority. They also identified literary property as the highest form of property – most personal and yet alienable. French philosopher Denis Diderot (1713–1784) advocated in favor of a "personalized" yet fully alienable literary property. While he followed the Lockean argument that property arises when labor is mixed with resources, he did not equate literary property and writing to land or the products of manual labor.[254] Provincial booksellers and their representatives, such as the lawyers Gaultier (likely Jean-François Gaultier de Biauzat, 1739–1815) and Nicolas de Condorcet (1743–1794),[255] denied the existence of authors' personal rights and the notion of literary property. Instead, they claimed that an author merely gives expression to the ideas of society, showcasing that the concept of the idea/expression dichotomy was already present in France during the second half of the eighteenth century.[256] They argued that the public should have access to books because they expressed ideas created by society and anyone should be able to improve upon their expression.[257]

A change took place when on August 30, 1777, a decree was passed to secure literary property to the author in the form of authors' rights and to modify the nature of book privileges.[258] In its decree the court differentiated between an author's labor and a bookseller's industry and awarded the author more extensive rights and longer privileges than the bookseller. In article V the author received a perpetual property right based on his or her labor. Authors were also granted the right to sell their own creations.[259] If the author published

252 Rideau, "Aspects," 396.

253 Joseph-Félicité Cochu. "Requête Au Roi et Consultations Pour La Librairie et L'imprimerie de Paris" in *La Propriété Littéraire Au XVIIIe Siècle*, ed. Édouard Laboulaye and Georges Guiffrey (Paris: L. Hachette, 1859), 151–220; Simon Nicolas Henri, *Mémoire sur les propriétes et privileges exclusifs de libraire*. 1774.

254 Rideau, "Aspects," 397–398. Denis Diderot, Lettre historique et politique addressee à un magistrat sur le commerce de la libraire. 1764.

255 Gaultier. *Mémoire à consulter pour les Libraires et Imprimeurs de Lyon, Rouen, Toulouse, Marseille et Nisme, concernant les privileges de libraire et continuation d'iceux*. 1776; de Condorcet, Nicolas. *Fragments sur la liberté de la presse*. 1776.

256 Rideau, "Aspects," 399–400.

257 Rideau, "Aspects," 400–401.

258 *French Decree of 30 August 1777, on the duration of privileges, Paris (1777)*. Primary Sources on Copyright (1450–1900), ed. L. Bently and and M. Kretschmer, www.copyrighthistory.org.

259 Rideau, "Aspects," 405–406.

their own work, they retained the perpetual printing privilege – if the author assigned the right to print to a publisher the right was limited to the author's lifetime.[260] Legislation changed again during the revolutionary period.

3.2.1.1 Revolutionary France

In 1793, during the French Revolution, the *Literary and Artistic Property Act* was passed to further secure authors' rights.[261] Rideau argues that this act attempted to "see[k] an acceptable balance between divergent interests while upholding natural property as a legal basis for the author's right."[262] The act confirmed the existence of a literary property to be protected by statutes rather than royal privileges. Under certain conditions authors received the exclusive right to their works for their lifespan, plus an additional ten years following the death of the author. This span was extended to twenty years in 1810. Once the term of protection expired, all works entered the "domaine public" and became "propriété nationale."[263] This act influenced the next century of copyright legislation in France, though the span of protection and the balance between authors' rights and public interest remained disputed in the following decades. It also evoked fundamental questions of which works qualified as property and how to apply such a "sacred" property in court. The courts also considered protecting the non-pecuniary rights of authors (later called moral rights) through requirements such as including the name of the author in a work or keeping the work intact and unchanged.[264]

Focusing on the revolutionary period, Jane C. Ginsburg proposes that while the French copyright system is often contrasted with the Anglo-American copyright system, the differences between the two systems are not as substantial as often claimed.[265] According to Ginsburg, scholars often argue that the French copyright regime centered on authors' rights while US state laws ignored them. She points out that both France and the US recognized and rewarded an author's labor to encourage the creation of works beneficial to national social goals.[266] Public welfare and the enrichment of the public

260 Gieseke, *Privileg*, 142.

261 *French Literary and Artistic Property Act, Paris (1793)*. Primary Sources on Copyright (1450–1900), ed. L. Bently and and M. Kretschmer, www.copyrighthistory.org.

262 Rideau, "Aspects," 409.

263 Gieseke, *Privileg*, 143.

264 Rideau, "Aspects," 413–418.

265 Ginsburg, "Tale," 994.

266 Ginsburg, "Tale," 995.

domain were also a concern in the French act of 1793.[267] She also finds "at least a strong instrumentalist undercurrent to the French decrees of 1791 and 1793" and "author-oriented rationales" in early US states' copyright laws.[268] Ginsburg summarizes that the distinctions between both systems are "neither original nor immutable" and that the US system has not always been quite as different from European systems of copyright.[269]

The issue of copyright stayed the subject of debates throughout the nineteenth century in France. Between 1837 and 1838 three treatises on copyright were published in rapid succession. Luther S. Cushing (1803–1856) examined the different treatises in the *American Jurist*.[270] Adrien Gastambide (1808–1880) published *Traité théorique et pratique des Contrefaçons en tous Genres, ou de la Propriété en matière de Littérature, Théâtre, &c.* in Paris in 1837, a short and practical examination of literary property and counterfeits. Merely a year later Etienne Blanc (1805–1874) published *Traité de la Contrefaçon, et de sa Poursuite en Justice, concernant: les Brevets d'Invention, &c., la Propriété littéraire, &c* in Paris. Blanc also examined the relationship between counterfeits and literary property in conjunction with possible court action. His examination was longer and more practical than Gastambide's and furnished with a collection of related court cases. Last but not least, Augustine-Charles Renouard (1794–1878) published the first volume of his *Traité des Droits d'Auteurs dans la Littérature, les Sciences, et les Beaux-Arts* in 1838, in which he examined the rights of authors in literature, science, and art, and coined the term "droits d'auteurs," meaning authors' rights ("French Works," 225). The publication of three treatises on the subject illustrates the relevance of the question of authors' rights in France. The debate on "droits d'auteurs" reached the United States through the translation and publication of a part of Renouard's first treatise. The translation was published in the form of an article under the headline "Theories of the Rights of Authors" in the *American Jurist and Law Magazine* in October 1839.[271] The reception and discus-

267 Ginsburg, "Tale," 1006.

268 Ginsburg, "Tale," 995.

269 Ginsburg, "Tale," 996.

270 Cushing, Luther S, "French Works on Copyright and Patents," *American Jurist and Law Magazine from April 1838 to January 1843*, 22.42 (1839): 225–26. Hereafter abbreviatd as "French Works."

271 According to the introductory paragraph added by editor Luther S. Cushing, this dissertation was originally read by Charles Renouard (1794–1878) before the *Academy of Moral and Political Sciences* in Paris in 1837. It was then published in M. L. Wolowski's *Review of Legislation and Jurisprudence*. Afterwards, a revised version was inserted into the first volume of Renouard's *Traité des Droits d'Auteurs dans la Litterature, les Sciences, et les Beaux-Arts* as "Part III: Théorie du droit des auteurs." That third part was then translated

sion of Renouard's work highlights that national discourses on copyright, authors' rights, and literary property permeated borders and were received in other countries. Lawyers, jurists, and politicians in the US read works from Europe and reflected on contrasting ideas. The debate on copyright was not localized but inherently transnational. In Lieber's case, the strong authors' rights protection and the concept of an author's aesthetic rights inspired him and he refers to French law in his entries on literary property and copyright in the *Encyclopædia Americana* and in *On International Copyright.* Even more influential for Lieber was the German understanding of Urheberrecht, a concept Lieber had grown up with in Prussia.

3.2.2 Prussia and the German States

In the German states, copyright regulation remained disparate and fragmented throughout the eighteenth and nineteenth centuries. Before 1845 no uniform legislation on reprinting existed in the German states and the states could not agree on a generally accepted dogmatic justification for the protection of authors' rights to their work.[272] While France recognized a literary and artistic property as early as 1793, German jurists refused to acknowledge a literary or intellectual property ("dominium literarum") and limited property to physical objects. Gieseke argues that jurists hesitated to recognize property that was not already embedded in the Roman *corpus iuris.*[273] While the term literary property ("Literarisches Eigentum") was used colloquially to designate an author's right to their work, it was not used in a legal sense.[274] Initially, royal printing privileges were granted to printers and booksellers for their publications, later to authors as well. In the wake of the Enlightenment, the French Revolution, and following discussions on natural rights, many denounced privileges but individual German states still granted them far into the nineteenth century. Each state had its own copyright legislation and while the German Confederation resolved common principles concerning Urheberrecht in 1837, not all states promptly implemented those principles as law. Prussia, Lieber's home state, passed a comprehensive copyright act in 1837. Only in 1845 were uniform copyright regulations adopted in all German states, following a long process of normative and legal transformation.

---

and published as an article titled "Theory of the Rights of Authors" in the *American Jurist and Law Magazine* in 1839.

272 Gieseke, *Privileg*, 220.

273 Gieseke, *Privileg*, 210.

274 Gieseke, *Privileg*, 211–213.

Following the introduction of the printing press in the Holy Roman Empire during the fifteenth century, royal printing privileges were granted to printers and booksellers within the empire's territory, as was the case in England and in the French *Ancien régime*.[275] Privileges served to protect economic interests, to disseminate ideas, and to educate the public, but also to censor unwelcome sentiments in books prior to publication.[276] Following the Thirty Years' War (1618–1648), natural law dominated political theory and jurisprudence, prompting a renegotiation of power relations and a substitution of theological arguments with rationality. Natural law also laid the groundwork for the development of the philosophy of liberalism.[277] Privileges were categorically rejected by natural law theorists as tools of control used by the absolutist-mercantilist state to promote inequality. Instead, they proposed new humanist goals such as equality and freedom of trade and property.[278] The perception of the figure of "the author" also changed throughout the eighteenth century. Using analogies borrowed from natural law, Roman law, and German trade law, "the author" was conceptualized by authors and by publishers as a proprietor entitled to reap the fruits of their labor.[279] While writers were previously seen as the hand that expresses God's creation through writing, more authors understood themselves as original creators of their works during the second half of the eighteenth century. Moral, philosophical, and aesthetic debates shaped the image of the author as originator and proprietor. Consequently, authors called for more rights to their works. Many demanded to be in charge of their own works rather than to have printers or publishers control them, pushing back against the established publication system.[280] Ludwig Gieseke argues that since the inadequacies of the German privilege system were already prevalent during the seventeenth and eigh-

275 Diethelm Klippel, "Das Privileg in der deutschen Staatsrechtslehre des 19. Jahrhunderts" in *Das Privileg im europäischen Vergleich. Band 2*, ed. Barbara Dölemeyer and Heinz Mohnhaupt (Frankfurt a.M.: Klostermann, 1999), 285–308, 289.

276 Diethelm Klippel, "Das Privileg im deutschen Naturrecht des 18. und 19. Jahrhunderts" in *Das Privileg im europäischen Vergleich. Band 1*, ed. Barbara Dölemeyer and Heinz Mohnhaupt (Frankfurt a.M.: Klostermann, 1997), 329–346, 337.

277 Klippel, "Deutsches Naturrecht," 332–334.

278 Klippel, "Deutsches Naturrecht," 338–339.

279 Hannes Siegrist, "Geschichte des geistigen Eigentums und der Urheberrechte. Kulturelle Handlungsrechte in der Moderne" in *Wissen und Eigentum. Geschichte, Recht und Ökonomie stoffloser Güter*, ed. Jeanette Hoffmann (Bonn: Bundeszentrale für politische Bildung, 2006), 64–80, 69.

280 Siegrist, "Geschichte," 68.

teenth centuries, the concept of Urheberrecht did not develop *out of* the privilege system but rather *in conflict with* and *against* the privilege system.[281]

Notably, some booksellers and authors spoke out in favor of reprinting. Ulrike Andersch proposes that advocacy for reprinting followed five major lines of reasoning: Firstly, those in favor of reprinting argued that the mere existence of royal privileges proved that anything not awarded a privilege could be reprinted freely – if reprinting was never legal, privileges would not need to exist in the first place.[282] Reprinters claimed that since no law prohibited reprinting in all the German states, reprinting books without privilege protection must be legal. Some even admitted that reprinting might not be *moral* but they insisted it was not *illegal*. Reprinters could thus be condemned but they could not be punished.[283] Secondly, reprinters referred to historical arguments. They argued that reprinting had never been illegal and that copying and selling books had been common in ancient Rome and the Middle Ages – therefore, it should be embraced. Those in favor of reprinting denied any difference between copying a work by hand and mechanically reprinting it; neither would qualify as theft.[284] Thirdly, they used economic arguments. They claimed that reprinting books promotes positive competition, regulates prices, makes books easily accessible and disseminates knowledge. As with any other product sold on the market, a publisher must be aware of the risk that any book published might be reprinted and sold for a cheaper price. Books deserve no special protection, they claimed, and publishers and authors merely complained out of greed. Actually, they argued, an author profits from reprinting, as every reprint promotes the author's work, makes it more accessible, and encourages them to write more.[285] This argument goes hand in hand with the fourth claim: Cheaper reprints make knowledge more widely accessible and thus promote enlightenment and education among underserved populations and territories. Reprinting, they claimed, supports public welfare.[286] Lastly, reprinters argued against the concept of intellectual property itself. They denied the notion that an author could hold a property right to their work as well as the claim that an author could transfer this property right to a publisher in the form of an exclusive publisher's right ("Verlagsrecht"). They referred to Roman law, which only recognized property in physical

281 Gieseke, *Privileg*, 145.

282 Ulrike Andersch, *Die Diskussion über den Büchernachdruck in Deutschland um 1700 bis 1815* (Tübingen: Mohr Siebeck, 2018), 227, 420.

283 Andersch, *Diskussion*, 420.

284 Andersch, *Diskussion*, 421.

285 Andersch, *Diskussion*, 422–427.

286 Andersch, *Diskussion*, 430.

objects, and argued that only the unpublished manuscript was property. Copying a published book would not injure the author's property in the manuscript, they claimed.[287]

Those in favor of reprinting also denied that thoughts could be sold in the first place and concluded that they could not possibly steal an author's thought or intellectual property by reprinting a book. Since an author could only decide whether to publish a work at all, not who could print the published work, an author could not grant a publisher any exclusive publishing right. Consequently, they claimed, reprinting did not injure an author's property rights or a publisher's exclusive publishing rights – therefore it could not be unlawful.[288] Reprinting advocates also criticized that many who opposed reprinting and claimed property rights to a work still accepted reprinting in specific cases, such as in the case of foreign books, and did not claim a worldwide and permanent exclusive property right. This understanding of property, they stated, was inherently contradictory and invalidated authors' and publishers' positions.[289] Interestingly, all arguments expressed by reprinting advocates in the German states were also present in debates in the US. While the early German system of printing privileges differed significantly from the later US system of copyright, the arguments in favor of reprinting were largely interchangeable. Thus, it is not surprising that Lieber later included these arguments in his work on US copyright in an effort to refute them – they were not new to him.

The eighteenth century saw many lively discussions on the matter of reprinting in the German states.[290] Many treatises were published on the legitimacy, appropriateness, and reprehensibility of reprinting. To name only a few examples, German poet Friedrich Gottlieb Klopstock (1724–1803) wrote about the property rights of authors to their works,[291] and philosopher Johann Gottlieb Fichte (1762–1814) explored theories of intellectual property.[292] Johann Albert

287 Andersch, *Diskussion*, 432–433.

288 Andersch, *Diskussion*, 435–436.

289 Andersch, *Diskussion*, 441.

290 For an in-depth examination of the discussion surrounding reprinting in the Holy Roman Empire between 1700 and 1815, see Andersch's work. *Die Diskussion Über Den Büchernachdruck in Deutschland Um 1700 Bis 1815*. Andersch analyzes the discussion in great detail and presents a comprehensive summary of the participants and the arguments in favor of and against reprinting. All those mentioned in this paragraph are discussed in more detail in Andersch's monograph and in Ludwig Gieseke's earlier work.

291 Friedrich Gottlieb Kloppstock, *Die Deutsche Gelehrtenrepublik* (Berlin: Walter de Gruyter, 1774).

292 Fichte, Johann Gottlieb. "Beweis Der Unrechtmäßigkeit des Büchernachdrucks. Ein Räsonement Und Eine Parabel." *Berlinische Monatsschriften*, 21 (1793): 443–483.

Heinrich Reimarus (1729–1814), Christian Heinrich Wilke (no date of birth and death), and Adolph F. F. L. Freiherr von Knigge (1752–1796) all published treatises in favor of reprinting,[293] and Gotthold Ephraim Lessing (1729–1781) and Philipp Erasmus Reich (1717–1787) both authored treatises against reprinting.[294] These examples only offer a small window into the eighteenth-century discourse on reprinting, but they emphasize the richness of the discussion and the variety of standpoints. Interestingly, the English *Statute of Anne* (see chapter 3.1) remained largely unacknowledged in the German states. As Gieseke points out, only few commented on the statute and they largely agreed that it was an unreasonable limitation of copyright. The French acts of 1777 and 1793 (see chapter 3.2.1) were acknowledged in the German states but not considered in detail.[295]

The discussion on reprinting quieted down following the 1740s but was revived in the 1770s, when power structures within the book trade shifted and the rate of reprinting increased.[296] Several German states signed mutual agreements prohibiting the sale of reprints but efforts failed to establish a North-German convention against reprinting.[297] During the political upheav-

---

293 Knigge, Freiherr von, Adolph. *Über Den Büchernachdruck.* 1792; Reimarus, Johann Albert Heinrich. *Der Bücherverlag in Betrachtung Der Schriftsteller, Der Buchhändler Und Des Publikums Erwogen.* 1773; Reimarus, Johann Albert Heinrich. "Der Bücherverlag in Betrachtung Der Schriftsteller, Der Buchhändler Und Des Publikums Abermals Erwogen." *Deutsches Magazin* (1791): 383–414; Wilcke, Christian Heinrich. *Der Gerechtfertigte Nachdrucker, Oder: Der Gerechtfertigte Nachdrucker, Oder: Johann Thomas Von Trattners, Des Heil. Römschen Reichs Ritter, Wie Auch Kayserl. Königl. Hofbuchdruckers Und Buchhändlers in Wien Erwiesene Rechtmäßigkeit Seiner Veranstalteten Nachdrucke. Als Eine Beleuchtung Der Auf Ihn Gedruckten Leipziger Pasquille.* 1774.

294 Lessing, Gotthold Ephraim. "Leben Und Leben Lassen. Ein Projekt Für Schriftsteller Und Buchhändler." *Gotthold Ephraim Lessing – Gesammelte Werke in 10 Bänden*, edited by Paul Villa (Berlin: Aufbau, 1968), 535–549; Reich, Philipp Erasmus. *Der Bücher-Verlag in Allen Absichten Genauer Bestimmt. An Den Herren Verfasser Des Bücher-Verlags in Betrachtung Der Schriftsteller, Der Buchhändler Und Des Publikums Erwogen.* 1773.

295 Gieseke, *Privileg*, 140–143.

296 Gieseke elaborates on the changes in the book trade in chapter IX of his work. In section 3 of that same chapter, he analyzes the different contributions to the discussion of reprinting in the late eighteenth century. The section includes examinations of the works of Johann Albert Heinrich Reimarus, Philipp Erasmus Reich, Johann Stephan Pütter (1725–1807), Johann Georg Heinrich Feder (1740–1821), Heinrich Gottfried Scheidemantel (1739–1788), Martin Ehlers (1732–1800), Johann August Schlettwein (1731–1802), Johann Jakob Cella, Immanuel Kant (1724–1804), Gottlob August Tittel (1739–1816), Jakob Fauth (1757–1807), Justus Friedrich Runde (1741–1807), Wilhelm August Friedrich Danz (1764–1803), and Karl Salomo Zachariae (1769–1843). See Gieseke, *Privileg*, 161–173.

297 Gieseke, *Privileg*, 155.

als of the 1790s in Europe publishers saw a chance to promote a general law against reprinting and coordinated their efforts. They lobbied for the inclusion of such a law in the electoral capitulation of Emperor Leopold II. (1747–1792) and soon after in the electoral capitulation of Emperor Franz II. (1768–1835).[298] While both emperors did not cover such a law in their respective capitulations, they included the remark that an expert opinion on reprinting should be obtained.[299] Publishers continued their efforts for several years, mostly to protect their own rights rather than the rights of authors – at the time most considered reprinting a problem facing publishers, not authors.[300] Authors did not yet lobby strategically for their own rights. Usually, they were paid a patronage and did not make a living exclusively from selling books, wherefore some were less concerned with reprinting. This would change during the nineteenth century as the reading public grew, the imbalance between authors' remuneration and publishers' profits increased, and authors' self-conception changed.[301]

Toward the turn of the century the issue of reprinting moved further into the background due to the French Revolution, the French Revolutionary and Napoleonic Wars, the end of the Holy Roman Empire, and the subsequent reorganization of Europe.[302] Until the *Congress of Vienna* (1814–1815) individual German states were responsible for negotiating the matter of reprinting.[303] While some states implemented individual legislation, most did not. Andersch argues that individual state laws passed at the time focused on promoting the book trade. The author increasingly became the subject of protection ("Schutzsubjekt") but intellectual property was not legally recognized. Instead, the goal was to balance the interests of publishers, authors, and the public, to protect and promote local trade, and to implement new censorship laws.[304] In most states, though, the privilege system continued because civil

298 Prospective emperors of the Holy Roman Empire signed an electoral capitulation ("Wahlkapitulation") that comprised different provisions laid down by the prince-electors. The future ruler agreed to adhere to these provisions during his reign.

299 Andersch, *Diskussion*, 445, 454.

300 Gieseke, *Privileg*, 137, 162.

301 Andersch, *Diskussion*, 454; Gieseke, *Privileg*, 162, 173. Some authors attempted to publish works without the assistance of professional publishers between 1760 and 1780. They believed that they should be awarded more rights and control over the process of printing and selling their works (Gieseke, *Privileg*, 174). Gieseke examines different authors' contributions to the discussion of reprinting in section 3, chapter IX of his book (*Privileg*, 173–181).

302 Andersch, *Diskussion*, 445.

303 The Congress of Vienna followed the fall of Napoleon Bonaparte and consisted of a series of diplomatic meetings during which the future political order of Europe was discussed.

304 Andersch, *Diskussion*, 456–457.

and public law offered no legal alternatives to replace it with. Privileges awarded by birth and those not accessible to all citizens were dismantled first, while privileges accessible to anyone, such as authors' or inventors' privileges, existed for several more decades.[305]

Gieseke argues that the eighteenth-century discussions on reprinting eventually resulted in a general consensus to reject the practice as morally wrong. Nevertheless, the law lagged behind and consequently individual states treated the issue very differently.[306] While several states continued to tolerate reprinting – for example Bamberg, Baden, and Württemberg – Prussia passed the *General Prussian Land Law* ("Allgemeines Preußisches Landrecht," abbreviated APLR in the following) in 1794, which broached the issue directly and introduced the first detailed legislation concerning derivate publishing rights ("Verlagsrecht")[307] and reprinting.[308] According to the APLR, books may not be reprinted if a Prussian subject holds the derivative publishing rights for them[309] and no new editions may be printed without an author's consent.[310] This exclusive right does not pass on to an author's heir and if no publisher holds the publishing rights and the author's rights to the work have expired, a new publisher may reprint the work.[311] Nonetheless, if the author's descendants are still alive, the new publisher has to negotiate the matter with them.[312] The APLR also permits the reprint of new editions of foreign language works by non-Prussian authors published outside the German States, as long as their

305 Klippel, "Deutsches Naturrecht," 330, 341.

306 Gieseke, *Privileg*, 181.

307 Derivative publishing rights constitute a publisher's right to print and distribute a work. The publisher obtains this right through a contract with the author, according to the Allgemeines Preußisches Landrecht, Erster Theil, Elfter Titel, Achter Abschnitt: Von Verträgen; wodurch Sachen gegen Handlungen, oder Handlungen gegen Handlungen versprochen werden," 7): "Verlagsverträge" §§ 996–1035, see for example: "Allgemeines Landrecht für die Preußischen Staaten (01.06.1794), Erster Theil." Opiniojuris.de, https://opinioiuris.de/quelle/1622#Achter_Abschnitt._Von_Vertraegen_wodurch_Sachen_gegen_Handlungen_oder_Handlungen_gegen_Handlungen_versprochen_werden. Accessed 28 Aug. 2023.

308 Andersch, *Diskussion*, 458. Zweyter Theil, Zwanzigster Titel, Fünfzehnter Abschnitt: "Von Beschädigungen des Vermögens durch strafbaren Eigennutz und Betrug," 6): "Büchernachdruck" §§1294–1297 d.), 01.06.1794, see for example: "Allgemeines Landrecht für die Preußischen Staaten (01.06.1794), Zweyter Theil." https://opinioiuris.de/quelle/1623#Fuenfzehnter_Abschnitt._Von_Beschaedigungen_des_Vermoegens_durch_strafbaren_Eigennutz_und_Betrug. 28 Aug. 2023.

309 Zweyter Theil, Zwanzigster Titel, Fünfzehnter Abschnitt, §1294.

310 Erster Theil, Elfter Titel, Achter Abschnitt, §1020.

311 Erster Theil, Elfter Titel, Achter Abschnitt, §1029.

312 Erster Theil, Elfter Titel, Achter Abschnitt, §1030.

publishers do not visit the Frankfurt or Leipzig book fair and have not been granted an exclusive privilege for the work.[313] New translations of previously translated works do not qualify as reprinting according to the APLR.[314] §1033 declares that if a publisher's book is reprinted outside of Prussia, the injured publisher may reprint any other books published by the reprinter. §1034 states that if illegal reprints are produced, publishers are entitled to compensation, detailed in §1035, and that the reprints must not be imported to Prussia.[315]

Andersch posits that the APLR constituted a threshold between the theory of derivative publishing rights ("Verlagsrecht," a publisher's contractual right to print and distribute an author's work) and the theory of intellectual property; it originated through a conflict between both theories. The idea of intellectual property began to emerge, but derivate publishing rights prevailed. Andersch concludes that the drafters of the APLR could not reconcile the civil law notion of an author's intellectual property with the criminal law prohibition of reprinting.[316] Instead, the APLR focused on the relationship between publisher and author, and the role of the author came to the fore. Due to changing market conditions authors now often made a living by selling their works and it proved necessary to revise authors' relationships with publishers and the market.[317] On a broader scale the APLR proved to be a turning point in the history of copyright, because it framed publishers' derivative publishing rights as rights of *use* rather than as rights of *property* – a publisher did not own the works they published; they merely acquired the right to use them. The APLR remained the most comprehensive publishing rights legislation until the *Prussian Copyright Act of 1837* was passed.[318] Two decades after Prussia passed the APLR, European rulers convened during the *Congress of Vienna* (1814–1815) to renegotiate power relations in Europe following the defeat of Napoléon Bonaparte. Several German booksellers chose to present a memorandum on reprinting in the hopes of effectuating pan-German legislation against reprinting.[319]

---

313 Erster Theil, Elfter Titel, Achter Abschnitt, §1026.

314 Erster Theil, Elfter Titel, Achter Abschnitt, §1028.

315 Erster Theil, Elfter Titel, Achter Abschnitt, §1033–1036.

316 Andersch, *Diskussion*, 458, 467–468.

317 Andersch, *Diskussion*, 466–467.

318 Andersch, *Diskussion*, 468–469.

319 The memorandum was titled *Denkschrift gegen den Büchernachdruck; zugleich Bittschrift um Bewürkung eines deutschen Reichsgesetzes gegen denselben*, 1814. Carl Bertuch's diary entries detail the events during the congress: Bertuch, Carl. *Carl Bertuchs Tagebuch vom Wiener Kongreß*, edited by Hermann Freiherrn v. Egloffstein, Gebrüder Paetel, Berlin, 1916, http://ds.ub.uni-bielefeld.de/viewer/resolver?urn=urn:nbn:de:0070-disa-685224.

3.2.2.1 The Congress of Vienna

When the *Congress of Vienna* commenced in 1814 many publishers and authors felt that intellectual works were not properly protected in the different German states. As Gieseke points out, the protection offered for intellectual works in many German states fell short of the demands and possibilities of the time. While reprinting flourished in the South and Austria, better measures existed in the Middle and Northern territories. Reprinted works from Southern regions were imported to Middle and Northern states and threatened the local book trade.[320] In preparation for the *Congress of Vienna* booksellers from Austria and the German states convened at the 1814 Easter Mass in Leipzig to organize lobbying activities against reprinting at the *Congress*. They elected a delegation of six publishers, who selected two publishers from their midst to travel to Vienna and lobby on-site for booksellers' and publishers' interests. The delegation chose Johann Friedrich Cotta (1764–1832) and Friedrich Justus Bertuch (1747–1822). Bertuch fell ill and his son Carl Bertuch (1777–1815) attended the congress in his stead.[321] The delegation also commissioned August von Kotzebue (1761–1819) to draw up a memorandum against reprinting. Kotzebue was a playwright, not a jurist, and Bertuch and Cotta criticized that the resulting memorandum lacked legal depth. Kotzebue did not include any new thoughts on reprinting in his memorandum. Instead, he recalled the arguments made by Johann Stephan Pütter (1725–1807) in 1774,[322] focused on derivate publishing rights ("Verlagsrecht"), and did not denounce censorship.[323] Consequently, Bertuch and Cotta drafted their own statements and added them to Kotzebue's memorandum. The collected documents were passed on to the attendees of the *Congress*, along with a request to consider the issue of reprinting. The delegation also demanded

---

Accessed 15 September 2021. Among the booksellers was Francis Lieber's later contact Johann Friedrich Cotta (1764–1832) (*Preußisches Gesetz* 22–24; Andersch, *Diskussion*, 497).

320 Gieseke, *Privileg*, 203–204.

321 Siegfried Seifert, "Der weimarer Verleger Carl Bertuch und der Wiener Kongreß. Mit einem Anhang bisher ungedruckter Dokumente aus dem Weimarer Goethe- und Schiller-Archiv" in *Beiträge zur Geschichte des Buchwesens im frühen 19. Jahrhundert: Ausgewählte Referate der Tagung des Leipziger Arbeitskreises zur Geschichte des Buchwesens vom 25. bis 27. September 1992*, ed. Mark Lehmstedt (Wiesbaden: Harrassowitz, 1993), 25–52, 45–47. In the appendix Seifert includes transcripts of Bertuch's draft for an act against reprinting, which defines reprinting and illustrates the concerns of publishers at the time.

322 Pütter, Johann Stephan. *Der Büchernachdruck nach ächten Grundsätzen des Rechts geprüft*. Göttingen, 1774.

323 Gieseke, *Privileg*, 204–205.

an end to the system of privileges and lobbied for the introduction of a universal law against reprinting in all German states.[324] They advocated for freedom of printing (then called "Pressfreiheit") and protested against state censorship.[325] Following the presentation of Kotzebue's memorandum at the *Congress of Vienna,* Austrian reprinters published their own memorandum to protest against the criticism leveled at them.[326] They argued that an exclusive copyright would constitute a monopoly and thus harm the public good. If one buys a copy of a book, they claimed, the copy becomes one's property and thus one can do with it as one pleases. They believed this included the right to copy and sell it. Reprinting a book was thus no different from copying a painting or reproducing manufactured goods. They concluded that book prices would rise and cause harm to the public if it were to become illegal to reprint books.

Two other works on reprinting were published in 1814: Heinrich Luden (1780–1845) published *Vom freien Geistesverkehr* and August Gottlieb Eberhard (1769–1845) published *Die deutschen Schriftsteller. Was sie thaten, was sie für Unrecht leiden, und was ihnen für Lohn gebührt.* Both works were no legal treatises. Gieseke claims that jurists kept a low profile at the time: No new legal text on the rights of authors was published until 1823.[327] Andersch presents excerpts from Luden's text, which prove very interesting: Luden argues that authors contribute to the education and culture of a country through their works and thus their works must not be threatened by reprinting or censorship. Reprinting, he claims, is a crime against country and people, against the formation of the spirit, and against the purpose of human existence.[328] Andersch points out that this passage and others from the work demonstrate the growing awareness of German unity, the increasing resistance against Napoleon, and the desire for the formation of a German nation.[329] The sentiments presented by Luden will also appear in Lieber's work on copyright roughly fifteen years later (see chapter 4).

---

324 Andersch, *Diskussion*, 498–500.

325 Andersch, *Diskussion*, 503.

326 *Denkschrift Gegen Den Büchernachdruck. Den Am Wiener Congresse Versammelten Gesandten von Einer Deputation Der Leipziger Buchhändler Überreicht, Mit Berichtigungen Der Darin Aufgestellten Irrigen Ansichten, von Einem Österreicher.* Wien, 1815.

327 Gieseke, *Privileg*, 204. Schmid, Karl Ernst. *Der Büchernachdruck aus dem Gesichtspunkt des Rechts, der Moral und Politik, mit Berücksichtigung der wichtigsten in- und ausländischen Gesetzgebungen, gegen L. Fr. Griesinger. Der Deutschen Bundesversammlung zugeignet.* Jena 1823.

328 "Ein Frevel gegen Volk und Vaterland, gegen die Ausbildung des Geistes überhaupt, also gegen den Zweck des Lebens der Menschheit," quoted in Andersch, *Diskussion*, 501.

329 Andersch, *Diskussion*, 501.

During the year-long *Congress of Vienna* Prussia introduced drafts for a law against reprinting while the Southern German states Bavaria and Württemberg commented in favor of reprinting. The majority of representatives at the *Congress* spoke out against reprinting, some did not consider the topic important enough to be discussed at the *Congress*, and some demanded that booksellers guarantee affordable book prices first.[330] As a result of the *Congress of Vienna*, the German Confederation ("Deutscher Bund") adopted the *German Federal Act of 1815* as its constitution on June 6, 1815. In article 18 the constitution determined that the Federal Convention ("Bundesversammlung") of the German Confederation must, during its first meeting, draft uniform legislation concerning freedom of the press and authors' and publishers' protection against reprinting.[331] Andersch argues that this article implied the unlawfulness of reprinting and accepted the rights of authors alongside the rights of publishers.[332] Following the *Congress of Vienna*, the discussion shifted from whether reprinting *could be* lawful to how to prevent reprinting and how to protect authors and publishers. The duration and extent of protection as well as whether foreign works should be protected remained points of contention.[333]

3.2.2.2 Literary Property and Authors' Rights

The first decades of the nineteenth century also brought changes in literary production. More authors created a greater variety of works, which were consumed by more readers. New forms of media emerged as better printing procedures were developed. German infrastructure improved, allowing for easier trade and transportation of books to satisfy increasing demand by the reading public.[334] Following the end of the Napoleonic Wars and the foundation of the German Confederation in 1815, the nationalization of culture and society led to the stylization of "the author" as a central figure of national culture and identity.[335] Printers and publishers were increasingly portrayed as antagonists

330 Andersch, *Diskussion*, 500–502.

331 "Die Bundesversammlung wird sich bei ihrer ersten Zusammenkunft mit Abfassung gleichförmiger Verfügungen über die Preß-Freiheit und die Sicherstellung der Rechte der Schriftsteller und Verleger gegen den Nachdruck beschäftigen." "Deutsche Bundesakte vom 8ten Juni 1815," Artikel Achtzehn, No. 4, *Gesetz-Sammlung für die Königlichen Preußischen Staaten*, Georg Decker, Berlin, 1818, p. 143–155, https://www.digizeitschriften.de/dms/toc/?PID=PPN781538416. Accessed 15 September 2021.

332 Andersch, *Diskussion*, 503.

333 Andersch, *Diskussion*, 504.

334 Siegrist, "Geschichte," 76.

335 Siegrist, "Geschichte," 72.

of authors, while readers understood themselves as "equal partners of the artist and author" ("gleichwertig[e] Partner des Künstlers und Autors"), as Hannes Siegrist argues.[336] Authors lobbied for formal recognition and longer protection of their rights. They began framing their works as their literary property ("literarisches Eigentum") and argued that states' governments had to protect it as a form of property. During the 1830s and 1840s interest groups formed and later turned into professional associations with the goal of putting the issue of literary property and authors' rights on the political agenda.[337] Siegrist posits that the revolutions and reforms of the eighteenth and nineteenth centuries changed institutional, political, and ideological frameworks and enabled the breakthrough of intellectual property as an institution.[338] The modern state functioned as legislator, bureaucratic administrator, producer, and mediator of knowledge and culture.[339] The slow process of dismantling the system of printing privileges in the German Confederation commenced.

Legislators had three options to replace the former system of royal printing privileges and to protect intellectual property following the foundation of the German Confederation, as Diethelm Klippel summarizes: They could substitute the privilege system with a general privilege or criminal law act, they could expand the concept of property to include intellectual creations, or they could develop new categories of legitimation, such as personal rights. Any option would have to justify the existence of temporary and exclusive monopolies in constitutional law.[340] While the civil liberties of natural law theory clearly dismissed privileges as well as legal positions protected through privileges, the privilege system continued to exist as a "necessary evil" for several more decades, up until 1870.[341] In 1818/1819 and in 1864, drafts for universal copyright legislation ("Urheberrechtsgesetz") were drawn up but never implemented.[342] Elmar Wadle finds that until 1837 several new applications for privileges were submitted in Prussia, but most were rejected.[343] Prussia passed its own copyright act to protect scientific or artistic works against

---

336 Siegrist, "Geschichte," 73.

337 Siegrist, "Geschichte," 71–72.

338 Siegrist, "Geschichte," 77.

339 Siegrist, "Geschichte," 74.

340 Klippel, "Deutsches Naturrecht," 344–345.

341 Klippel, "Deutsche Staatsrechtslehre," 292.

342 Elmar Wadle, "Der Langsame Abschied vom Privileg. Das Beispiel des Urheberrechts" in *Das Privileg im Europäischen Vergleich. Band 1*, ed. Barbara Dölemeyer and Heinz Mohnhaupt (Frankfurt am Main: Vittorio Klostermann, 1997), 377–399, 380.

343 Elmar Wadle, "Privilegienpraxis in Preußen: Privilegien zum Schutz gegen Nachdruck 1815–1837" in *Das Privileg im Europäischen Vergleich. Band 2*, ed. Barbara Dölemeyer and Heinz Mohnhaupt (Frankfurt am Main: Vittorio Klostermann, 1999), 335–362, 336–340.

reprinting on June 11, 1837 (examined in detail in chapter 5.3). The German Confederation passed a federal provision ("Bundesbeschluss") on November 9, 1837, which contained principles for the protection of literary and artistic productions within the territory of the German Confederation.[344] Nevertheless, the Federal Convention still granted a few select privileges until 1867, for example to the heirs of popular authors Friedrich Schiller (1759–1805) and Johann Wolfgang von Goethe (1749–1832).[345] Another federal decision from June 19, 1845 required all German states to enhance protection for literary works. Some states adhered to the decision, others continued to allow or even require privileges.[346] The *Paulskirchenverfassung* of March 28, 1849, a constitution drafted during the German revolutions of 1848 and 1849, intended to do away with privileges as a legal category but was not accepted by several large German states.[347] The German Confederation did not succeed in abolishing privileges altogether. The first universal German copyright act to grant protection to the creators of a work ("Urheberrechtsgesetz") passed on June 11, 1870 and subsequently outlawed privileges, granting statutory protection instead.[348] Following the foundation of the German Empire in 1871, authors, publishers, jurists, and politicians lobbied for the internationalization of copyright regulation during international conferences and in 1886 the German Empire joined the international *Berne Convention for the Protection of Literary and Artistic Works* and consequently implemented domestic protection for international works.[349]

Francis Lieber was certainly most influenced by the period from the foundation of the German Confederation in 1815 until the enactment of the *Prussian Copyright Act* of 1837 ("Preußisches Urheberrechtsgesetz"), which he discusses in his diary entries, translated for the American public, and which inspired him while drafting *On International Copyright* (see chapter 6). Within the German Confederation the individual states functioned as legislators. Prussia lobbied for more comprehensive copyright protection during the early years of the German Confederation and when the *Prussian Copyright*

344 "Separat-Protokoll Der 31. Sitzung Der Deutschen Bundesversammlung," in *Protokolle Der Deutschen Bundesversammlung Vom Jahre 1837*, vol. 22, Bundes-Präsidial-Druckerei, 1837, 846a-846h. For a detailed examination of the negotiations preceding the passage of the act, see Elmar Wadle, "Der Bundesbeschluß vom 9. November 1837 gegen den Nachdruck. Das Ergebnis einer Kontroverse aus preußischer Sicht," *Zeitschrift der Savigny-Stiftung für Rechtsgeschichte: Germanistische Abteilung* 106.1 (1989): 189–238.

345 Wadle, "Langsamer Abschied," 368

346 Wadle, "Langsamer Abschied," 388–389.

347 Klippel, "Deutsche Staatsrechtslehre," 295–296.

348 Wadle, "Langsamer Abschied," 377.

349 Siegrist, "Geschichte," 74.

Act passed in 1837, it inspired other states and the Confederation to adopt new copyright regimes.[350] In 1838, Eduard Julius Hitzig, a Prussian jurist and bookseller, published a commented version of the *Prussian Copyright Act* of 1837.[351] Hitzig was consulted during the drafting of the act and he was one of Lieber's German contacts. Lieber mentions Hitzig in a speech at the *International Copyright Association* in 1868, suggesting that Lieber read Hitzig's commented version of the act and was inspired by it.[352] In the preface to this commented version Hitzig explains that he felt called to comment on the copyright act due to his personal experiences as a legal scholar and a bookseller (*Preußisches Gesetz*, VI). His aim was to offer information to authors and artists whose rights were secured by the act, and also to judges who would have to judge on the matter of copyright (*Preußisches Gesetz*, VII–VIII). He argues that the rights of literary workers had been wholly unprotected until the enactment of this copyright act. Consequently, he questions how judges were able to rule on matters of copyright at all since the copyright legislation drafted by experts was faulty until recently. "Monstrous decisions saw the light of day,"[353] Hitzig argues, before the new copyright act passed (*Preußisches Gesetz*, 11). Prussia had not only passed the first comprehensive copyright regulation in the German states, it also influenced the genesis of federal copyright legislation in the German Confederation.

3.2.2.3 Prussian Influence on Federal Copyright Regulation

The members of the Federal Convention decided in 1817 to commission Günter Heinrich von Berg (1765–1843) to collect and review all regulation on printing and reprinting in the German states.[354] Following von Berg's advice,

---

350 Elmar Wadle, "Entwicklungsschritte des Geistigen Eigentums in Frankreich und Deutschland. Eine vergleichende Studie" in *Eigentum im internationalen Vergleich (18.–20. Jahrhundert)*, ed. Hannes Siegrist and David Sugarman (Götting: Vandenhoeck & Ruprecht, 1999), 245–263, 249.

351 Julius Eduard Hitzig, *Das Köngl. Preußische Gesetz vom 11. Juni 1837. Zum Schutze des Eigenthums an Werken der Wissenschaft und Kunst gegen Nachdruck und Nachbildung dargestellt in seinem Entstehen und erläutert durch Dr. Julius Eduard Hitzig* (Berlin: Ferdinand Dümmler, 1838). Hereafter abbreviated as *Preußisches Gesetz*.

352 Francis Lieber, "Speech of Francis Lieber" in *International Copyright. Meeting of Authors and Publishers, at the Rooms of the New York Historical Society, April 9, 1868 and Organization of the International Copyright Association* (New York: International Copyright Association, 1868), 20–24. Hereafter abbreviated as "Speech."

353 My translation, in the original: "Die monströsesten Entscheidungen kamen zum Vorschein."

354 Gieseke, *Privileg*, 206–207.

the members of the Federal Convention decided in their thirty-fourth session of the year 1818 to appoint a committee to issue an expert opinion on the matter of copyright protection. The committee presented its expert opinion in the fourth session of 1819 and the states discussed it within their own governmental institutions. Prussia's Royal State Ministry ("Königliches Staatsministerium") responded in 1823, but other states came to different conclusions – it seemed unlikely the states would reach an agreement (*Preußisches Gesetz*, 22–24). Therefore, the Prussian ministry decided to work on individual legislation. The drafters assumed that all states would agree that the prohibition of reprinting was a prerequisite to protecting authors' and publishers' rights and would therefore implement the necessary legislation. Thus, they focused on establishing means of protection *within* their own state. In 1827, Prussia began drafting agreements between individual states to ensure inter-state protection and entered into more than thirty different bilateral agreements.[355] In the twenty-fourth session of the Federal Convention in 1829, Prussia requested that all states grant equal protection against reprinting to the subjects of their own state and the subjects of all other member states of the German Confederation. In 1832, the Federal Convention agreed to stop differentiating between one's own subjects and subjects of other German states with regard to protection against reprinting: All publishers, booksellers, and authors should enjoy equal legal protection against reprinting in all German states. Prussia decided to grant these protections to all Prussian provinces, even those that were not members of the German Confederation.[356] Other states applied different standards of protection, wherefore the legal protection against reprinting again remained inconsistent between states. Granting equal protection to all citizens seemed impossible as long as some states (e.g., Württemberg) stuck with the privilege system, while others implemented general protection against reprinting for all Germans.[357]

During the ministerial conference in Vienna on June 7, 1834 sixty new federal articles were proposed, including article 36, which proclaimed that all state governments agreed to prohibit reprinting across federal territory and to protect authorial property ("schriftstellerisch[es] Eigenthum") following uniform principles (*Preußisches Gesetz*, 29).[358] The article was uniformly

355 Gieseke, *Privileg*, 230.

356 This included the provinces East Prussia, West Prussia, and Posen.

357 Gieseke, *Privileg*, 231.

358 "Die Regierungen vereinbaren sich dahin, daß der Nachdruck im Umfange des ganzen Bundesgebiets zu verbieten, und das schriftstellerische Eigenthum nach gleichförmigen Grundsätzen festzustellen und zu schützen sei." "Schlußprotokoll der Wiener Ministerial-Konferenz vom 12. Juni 1834" in *Quellen und Aktenstücke zur deutschen Verfassungs-*

accepted during the Federal Convention on April 2, 1835, and through the official usage of the term "authorial property" ("schriftstellerisch[es] Eigenthum") an author's property in their works was legally established (*Preußisches Gesetz*, 39). All states were required to present their own concept to implement these principles within two months, but some states claimed a different understanding of the clause: They argued that it was not clear whether the clause itself prohibited reprinting or whether it merely directed states to draft such a prohibition (Gieseke 232).

In the sixteenth session of the year 1835, Prussia complained about the lack of concreteness in the wording of the agreement. The Prussian representatives demanded that the Confederation determine which manners of reproduction were prohibited and which period the article applied to. Prussia also proposed that all works of science and art must only be copied with the consent of the creator. The creator could alienate these rights to another person – either via purchase or via inheritance – who would then hold these rights for at least fifteen years (*Preußisches Gesetz*, 30–32). The Federal Convention postponed a decision on these demands but clarified key principles of the agreement in the thirty-seventh meeting on November 11, 1835: All states *had to* adhere to the agreement and no works of science or art could be copied without consent of the author, no matter if they had been printed prior to April 1835. Additionally, the copyright could be inherited by the heirs or legal successors of an author for at least ten years following the publication of the work, not the death of the author. In particular cases the period of protection could be prolonged by federal decision. In the case of illegal reprinting, author, editor, and publisher were entitled to compensation and all copies as well as all respective printing plates would be seized (*Preußisches Gesetz*, 29–33).[359]

In his assessment of the *Prussian Copyright Act*, Hitzig summarizes the state of copyright regulation that preceded the act in the German Confederation up until 1835: All federal states had prohibited reprinting, the system of privileges ought not to be employed anymore, but no general legislation protecting literary property existed yet. Hitzig then turns to the situation within the Kingdom of Prussia. On February 20, 1836, a commission convened to decide whether the recent federal resolutions granted comprehensive and unified protection or whether Prussia needed to implement additional protective measures. The commission concluded that the protective measures on the

geschichte: Von der Gründung des deutschen Bundes bis zur Eröffnung des Erfurter Parlaments und dem Vierkönigsbündnisse, ed. Karl Weil (Berlin, Boston: De Gruyter, 2018), 68–83.

359 Gieseke, Privileg, 231–233.

Prussian state level were still insufficient and more effective state protection was needed before the federal measures could be put into practice. New state legislation would determine which works qualified for protection, how long they were protected for, and which civil and criminal penalties would be appropriate in cases of reprinting. The commission presented a draft bill, which the foreign minister in turn presented to the State Ministry. The Ministry modified the bill and proposed it to the King of Prussia, Friedrich Wilhelm III. (1770–1840). The king instructed the State Council to examine the bill and in 1837 the Council determined that a new Prussian law was necessary to adhere to federal law provisions (*Preußisches Gesetz*, 38–39). The State Council called together another commission, which presented a draft bill to the State Council in 1837. The State Council discussed and voted on the bill four times until it was again presented to the king, who accepted the *Prussian Copyright Act* on June 11, 1837.[360] Prussia then let the Federal Convention know that uniform provisions were now needed in all states of the German Confederation. The Convention discussed the matter since Prussia advocated for a thirty-year period of protection following the death of the author, a demand other states such as Austria and Württemberg rejected. Eventually, the Federal Convention resolved federal provisions on November 9, 1837, which included a ten-year post mortem period of protection (*Preußisches Gesetz*, 35–41).[361]

3.2.2.4 The Prussian Copyright Act of June 11, 1837

The *Prussian Copyright Act* of June 11, 1837 includes 38 articles and copyright scholars generally consider it the first modern German law that offers protec-

360 The State Council voted on April 26, April 29, May 3, and May 5, 1837. The act was passed as *Gesetz zum Schutze des Eigenthums an Werken der Wissenschaft und Kunst gegen Nachdruck und Nachbildung. Vom 11. Juni 1837*. Verlag der Deckerschen Geheimen Ober-Hofbuchdruckerei, 1855.

361 Laid down first in the protocols of the Federal Convention: "Separat-Protokoll Der 31. Sitzung Der Deutschen Bundesversammlung," in *Protokolle Der Deutschen Bundesversammlung Vom Jahre 1837*, vol. 22, Bundes-Präsidial-Druckerei, 1837, 846a-846h. The provisions were published in Berlin on December 11, 1837, and later included in "Publikations-Patent über den, von der deutschen Bundesversammlung unter dem 9. November d. J. gefaßten Beschluß wegen gleichförmiger Grundsätze zum Schutze des schriftstellerischen und künstlerischen Eigenthums gegen Nachdruck und unbefugte Nachbildung" in *Gesetz-Sammlung Für Die Königlichen Preußischen Staaten. 1837* (Berlin: Vereinigtes Gesetz-Sammlungs-Debits- und Zeitungskontoir, 1838), 161–164. Hereafter abbreviated as *Publikations-Patent*.

tion for authors ("Urheber").[362] The act was published in the Prussian statute book for the year 1837[363] and Julius Eduard Hitzig published his commented version of the act in 1838. The act will be examined in detail here because – coming from Lieber's home state – its contents significantly inspired Lieber's work on copyright (see chapter 6). §1 of the act declares that only the author (or those who have been granted permission by the author) holds the right to commission the publication of a new partial or complete edition of their work, either in print or through any other mechanical way of reproduction. §2 defines reprinting as the reproduction of a work without the consent of the author or rightful appointees and declares it forbidden. The third paragraph clarifies that reprinting of manuscripts or transcribed sermons and lectures also constitutes an act of illegal reprinting, even if the original manuscript or transcript was rightfully purchased ("Gesetz," 165). These paragraphs establish a difference between the manuscript or copy of a work, which can be purchased, and the work itself, which remains the author's. They also demonstrate that the author has become the central focus of the German Urheberrecht: As the Urheber or creator of the work, the author holds all rights to the work and merely passes the publication rights on to the publishers for one edition. Even if the author decides to sell the manuscript of a work, the new owner only owns the manuscript, not its content.

§4 details what is not considered reprinting, namely quoting of specific passages (though it might constitute plagiarism), printing individual articles or poems in a literary collection or historical work to be used in educational contexts, and translating published works. Translations from a "dead language" ("todten Sprache") without an author's consent are considered a reprint. If a translation into the target language already exists or has been announced by the author, translating the work also constitutes a reprint ("Gesetz," 165–66). §5 grants the author protection against reprints for life and §6 states that the author's heirs also receive protection for up to thirty years following the author's death. To receive protection, the author's name must be stated on the title page or in the preface (§7). If the author chooses to remain anonymous or uses a pseudonym, the work will only be protected for fifteen years, unless the work is reissued with the author's true name within those fifteen years ("Gesetz," 166). These paragraphs are interesting for several reasons: That works may be reprinted for school books demonstrates that public education

362 Gieseke, *Privileg*, 241.

363 "Gesetz zum Schutze des Eigenthums an Werken der Wissenschaft und Kunst gegen Nachdruck und Nachbildung. Vom 11. Juni 1837" in *Gesetz-Sammlung für die königlichen preußischen Staaten 1837* (Berlin: Gesetz-Sammlungs-Debits- und Zeitungs-Kontoir, 1838), 165–171. Hereafter abbreviated as "Gesetz."

is a concern for the drafters. Universities and academies are also granted the exclusive right to reissue their works for thirty years ("Gesetz," 166–167). It is also noteworthy that the act does not consider the translation of a work a reprint – this notion is also part of Lieber's own line of argument. It is also significant that copyright protection automatically passes on to an author's heirs because its transmissibility underlines the property-like qualities of the copyright. This is reinforced by §9, which states that authors and their heirs can alienate the exclusive publication right partially or completely to others.

The act determines that a reprinter must compensate the author or those who hold the rights to the original work (§10). Any reprinted copies will be confiscated and a penalty of 50 to 1,000 Taler must be paid. A judge determines the appropriate penalty, which should be equivalent to the price of 50 to 1,000 copies sold, unless the author can prove an even higher financial loss (§11). Any confiscated copies have to be destroyed or handed over to the author (§12) and anyone who knowingly sells illegal reprints must pay the compensation together with the reprinter, plus an extra fine (§13) ("Gesetz," 167). A legal enquiry into a possible violation of the act does not take place unless requested by the publisher whose edition was reprinted, by its author, or by the heirs (§15). If a judge is not certain whether an act of reprinting has been committed or how large the fine should be, a committee of experts must be consulted (§17). The following paragraphs detail that the reproduction of works of art, maps, pieces of music, and sculptures is also illegal and that §1, §2, and §5–17 equally apply to them ("Gesetz," 168).[364] §36 declares that anyone who holds a printing privilege is free to continue to use it rather than accept the protection offered by the act, but it overrides all other previous or contrary provisions (§37). Lastly, the act applies to works published in other states ("in einem fremden Staate") insofar as the rights in those states correspond to Prussia's act, implementing a reciprocal inter-state copyright for the German states (§38) ("Gesetz," 171).

3.2.2.5 The Federal Provisions of November 9, 1837

The federal provisions of November 9, 1837, which followed the *Prussian Copyright Act*, were first published in the protocol of the thirty-first session of the German Federal Convention[365] and later in the Prussian statute book of 1837

364 The paragraphs 18 to 35 detail the protection offered for works of music and art and will not be examined here.

365 "Separat-Protokoll Der 31. Sitzung Der Deutschen Bundesversammlung," in *Protokolle Der Deutschen Bundesversammlung Vom Jahre 1837*, vol. 22, Bundes-Präsidial-Druckerei, 1837, 846a-846h.

(*Publikations-Patent*, 161–164). The provisions contain six articles. Article 1 declares that literary products of any sort ("literarische Erzeugnisse aller Art"), published prior to or after this date, must not be reprinted without the consent of the author or the author's legal successor. Article 2 declares that this exclusive right to copy passes on to heirs or legal successors, who hold that right in all federal states for at least ten years.[366] Article 3 states that the period of protection can be extended to a maximum of twenty years in the case of major publications, which require publishers to invest a large advance payment. Article 4 determines that author, editor, and publisher are entitled to full compensation, if their works are reprinted without consent. This includes financial compensation and the seizure of all printing plates and copies. Article 5 prohibits the sale of reprints in all federal states but grants individual states the right to determine whether the sale of older reprints will be allowed in the future. Article 6 urges individual states to report to the Federal Convention on how they plan to implement these provisions. Wadle states that the federal provisions offered a minimum level of agreement between all states and obliged states which had previously hesitated to implement copyright legislation to do so now. Nevertheless, the provisions were not the uniform decrees the *Congress of Vienna* had promised and Prussia expected. Rather, they constituted a compromise which was not equivalent to what was necessary or possible at the time when compared with regulations in other countries.[367]

In June 1842, the Federal Convention began negotiating a possible extension of the period of protection since other states had introduced a longer thirty-year protection period. The Reprinting Commission submitted an expert opinion and the individual states voted on the matter. In June 1845, the Federal Convention unanimously agreed to implement a uniform federal protection period against reprinting of thirty years following the death of the author, and thus officially implemented a clear federal prohibition against reprinting. Gieseke argues that it took until 1845 to implement uniform federal regulations due to the territorial fragmentation of the German states, due to extensive dogmatic discussions, and due to a cultural preference for examining legal changes in great detail before agreeing on them. The period of protection

366 For all works published on federal territory within the last twenty years, the span of ten years begins on November 9, 1837. For all future publications, that span begins on the day of publication. In the case of serial publications the span begins on the day the last work is published, as long as no more than thirty years have passed between first and last publication (*Publikations-Patent,* 161–162).

367 Wadle, "Bundesbeschluß," 189–190.

remained unchanged until 1934, when it was extended to fifty years following the death of the author.[368]

3.3 Summary

The legal and cultural environments sketched out in this chapter differ significantly, but they also share similarities. The Anglo-American sphere developed a copyright regime focused on broad access to literature and the promotion of sciences and art through exclusive but temporary printing monopolies, which offered financial benefits to authors. Different countries in the continental-European sphere cultivated an authors' rights regime focused on the advancement of national literature and identity through comprehensive protection of authors' moral and aesthetic rights to their work, its integrity, and the right to control its printing and distribution. British and US-American copyright systems were closely related and both cultural-legal spheres weighed the benefits of offering a financial incentive to authors to produce more science, literature, and art, against the benefits of offering the public broad access to literature and thus promoting public welfare. Both systems resorted to temporary printing monopolies but with significant differences: The British copyright, on the one hand, evolved from a long history of printers' advocacy and dates back to the *Stationers' Company*'s printing privileges. For more than a century the printers' guild emphasized and protected printers' and booksellers' rights to a published work and offered protection against the financial damages they suffered through reprinting. In 1710, these privileges were superseded by the *Statute of Anne*, which instead gave priority to authors' rights to their work but also to the encouragement of learning. While the statute protected an author's exclusive right to print and distribute copies of their work, this right was limited to fourteen or twenty-eight years. Instead of a publishers' copyright, the statute offered an authors' copyright, but it did not frame it in terms of property rights. The US-American copyright, on the other hand, developed out of the individual states' statutes and British colonial influence. The states' statutes differed in their conceptualization of authors' rights and copyright but several spoke explicitly of an author's literary property, while also addressing the encouragement of learning. These statutes balanced both the interests of the authors and the public, proving that tendencies to protect authors through property rights existed on the American continent. The *Copyright Clause* in the US Constitution as well as the resulting *Copyright Act of 1790*

368 Gieseke, *Privileg*, 229, 242–44, 247

did away with the conceptualization of literature as an author's property. Instead, they emphasized the progress of science and useful arts through exclusive printing and distribution rights for authors, which were granted for a period of fourteen to twenty-eight years. Congress' century-long refusal to implement copyright protection for foreign authors highlights the influence of printers and publishers in the US, but it also underlines the importance placed on general education and on broad and cheap access to literature in the public domain. Copyright became the subject of passionate cultural, legal, and political discussions in the US during the nineteenth century. This is hardly surprising: Considering the recent foundation of the republic, governmental and legal systems in the US were still in flux.

When Francis Lieber arrived in the US and voiced his interest in copyright protection, he entered into a rich and complex domestic discourse within a country still cultivating its own national identity. This included both a reliance on British law – due to the recent constitution of the US government and novel inception of the legal system – and a desire to distance the country from Great Britain by developing a uniquely US-American identity and putting national interests first. Lieber eagerly participated in this discourse, quickly siding with those who called for more comprehensive copyright protection for domestic and foreign authors and with those who framed authors' rights in terms of property, rather than as exclusive but temporary copyrights. But Lieber did not enter into the discourse without any preconceived notions; rather, he brought with him his own preexisting assumptions about authors' rights and copyright protection from continental Europe. It is exactly this transnational influence which makes Lieber's contribution to the copyright debate in the US so interesting: He introduced continental-European notions of Urheberrecht and droit d'auteur to the US, combining them with Anglo-American notions of copyright and thus cultivating his own transnational understanding of literature as property.

Francis Lieber grew up in Prussia during a time of political upheaval, which resulted in profound political shifts. Born during the reign of Napoleon Bonaparte, Lieber witnessed the disintegration of Napoleon's empire as well as the dissolution of the Holy Roman Empire. He observed the political reorganization of the European continent and the foundation of the German Confederation. He was no stranger to an environment of federalism and competing political interests and as a writer Lieber took an early and personally motivated interest in the protection of authors' works. Prussia was the German forerunner in matters of comprehensive protection of Urheberrecht and this advocacy for authors' rights likely shaped Lieber's opinion on the matter before he left Prussia. While Lieber fostered a strong dislike of the French due to his experiences as a child in French-occupied Prussia and as a soldier during the Napoleonic Wars, a strong French influence in his life cannot be denied. French notions of droit d'auteur emerged during and after the French revolution and likely influenced Lieber's strong stance on authors' rights protection, as did the resonances of the complex and controversial discourse on the subject in the German Confederation. Even after he had migrated to the US, Lieber monitored legal and political changes in Europe and especially in Prussia. These changes continued to influence Lieber, who still considered Germany – as he referred to the German Confederation – his home, though he also identified as a true US citizen.

Naturally, opponents of authors' rights existed in the German Confederation and France as well – some publishers claimed the right to an author's work for themselves, others thrived by reprinting works published in other German states. In all legal-political environments copyright regulation was in flux. As national and international politics shifted during the long nineteenth century, so did conceptualization of authors' rights, literary property, and copyright. At this point in time no country in Europe or North America existed in isolation and legal-political changes did not transpire in a vacuum. Young countries such as the US looked to more established legal regimes for guidance but they also developed in opposition to them. Their emerging national literature and identity was shaped by transnational influences as well as conflicts. As a transnational figure Francis Lieber's understanding of copyright, literary property, and authors' rights was shaped by different legal environments and against this diverse backdrop Lieber developed his own framework of literary property. He amalgamated the legal-political notions gathered in continental Europe with what he learned in England and the US and then introduced his transnational perspective to the US discourse. As an immigrant, an author, an editor, an educator, and a political scientist, Francis Lieber thus contributed in a unique way to the (inter)national copyright debate in the US during the nineteenth century. Detailed analyses of his different contributions – published works, diary entries, speeches, and correspondence – on the basis of the established historical context are the subjects of the following chapters.

CHAPTER 4

The 1820s: Authors' Rights and Literary Property in the *Encyclopædia Americana* Entries

During the nineteenth century, Germans constituted the largest migrant group in the US. They had brought with them their own preconceived notions and categories of thinking and thus influenced US society, culture, and politics. Simultaneously, Nativism as a political movement flourished and not all US citizens welcomed German immigrants.[1] Still, the nineteenth century saw an "unusually broad influx of German ideas and cultural practices into American life, from religion to education, food, farming, political and intellectual life."[2] German influences also shaped US higher education and many US-Americans left their home country to study in the German states.[3] Many Germans saw the US as "a new stage in the progress of humanity", but others remained critical of the institution of slavery – despite Prussia's economic dependence on cotton imported from the US.[4] US republicanism was critically and enthusiastically discussed in the German States, as well as during the German revolution of 1848/1849.[5] Many larger societal trends in the US and in the German States during the nineteenth century resemble one another. Rising industrialization shaped society, factories replaced workshops, many left the countryside and moved to the city, the wealth gap widened, sectional conflicts arose between different parts of the population, and during the second half of the century, both Germans and US-Americans engaged in processes of nation-building.[6]

Francis Lieber, who was one of these German migrants and spent his life both in Europe and in the United States, was born under the name of Franz Lieber in Alt Cölln (today Berlin-Mitte) on April 8, 1798, as one of eleven children of a merchant family.[7] His parents were well-connected and Lieber was

1 Hermann J. Rupieper, "Epilogue: The United States and Germany in the Time of Francis Lieber, 1798–1872," in *Francis Lieber and the Culture of the Mind*, ed. Charles R. Mack and Henry H. Lesesne (Columbia: University of South Carolina Press, 2005), 149–163, 155.

2 Rupieper, "Epilogue," 149.

3 Rupieper, "Epilogue," 149–150.

4 Rupieper, "Epilogue," 1450, 156.

5 Rupieper, "Epilogue," 150–151.

6 Rupieper, "Epilogue," 150–160.

7 During his time in the US, Lieber changed his date of birth and claimed he was born in 1800, effectively making himself younger. Consequently, scholars do not always agree on Lieber's actual date of birth. James Farr, for example, cites both March 18, 1798, and March 18, 1800,

 | HTTPS://DOI.ORG/10.1515/9783112239407-004

raised in relative freedom.[8] As a child he showed interest in medicine, botany, mathematics, and religion, though he did not enjoy his time at private school.[9] Lieber claimed that his childhood was heavily influenced by the Napoleonic wars. Young Lieber fostered a hatred of Napoleon and the French after witnessing the march of Napoleonic occupying forces through Berlin in 1806. This hatred resulted in growing nationalist convictions and made Lieber more susceptible to the teachings of Friedrich Ludwig Jahn (1778–1852), a German nationalist who advocated for the unification of the German states. Lieber started attending Jahn's *Turner* lessons in 1811.[10] In 1815, after Napoleon had returned from Elba, Lieber volunteered for the Pomeranian regiment *Colberg*. He fought in the war for several months until he was gravely wounded at Namur.[11] He barely survived his injuries, contracted typhus during his stay in a military hospital, and remained deaf in one ear.[12]

In 1816, Lieber attended the secondary school *Zum Grauen Kloster* but left without a diploma in 1818 and then likely took private lessons with Friedrich Schleiermacher (1768–1834).[13] In July 1819, Lieber was arrested for the first time, in response to the murder of August von Kotzebue (1761–1819) by the hands of fellow *Turner* Karl Ludwig Sand (1795–1820) on March 23, 1819.[14]

---

in the *American National Biography*, see James Farr, "Lieber, Francis (18 Mar. 1798 or 1800–02 October 1872), educator and political writer," *American National Biography*. February, 2000. Oxford UP. Accessed 24 October 2023, https://www.anb.org/view/10.1093/anb/9780198606697.001.0001/anb-9780198606697-e-1400365. Claudia Schnurmann argues that Lieber was born on April 8, 1798, as stated by Lieber's cousin Albert Baur. Hamilton Lieber, Francis Lieber's son, claimed that Francis Lieber and his ten siblings all shared similar birthdays and that their parents therefore changed their birthdays to avoid celebrating all eleven birthdays within a few days. This accounts for the change in month and day (Schnurmann, *Brücken*, 37).

8 Schnurmann, *Brücken*, 37–40.

9 Schnurmann, *Brücken*, 43, 52–54.

10 Lieber harbored a strong dislike of the French for years following, until he met and befriended Joseph Bonaparte (1768–1844), brother of Napoleon Bonaparte, in the US in 1828 (Schnurmann, *Brücken*, 44–47, 57).

11 Annexed by the French in 1794, today Belgium.

12 Schnurmann, *Brücken*, 49–51. In his later retellings, Lieber claimed he was merely fifteen (instead of seventeen) at the time and asserted he was wounded in the battle of Waterloo/Bellealliance, rather than at Namur (Schnurmann, *Brücken*, 50). Nonetheless, his experiences on the battlefield and especially his feelings of powerlessness, mortal fear, and the dread of being a prisoner of war likely paved the way for his interest in military law and the publication of the *Code 100* (see chapter 7.2).

13 Schnurmann, *Brücken*, 56.

14 The same August von Kotzebue who booksellers from Austria and Prussia hired to author the first draft of their letter expressing protest against reprinting at the *Congress of Vienna*, see chapter 3.2.2.

Due to Lieber's activities in Jahn's *Turner*-Movement he was accused of demagogy and incitement.[15] While Lieber was released soon, his confrontation with the Prussian authorities destroyed any long-term future chances he might have had in Prussia. The authorities subjected him to constant surveillance and suspicion as they considered him a fanatic follower of Jahn and an outspoken advocate for a united greater-German state. Lieber passed his *Abitur* exams in 1819, but the Prussian government and police denied his matriculation at Berlin University due to his previous arrest. In a letter to the responsible ministry Lieber requested matriculation but his application was again denied. The pleadings of his parents and pastor could not change the decision of police and ministry and Lieber left Berlin in March 1820 without giving notice of his departure.[16]

He then attended the theological faculty at the University of Jena as a mathematics student and received his doctorate after only four months in June 1820.[17] He did not cease his political activities and continued to advocate for a unified Germany. Prussian minister Freiherr von Stein zum Altenstein (1770–1840) urged Lieber's father to convince his son to study at Halle University, where he could be closely monitored. In Halle, Lieber studied mathematics and engineering and apparently ceased his subversive activities for some time until he was again accused of delivering agitating speeches and songs. He left Halle, travelled to Dresden, and eventually departed to Greece via Saxony, Bavaria, Switzerland, and France, with the intention of fighting in the Greek War of Independence. He spent three months in Greece but soon left for Italy and resided at the residence of historian and Prussian envoy Barthold

15 Schnurmann highlights that the members of the *Turner*-Movement were an emotionally-bonded community and differed from other communities through their idiosyncratic idiom, rituals, extreme xenophobia, antisemitism, misogyny, and religious fundamentalism ("Insgesamt bildete die Turnerschar eine emotionale Gemeinschaft, die sich mit einem eigenwilligen Idiom, Ritualen und extremer Xenophobie, Judenhass, Misogynie und religiösem Fundamentalismus gegenüber anderen Gruppen abgrenzte.") (Schnurmann, Brücken, 59). For a detailed examination of Lieber's activities in the *Turner*-movement as well as his antisemitic convictions, see Schnurmann, *Brücken*, 57, 62–71.

16 Schnurmann, *Brücken*, 67–71.

17 Lieber was matriculated in Jena on April 21, 1820, see: Francis Lieber Matriculation paper. Printed form, filled in. April 21, 1820. Francis Lieber papers. mssLI. Box 85, no. 4. LI4689. The Huntington. San Marino, CA. Lieber's ten-page dissertation *Ein in einigen Stücken ausgeführter Plan zur Darstellung der Theorie der höheren Reihen für den Unterricht* focuses on teaching, signaling Lieber's interest in education (Schnurmann, *Brücken*, 72).

Georg Niebuhr (1776–1831) in Rome, where he wrote and later published a book recollecting his stay in Greece.[18]

In the summer of 1823 Lieber returned to Berlin after Niebuhr elicited the promise from King Friedrich Wilhelm III. that Lieber would be able to move freely in Prussia. Lieber spent some time in Berlin and studied – again – in Halle, where he was – again – arrested and jailed on suspicion of subversive activities in 1824. He was imprisoned for seven months and released on bail in April 1825, but his freedom of movement was restricted. Lieber now attempted to distance himself from his image as a demagogue and instead socialized with writers, artists, politicians, and reformed *Turner* members, expanding his circle and improving his social standing. Nonetheless, the Prussian authorities summoned him again for extensive interrogations, lasting for hours a day and weeks on end. Lieber eventually decided to plan his escape from Prussia.[19]

On May 17, 1826, Lieber left Prussia secretly and without giving notice of his departure.[20] He spent several days in Hamburg and then departed for London, where he arrived on May 27, 1826. Lieber spent a year in London, where he worked as a language teacher, established social relationships, and fell in love with his student Mathilde Oppenheimer.[21] He collected letters of recommendation and applied for a position as a swimming instructor in Boston, as well as for a professorship in German studies at London University.[22] He was unofficially accepted in Boston during the winter of 1826–1827 and began preparations for his migration to the US. Claudia Schnurmann argues that it was at this time that Lieber began to portray himself as a scientist, a literate, and an artist. On April 3, 1827, Lieber officially accepted the position as a swim instructor at the Boston gymnasium in his first transatlantic letter.[23] To his

18 Schnurmann, *Brücken*, 72–74. Lieber, Francis. *Tagebuch meines Aufenthaltes in Griechenland während der Monate Januar, Februar und März im Jahre 1822*. F. A. Brockhaus, 1823.

19 Schnurmann, *Brücken*, 74–77. Interestingly, Julius Eduard Hitzig signed the interrogation protocols (Schnurmann, *Brücken*, 77). For more on Hitzig, see chapter 3.2.2 and 6.4.

20 Lieber always portrayed his departure as a spontaneous decision but, as Schnurmann points out, a journey to another country requires careful preparation and Lieber likely secretly planned his escape for several weeks. He had also started studying English in February 1826, months before his departure. But a spontaneous escape by moonlight simply seems more romantic and that version of events also protected his parents, as it exempted them from the accusation of helping their son escape (77–78).

21 During his stays in Berlin, Rome, Hamburg and London he became acquainted with influential persons, such as the families Beneke, Sieveking, Krutisch, and de Chateauneuf in Hamburg, and the families Rothschild, Fould, Goldschmidt, Levy, and Oppenheimer, as well as Lucie Domeier and Henriette Herz (Schnurmann, *Brücken*, 79–80).

22 Schnurmann, *Brücken*, 112.

23 Schnurmann, *Brücken*, 116.

future employer, John Collins Warren (1778–1856), Lieber sent these words on April 27, 1827: "I leave Europe which began to know my literary name, for a real activity in your country [the US]."[24] To his family members, who did not approve of his decision to move to such a distant country, he wrote that "[in the US] I shall feel that I am in a land of progress, where civilization is building her home, while in Europe we can scarcely tell whether there is progression or retrogression" (*Life and Letters*, 70).[25] Before Lieber left England on May 16, 1827, he had proposed to Mathilde Oppenheimer, who remained in London to follow him to the US later.[26] On the ship *Britannia* he travelled across the Atlantic; the journey took a little over a month.[27] Within that liminal space between his former home and his new country, Lieber reflected on his past and planned his future. He would only return to Europe thrice.[28]

His migration offered Lieber a fresh start in the US. He arrived in New York City on June 22, 1827. On his way to Boston, he laid down his first impressions of the US in his diary:

> [N]ew and greater ideas are dawning which Europe is too petrified and ossified to accept or adopt [...] These new ideas will find their soil in America, and many have already taken root. There never has existed, to my knowledge, a government that has been formed so entirely for the good of the people. Never in the history of the world has so much wisdom and humanity been shown as in their civilization [...] No nation has ever made such rapid progress (*Life and Letters*, 70).

Lieber stayed in Boston until 1832. Here he made his first acquaintances in the US and expanded his international network of contacts. He worked as a swimming instructor and socialized with the Bostonian intellectual, political, and literary elites. He also engaged in journalism as a foreign correspondent for several German newspapers and journals and entertained plans for the foun-

24 Cited in Schnurmann, *Brücken*, 117.

25 This and the following quote are likely translated into English by Mathilde Lieber or Thomas Perry.

26 Mathilde Oppenheimer left England two years later and arrived in New York City on September 16, 1829. They married on September 21, 1829.

27 Lieber left Europe via Liverpool on May 16, 1827. On board the *MS Britannia* he crossed the Atlantic Ocean and arrived in New York City on June 22, 1827 (Schnurmann, *Brücken*, 121).

28 From April 1844 to January 1845, in 1848, and finally in 1851 to visit the *Great Exhibition* in London.

dation of his own US newspaper.[29] In his articles, he conveyed knowledge about life and customs in the US to German readers and engaged in international knowledge transfer. In 1830 he terminated his business relationship with publisher Johann Friedrich Cotta, inter alia because Lieber took offence to changes made to his manuscripts by the publishing house.[30]

He was "always scrambling, always proposing projects and looking for work, always reading and thinking and investigating,"[31] or, in the words of his contemporary Rufus Choate, he was "the most fertile, indomitable, unsleeping, combative and propagandizing person of his race."[32] Lieber worked "twelve and fourteen hours [a day] frequently, scarcely leaving [his] chair" and when he wished to rest, he found himself pressed to write more (*Life and Letters*, 135). He mused that "there must be such beings as literary furies, or a pressing and irresistible inspiration" that often seemed to possess him. He researched and published on a variety of topics from different disciplines, including property, labor, copyright, penology, education, and linguistics. He also issued pamphlets commenting on contemporary political affairs and passionately composed poems and songs. While writing, he created many English neologisms widely popular today.[33]

In the fall of 1827, Lieber began to make plans for the publication of the *Encyclopædia Americana*. This work was Lieber's new quest in knowledge transfer, as well as his great breakthrough as an author and publicist. In 1827, he sent a circular letter to his acquaintances, pitching his idea to translate and adapt the popular German *Brockhaus Conversations-Lexicon*.[34] He then sent this letter – along with responses by Edward Everett, George Bancroft, Charles

29 For example *Allgemeine Zeitung, Morgenblatt für gebildete Stände, Das Polytechnische Journal, Politische Annalen,* and *Das Ausland.* His plans for his own newspaper failed due to the lack of support from publisher Johann Friedrich Cotta, who also denied support for Lieber's early plans to publish the *Encyclopaedia Americana* (Schnurmann, *Brücken*, 126–130.) Claudia Schnurmann dedicates several pages to Lieber's journalistic endeavors and comments that Lieber's journalism consisted of a mixture of facts, fiction, his own and collective stereotypes, history, gossip, and anecdotes (Schnurmann, *Brücken*, 124–133).

30 Schnurmann, *Brücken*, 132–133.

31 Soifer, "Facts,“ 2305.

32 Rufus Choate, Boston lawyer, in a letter to Charles Sumner, dated January 7, 1842; quoted in Soifer, "Facts," 2305.

33 These included words such as 'bureaucracy', 'jural', 'publicist', 'nationalism', 'individualism', 'city-state', 'interdependence', 'commonwealth of nations', and 'Pan-American' (Mueller-Vollmer, "Cultural interaction," 4; Soifer, "Facts," 2305).

34 Lieber, Francis. Circular letter proposing to translate the *Brockhaus Conversations Lexicon*, together with responses. November 14, 1827. Francis Lieber papers. mssLI. Box 81, no. 1. LI88. The Huntington. San Marino, CA.

Follen, George Ticknor, and Moses Stuart – as a book proposal to booksellers. After he signed a contract with publishers Carey and Lea, the *Encyclopædia Americana* became a commercial success and laid the foundation for Lieber's career in the US.[35] In 1828 he resigned from his position as a swimming instructor to focus on the *Encyclopædia Americana*. Lieber worked with Joseph Story (1779–1845), John Pickering (1777–1846), Edward Everett (1794–1865), George Ticknor (1791–1871), and Moses Stuart (1780–1852) and became well-known among the US intellectual elite, expanding his network of contacts in the US. Many articles he wrote himself, some were inspired by the *Brockhaus Conversations-Lexicon,* others were entirely new. The *Encyclopædia Americana* became the first genuinely US-American multivolume encyclopedia, published in 13 volumes between 1830 and 1834. It was co-edited by Francis Lieber, Edward Wigglesworth (1804–1876), and Thomas Gamaliel Bradford (1802–1887) and became a great success. Lieber had, as Claudia Schnurmann points out, his finger on the pulse of a literary market that longed to distance itself from British culture but craved general knowledge from Europe.[36] With his first major US publication Lieber established himself as a well-known literary figure in the US and positioned himself as cultural negotiator and an authority on US politics and culture.[37]

This chapter offers a detailed examination of Francis Lieber's first work with regard to the conceptualization of literature as a form of transnational property. His publications served as tools for the transmission of knowledge to a larger audience and the examination of these works showcases the broadness and robustness of Lieber's thought on literary property and copyright. It also constitutes his emergence as an issue entrepreneur for the causes of literary property protection and international copyright. In this work he presents his initial framing of these issues and due to its success with a large audience in the US, the work constitutes one of his most impactful appeals to the public. This chapter also captures the different continental-European and US-American influences on Lieber's work and highlights how Lieber contrasts and combines these disparate frameworks while cultivating his own theory of copyright and literary property.

35 Ironically, Henry Charles Carey of Carey and Lea would later become one of the most resolute opponents to Lieber's fight for an international copyright, see chapter 7.2.2.

36 Schnurmann, *Brücken*, 134.

37 For a thorough examination of the role Francis Lieber claimed for himself in US culture, see Fenja Heisig, "Travel Writing and Transnational Relations: Francis Lieber As The Stranger in America," *Current Objectives of Postgraduate American Studies*, 23.1 (2022): 24–40, doi:10.5283/copas.355.

4.1 Context

Lieber's first preserved comments on copyright and literary property can be found in the respective entries on "copyright," "property," and "literary property" of the *Encyclopædia Americana*. Since the articles do not contain the authors' names, it must first be determined whether Lieber himself wrote the article or whether a guest writer created them. Lieber's later works on copyright, such as *On International Copyright* (1840), echo the earlier entries in the *Encyclopædia Americana* in detail. Not only the line of argument but also the writing style corresponds to Lieber's recognizably German style of writing and it can reasonably be assumed that these entries were written by Lieber himself. Evidently, the entries are also no direct translations from the German *Brockhaus* lexicon, which offers no entries on literary property ("Literarisches Eigentum") or German copyright ("Urheberrecht") in the seventh edition from 1827.[38] Volume 2 contains an article on copies,[39] which focuses on the copying of visual art rather than literature, and articles on copy machines,[40] and the printers' guild,[41] which do not address the legal issues associated with mechanical copying and printing. The article on property in volume 3 does not mention literary property,[42] neither does the article on literature ("Literatur").[43] The entry on reprinting ("Büchernachdruck") contains several arguments brought forward against reprinting,[44] which Lieber echoes in his own early work on copyright. Nevertheless, a comparison of this article with Lieber's *Encyclopædia Americana* entries proves that Lieber's entries are no mere translations of this German article – though it may have served as a reference work. Lastly, the entry which covers both publishers and publication rights offers many of the same criticisms of reprinting that Lieber brings forward, while also arguing in favor of an author's property rights and a

38 As indicated on the title page of the *Encyclopædia Americana* the work is "an American Biography on the Basis of the Seventh Edition of the German Conversations-Lexicon."

39 "Copie" in *Allgemeine deutsche Real-Encyklopädie für die gebildeten Stände* (*Conversations-Lexikon*) (Leipzig: Brockhaus, 1827), 869.

40 "Copirmaschinen" in *Allgemeine deutsche Real-Encyklopädie für die gebildeten Stände* (*Conversations-Lexikon*) (Leipzig: Brockhaus, 1827), 869–870.

41 "Buchdruckerzunft" in *Allgemeine deutsche Real-Encyklopädie für die gebildeten Stände* (*Conversations-Lexikon*) (Leipzig: Brockhaus, 1827), 263–267.

42 "Eigenthum" in *Allgemeine deutsche Real-Encyklopädie für die gebildeten Stände* (*Conversations-Lexikon*) (Leipzig: Brockhaus, 1827), 454.

43 "Literatur" in *Allgemeine deutsche Real-Encyklopädie für die gebildeten Stände* (*Conversations-Lexikon*) (Leipzig: Brockhaus, 1827), 615.

44 "Büchernachdruck" in *Allgemeine deutsche Real-Encyklopädie für die gebildeten Stände* (*Conversations-Lexikon*) (Leipzig: Brockhaus, 1827), 271–273.

publisher's exclusive printing rights.[45] Lieber may have referred to this article while writing his own, yet it is not a translation. Consequently, the entries on copyright and literary property constitute Lieber's first recorded comments on these topics and prove highly interesting sources.[46] While Lieber had only lived in the US for a few years when the respective volumes of the first edition of the *Encyclopædia Americana* were published, he used these entries to frame the issues of literary property and copyright for the public in an understandable and easily accessible way. He presented a narrative designed to educate his audience on the perceived wrongs of the copyright system in the US. By presenting his conclusions in the form of encyclopedia entries, Lieber framed them as facts rather than opinions and claimed their general validity.

4.2 Copyright in the *Encyclopædia Americana*, 1830

In his entry on copyright in the *Encyclopædia Americana,* Francis Lieber emphasizes that an author has a *property* right in their work, rather than merely controlling the right to copy and distribute the work ("Copyright," 527). He takes a decisive stand and openly expresses his critique of existing US copyright legislation, framing it as an issue that requires political and legal action. Clearly, European and especially German influences shape his opinion on the protection of literary works through property rights. His criticism is consistent with the conceptualization of copyright as a property right, which – following Lieber – ought to be exclusive and perpetual, as other forms of property are. While he lays the foundation for his theory of an adequate copyright regime in this entry, he does not yet comprehensively discuss the international dimension of copyright.

Lieber opens the article with his definition of copyright. He states: "Copyright denotes the property which an author has in his literary works, or which any other person has acquired by purchase, and which consists of an exclusive right of publication" ("Copyright," 527). Immediately, this entry proves saturated with Lieber's personal notions of copyright. In this initial sentence Lieber is already at variance with the *Copyright Act of 1790*: He defines copyright as a *property* which an author has in a literary work. The *Copyright Act of*

45 "Verlag, Verlagsrecht, Verleger" in *Allgemeine deutsche Real-Encyklopädie für die gebildeten Stände* (*Conversations-Lexikon*) (Leipzig: Brockhaus, 1827), 668–671.

46 The earlier entries from 1830 and 1831 serve as the basis of this analysis. The entries remain entirely unchanged in the last edition of the *Encyclopædia Americana*, published in 1851 and 1854.

1790, on the other hand, defines copyright as the author's "sole right and liberty of printing, reprinting, publishing and vending such map, chart, book or books, for the term of fourteen years from the recording the title thereof in the clerk's office."[47] Lieber does not define his understanding of property more closely, but he frames it as a right that is exclusive, focused on controlling the act of publication, and without temporal limitation. The conceptualization of copyright varies greatly; while Congress merely grants an exclusive right to print and publish, contingent on registration, Lieber claims an exclusive and unlimited property right. This proves especially interesting due to the supposedly objective format of an encyclopedia – within the first sentence Lieber claims authority over the "right" definition of copyright, though a legal one already exists. As early as 1830 Lieber thus introduced the notion of copyright as a property right to a broad US audience. He was certainly not the first one to frame copyright in terms of property; the early state statutes in the US often understood literature as property (see chapter 3.1.2). As Justin Hughes points out,

> any claim that copyrights have only recently been understood as 'property' within the legal system appears to be historically wrong. 'Intellectual property' is certainly a newer phrase, but not as new as some have claimed or intimated [...] this long history has to be acknowledged – that is, we must recognize that people have called copyright 'property' for the past two hundred years.[48]

Nevertheless, in the US the notion of copyright as property had largely been replaced by an understanding of copyright as a temporary monopoly and an incentive for authors to produce new works following the *Copyright Act of 1790*. In this entry Lieber therefore reintroduced a familiar but largely forgotten idea to his audience. He then strategically points out that an author's right to the literature they produce is, indeed, perpetual in some countries in Europe – though not in the US ("Copyright," 527). By emphasizing the existence of perpetual copyright in some European countries, Lieber adds credibility to his own claim of perpetual property rights in literature and includes an international dimension. Following Lieber's argument, copyright should be

47 Congress of the United States. *An Act for the encouragement of learning, by securing the copies of maps, Charts, And books, to the authors and proprietors of such copies, during the times therein mentioned.* May 31, 1790. See for example: *Copyright Act of 1790: U.S. Copyright Office*. Edited by US Copyright Office, copyright.gov/about/1790-copyright-act.html. Accessed 16 November 2022.

48 Hughes, "Copyright," 1040–1041.

evaluated in comparison with other legal regimes, not just within the national context.

A fairly detailed summary of the history of copyright in England follows, indicating that Lieber believed that this example would interest US readers. He addresses the *Licensing Act of 1662*,[49] as well as the *Statute of Anne* (1710),[50] which he criticizes for burdening the publisher with the "heavy tax" of delivering nine copies of each book to public libraries to "guar[d] the property of copyright against intruders" ("Copyright," 527). Lieber emphasizes that "[n]otwithstanding the statute of Anne, it was, for some time, the prevailing opinion, in England, that authors had a permanent, exclusive copyright, at common law" ("Copyright," 528). He underlines his claim with a reference to the "celebrated case" *Miller v Taylor* (1769), which granted a "common law right in perpetuity, independent of the statute," until it was repealed in 1774 ("Copyright," 528.) The arrangement and presentation of select statutes and cases serves to underline Lieber's framing of copyright as an exclusive and perpetual property right, akin to other property rights.

An outline of the legal copyright regime in the US follows with references to Art. 1, § 8, cl. 8 of the Constitution, the Constitutional Copyright Clause,[51] as well as to the Congressional acts of May 31, 1790 (*Copyright Act of 1790*), and April 29, 1802. As Lieber points out, an author must be a citizen or resident of the US to qualify for the exclusive right of publishing for fourteen years and for a contingent fourteen year renewal ("Copyright," 528). He then compares the US copyright to English law again, which he claims "does not distinguish between resident and non-resident aliens, like the American law" ("Copyright," 528). Here Lieber emphasizes the lack of international copyright regulation in the US, a point of criticism he raises frequently throughout his life. Lieber then expands the scope of his discussion of copyright by referring to the situation in continental Europe, namely in France and the German states, including Austria. This selection of countries demonstrates Lieber's main focus: In his comparisons, he relates the US mostly to England, different Ger-

49 Licensing Act (parchment copy), London (1662), Primary Sources on Copyright (1450–1900), ed. L. Bently and and M. Kretschmer, www.copyrighthistory.org. Accessed 16 November 2022.

50 A Bill for Encouragement of Learning, London (1710), Primary Sources on Copyright (1450–1900), ed. L. Bently and and M. Kretschmer, www.copyrighthistory.org. Accessed 16 November2022.

51 The Constitutional Copyright Clause, Philadelphia, Pennsylvania (1789), Primary Sources on Copyright (1450–1900), ed. L. Bently and and M. Kretschmer, www.copyrighthistory.org. Accessed 16 November 2022.

man states, and France – he considered them closely related and united on their path towards civilization.

In France, Lieber writes, the law of copyright from 1793[52] "gave authors a right in their works for life, and to their heirs for 10 years after their deaths," while the decree of 1810[53] "gave the right to the author for life, and to his wife, if she should survive him, for her life, and to their children for 20 years" ("Copyright," 528). The term of protection is thus significantly longer than in the US and it might possibly be extended further in the future, Lieber claims, but works published in a different country may still be reprinted in France without the consent of the author ("Copyright," 528). An examination of the copyright regime in Lieber's home country, the German Confederation, follows: "In Germany, the laws respecting copyright vary in the different countries; but, in general, there is no fixed time. The copyright is almost always given for the lifetime of the author," Lieber writes ("Copyright," 528). By granting copyright for an author's lifetime, rather than a few years, German law partly corresponds to Lieber's demands. But, as he points out, "the Germanic federation has not, as yet, succeeded in agreeing upon a general law, and an author's works may be printed in any of the states in which he has not taken out a copyright." Austria, on the other hand, is mentioned dismissively: "Austria is famous for piratical, incorrect, cheap editions; the government seeming to calculate according to the old maxim of political economy – if the book is pirated there, the cost of it does not go out of the country" ("Copyright," 528). This criticism equally applies to the US, where no copyright is granted for foreign authors' works. Interestingly, Lieber does not directly criticize the US here; instead, he uses the case of Austria as a substitute. He likely assumed that his US audience would be more perceptive to his criticism if applied to a different country. He underlines his disapproval by stating that disputes between German and Austrian booksellers caused by reprinting could easily be settled at the bookfair in Leipzig, where publishers from both countries convened and "no member of the community would like to appear in the character of a piratical publisher" ("Copyright," 528). Lieber thus adds a normative dimension to his criticisms and uses the entries in his *Encyclopædia Americana* as a way to express disapproval of existing copyright systems. He

52 French Literary and Artistic Property Act, Paris (1793), Primary Sources on Copyright (1450–1900), ed. L. Bently and and M. Kretschmer, www.copyrighthistory.org. Accessed 16 November 2022.

53 Imperial decree on the book trade, Paris (1810), Primary Sources on Copyright (1450–1900), ed. L. Bently and and M. Kretschmer, www.copyrighthistory.org. Accessed 16 November 2022.

thus aims to carve out and frame the relevant issue of copyright, to then present it to his audience in an understandable manner.

A more explicit criticism of the copyright regime in the US and England follows. An abridgement of a book written and published by a person who is not the original author is not considered a violation of copyright in the US or England, he points out, while this is not possible in the German Confederation. Such Anglo-American laws, Lieber claims,

> tend greatly to the prejudice of the authors of original works, who are liable to have the most valuable fruits of their toils given to the public in the shape best fitted to command a rapid sale, for the benefit of others, while the original works are comparatively excluded from the market ("Copyright," 528).

Lieber frames these laws as exploitative, rather than economical. While they make works accessible to a larger audience, to Lieber these laws constitute a violation of the author's privilege to sell their work as they see fit. The copyright term in the US, he criticizes, is short and he suggests that "it would seem but just to allow a man the exclusive property in his own book during his life, and even to extend the same, for a given period, to his heirs, in certain cases" ("Copyright," 528). He also categorizes works by their perceived literary value and laments that limited copyright protection discriminates against "the most valuable books [which] are, in many cases, those which have the slowest sale" ("Copyright," 529).

While Lieber demands a lifelong, transmissible copyright in the form of property protection, he also advocates to remove obstacles to the import of foreign literature, such as book tariffs. Any restrictions on the import of educational material ultimately harms society, he argues, since "the intelligence of the people" forms the foundation of a country's government ("Copyright," 529). "[I]t does not seem advisable to throw this obstacle in the way of intellectual improvement," Lieber states, emphasizing the role authors play within a nation: Rather than offering simple entertainment, many further progress and intellectual advancement through their works ("Copyright," 529). Interestingly, this argument echoes the purpose of Art. 1, § 8, cl. 8 of the Constitution, which endows Congress with the power to "promote the Progress of Science and useful Arts."[54] Congress has not used this power, Lieber implies, but rather impeded its very purpose. Additionally, the sums paid to authors for their

54 The Constitutional Copyright Clause, Philadelphia, Pennsylvania (1789), Primary Sources on Copyright (1450–1900), ed. L. Bently and and M. Kretschmer, www.copyrighthistory.org. Accessed 16 November 2022.

copyright by publishers vary depending on the type of literature and the calculability of success. Thus, rather than promoting scientific or poetic works, higher sums are paid for works which "promise a rapid sale," such as compilations, dictionaries, or novels ("Copyright," 529). This is the case in the US and in Europe, Lieber claims, and makes it very difficult to make a living as an author of scientific or historical works, those works that promote scientific progress and education – an author like Lieber himself.

Throughout this entry, Lieber cultivates a comparative transnational perspective on copyright regulation. He creates a dichotomy between Anglo-American copyright, with British regulation being the forerunner to US regulation, and continental-European notions of copyright, present in the German Confederation and France. Throughout the article Lieber outlines his personal position on copyright protection: He is in favor of lifelong and transmissible copyright protection in the form of a property right. Authors should be granted such protection due to the central role literature plays for the progress of the entire nation. Lieber is also critical of reprinting, which he calls "piratical," and of the promotion of "light reading." In this entry, Lieber implies the existence of a universal and morally correct standard of copyright protection – a standard which all countries must strive to meet eventually. He measures copyright legislation in all countries against his own requirements for copyright protection – lifelong, transmissible property rights – and thus promotes his own understanding as the gold standard of copyright protection. He aims for normative change with regard to copyright regulation and tries to put the issue on the national political agenda. By harnessing the entries in an encyclopedia, Lieber hopes to address a broad audience and to mobilize support for the issue by framing it as relevant to all citizens. Lieber follows up this entry with an entry on literary property in volume VIII.

4.3 Literary Property in the *Encyclopædia Americana*, 1831

To begin with, it is noteworthy that no entry for property exists in the 1831 or the 1851 edition of the *Encyclopædia Americana*. The keyword "property" merely contains the reference "See *Literary Property*, and *Copyright*."[55] This stresses the importance Lieber as editor placed on literature as a form of property and anticipates his belief that literature constitutes the most genuine

55 Francis Lieber, "Property" in *Encyclopædia Americana. A Popular Dictionary of Arts, Sciences, Literature, History, Politics and Biography. Vol. X*, ed. Francis Lieber et al. (Philadelphia: Carey and Lea, 1832), 373.

form of property.[56] In the specified entry, Lieber identifies literary property as *the* quintessential human product, the only one produced without exterior aid ("Literary Property," 14). The production of literary property requires no external resources, he claims, it comes from the mind alone: "In the whole compass and variety of the products of human labor, no one thing is more exclusively such than intellectual works" ("Literary Property," 14). He positions intellectual works as the quintessential product of human labor because "[i]n the fabrication and production of almost all other subjects of value and property, the materials are supplied, directly or indirectly, by the earth or the water; and man only cöoperates [sic] with nature in furnishing the article" ("Literary Property," 14). During the creation of an intellectual work, on the other hand, external supplies are merely used to record the fruits of the intellectual labor process and are "no more a part of the thing produced, than a deed, conveying an estate, is a part of the thing conveyed" ("Literary Property," 14). Thus – according to Lieber – the property right to these products must be granted unconditionally.

Lieber's argument stems from John Locke's definition of the origins of property: Locke claims that property is created when labor is exerted upon resources. Whoever invests labor into transforming natural resources is entitled to the products of that labor and becomes the owner of the resulting property according to Locke. Lieber argues that only the production of literary property requires no external natural resources; therefore, the author produces an inherently human property. He frames literature as a product of pure human labor, "the offspring of the unaided labor of the mind" and, consequently, "the right to the products of intellectual labor [as] peculiarly positive and absolute" ("Literary Property," 14). This property is intrinsic to the creator, it is personal, and must therefore be recognized as unconditionally the author's own. Lieber frames the ideas expressed in literary works as original ideas, as the author's own thoughts, and echoes the ideology of literary genius, of the author as the source of creation. This view rejects the understanding of creation as a shared process in which authors are inspired by others and give expression to common ideas. Instead, he attributes the process of creation solely to the author and, consequently, assigns ownership of the resulting product, the work, to

56 It is especially noteworthy that Lieber did not add an entry on property to the new edition of the Encyclopædia Americana published in 1851. He focused on the topic of property in *On International Copyright, in a Letter* and published an entire essay collection titled *Essays on Property and Labor as Connected with Natural Law and the Constitution of Society* in 1841. Lieber positions property as a central category of human existence in these works and it is surprising that he did not dedicate a proper entry to the topic in the later edition of the *Encyclopœdia Americana.*

the author alone. Nonetheless, Lieber laments, the property right to the products of intellectual labor is "among the latest rights of property recognized in a community" ("Literary Property," 14). He attributes this to the fact that such intellectual products are "only the result of an advanced state of civilization," to the abstract and incorporeal nature of this form of property, and to the difficulty in identifying and defining intellectual property ("Literary Property," 14).

Lieber also introduces an economic argument in favor of the protection of literary works: Authors who further progress and civilization might live in poverty because the government neither protects nor rewards them for their work, he claims ("Literary Property," 15). These authors cannot support cultural progress, if they cannot feed their families, and their contribution to the advancement of society may be lost. Lieber also repeats his criticism of the temporal limitation of protection and mentions favorably the lifelong copyright protection in France, Russia, and the German states ("Literary Property," 15). Hereinafter, Lieber approaches the subject of literary property from a historical perspective. He mentions English court cases such as *Millar v Taylor*[57] and *Donaldson v Becket*,[58] which discussed whether an author has a property right to his intellectual works "as unquestionable and absolute as any other producer" ("Literary Property," 14). These cases investigate whether an author has, by common law, a property right in their intellectual products and Lieber highlights the inherent conflict between perpetual common law copyright and limited statutory copyright for intellectual works in England ("Literary Property," 14). He also refers to a French case from 1831 in which the court confirmed an artist's exclusive right to create and sell copies of a statue he created, even if he sold the original piece ("Literary Property," 14–15). Lieber compares this French case to *Donaldson v Becket*, where the House of Lords ultimately decided that an author "had no exclusive right [to a work] after the expiration of the period limited in the statute," a decision Lieber finds unsatisfactory and difficult to understand ("Literary Property," 15).

57 In the initial case the Court decided that an author retains exclusive publishing rights to their work, regardless of the statutory provisions of the *Statute of Anne*. Millar v. Taylor, London (1769), Primary Sources on Copyright (1450–1900), ed. L. Bently and and M. Kretschmer, www.copyrighthistory.org. Accessed 16 November 16, 2022.

58 In this later case the House of Lords focused on copyright and concluded the British literary property debate of the eighteenth century. They ruled that while a common law copyright existed, the provisions of *the Statute of Anne* nevertheless superseded it. Donaldson v. Becket, London (1774), Primary Sources on Copyright (1450–1900), ed. L. Bently and and M. Kretschmer, www.copyrighthistory.org. Accessed 16 November, 2022.

Lieber accuses the British government of depriving authors of the fruits of their labor, keeping them in poverty, and inhibiting the progress of civilization and intellectual advancement by denying authors definitive and unlimited copyright. He states:

> Thus, while the poverty of authors and scholars – the great leaders and champions of civilization and intellectual advancement – has been proverbial all the world over, the government has interposed [...] with its mighty arm, not for their protection and reward, but to despoil them of their property, the fruits of their own labor, and sequestrate it for the public use ("Literary Property," 15).

In Lieber's opinion, the property right of an author to their work is as indisputable as the property right of those who cultivate land and own the fruits of that labor, a perpetual right which they pass on to their heirs. Instead, an author may only keep the fruits of their labor for fourteen years, as Lieber points out. "The injustice of such a doctrine is so obvious, that its legality, though sanctioned by an acquiescence of half a century, may well be questioned," Lieber writes, and bitterly states that any attempts to extend the term of copyright protection beyond 14 years is merely "entitled to the commendation of being less unjust than that of Anne" ("Literary Property," 15).

In this entry Lieber also offers a comparative perspective by examining the situation in England and the US in contrast to that in continental-Europe. He echoes his comments on copyright law in France and the German states from his earlier entry on copyright (see chapter 4.2). Based on this comparative framework Lieber turns to the US – an interesting order of argument in an entry written for an American audience. Likely, Lieber discussed English and continental-European law first to introduce notions of perpetual copyright protection to an audience in the US, which might be unfamiliar with this concept. As in his entry on copyright Lieber discusses Art. 1, § 8, cl. 8 of the Constitution, as well as the *Copyright Act of 1790*. He criticizes limited terms of protection as well as the fact that copyright must be registered, rather than being granted automatically. In the following he also examines the very recent and "more liberal, or, rather, less illiberal" act of 1831, which extends the copyright term in the US to 28 years, along with a possible renewal for life, and discards some of the provisions required of authors to maintain their copyright ("Literary Property," 15).

With this entry on literary property, Lieber published an assertive piece in a popular publication, read by many at the time. While the entry on copyright is already an opinionated piece which differs from the prevailing understanding of copyright at the time in the US, the concept of property in literature introduced in this entry goes entirely against US copyright legislation at the time. The *Copyright Act of 1790* did not frame copyright as a property right but as a limited monopoly on printing.[59] Unswervingly, Lieber asserts the existence of literary property as a given. To acknowledge literature as a form of property is unavoidable, he claims, and any nation which does not yet recognize literary property has not yet reached the advanced stages of civilization. Lieber paints a picture of teleological progression towards a perfect state of civilization, in which all forms of property will be recognized and protected as such. He does not allow for different models of copyright protection and dismisses cultural specifics or differences. Instead, he presents the protection of literature through property rights as the only morally acceptable and inherently correct approach. To support his argument Lieber integrates aspects from US-American and German understandings of authorship, literature, and copyright. He frames literature as a source of progress and learning, echoing the *Copyright Act of 1790*, and agrees with the goal of granting authors the exclusive right to print and publish their work in the form of a copyright. However, Lieber frames this right to copy as a property right and rejects limited time frames. He speaks instead in favor of strong authors' rights and demands lifelong and transmissible protection to ensure the financial security of an author and their heirs. Here, Lieber echoes French and German authors' rights sentiments and German legislation, which occasionally allow for lifelong copyright protection (see chapter 3.2.1 and 3.2.2).

Interestingly, the views Lieber expresses in these entries align much more closely with the copyright statutes of the original thirteen US states, which preceded the *Constitutional Copyright Clause* and conceptualized literature as a form of property (see chapter 3.1.2). Lieber did not introduce radically new notions by framing literature as property – rather, he retrieved sentiments already present during the founding period of the US. All original state statutes secure an author's profits in their work to encourage learning and civil progress. Several states – namely Massachusetts, Maryland, New Hampshire, North Carolina, and Virginia – explicitly frame an author's work as a form of property, while other states grant an exclusive right to print, copy, and sell. Though the *Copyright Act of 1790* supersedes these acts and eliminates the legal representation of copyright as a property right, it is noteworthy that almost half of all original states recognized a property right in literature. Evi-

59 Congress of the United States. *An Act for the encouragement of learning, by securing the copies of maps, Charts, And books, to the authors and proprietors of such copies, during the times therein mentioned.* May 31, 1790. See for example: *Copyright Act of 1790: U.S. Copyright Office.* Edited by US Copyright Office, copyright.gov/about/1790-copyright-act.html. Accessed 16 November 2022.

dently, Francis Lieber's account of literature as property in the *Encyclopædia Americana* aligns much more closely with the sentiments expressed in these state laws, rather than the later *Copyright Act of 1790*. In fact, his standpoints in the *Encyclopædia Americana* entries resemble the preambles of Massachusetts and North Carolina so closely (see chapter 3.1.2) that it seems possible that Lieber read these acts and was inspired by their understanding of literature as property. Either way, he does not mention or quote any state statutes in his entries in the *Encyclopædia Americana* or in his later work on copyright. Lieber definitely read the *Statute of Anne* as he refers to it in the entries. Whether he knew the original version of the bill, which framed literature as property, is uncertain.

It is noteworthy that in his earliest work on copyright, Lieber echoes the sentiments of the drafters of the original *British Bill for Encouragement of Learning, and for Securing the Property of Copies of Books to the Rightful Owners thereof* from 1710 (see chapter 3.1) – the same sentiments present in the state statutes of Massachusetts, Maryland, New Hampshire, North Carolina, and Virginia (see chapters 3.1.1 and 3.1.2). All state statutes resemble either the original and or the enacted version of the *Statute of Anne*, sometimes literally copying from the British original. Thus, while Lieber criticizes the *Statute of Anne* and British regulation in these early entries on copyright and literary property, he nonetheless echoes sentiments that were present in Britain a century earlier and popular in the US less than fifty years ago. While Lieber promotes a strong authors' rights-perspective in the US, utilizing his successful publication as a platform to disseminate his views, his objections were not new. Instead, he replicates concerns voiced in the original thirteen states but superseded by the *Copyright Act of 1790*. Consequently, Lieber does not introduce an entirely new view of copyright but rather retrieves early US-American understandings of literary property and connects them with Continental-European authors' rights tendencies. While this view of literature as property was no longer reflected in US state and federal legislation following the *Copyright Act of 1790*, copyright activists continued to promote the issue of the protection of literary property until the late nineteenth century and Lieber remained a central figure of this reform movement.

4.4 Summary

In his earliest work on copyright and literary property Lieber censured different aspects of existing copyright legislation in the US through comparison with German and French authors' rights notions: He criticized that copyright was only granted for a limited term and that the copyright title was not automatically transferred to the respective heirs after the death of an author. He also reprehended that copyright protection was not granted to foreign authors unless they resided in the US. Though this criticism is not spelled out explicitly in these early works, the denial of copyright protection for foreign authors would transform into Lieber's greatest complaint. His disapproval of US copyright law stems from one singular source: It was the result of his belief that written works were the literary *property* of the author. Literary works had to be protected through property rights, not copyrights, he claimed. Merely granting the author the right to control copying and distribution did not go far enough for Lieber – he demanded the recognition of literature as an author's property and its protection through exclusive, unlimited, transmissible property rights. The subject was of such importance to Lieber because he perceived it as an injustice towards authors as the champions of civilization; an injustice that could only be corrected through legal change. In these entries Lieber framed the issue of literary property through the narrative of the disadvantaged author, who lived in poverty despite – or because of – their service to society. He thus appealed to the sentiments of his readers to effect normative change and mobilize support for this issue.

Initially, few in the US agreed with Lieber. Most did not consider literature a form of property, but other authors also complained: British authors condemned the reprint of their works and US authors feared their works could not contend with cheaper, copyright-free works. Others were concerned that the development of a national literary culture was stifled by the import of British works because emancipation from Britain could only be successful if British cultural influence was reduced. Like these authors, Lieber became an issue entrepreneur for the cause of literary property, a role which would lead him to utilize his network to lobby politicians and publish an entire work dedicated to international copyright later.

Soon after publishing the first edition of the *Encyclopædia Americana*, Lieber busied himself with other projects. In 1829 he lectured at the *Boston Society for Useful Knowledge* and entertained plans for his own geographical, statistical, and ethnographical periodical (*Life and Letters*, 87). He also planned to publish a catalogue of recent books and pamphlets, a plan that never came to fruition.[60] In 1832 he moved his family to Manhattanville, outside New York City, to be closer to the University of the City New York (today NYU) and his publishers in Philadelphia. He had been invited to a foundational meeting at the university and likely hoped for a permanent position there – his second

60 Schnurmann, *Brücken*, 137.

child had been born at the beginning of that year and he struggled to support his family financially.[61] Lieber received a teaching assignment as "lecturer in History of Commerce, Agricultures, and the Mechanic Arts" and translated Alexis de Tocqueville's and Gustave de Beaumont's *Du système pénitentaire aux États-Unis et de son application en France*.[62] After five years in the US, he adopted US citizenship in 1832.[63]

In 1833, the Liebers moved to Philadelphia. Here, Lieber drew up a draft for the educational organization of the prospective *Girard College for Orphans*, once again hoping for a permanent position.[64] Despite his best efforts, his draft was rejected and he was not employed once the college opened.[65] He continued his search for a permanent position while he wrote and published *The Stranger in America; Or, Letters to a Gentleman in Germany: Comprising Sketches of the Manners, Society, and National Peculiarities of the United States*, engaging in international knowledge transfer as a mediator between two cultures.[66] Lieber utilized his European and US-American connections in hopes of attaining a higher position within the US educational system, but his search continued for another two years. In the meantime, Lieber even considered returning to university to study law and become a lawyer.[67] Finally, through

61 Schnurmann, *Brücken*, 139.

62 Schnurmann, *Brücken*, 140–142. Published as: de Beaumont, Gustave, and Alexis de Tocqueville. *On the Penitentiary System in the United States, and Its Application in France; with an Appendix on Penal Colonies, and Also, Statistical Notes.* Carey, Lea & Blanchard, 1833.

63 Lieber was admitted to become a citizen of the United States on February 7, 1832, by the U.S. district court in Boston. District Course Massachusetts. Francis Lieber Citizenship Paper. February 7,1832. Francis Lieber papers. mssLI. Box 85, no. 16. No LI number. The Huntington. San Marino, CA.

64 Lieber, Francis. *A Constitution and Plan of Education for Girard College for Orphans, with an Introductory Report, Laid before the Board of Trustees.* Carey, Lea & Blanchard, 1834. Here, Lieber again combined German and European approaches to education with the practical US model, demonstrating his ability to combine diverse cultural and scientific knowledge.

65 Schnurmann, *Brücken*, 141.

66 Francis Lieber, *The Stranger in America: Comprising Sketches of the Manners, Society, and National Peculiarities of the United States, In a Series of Letters to a Friend in Europe* (London: Richard Bentley, 1835). I analyze Lieber's efforts at international knowledge transfer more closely in my article on *The Stranger in America*, see Fenja Heisig, "Travel Writing and Transnational Relations: Francis Lieber As The Stranger in America," *Current Objectives of Postgraduate American Studies*, 23.1 (2022): 24–40, doi:10.5283/copas.355.

67 Lieber's interest in law became apparent in his correspondence with jurists. He imparted his wish to study law to judge Story, who apparently supported it, and also communicated it to C. J. A. Mittermaier in 1834 (Lieber, *Life and Letters*, 99). He also proposed an

the shared efforts of influential acquaintances such as Carl August Heckscher, Nicholas Biddle (1786–1844), James Kent (1763–1847), James Hamilton Jr. (1786–1857), and again, Joseph Story, Lieber received a position as professor of history, political philosophy and economy at South Carolina College, Columbia, in 1835.[68] He should remain there for more than twenty years, but he spent, as Michael Herz points out, "most of them [...] trying to leave."[69]

Lieber was reluctant to move to South Carolina. He would have preferred to stay in the North, where his friends resided, where his publishers dwelled, and where the intellectual life boomed. He considered South Carolina, an eager slave-holding state, an exile: "I can not [sic] help it," he wrote in his diary in May 1835, only shortly after his arrival, "to have a sense for the higher life of the arts, of the sciences, of an elevated social intercourse and then, to be in this exile, I feel greatly tempted to study the insects here [...] Something I must have to divert my mind."[70] To distract himself Lieber dedicated himself to his work and entered a highly productive phase of his life. As professor of history, political philosophy and economy Lieber focused on his research and published two of his more popular full-length publications, his *Manual of Political Ethics* and the derivative work *Legal and Political Hermeneutics*, which will be examined in the following chapter.

---

advertising paper to the editor of the New York *Commercial Advertiser* and applied for a position as literary assistant with the paper, but was rejected. Lieber suffered greatly from each rejection, as can be deduced from his diary entries at the time (Lieber, *Life and Letters*, 101–102).

68 Schnurmann, *Brücken*, 142–148. Catalogue of the Trustees, Faculty and Students, of the South Carolina College. January 1847. Francis Lieber papers. mssLI. Box 88, no. 7. No LI number. The Huntington. San Marino, CA.

69 Herz, "Rediscovering," 2111.

70 Schnurmann, *Brücken*, 148.

CHAPTER 5

The 1830s: Property, Political Ethics, and Legal Hermeneutics

As an issue entrepreneur, the topic of property as an institution occupied Francis Lieber throughout his life. He considered it a central concept and structuring element of society and politics, which influences all other areas of political life within a nation. Lieber's interest in property theory was likely sparked by his examination of copyright and literature *as* property in the *Encyclopædia Americana*. When Lieber drew up these entries in his earliest years in the US, he formulated his first tentative thoughts on property, but the short entries do not constitute a comprehensive property theory. Lieber continued to reflect on the topic for several more years until he recorded a triumphant moment in his diary on August 18, 1837:

> On the stage to Hartford I think out the theory of property, and now I have it. Property is realization or enactment of man's individuality. Without it, no individuality; thence the constant tendency to acquire property. Man feels awe at the idea of being merged in the species without individuality. It is acquired differently: by production, labor stored, occupancy, violence, law. A child wishes to have a bed in a garden for itself. If they look at birds, children will say, "This is my bird," &c. Civil liberty is that political condition in which we may do (without compulsion) what ethics allows us to do. Hence, I must have the right to be a fool and spend my property badly; for if not, I should be forced to spend it well, which would not be liberty. Liberty always involves the possibility of abuse [...] (*Life and Letters*, 119–120).

Evidently, Lieber wanted to record his epiphany. At the time of this revelation, Lieber lived in Columbia but most summers he traveled North, to New York, Boston, and Philadelphia, to spend time with his friends and those who inspired him. He craved intellectual stimulation and exchange, writing many letters during his evening hours in Columbia. In 1837 he spent some weeks in the North and two days before writing the diary entry above, Lieber and his friend Charles Sumner (1811–1874) visited Joseph Story (1779–1845), Supreme Court justice and professor of law at Harvard College in Cambridge. Lieber admired Story and that evening he experienced, in his words, "an hour which was worth living for many a year, – one of those full, intense, entire hours, as I

 | HTTPS://DOI.ORG/10.1515/9783112239407-005

call them, in which you quaff life itself out of the deep and full goblet" (*Life and Letters*, 118). This experience strengthened his resolve to write and heightened his confidence in his works.

On August 27, 1837, Lieber took the time to share his thoughts on property in a letter to his friend Charles Sumner, requesting his opinion. In this letter to Sumner Lieber lays out his property theory, based on the assertion that man is an individual and "his individuality is an insoluble inalienable attribute of his humanity" (*Life and Letters*, 120–121). Man's individuality determines the nature of all his relations: Because man is an individual, he enjoys moral liberty. Because he is an individual, he has to bear responsibility for his actions. As an individual, man stands in a jural relation to his fellow humans but also enjoys the benefits of civil and mental liberty. As an individual, he can freely think, produce and create. If man then applies his individuality to a thing, it becomes his property. Property, Lieber writes, "is the realization of man's individuality in the material world" (*Life and Letters*, 121). To individualize things and thus to appropriate is natural to man, Lieber asserts: "Man cannot be, never was, without *mine* and *thine*" (*Life and Letters*, 121). He argues that even small children single out objects and call them their own, thus individualizing them in order to assert their own individuality.[1] Humans crave the clarity and stability of ordered property relations; by claiming something as their own, humans position themselves as clearly delineated individuals – they recognize themselves in their property, as Lieber claims, and "see [their] *humanity* reflected" (*Life and Letters*, 121). Going further, Lieber argues that "hell" could best be described as loss of individuality; individualization ensures the immortality of the soul. Following Lieber, property can be established in different ways: through production, mixed production, appropriation, occupancy, preemption, positive legal declaration and through conveyance (*Life and Letters*, 121–122).

In this letter to Charles Sumner from 1837 Lieber writes out the first draft of his property theory – and quickly declares himself "perfectly master of it" (*Life and Letters*, 122). He does not name any sources that inspired him and presents his theory as entirely his own. This corresponds to Lieber's general understanding of ideas as an author's original creation, rather than a common creation dependent on previous ideas and works. Nevertheless, Lieber's understanding of property as the result of free will and as an expression of his

1 Evidently, Lieber interprets the behavior of small children as an indicator of the natural, primal state of man, neglecting to consider the role nurture plays even in small children's behavior. The tendency of small children to appropriate objects might as well be a reflection of their environment, not an indicator of an assumed primordial state of nature.

individuality through possession clearly resembles Georg Wilhelm Friedrich Hegel's (1770–1831) earlier personhood theory. Hegel presented his property theory in his 1820 work *Grundlinien der Philosophie des Rechts.*[2] He believed that property was a means to self-realization: Through property the individual could further the development of the personality and the self. Following Hegel, property is the medium through which the personality can relate to the external world. By imposing its free will on the world through an act of possession, the individual externalizes its free will and realizes itself in relation to others.[3] Lieber's theory of property as the realization of one's individuality in relation to others echoes Hegel's understanding of possession as an act of externalizing an individual's free will. Lieber's property theory continued to develop through the confrontation with questions of constitutional and international law, political ethics and the rights and duties of citizens. It informed his works throughout the following years, including *Manual of Political Ethics* (1838, 1839) and *Legal and Political Hermeneutics* (1839), two works preceding *On International Copyright* and *Essays on Property and Labor*. While these early works do not focus on property in detail, Lieber's understanding of political ethics, the state, and civic duties cannot be separated from his perception of property as a central structuring element of society.

Lieber's work on political ethics started years before the publication of the two volumes of *Manual of Political Ethics Designed Chiefly for the Use of Colleges and Students at Law* in 1838 and 1839. In 1836, Lieber sent a letter to his friend Carl Joseph Anton Mittermaier in Heidelberg, explaining his intention behind writing on political ethics. He stated that

> it is time that the many subjects which have such strong influence on politics, and yet do not belong to political or legal science, should be treated soundly and truthfully. I mean subjects such as public opinion, parties, factions, opposition, whether there is an obligation to vote if one has that right, what is to influence a citizen to vote one way or the other, friendship in politics, love of truth, perseverance, newspaper publishing, the duty of representatives, judges, advocates, and office-holder [...] and the pardoning power.[4]

2 Hegel, Georg Wilhelm Friedrich. *Grundlinien der Philosophie des Rechts.* (Berlin: In der Nicolaischen Buchhandlung, 1821).

3 Alexander and Peñalver, *Introduction*, 56–57.

4 Lieber, Francis. Letter to C. J. A. Mittermaier. May 10, 1836. Francis Lieber papers. mssLI. Box 39, no. 41. LI2867. The Huntington. San Marino, CA.

Lieber considered the question of ethical conduct in politics "a new and dangerous field," the work on which enticed him.[5] He researched the topic comprehensively, writing to Carl Joseph Anton Mittermaier that he had "gathered eight hundred notes, papers, extracts &c, and the plan of the work, in all its details, is clearly in my mind." With this work, he aimed to introduce political ethics "into the circle of Political Sciences" in the US but also in the German states, as proven by his hopes for a German translation.[6] Lieber also believed that this matter should become a part of the study of legal science, considering he intended the manual specifically for the use of law students. Lieber was convinced of the central importance of this work and did not hesitate to write to his friend Charles Sumner that

> [w]hether the book will take here I can not know; nobody can: but I am conscious, calmly and fully, that I have had the power of elevating my mind above the vast struggle of our times, and the energy of penetrating their many relations without being affected, for the time, by them.[7]

Lieber was determined to break new ground in his work and even succeeded in convincing his paragon Joseph Story to read and comment on the manuscript for the second volume prior to publication.[8] Lieber's work on political ethics indeed focuses on a myriad of issues related to politics, the organization of the state, and the conduct of politicians and citizens. With more than a thousand pages the work is so extensive that it had to be published in two volumes, containing seven books in total. While Lieber's understanding of political ethics is ingenious, this chapter focuses mainly on his perspective on property and copyright as presented in this publication.

---

5 Lieber, Francis. Letter to C. J. A. Mittermaier. May 10, 1836. Francis Lieber papers. mssLI. Box 39, no. 41. LI2867. The Huntington. San Marino, CA.

6 Lieber, Francis. Letter to C. J. A. Mittermaier. May 10, 1836. Francis Lieber papers. mssLI. Box 39, no. 41. LI2867. The Huntington. San Marino, CA.

7 Lieber, Francis. Letter to Charles Sumner. August 13, 1838. Francis Lieber papers. mssLI. Box 104, no. 7. No LI no. The Huntington. San Marino, CA.

8 Story, Joseph. Letter to Francis Lieber. August 14, 1837. Francis Lieber papers. mssLI. Box 104, no. 6. No LI no. The Huntington. San Marino, CA. In his letter, Story wrote that it "constitutes one of the best theoretical treatises on the true nature and objects of government, which has been produced in modern times, containing much for instruction, much for admonition, and much for deep meditation, addressing itself to the wise and virtuous of all countries."

5.1 *Manual of Political Ethics*, 1839

In *Manual of Political Ethics*, Lieber examines property in relation to several fundamental aspects of the organization and ethical conduct of a government and its people. He incorporates his developing theory of property into this work because he considers property an inherent and natural institution present in all human societies. As James Farr summarizes, Lieber defined an institution as "an objective system or body of laws or usages, of extensive operation, in a delimited field, lasting beyond the lives or contributions of the individuals acting within and perpetuating it."[9] Property as an institution therefore constitutes an important aspect of political ethics and the relationship between the citizen and the state. As Farr showcases, Lieber approached the state in a novel way and proposed a more comprehensive understanding than many others at the time: He framed the state not just as the government but as "society itself, understood jurally and organically. The government was but an organ of the more extensive legal organism of state."[10] The state as Lieber outlines it "deepened and advanced man's existence as both a social being and a free individual, predicated with rights and duties in relation to others. Far from being static or timeless, the state evolved along different trajectories in different social and cultural environments," as Farr points out.[11]

Preceding the state, Lieber argues that property rights arise from natural law and are therefore rights derived from "the essential nature of men" (*Political Ethics I*, 65). These natural rights, he claims, must be acknowledged by the government on the grounds of ethics and conscience – as natural rights they are non-negotiable (*Political Ethics I*, 45). Politics proper, defined by Lieber as applied law, merely ascertains the best means to secure these pre-existing rights (*Political Ethics I*, 65–66). Consequently, applied to the matter of literary property, the government does not decide *whether to recognize* literary property but merely *how to protect it* through effective copyright legislation. Lieber proposes that the institution of property originally resulted from a scarcity of resources and the investment of individual labor: By investing labor into an object, one cultivates an exclusive relationship with that object (*Political Ethics I*, 116–117). The right of property is thus acquired "by assimilation or imprint of labor or industry" (*Political Ethics I*, 118). Here, Lieber again echoes Locke's

9 James Farr, "From Moral Philosophy to Political Science: Lieber and the Innovations of Antebellum Political Thought" in *Francis Lieber and the Culture of the Mind*, ed. Charles R. Mack and Henry H. Lesesne (Columbia: University of South Carolina Press, 2005), 113–128, 120.

10 Farr, "Moral Philosophy," 119–120.

11 Farr, "Moral Philosophy," 120.

labor theory and later on – in *On International Copyright* – applies the same reasoning to the creation of literary property: The author's labor is writing the text and they thus create an object of property. This literary property is fully their own due to the labor they invested in its creation.

Lieber then expands on the assimilation of property by focusing on the relationship between private property and individuality. Private property is, he claims, "nothing else than the application of man's individuality to external things, or the realization and manifestation of man's individuality in the material world" (*Political Ethics I*, 120). He echoes the thoughts laid down in his earlier diary entries, where he stated that property "is the realization or enactment of man's individuality" and framed individuality as a requirement for humanity (*Life and Letters*, 119–120). The emphasis on the role of individuality in property relations is reflected in his understanding of literary works as a deeply personal form of property. To Lieber, literary property is more personal and individual than other objects of property. The written word is intertwined with the author's personality and thus, his individuality: A book contains an author's thoughts and beliefs; it comes from the author's mind only. If an author decides to share a piece of their inner world with readers, their written work should be protected from both theft and financial exploitation. Therefore, in Lieber's opinion, an author should always be able to control the distribution of their works, property, and the testament of their individuality reflected in the world. Lieber thus incorporates elements of both Hegel's and Locke's theories of property in this work by emphasizing both the constitutive relation between property, free will, and the externalization of individuality through possession, and the importance of investing labor in the creation of property.

Lieber then introduces another central aspect in relation to property: The advancement of civilization. Far from being relevant only to the individual, private property also promotes the progress of civilization, he claims. While private property originates from one's individuality, it nevertheless secures and stabilizes society as a whole (*Political Ethics I*, 120). Property as a natural right has always existed but it "has been but gradually recognised; each step in the way of civilisation has obliged men to acknowledge [the right of property] in one more of its many ramifications and peculiar forms," Lieber asserts (*Political Ethics I*, 130). This is to be expected, he claims, as that which "is truly natural to men [...] unfolds itself more perspicuously with the progress of civilization" (*Political Ethics I*, 130–131). The process of civilization requires constant reflection and revision and positive law must change accordingly (*Political Ethics I*, 132).

Lieber identifies literature as one of these "peculiar forms" of property and directly addresses copyright as the protection of literary property through law. Copyright legislation only became necessary when reprinting of works became possible. Due to its recent nature, Lieber criticizes, many believe copyright to be "an invented thing [...] a grant bestowed by the mere grace and pleasure of society" (*Political Ethics I*, 132). He rejects claims that an author can have no right to ideas since they cannot have entirely original thoughts and are merely inspired by freely-available ideas. Since the author owes those ideas to society, the author cannot claim them as his own or profit from selling them. Lieber decidedly disagrees: While an idea cannot be property, the specific arrangement of ideas in a composition is an author's invention and therefore their private property (*Political Ethics I*, 132). In Lieber's understanding, the title to literary property originates from preoccupancy and actual production (*Political Ethics I*, 132). Literary property should therefore be treated like any other form of property, Lieber argues, criticizing that "[i]t strikes every one [sic], now-a-days, as very barbarous, that in former times, commodities belonging to any foreign nation were considered as good prize, yet we allow robbing in the shape of reprint, to the manifest injury of the author" (*Political Ethics I*, 133). Evidently, his support for authors' rights and his critique of the lack of international copyright regulation in the US began to inform his major works on other subjects.

US legislation does not yet recognize this form of property rights, Lieber admits, while other copyright systems, such as the "extensive and well-grounded copy-right law" in Prussia, do (*Political Ethics I*, 133). This lack of protection is emphasized by the fact that the US allows persons to claim the abridgement of another's work as their own. Existing copyright legislation also does not protect works by foreign authors through copyright (*Political Ethics I*, 133). In this work from 1838, Lieber still claims that a perpetual copyright is not "absolutely necessary according to natural justice," a position he would alter in *On International Copyright* (*Political Ethics I*, 131). Instead, he suggests that copyright should be protected for a century and that an author should be able to bequeath the copyright to his heirs. It is now time, Lieber asserts, for positive law to change in order to protect literary property. He lays out the issue clearly for his readers: Books provide knowledge and educate the public; authors thus promote progress and civilization. But an author will only write and share their ideas and knowledge with society if their property is protected. Besides, Lieber claims, only a society which respects all forms of property and protects all citizens equally can truly become more civilized. He thus offers a relatable narrative framing for his readers in an effort to sway their opinion on copyright protection and to mobilize their support. He also embeds the issue within the larger context of proper political and ethical conduct and thus engages in frame bridging by building conceptual links with other issues.

In *Manual of Political Ethics*, Lieber elaborates on ideas introduced in his *Encyclopædia Americana* entries. He places property in relation with central categories such as labor, individuality, and civilization, and draws connections to literary property and copyright protection. He then considers copyright within an international context and criticizes US copyright legislation for its refusal to offer protection against reprinting for foreign works. Drawing on international comparisons, he cites the Prussian copyright regime as a better example. He does not, however, offer any real alternatives to copyright as the protection of literary property. Instead, he focuses on copyright extension. He does not yet demand absolute, exclusive, and perpetual property rights to literature. But in this work Lieber laid the groundwork for the fully-formed property theory he presented two years later in *On International Copyright.*

5.1.1 Reception

Lieber's *Manual of Political Ethics*, a work he believed to be "new and dangerous,"[12] was largely well-received in the US. George Stillman Hillard (1808–1879), a friend of Lieber's, reviewed the work in *The North American Review*[13] and ensured Lieber that "as I learn from the booksellers, [the book] meets with a good sale."[14] A few months later, Hillard informed Lieber that according to the publishers the work did not sell rapidly – as anticipated due to the subject nature – but that it performed according to expectations.[15] Lieber responded that the "news respecting the sale of my Political Ethics, namely, that it meets with the expectation of the publishers, however limited that may have been, is most grateful to me."[16] Lieber originally feared not finding a publisher and that the work would "sell no swifter than an oak grows." He was eager to distribute the work to the German states and thus sent C. J. A. Mittermaier a copy to

---

12 Lieber, Francis. Letter to C. J. A. Mittermaier. May 10, 1836. Francis Lieber papers. mssLI. Box 39, no. 41. LI2867. The Huntington. San Marino, CA.

13 "Review: Manual of Political Ethics, Designed Chiefly for the Use of Colleges and Students at Law. Part I by Francis Lieber." *The North American Review*, 47.101 (1838): 494–495.

14 Hillard, George Stillman. Letter to Francis Lieber. October 21, 1838. Francis Lieber papers. mssLI. Box 16, no. 21. LI1914. The Huntington. San Marino, CA.

15 Hillard, George Stillman. Letter to Francis Lieber. November 19, 1838. Francis Lieber papers. mssLI. Box 16, no. 22. LI1915. The Huntington. San Marino, CA.

16 Lieber, Francis. Letter to George Stillman Hillard. December 3, 1838. Francis Lieber papers. mssLI. Box 103, no. 8. No LI no. The Huntington. San Marino, CA.

review in a German periodical.[17] Lieber's acquaintances in the US received his work warmly. Influential legal scholar and jurist James Kent (1763–1847), whom Lieber greatly admired, called *Manual of Political Ethics* a "profound work, full of deep reflection and solid principle and sound apporite [sic] illustrations."[18] Lieber, clearly flattered, dedicated the second volume of the work to Kent. William Pinckney Starke[19] applauded Lieber for his innovative thinking, calling his "idea of property being the reflection of a man's individuality in the material world [...] striking."[20] Historian William H. Prescott (1796–1859) praised Lieber's sentiments as "not merely liberal, but [...] distinguished by a warm philanthropy and a reliance on the capacities and good principles of your nature."[21] He also stated that he "shall say nothing of the style of the work, which is a wonderful achievement for a foreigner," hinting at the fact that not everyone enjoyed Lieber's lengthy and complicated style of writing, which betrays his German origins. Others were not fond of Lieber's work: A Mr. F. Bower went to great lengths to publish a negative review of the book, as Hillard warned Lieber:

> You know I told you that Bower was preparing an article on the political Ethics for the N.A.R. [North American Review] and that there would be pepper and mustard in it, but the truth was not half told you. Dr. Palfrey submitted it to me in M.S. and such a piece of savage slaughtering I never read. It was written with considerable ability but was mostly occupied with [?] upon subjects suggested by your work, and not more than two or three pages were devoted to a proper review and those were unqualified damnation. He said it was crude, full of digressions and inquisitions [?] of no value, pedantic, pretending to originality and having none, starting many interesting questions, but settling none &c. I need not say to you that I considered it a very unfair review.[22]

17 Lieber, Francis. Letter to C. J. A. Mittermaier. August 28, 1838. Francis Lieber papers. mssLI. Box 39, no. 42. No LI no. The Huntington. San Marino, CA.

18 Kent, James. Letter to Francis Lieber. September 8, 1838. Francis Lieber papers. mssLI. Box 103, no. 10. No LI no. The Huntington. San Marino, CA.

19 Birthdate of William Pinckney Starke is unknown. He lived in South Carolina, was a correspondent of vice president John C. Calhoun (1872–1850), and died in 1886.

20 Starke, William Pinckney Starke. Letter to Francis Lieber. July 18, 1842. Francis Lieber papers. mssLI. Box 63, no. 33. LI3238. The Huntington. San Marino, CA.

21 Prescott, William H. Letter to Francis Lieber. September 22, 1838. Francis Lieber papers. mssLI. Box 104, no. 5. No LI no. The Huntington. San Marino, CA.

22 Hillard, George Stillman. Letter to Francis Lieber. January 12, 1839. Francis Lieber papers. mssLI. Box 16, no. 23. LI1916. The Huntington. San Marino, CA.

The *North American Review* rejected the critique, but it was later published in the *Christian Examiner*.[23] Lieber's friend, professor of law Simon Greenleaf (1783–1853) called the review "bitter & fault-finding"[24] and Hillard replied to it in "a short communication in the Daily Advertiser [...] but which had its claws somewhat pared before it went in."[25] Greenleaf continued to support Lieber, informing him of other reviews published in the North and any informal comments on the work. His friends, Greenleaf states, might have wished for a "higher finish & elaborateness" but praised the work's "freedom & boldness, and vigor of conception."[26] Three years after Lieber's death, his *Manual of Political Ethics* was edited and republished by Theodore Dwight Woolsey (1801–1889), president of Yale College, who stated that for the new edition "[w]e have looked carefully for passages which the recent advances in historical criticism and sociological research, or the political experience of this country or of Western Europe, might have deprived of their value, and we confess we have not found one."[27] This praise of the work's relevance is only dampened by Woolsey's assertion that "[t]he fault of this book, as of Dr. Lieber's other works, is discursiveness [...] The temptation, therefore, to ramble in the byways of a various learning he was very apt to find irresistible." Woolsey argues that while the "ramblings" in Lieber's works make them more attractive to the class of people they were intended for, they diminish its value as a scientific work. With the statement that "if Dr. Lieber had had more capacity for scientific arrangement he would probably have had less success as a preacher," Woolsey finishes his review – an assertion he likely purposefully kept to himself until Lieber's death.

During Lieber's work on the *Manual of Political Ethics*, he closely considered the subject of interpretation and construction and decided to lay his views down in an article rather than in an extensive chapter. This article was pub-

---

23 Greenleaf, Simon. Letter to Francis Lieber. April 15, 1839. Francis Lieber papers. mssLI. Box 13, no. 62. LI1574. The Huntington. San Marino, CA. The review is still available, see Bower, F. "Review: Manual of Political Ethics. By Francis Lieber." *The Christian Examiner and General Review*, vol. XXVI, Third Series, VIII (1839): 32–54.

24 Greenleaf, Simon. Letter to Francis Lieber. December 12, 1838. Francis Lieber papers. mssLI. Box 13, no. 61. LI1573. The Huntington. San Marino, CA.

25 Hillard, George Stillman. Letter to Francis Lieber. 22 March 1839. Francis Lieber papers. mssLI. Box 16, no. 26. LI1919. The Huntington. San Marino, CA.

26 Greenleaf, Simon. Letter to Francis Lieber. June 12, 1842. Francis Lieber papers. mssLI. Box 13, no. 63. LI1575. The Huntington. San Marino, CA.

27 Woolsey, Theodore. Review of the new edition of Political Ethics by Theodore Woolsey. 1875. Francis Lieber papers. mssLI. Box 86, no. 8. No LI no. The Huntington. San Marino, CA.

lished in the *American Jurist* and was well received.[28] Lieber claims several jurists separately asked him to publish the article as a book and after rewriting and extending the piece, Lieber published it as a book titled *Legal and Political Hermeneutics, Or of Principles of Interpretation and Construction in Law and Politics, with Remarks on Precedents and Authorities* in 1839.[29] Again, Lieber dedicated the work to James Kent, who had apparently approved of the article in the *Jurist* – a fact Lieber eagerly shared in the preface, but only after consulting with George Stillman Hillard on whether such a dedication would be appropriate (*Hermeneutics*, V).[30]

5.2 *Legal and Political Hermeneutics*, 1839

Francis Lieber composed and published *Legal and Political Hermeneutics* with the support of his friends in the North. In the work Lieber elaborates on how to properly interpret the meaning of written documents, following the principles of good faith and common sense. While the work did not necessarily include new insights into the subject of hermeneutics, it collected the information in one place and thus constituted a handy guide for lawyers and jurists.[31] Initially, Lieber's acquaintance and lawyer Simon Greenleaf (1783–1853) advised him to publish his work on hermeneutics as an "avant courier" to the *Manual of Political Ethics* to draw in jurists and lawyers.[32] Lieber declined and asked Greenleaf to propose the full-length book manuscript to publishers Little and Brown, who rejected it.[33] A few months later, Greenleaf followed up his request with another letter, asking Little and Brown to reconsider publishing

28 The article was published in two parts, in October 1837, and in January 1838, see Francis Lieber, "Art. III On Political Hermeneutics, or on Political Interpretation and Construction, and Also on Precedents," *The American Jurist and Law Magazine* 18.35 (1837): 37–101, and Francis Lieber, "Art. I On Political Hermeneutics–Precedents," *The American Jurist and Law Magazine* 18.38 (1838): 282–294.

29 Lieber, Francis. Legal and Political Hermeneutics, Or of Principles of Interpretation and Construction in Law and Politics, with Remarks on Precedents and Authorities. Charles C. Little and James Brown, 1839.

30 Hillard, George Stillman. Letter to Francis Lieber. January 13, 1839. Francis Lieber papers. mssLI. Box16, no. 23. LI1916. The Huntington. San Marino, California.

31 Peter Becker, "Prologue: Lieber's Place in History" in *Francis Lieber and the Culture of the Mind*, ed. Charles R. Mack and Henry H. Lesesne (Columbia: University of South Carolina Press, 2005), 4.

32 Greenleaf, Simon. Letter to Francis Lieber. December 12, 1838. Francis Lieber papers. mssLI. Box 13, no. 61. LI1573. The Huntington. San Marino, CA.

33 Apparently Little and Brown were financially taxed as they prepared the publication of an extensive collection of works by Joseph Story. Greenleaf, Simon. Letter to Francis

Lieber's work which would be "eminently useful to our profession – not merely to students, but to men of long experience at the bar [...] a valuable contribution to the law [which will] incorporate itself into the more enduring fabric of solid science."[34] Apparently Greenleaf's praise did not go unheard as Little and Brown published the first edition of *Legal and Political Hermeneutics* in 1839. Lieber called upon George Stillman Hillard to proof-read the manuscript and improve the language, writing

> I beg you, I implore you, I charge you by your allegiance. I depend upon it, and although I know to the fullest extent that this is asking very much [...] This time I can not help it. Let me then sleep quietly in the confidence that you will yield change whatever English you choose. I give you unlimited power.[35]

Hillard agreed, though he advised Lieber that "[m]any of the chapters I think might be favorably condensed into a smaller compass."[36] He made corrections to the content and in Boston he oversaw the printing and publication process of the "neat, well-dressed book [whose] substance will do you much honor."[37] Simon Greenleaf also modified the manuscript with regard to a specific legal case discussed in the work.[38] The result is a – by Lieber's standards – short work of 240 pages, focused on hermeneutics, the method of systematic interpretation and construction of language in legal and political contexts. Lieber argues that interpretation and construction are indispensable to the methodical study and understanding of a text. Only through mathematical – meaning systematic – analysis of the text can its true meaning be discovered but in "the hands of the disingenuous" and "without good faith [interpretation and construction] become desperate weapons" (*Hermeneutics*, VII). With this work, Lieber aimed to systematize the act of properly interpreting texts and speech acts within the legal and political context. He believed that in common law countries, such as the US and Great Britain, where "the law is allowed to make

---

Lieber. April 11, 1838. Francis Lieber papers. mssLI. Box 13, no. 59. LI1570. The Huntington. San Marino, CA.

34 Greenleaf, Simon. Letter to Messrs. Little & Brown. July 3 1838. Francis Lieber papers. mssLI. Box 14, no. 5. LI1588. The Huntington. San Marino, CA.

35 Lieber, Francis. Letter to George Stillman Hillard. January 1839. Francis Lieber papers. mssLI. Box 103, no. 8. No LI no. The Huntington. San Marino, CA.

36 Hillard, George Stillman. Letter to Francis Lieber. September 17, 1839. Francis Lieber papers. mssLI. Box 16, no. 29. LI19122. The Huntington. San Marino, CA.

37 Hillard, George Stillman. Letter to Francis Lieber. March 22, 1839. Francis Lieber papers. mssLI. Box 16, no. 26. LI1919. The Huntington. San Marino, CA.

38 Greenleaf, Simon. Letter to Francis Lieber. April 15, 1839. Francis Lieber papers. mssLI. Box 13, no. 62. LI1547. The Huntington. San Marino, CA.

its own way," clear and consistent rules for the interpretation and construction of such laws must exist (*Hermeneutics*, VIII). These principles and rules must be implemented alongside the law and mastered by all in the legal field.

5.2.1 Text Analysis

To understand the importance Lieber placed on hermeneutics, it is essential to know that Lieber assumed that any text only has one true meaning, the meaning the author intended. But different readers bring with them different preconceptions and might therefore come to different conclusions while reading the same text. This, to Lieber, is an issue, especially with regard to legal texts, which should lead all to the same conclusions. Interpretation and construction are the tools necessary to identify the one meaning the author meant to convey through the text. Lieber identifies a "primeval principle" in all humans to express outward what is happening inward, a "pressing urgency of utterance" (*Hermeneutics*, 15). While humans have the frequent urge to communicate, there can be no "direct communication between the minds of men," as Lieber points out. Humans must resort to outward manifestation to communicate what happens inwardly (*Hermeneutics*, 13).

To facilitate communication, humans use signs. Lieber defines signs as all "expressions perceptible by the senses" (*Hermeneutics*, 13). Understanding signs, such as language, requires interpretation; only through interpretation can we arrive at the "true meaning" of a sign – that meaning "which those who used them were desirous of expressing" (*Hermeneutics*, 17). Lieber assumes that there is no way to be absolutely clear and precise in our expression of meaning because language is too limited to convey our exact signification (*Hermeneutics*, 30–31). Additionally, language is flexible and changes with time and context. To discern the exact original meaning of someone's words or signs, we must therefore always resort to interpretation (*Hermeneutics*, 31). It is important to narrow down the exact meaning of signs through interpretation, in order to understand the true meaning of a text (*Hermeneutics*, 22). Only through methodical interpretation and construction can humans understand each other and "attach the same signification or sense to the words which the speaker or writer intended to convey" (*Hermeneutics*, 23). Understanding that Lieber believes there to be only one true meaning of a text clarifies why the integrity of an original text is so important to Lieber – if a text is changed in any way, for example by a typesetter, printer or publisher, the true meaning of the text may no longer be discernable through interpretation. Methodical interpretation and construction are only possible if the signs that constitute the text remain unchanged. While Lieber does not spell it out, it follows that a comprehensive and perpetual authors' copyright for all texts would be an effective measure to preserve the original text. If the author controls the printing and distribution of the text, the actual meaning of the text can be protected against faulty reprints. Through interpretation and construction, which follow strict rules and are conducted in good faith and with common sense, the reader is able to understand the text as the author intended (*Hermeneutics*, 64).

Lieber defines interpretation as "the art of finding out the true sense of any form of words: that is, the sense which their author intended to convey, and of enabling others to derive from the same idea which the author intended to convey" (*Hermeneutics*, 23). Since humans communicate continually, we must resort to interpretation all the time (*Hermeneutics*, 23). While interpretation is essential in all acts of communication, clear principles of interpretation are of great importance with regard to legal and political texts, which offer written rules of action (*Hermeneutics*, 40). While lawmakers usually aim to draft clear and concise laws, no law or code exists which does not require interpretation. Lieber even claims that an exact code which requires no interpretation would not be a good thing. He argues that

> [i]t is one of the most efficient agents in the civil progress of a nation, that, certain principles being established, they should be left to unfold themselves gradually, and to be expanded, modified, and limited, by the civil action of the nation itself, by the practical political intercourse of society (*Hermeneutics*, 40).

Laws could only be definite and permanent in an unchanging society, a society which ceased to grow and evolve. Such a society is not desirable, Lieber argues (*Hermeneutics*, 49). Instead, the integrity of the law must be ensured through a separation of powers. As long as those who administer laws do not also write them, interpretation will always be necessary and safeguard the supremacy of the law (*Hermeneutics*, 53). Furthermore, it is the duty of every citizen to interpret existing law and to "form his opinion upon all prominent features of his government, fundamental laws, public men, and important measures" (*Hermeneutics*, 76).

Frequently, the entire meaning of the text cannot be deduced strictly from the written words available. This may be the case if the text is in itself contradictory or if it is at variance with another text or law by the same author or responsible authority. This may also be the case if one is bound to act under unforeseen circumstances or during events not anticipated by the author of a text or the drafter of a constitution (*Hermeneutics*, 56). In those situations, construction becomes necessary. Lieber defines construction as "the drawing of conclusions respecting subjects, that lie beyond the direct expression of the text, from elements known from and given in the text – conclusions which are in the spirit, though not within the letter of the text" (*Hermeneutics*, 56). Construction must be guided by "the spirit, principles, and rules" of the text to ensure that the true meaning of the text can be constructed in good faith and through common sense, analogy and parallel reasoning (*Hermeneutics*, 59). Construction is a dangerous procedure: As it goes beyond the available signs, we risk projecting too much of our own understanding and biases into the text and thus change its true meaning. Accordingly, rules are necessary to guide the process and Lieber defines these guiding principles as hermeneutics, "that branch of science which establishes the principles and rules of interpretation and construction" (*Hermeneutics*, 64).[39] He presents different types of interpretation (*Hermeneutics*, 120) and construction (*Hermeneutics*, 143–144) and explains the two processes, including what to avoid. These explanations include hermeneutic rules for the interpretation and construction of different text forms, such as speeches, letters, diary entries, contracts, deeds, and wills (*Hermeneutics*, 145–161), laws (*Hermeneutics*, 163–172), constitutions (*Hermeneutics*, 172–189), and treaties (*Hermeneutics*, 190–191). Lieber wraps up his guide on the principles of interpretation and construction by referring to the importance of precedents (*Hermeneutics*, 192–221), the role of authorities (*Hermeneutics*, 223–227), and the rules of fair criticism (*Hermeneutics*, 227–239). To substantiate his claims, Lieber uses international comparisons and refers to the authority of other countries' legal systems. As Lawrence Lessig points out, these references to foreign legal systems may strike legal scholars today as odd or fruitless. Lessig rejects this judgement and argues that Lieber "wrote in a world where cross-cultural constitutional experience was a relevant and salient authority" and that cross-national comparisons were – and still are today – a valuable tool in legal studies.[40] In this work, Lieber once again creates a synthesis of different international frameworks to substantiate his own ideas on the true meaning of texts and how to interpret them.

39 Hermeneutics designates the theory and methodology guiding the interpretation of texts, including biblical and philosophical texts. Theologians in the US and in England use the term hermeneutics to designate the principles of methodological interpretation of the bible, while in Germany it applies to philology and divinity. Lieber believes that the word should be adopted by all sciences that use interpretation and construction of signs (*Hermeneutics*, 64).

40 Lessig, "Limits," 2252–2253.

Lieber's work on hermeneutics and the rules of interpretation and construction is related to his understanding of literature as a form of property. As Peter Schneck argues in his talk "The Hermeneutics of Property: Francis Lieber on Copyright, Labor and Textual Interpretation," Lieber's understanding of authorial intention and the true meaning of a text explicated in *Legal and Political Hermeneutics* elucidates his demands for literary property protection in his other works.[41] As explained above, Lieber understands literary production as the intentional composition of speech and a political act by an author as a citizen in a free society. Writing as a creative and communicative act is an articulation of the author as a civil person. Literary production as the participation of the individual in social and political exchange leads to the creation of shared meaning. As Schneck points out, Lieber positions writing and literary production as "the purest manifestation both of individuality as such and of enjoyment of individual rights protected by the state."[42] Lieber understands the creation of literary property as the realization of the author's individuality. Consequently, an author should enjoy the full protection of his individual rights by the government, as Lieber claims. Literary property must be protected against theft, alteration, plagiarism and reprinting, but also against government censorship and control. Such comprehensive protection of authorial intention, literary property, and the enjoyment of individual rights is only possible through comprehensive copyright protection. As Schneck highlights, Lieber's demands for literary property protection are not merely founded in the financial benefits a copyright offers the author – they emerge from his understanding of the author as an individual and the free citizen as a subject of rights, which the state must protect.[43] Lieber's view of literary property "aligns the cultural and universal with the social and individual and, eventually, the political realization of the individual as a subject of rights," as Schneck points out.[44]

Since the subject of literary property protection relates to the rights of citizens and the relationship between the state and its subjects, as well as between different states, Lieber continued to promote the issue and increasingly emphasized its transnational dimension. He focused more on issue conveyance and worked to mobilize more public support and to put the issue on the agenda of policy makers. His most assertive demand for comprehensive

41 Peter Schneck, "The Hermeneutics of Property: Francis Lieber on Copyright, Labor and Textual Interpretation." *YouTube*, uploaded by rechtalskultur, March 12, 2019, https://www.youtube.com/watch?v=VSeTqYeWF24.

42 Schneck, "Hermeneutics," 53:20.

43 Schneck, "Hermeneutics," 53:20.

44 Schneck, "Hermeneutics," 53:38–53:45.

protection of literary property followed a year after the publication of *Legal and Political Hermeneutics*: In 1840 Lieber published *On International Copyright, In a Letter to the Hon. William C. Preston, Senator of the United States*, his impassioned call for copyright protection for all authors, domestic and foreign.

CHAPTER 6

The 1840s: Literature, Property, and International Copyright

Throughout the 1840s, Lieber continued to be unhappy in Columbia, South Carolina, a place he never considered his home. He fled to the North each summer, networking and seeking employment. In South Carolina he felt lonely, isolated, and trapped amongst people he had nothing in common with:

> It is not only unpleasant, it is a positive evil, to live in a place or community you feel no interest in, and every recollection of which would be wiped off from your memory the moment you leave it; in short, a place with which you are physically connected only. Life does not touch us; the world moves on, and we are left behind. I cannot remain here forever! (*Life and Letters*, 117).

He avidly searched for a professorship in the North and wrote letters to his friends, employing their help. Joseph Story offered to recommend Lieber for "a Professorship established in connection with the Law School at Cambridge," but nothing came of it.[1] To Charles Sumner Lieber wrote "I heartly wish myself and my family away from this place and region, which has now been my dwelling place for ten long years, but has never become and never will become the home of my heart." He pleaded with Sumner to mention his name to Edward Everett, president of Harvard University.[2] Lieber's efforts remained futile and he even considered moving back to "Germany," where he felt at home. Nevertheless, he declined an offer for a position as prison inspector from the Prussian ministry of justice in 1844.[3] He also declined an offer for a professorship from the Prussian king Friedrich Wilhelm IV. in 1845.[4] Schnurmann argues that Lieber likely waited for a better second offer, but none came. Only a year later, in a letter to C. J. A. Mittermaier, Lieber lamented: "Do you

1 Story, Joseph. Letter to Francis Lieber. March 11, 1844. Francis Lieber papers. mssLI. Box 104, no. 6. No LI number. The Huntington. San Marino, CA.

2 Lieber, Francis. Letter to Charles Sumner. June 30, 1846. Francis Lieber papers. mssLI. Box 104, no. 7. No LI number. he Huntington. San Marino, CA.

3 Schnurmann, *Brücken*, 389.

4 von Thiele, Ludwig Gustav, Minister of Justice in Prussia. Letter to Francis Lieber, conveying an offer from King Friedrich Wilhelm IV for a professorship in Prussia. May 22, 1845. Francis Lieber papers. mssLI. Box 85, no. 17. LI4340. The Huntington. San Marino, CA.

 | HTTPS://DOI.ORG/10.1515/9783112239407-006

know that I have thought frequently of retiring to Heidelberg. If only the Baden government would offer me but a small salary with a permanent professorship, I think I should come at once."[5] It seems that given the right opportunity, Lieber would have left the US and moved back to live in a German state. Eventually he decided to stay in the US but suffered from frequent homesickness. In 1854 he wrote to Mittermaier:

> Do you know, my dear friend, that tokens of esteem have reached me from many parts, only not from my own country. No German Academy has elected me a member, no Doctors degree has been sent to me from any German University. I am like a forgotten son of the fatherland for which I nevertheless could bleed at any moment, as I have bled for it in my earliest youth.[6]

At the same time, Lieber felt that his fellow Americans denied him job opportunities based on his German heritage. In 1850, Lieber privately complained in a letter to Sumner that Jared Sparks, president of Harvard College, had called him a foreigner and admitted that "to be spoken of a foreigner by so old a friend as Sparks – it made me feel sorry."[7]

Lieber focused more on his work, in part to combat his feelings of loneliness and isolation, and his interest in copyright regulation as a measure for property protection did not cease after the publication of the *Encyclopædia Americana* entries. *On International Copyright* was preceded by years of reflection on property, as showcased by Lieber's diary entries, correspondence, and sections of his new publications. The topic of copyright protection also continued to be discussed in Congress and before the US Supreme Court. In 1831, the federal copyright act was amended to include musical compositions. In 1834, the Supreme Court ruled in the landmark case *Wheaton v Peters*, affirming an author's perpetual right in their unpublished manuscript but also maintaining the statutory limitation of an author's copyright after publication. In 1837, 56 British writers entrusted senator Henry Clay (1777–1852, Whig party) with a

5 Lieber stated that he could teach "Politics, Penology, Parliamentary Right and Rules, the Constitution of England – of the United States and their History, Political Economy, the Administration of Justice." Lieber, Francis. Letter to C. J. A. Mittermaier. April 6, 1846. Francis Lieber papers. mssLI. Box 39, no. 46. LI2873. The Huntington. San Marino, CA. This letter is a translation of the original by Mathilde Lieber.

6 Lieber, Francis. Letter to C. J. A. Mittermaier. March 10, 1854. Francis Lieber papers. mssLI. Box 39, no. 50. LI2876. The Huntington. San Marino, CA. This letter is a translation of the original by Mathilde Lieber.

7 Lieber, Francis. Letter to Charles Sumner. December 27, 1850. Francis Lieber papers. mssLI. Box 104, no. 7. No LI number. The Huntington. San Marino, CA.

petition asking Congress to "grant to them the Exclusive Benefit of their Writings within the United States."[8] The authors claimed that "the want of a law by which the exclusive right to their respective writings may be secured to them in the United States of America" had inflicted "deep and extensive injuries [...] on their reputation and property, and on the interests of literature and science, which ought to constitute a bond of union and friendship between the United States and Great Britain." Along with the financial damage, British authors also complained about the possible mutilation and alteration of their works by which they "may be made responsible for works which they no longer recognise as their own."[9] US authors also suffered from current copyright regulation, they claimed, since

> American publishers can provide themselves with works for publication, by unjust appropriation, instead of equitable purchase, [and] they are under no inducement to afford to American authors a fair remuneration for their labors, under which grievance American authors have no redress but in sending over their works to England to be published; an expedient which has become an established practice with some, of whom their country has most reason to be proud.[10]

If the benefits of copyright law were extended to them, the petitioners claimed, then US authors and the public would profit as well. Clay presented this petition to Congress on February 2, 1837, arguing that

> [o]f all classes of our fellow-beings, there is none that has a better right than that of authors and inventors, to the kindness, the sympathy, and the protection of the Government. And surely nothing can be more reasonable than that they should be allowed to enjoy, without interruption, for a limited time, the property created by their own genius.[11]

---

8 Petition of British Authors, Washington D.C. (1837), *Primary Sources on Copyright (1450–1900)*, eds L. Bently and M. Kretschmer, www.copyrighthistory.org. Accessed 8 December 2022.

9 Petition of British Authors.

10 Debates in Congress, Washington D.C. (1837), Primary Sources on Copyright (1450–1900), ed L. Bently and M. Kretschmer, www.copyrighthistory.org. Accessed 6 December 2022.

11 Debates in Congress.

During the following debate in Congress, William C. Preston (1794–1860) also commented on the issue, explaining the conflict of interests at hand. He outlined that

> the subject was one of some difficulty; there was a large and meritorious class of authors in this country, who had a direct interest in securing to the authors of Great Britain the copy-right to their works, because copies of the works were sold without the expense of a copyright, and thus came in free and injurious competition with the works of American authors. But, then, publishers had an opposite interest, to seize upon foreign works without price and republish them.[12]

Consequently, Preston argued, "the subject [...] resolved itself into a complicated question of free trade and protection of mechanical arts" and proved too complicated to decide momentarily.[13] Andrew Buchanan (1789–1848) also weighed in, claiming that the consideration of this question would be "a vexed and difficult [one]" since what was at stake went far beyond the interests of the publishers – "the interest of the reading people of the United States" was in question.[14] Cheap editions were now readily available to the public but should copyright be granted to foreign authors then editions would become more expensive. Buchanan demanded to disregard the interests of publishers (and authors) and focus on the effects on public education.[15] Consequently, a special committee was assigned, consisting of Henry Clay, William C. Preston, and others.[16]

The committee's task was to summarize the state of current copyright law with regard to foreign authors and to outline whether changes to copyright regulation would be necessary. The committee drafted a report as well as a bill and presented both to Congress, recommending the introduction of international copyright for British authors. The bill did not pass; no action was taken to implement international copyright protection. Nevertheless, the report is highly interesting due to its radical notions, which differed significantly from

12 Debates in Congress.
13 Debates in Congress.
14 Debates in Congress.
15 Debates in Congress
16 The committee members were Henry Clay, William C. Preston, Andrew Buchanan (1780–1848), Daniel Webster (1782–1852), and William L. D. Ewing (1795–1846). Petition of British Authors, Washington D.C. (1837), Primary Sources on Copyright (1450–1900), ed. L. Bently and and M. Kretschmer, www.copyrighthistory.org. Accessed 6 December 2022.

the federal understanding of copyright and showcase that individual policy makers had picked up the issue of international copyright and campaigned for change – due in part to the lobbying efforts of issue entrepreneurs like Lieber.

In its report, the committee finds that the most current copyright legislation is the *Copyright Act of 1831*, which determines that the benefits of copyright protection are limited to citizens or residents of the United States. Consequently, no foreigner residing abroad can secure a copyright in the United States for any work of which they are the author, however important or valuable it may be.[17] The petition of certain British authors asked to remove this restriction with regard to British authors and the committee supports this demand. The report states

> that authors and inventors have, according to the practice among civilized nations, a property in the respective productions of their genius, is incontestable; and that this property should be protected as effectually as any other property is, by law, follows as a legitimate consequence.[18]

Notably, the committee members argue on the basis of property rights, even though the existing copyright act is careful to avoid framing copyright as a form of property. They justify this deviation from existing law by positioning authors as "among the greatest benefactors of mankind," who are often "dependent, exclusively, upon their own mental labors for the means of subsistence." The report constructs a class of authors that differs from other classes, a class "incapable of applying that provident care to worldly affairs which other classes of society are in the habit of bestowing." Thus, they deserve special protection of the law. The committee members believe it well established that "literary property is entitled to legal protection" and consequently, "this protection ought to be afforded wherever the property is situated." The report frames literature as a form of property which ought to be protected the same way other property is protected, even across national borders. To combat the unequal treatment of different classes of property the committee suggests "some safe and cautious amendment of the law," modelled on a recent reform of the patent law that extended protection to foreigners. This amend-

---

17 Senate Report, Washington D.C. (1837), Primary Sources on Copyright (1450–1900), ed. L. Bently and and M. Kretschmer, www.copyrighthistory.org. Accessed 8 December 2022.

18 Senate Report.

ment would provide reciprocal justice to Great Britain and France, jurisdictions that already offer copyright protection for US-American authors.[19]

The committee members were acutely aware of the conflict of interest between publishers and authors and state that they "have been anxious to devise some measure which, without too great a disturbance of interests, or affecting too seriously arrangements which have grown out of the present state of things, may, without hazard, be subjected to the test of practical experience." Therefore, they only suggest extending copyright protection to British and French subjects and only to works to be published in the future, not to works already published in the US. The legal measures for this protection are already in place, they argue, since the Constitution provides Congress with all the power necessary to protect the work of foreign authors and by no means limits that power to natives or residents of the US.[20] On the contrary, the committee members state they "perceive no objection to considering the republic of letters as one great community, and adopting a system of protection for literary property which should be common to all parts of it." They adopt a transnational perspective and speak of a global community with shared values, such as "the progress of science and useful arts" which "belong to no particular country, but to mankind generally." The promotion of "intellectual productions which have not yet been brought into existence, but lie buried in the mind of genius" justify the higher expenses that come with copyright protection for foreign works.[21] During the second session of the 24th Congress on February 16, 1837, Clay submitted bill no. 223 to Congress, which aimed to extend copyright protection to authors in Great Britain, Ireland, and France.[22] This constituted the first attempt to introduce an international copyright bill to Congress, but even though Clay reintroduced the bill on four separate occasions, Congress took no action.[23]

---

19 Senate Report.

20 The Constitution vests the power in Congress to "To promote the Progress of Science and useful Arts, by securing for limited Times to Authors and Inventors the exclusive Right to their respective Writings and Discoveries." It does not limit these provisions to residents or citizens of the US, see for example: "Constitution of the United States." *United States Senate*, Secretary of the Senate, 21 Jan. 2020, www.senate.gov/civics/constitution_item/constitution.htm. Accessed 8 Feb. 2023.

21 Senate Report.

22 Solberg, "Copyright in Congress," 33–34; Rudd, "Notable Dates," 138.

23 Solberg, "Copyright in Congress," 33–34; Rudd, "Notable Dates," 138–139. Clay reintroduced bill 223 on December 13, 1837, on December 12, 1838, on January 6, 1840, and on January 6, 1842. No action was taken by Congress (Solberg, "Copyright in Congress" 33–34). For detailed examinations of the proceedings of Congress regarding international copyright legislation, see the works of Thorvald Solberg, first register of copyright

The German Confederation passed federal policies concerning copyright on November 9, 1837 (see chapter 3.2.2). These policies prohibited all reprinting of literary products without an author's consent and framed literature as the property of the author ("Urheber"). The right of the author to his works would be protected federally, as long as his name is stated on the work – but only for ten years (*Preußisches Gesetz*, 42).[24] While the German Confederation did prohibit reprinting on a federal level in 1837, the act did not go far enough for Prussia, whose delegates made a first motion in 1829 to extend the provisions against reprinting to citizens of all German states, rather than limiting it to one's own citizens (*Preußisches Gesetz*, 41–45). Prussia – Lieber's former home – passed its own comprehensive copyright act in 1837 (see chapter 3.2.2). The *Prussian Copyright Act* strengthened an author's lifelong claim to their work, making authors' rights the central focus of copyright. An author automatically holds the rights to a work, prior to and following a publication, even if they transfer the rights for the publication of one edition to a publisher. The author's right is transmissible and – like other property – automatically passes on to the author's heir(s) following their death. Unlike with real property, though, an author's heirs only retain this right for the thirty years which follow the death of the author.

Julius Eduard Hitzig, an acquaintance of Lieber's, published a commented version of the *Prussian Copyright Act* in 1838. Lieber evidently read the *Prussian Copyright Act*; on July 2, 1839, Lieber wrote a letter to his wife, stating: "Almost all friends absent. I am translating the Prussian 'Copyright Law,' and read a good deal" (*Life and Letters*, 137). Clearly, he was still interested in the topic of copyright and sought inspiration from other works – nationally and internationally. After Lieber finished his translation of the *Prussian Copyright Act*, it was published in *The Law Reporter* in 1839.[25] The journal editors preface the translation by stating that they "believe the law will be read with great interest, as it relates to a subject to which public attention has of late been

---

in the US Copyright Office (in office from 1897 until 1930). His works on international copyright include, but are not limited to: Thorvald Solberg, *International Copyright in the Congress of the United States, 1837–1886* (Boston: Press of Rockwell and Churchill, 1886); Thorvald Solberg, *Copyright in Congress 1789–1904* (Washington: Government Printing, 1905); Thorvald Solberg, *Copyright Enactments of the United States 1783–1906* (Washington: Government Printing, 1906); Thorvald Solberg. *The United States and International Copyright* (New Haven: Yale UP, 1929).

24 In certain cases, if the publication of a work requires great expenses on the side of authors or publishers, the term of protection may be extended to 20 (Preußisches Gesetz 43).

25 Francis Lieber, "Prussian Law of Copyright of 1837." *The Law Reporter* 2.5 (1839): 129–133. Hereafter abbreviated as "Prussian Law."

earnestly turned, and appears to have been drawn up with great circumspection and patience, and with ample knowledge of existing copy-right laws" ("Prussian Law," 129). Lieber's translation of the *Prussian Copyright Act* proves his interest in the Prussian negotiation of copyright, as well as his desire to disseminate the Prussian perspective on copyright and authors' rights within the US. Clearly, Lieber wanted to make the Prussian legislation and framing of copyright accessible to a legal audience in the States. He pursued his goal to become a cultural negotiator by translating and publishing German law in the US and offered a different framing of the issue of literary property to a legal audience.

The editors of *The Law Reporter* introduce the translation as "a literal translation" but nevertheless, Lieber's subtle choice of words betrays his standpoint. Throughout the article Lieber translates the German word "Nachdruck" ("reprinting") with "piratical reprinting," adding a value judgement to the neutral term by likening it to acts of "piracy" ("Prussian Law," 129). In paragraph XIV Lieber even uses the term "literary piracy" to translate "[d]as Vergehen des Nachdrucks," more accurately translated as "the misdemeanor of reprinting" ("Prussian Law," 131).[26] He translates "Nachdruck" ("reprint," meaning the reprint without the author's consent of a work already published) as "pirated reprint" and thus underlines the violent connotations of "literary piracy," evoking the image of a robbery during which the reprinter wrenches the original edition from the author, making it their own through an act of violence.[27] This loaded language emphasizes Lieber's personal moral condemnation of the act of reprinting, arguably changing the tone of the German original and making it more poignant. It also constitutes the conveyance of an issue through an approachable narrative by Lieber as an issue entrepreneur. Through his use of emotionally charged language, Lieber frames the issue in a palpable narrative for his audience and appeals to their sentiments to elicit support for the issue of copyright protection.

The *Prussian Copyright Act* inspired Lieber, and he continued to mull over his own understanding of and demands for copyright protection. A year after his translation of the *Prussian Copyright Act* was published in *The Law*

26 Interestingly, Lieber writes of "piratical reprints" when referring to works of literature, but when referring to works of art he speaks of "unlawful copies" (Lieber, "Prussian Law," 131). Arguably, an act of piracy carries violent connotations, while the production of an "unlawful copy" sounds much less sinister.

27 In paragraph XVII. Lieber also translates "unerlaubter Abdruck" (meaning the printing of an unpublished work, such as a manuscript) as "illegal reprint" and juxtaposes it with pirated editions (Lieber, "Prussian Law," 131). This translation is misleading: An illegal print of an unpublished work cannot be a *re*print because no original print exists.

Reporter, Lieber began working on a treatise on international copyright protection. Early on, he decided to publish his thoughts in the form of a letter, addressed to William C. Preston, Whig senator of South Carolina. On March 19, 1840, Lieber noted in his diary:

> Finished my letter to Preston on International Copyright. It took me two days. I wished to be quite unencumbered, and read nothing on the subject, and had that mental comfort and *aisé d'esprit* which I always have when I intellectually produce and strike upon new paths [...] (*Life and Letters*, 143).

This short note highlights Lieber's aspiration to position himself as an original thinker, not inspired by others. As Claudia Schnurmann points out, Lieber carefully presented his works as entirely his own. While he inserts extensive footnotes into most of his other works, in his final letter to Preston Lieber purposefully keeps mentions of his sources brief in order to present his work as "original."[28] The fact that he published a translation of the *Prussian Copyright Act* proves that he did read other works on copyright very recently, as do the short references to other works on copyright within his letter to Preston and his earlier entries on copyright in the *Encyclopædia Americana*. Likely, his work on international copyright was also inspired by Henry Clay's copyright bill of 1837 and his continued efforts to reintroduce it, most recently on January 6, 1840. Lieber's efforts to bring about legal change in the copyright system had reached policy makers, since senator Clay sent Lieber several letters in 1839 suggesting that Lieber reach out to Clay to offer input on the new drafts of the copyright bill. Clay explained his strategy in Congress and commented on the probability of the bill's passage, claiming that

> I am afraid that the prospect [...] is bad of the passage of an International copy right [sic] law. The two last Committees to which it was referred were averse to it; and the activity of some of the large publishers has been such as to make strong impressions against it on the minds of many Senators.[29]

Clay continued to inform Lieber on the proceedings in the Senate. He also encouraged Lieber to become active and publicly support the bill, stating

---

28 "Pikanterweise verzichtete Lieber in seinem Plädoyer für die Eigentumsrechte von Autoren und bei der Diskussion von gedanklichem Eigentum darauf, seine Inspiration zu nennen und Hitzigs Schrift als Beleg seiner gedanklichen Übernahmen anzuführen" (Schnurmann, *Brücken*, 359).

29 Clay, Henry. Letter to Francis Lieber. December 28, 1839. Francis Lieber papers. mssLI. Box 9, no. 58. LI113. The Huntington. San Marino, CA.

> There are difficulties to be overcome; and they can only be subdued by enlightening public opinion, or causing it to flow in a correct channel. To this end, petitions numerously signed, the agency of the press and all other practicable demonstrations would be highly useful. And if a Committee of authors, well informed, sensible and judicious men could be got to attend Congress to answer and remove objections, before Committees of that body, I think it would be attended with the best effect.[30]

As Frank Freidel states, Lieber followed Clay's advice and reached out to historian William Hickling Prescott (1796–1859) to encourage him to contact other acquaintances, such as writer Washington Irving (1783–1859) and politician and lawyer Daniel Webster (1872–1852). None of them, though sympathetic to the cause, were willing to take the lead.[31] Consequently, as an issue entrepreneur Lieber decided to write an extensive letter to William C. Preston, whom he knew to be sympathetic to the cause. Lieber first sent the letter to Preston privately to use in Senate debates.[32] Preston then reached out to six publishers, who refused to print the letter if Lieber did not cover the expenses himself. This is hardly surprising considering most publishers did not share Lieber's radical standpoints on literary property protection. Eventually, Wiley and Putnam agreed to publish the letter as a pamphlet, printed at Lieber's own expense. Publisher George Palmer Putnam (1814–1872) was a vocal proponent of international copyright himself and approved of Lieber's message.[33] Unfortunately, Congress dismissed Clay's bill no. 223 again on July 17, 1840, before Lieber's pamphlet was published. Nevertheless, with *On International Copyright, In a Letter to the Hon. William C. Preston, Senator of the United States* Lieber issued his central work on international copyright in which he not only restates but expands the arguments presented in the entries of the

---

30 Clay, Henry. Letter to Francis Lieber. June 19, 1839. Francis Lieber papers. mssLI. Box 9, no. 57. LI112. The Huntington. San Marino, CA.

31 Freidel, "Contribution," 202.

32 Freidel, "Contribution," 202.

33 Putnam founded the first US-American international copyright association in 1837, the same year he published his own *Plea for International Copyright* (Andrew J. Eaton, "The American Movement for International Copyright, 1837–60," *The Library Quarterly: Information, Community, Policy*, 15.2 (1945): 95–122, 104). Putnam continued his efforts for copyright reform throughout his life, chairing the *International Copyright Association* in 1868. Lieber became a member of this association and delivered his final statements on copyright in front of association members (see chapter 7.3.1). After Putnam's death in 1872, his son continued his legacy and published *Authors and Publishers* (1882) and *Question of Copyright* (1891), see "Putnam, George Palmer." *The New International Encyclopædia*, (New York: Dodd, Mead and Company, 1905), 564–565.

Encyclopædia Americana. The pamphlet provides valuable insight into Lieber's understanding of literature as property, his demands for domestic and international copyright protection, and the transnational influences Lieber digests in this work. It is also directed towards the public and therefore illustrates Lieber's efforts to mobilize public support for policy change.

6.1 *On International Copyright, In a Letter to the Honorable William C. Preston*, 1840

Thorvald Solberg attributes central importance to Lieber's *On International Copyright* and outlined its influence on copyright debates in the US as follows

> A second wave of copyright agitation was set in motion during this year, 1840. Dr. Francis Lieber published a letter, addressed to Senator Preston, on International Copyright, and Dickens's visit to this country in 1841 increased the agitation to a flood-tide.[34]

Frank Freidel also assigns Lieber's pamphlet a central role in the international copyright movement, stating that "[f]rom New Orleans to Boston to Berlin, the pamphlet created comment and helped revive waning interest in international copyright."[35] Lieber's *On International Copyright* was certainly a key text in the copyright debate at the time, characterized by its unambiguous standpoints and acute demands. It positioned Lieber publicly as an issue entrepreneur and facilitated later exchange with policy makers in Congress.

In the letter, Lieber expresses his gratitude for Preston's "active part in bringing about a law which the plainest justice seems strongly to demand" and for not being "disheartened by repeated failures from persevering in this just cause" (*International Copyright*, 3). By sending a letter to Preston, Lieber hopes to "invit[e] through [Preston's] name, that degree of attention at the hands of the public, which it otherwise might not have felt inclined to bestow upon these fugitive lines" (*International Copyright*, 3). He fears that the matter of international copyright "does not appear to attract that general attention in our country, which fairness, justice, expediency, our own advantage and our reputation [...] call for" and believes that the topic would raise more

34 Thorvald Solberg, *International Copyright in the Congress of the United States, 1837–1886* (Boston: Press of Rockwell and Churchill, 1886), 9.

35 Freidel, "Contribution," 204.

attention if "the subject [was] more widely and more thoroughly understood" (*International Copyright*, 4). His intention with the letter is to "briefly exhibit the most important points connected with [international copyright] in as clear and popular a manner as the character of the subject may admit" (*International Copyright*, 4). He aims to raise public awareness of the issue with the explicit purpose of involving the public in the debate and to mobilize support, wherefore he frames the issue in the form of a conversational letter, an accessible narrative.

To Lieber, international copyright is elementary to international relations and of "great importance in political or civil intercourse" (*International Copyright*, 5). He laments that "radically erroneous notions" exist regarding copyright because its foundation, literary property, is not commonly understood, although it is situated at the heart of human society (*International Copyright*, 6). The protection of all forms of property should *concern everyone* because property *affects everyone*: Property precedes government and society, Lieber claims, and thus the laws referring to property must be "the large foundation of all enacted law" (*International Copyright*, 14). He considers individual property "absolutely necessary for society, peace and civilization" and thus demands that everyone should be familiar with the legal and political foundations of this central institution (*International Copyright*, 29). By involving the public, he also aims to mobilize support and exert political pressure on the legislature. Lieber disseminates knowledge about a legal issue in his letter: While it may be addressed to senator William C. Preston, its publication makes clear that it is also directed towards the public. In his letter he positions himself as a concerned citizen appealing to the legislature, thus presenting an accessible narrative to his readers. He offers detailed explanations in a conversational tone, elaborates on other laws and cases, as well as current and historical events. Lieber thus offers the reader a narrative to adopt, a moral stance rather than a legal one. As entrepreneur for an issue that has not yet garnered broad public support, he attempts to convince the public that a legal regime that they benefit from in the form of cheaper books is immoral and that, as citizens, they should speak out against it, demanding legal changes to their own economic disadvantages. To achieve this, Lieber had to make the incorporeal law regarding immaterial property graspable to the public, to make the abstract tangible. He conveys this issue by addressing feelings and essential values like justice, equality, and morality, rather than spelling out legal details. In his narrative framing he appeals to the peoples' understanding of themselves, their self-image, and questions how they position themselves within the state, as citizens.[36]

6.1.1 Text Analysis

In *On International Copyright* Lieber illustrates the relation between copyright, international copyright, literary property, and the importance of a transnational approach to all. He defines copyright as "the exclusive right to multiplying compositions and conceptions, which are represented upon paper, in other words of multiplying original books, music, maps, and engravings" (*International Copyright*, 4). Right away, Lieber considers this definition within an international context by comparing the given definition with the situation in England, Prussia, and France in a footnote (*International Copyright*, 4). He then defines the desired international copyright as "copyright, acknowledged and mutually protected by various independent nations, so that a copyright having originated in one nation, is of equal legal value among the people living under a different independent government" (*International Copyright*, 4). The "exclusive right of multiplying the copies" is also the essence of literary property, Lieber claims, following William Blackstone's definition of copyright (*International Copyright*, 5). But the scope of literary property, according to Lieber, goes beyond the exclusive right to multiply and includes other aspects, such as transmissibility and inheritance. Of these aspects the right to copy is the only right pertaining to literary property which Lieber considers of importance in international relations. This is because unauthorized reprints distributed in other countries hurt authors most acutely, while aspects such as inheritance usually concern individual domestic relations. Other countries have already passed international copyright regulation following the principle of reciprocity, Lieber points out, naming Great Britain and Prussia as examples (*International Copyright*, 5).[37] Lieber considers the necessity of international

36 I also analyze this letter and reiterate points made in this chapter but with a focus on Lieber's aim to educate the public on the subject of copyright and its political significance in my article "That general attention…which fairness, justice, expediency…call for." Strategies for Political Education in Francis Lieber's "On International Copyright", *in Political Education and American Studies*, ed. Astrid Franke, Uwe Küchler and Katharina Luther (Heidelberg: Winter, 2025), 81–100.

37 *The Prussian Copyright Act of 1837* act applied to works published in other states ("in einem fremden Staate") as long as the rights in those states correspond to Prussia's act. The act thus implements a reciprocal copyright between states ("Gesetz," 171). As Julius Eduard Hitzig explains in his commentary, this copyright extends to other German states, not all foreign states in general (*Preußisches* Gesetz, 108–109). But Lieber reads the act as applying to all foreign states, even those not part of the German federation.

copyright regulation within a transnational, rather than just the domestic context and advocates for a reciprocal relationship between nations in his letter.

Following Lieber, literary property comprises the property in the manuscript, the individual book, the thoughts within the book, and "the exclusive right freely to dispose of the conditions on which the composition or literary work shall be published" (*International Copyright*, 6–7). The "radically erroneous notions" regarding literary property originate from the false view that "by the very act of publication the author deliberately resigns any particular right in his manuscript" and from the idea that the rightful possession of a book grants the owner of the physical copy the right to "[do] with it whatever he chooses, and, consequently, also that of transcribing, reprinting, or multiplying it" (*International Copyright*, 6–7). The right to individual property is, Lieber claims, almost universally agreed to be established "by personal, individual production" (*International Copyright*, 8). To produce something means "changing by personal labor, skill, ingenuity or pains [...] the shape or substance of what exists" or to give "value, that is utility or desirableness, to what had none before, or increasing their degree of desirableness" (*International Copyright*, 8). Here, Lieber echoes John Locke's labor theory, arguing that the act of investing labor guarantees property rights to the product of said labor – including the literary labor an author undertakes to produce a work. To believe that the result of individual labor and effort would not belong to the one who invested the labor is, following Lieber, "so preposterous that no one would listen to this position, were it seriously advanced" (*International Copyright*, 8).

Lieber contests the notion of collectively held property – things, he believes, must belong to someone or they belong to no one (*International Copyright*, 10). Thus, individual property consists of "[t]he right of calling that my own which I have first appropriated, changed, fashioned and improved, upon which [...] I have first bestowed value, if it did not belong to some one else before I appropriated it to my particular use" (*International Copyright*, 9). If one owns a thing, one has the exclusive right to use or dispose of it accordingly (*International Copyright*, 16). Here Lieber expands on his earlier claims that property is the realization of man's individuality (*Life and Letters*, 120–122). A few years later, he now conceptualizes property as "a particularization of ownership," an "individual relation between the thing owned and the person owning" (*International Copyright*, 10). An individual's right to what they produce is a

---

Great Britain had recently introduced the *International Copyright Act 1 & 2 Vict. c.59* in 1838, which granted the British monarch the ability to offer copyright protection for international works, but limited this protection to Britain and British Dominions, see International Copyright Act, London (1838), Primary Sources on Copyright (1450–1900), ed. L. Bently and and M. Kretschmer, www.copyrighthistory.org, accessed 11 June 2024.

natural right and therefore foundational to society. Individual property is "absolutely necessary for society, peace and civilization" and "so direct an effect of man`s nature, that it precedes government," Lieber claims (*International Copyright*, 9). In fact, the protection of individual property from others necessitates government to begin with – following Lieber, property creates government (*International Copyright*, 11). Property also precedes society and law, he infers (*International Copyright*, 13): Since property precedes government and society, the law which refers to property arises from the interaction between people and must form "the large foundation of all enacted law" (*International Copyright*, 14). This "common law of the land" constitutes "the vast basis of all statute law" (*International Copyright*, 14) and is not created but merely acknowledged by government (*International Copyright*, 15). For Lieber, property is the central institution of human societies, which structures all human interaction and the rules and laws that govern human co-existence.

Intellectual labor, such as writing, generates a highly individualized form of property, Lieber claims. While no one can create an entirely new thing, intellectual labor bestows value upon a written work and "the more man's judgement and intellect are active in conferring value, the more he approaches to the creating of a new thing" (*International Copyright*, 16–17). For Lieber, literary production is the pinnacle of personal and intellectual labor:

> [I]f any product of individual activity has any claim whatever to an individual title of property, it is a literary composition; if there exists any species of property not made by government, but existing by its own spontaneous right, and which requires only to be acknowledged by way of protection on the part of the government, it is literary property; if there is any property which does not trench upon the rights of others, and exists without any sacrifice of theirs; in brief, if there is any property peculiarly innocent and inoffensive in its character, it is literary property (*International Copyright*, 17).

By framing literary property as the epitome of individual property, Lieber references a discourse which precedes the US Constitution: In his letter to representative Elias Boudinot in 1783, Joel Barlow stated that "[t]here is certainly no kind of property, in the nature of things, so much his own, as the works which a person originates from his own creative imagination" (see chapter 3.1.2).[38] As demonstrated earlier, this sentiment can also be found

38 Letter from Joel Barlow to the Continental Congress (1783), Primary Sources on Copyright (1450–1900), ed. L. Bently and and M. Kretschmer, www.copyrighthistory.org. Accessed 18 November 2022.

in the preambles of different state copyright acts, most explicitly in the preamble to Massachusetts' *Act for the Purpose of securing to Authors the exclusive Right and Benefit of publishing their Literary Productions, for Twenty-one Years*, passed on March 17, 1783.[39] Evidently, a conceptualization of literature as a uniquely individual form of property and worthy of legal protection was present in the US during the late eighteenth century. Lieber thus reiterates a discourse which emerged during the formative years of US state and federal law – a discourse in which both authors and jurists participated.

Fittingly, Lieber positions literary property within a long tradition of thought by claiming that the product of intellectual labor had always been accepted as the property of the writer, stating that "[i]t has always been so, until untoward circumstances have warped and distorted the notions respecting it" (*International Copyright*, 18). He refers to British common law and Martin Luther's (1483–1546) rejection of reprinting as proof for this long tradition, framing English and German standpoints as relevant to US law. He thus positions the question of literary property and international copyright as a transnational issue that concerns not just one country, but all. He points out that Luther's account of reprinting as "a right great robbery, which God assuredly will punish, and is ill-befitting for any honest christian [sic] soul" dates back to the very beginning of printed literature (*International Copyright*, 19).[40] Lieber thus insinuates that the notion of literary property has been prevalent since books could be printed, making "the title in literary property [...] just and clear, and correct" based on historical continuity and precedence (*International Copyright*, 19).

Lieber argues that literary property did not receive its "just title" as property – as opposed to other forms of property – because it only became marketable with the invention of the printing press, which made it possible to multiply texts cheaply and in large quantities (*International Copyright*, 20). Most

39 Massachusetts Copyright Statute, Massachusetts (1783), Primary Sources on Copyright (1450–1900), ed. L. Bently and and M. Kretschmer, www.copyrighthistory.org. Accessed 17 November 2022.

40 Here, Lieber refers to a preface by Luther where he condemns reprinting in general and especially the defacement of faulty reprinting. Nonetheless, the quote Lieber presents does not appear verbatim in the preface, see Luther, Martin. "Lutheri Vorrede Auf Die Verbesserte Edition Der Auslegung Der Episteln Und Evangelien, von Der H. Drey Könige Fest Bis Auf Ostern, An. 1525 in Druck Ausgangen." *D. Martin Luthers Sowol in Deutscher Als Lateinischer Sprache Verfertigte Und Aus Der Letztern in Die Erstere Übersetzte Sämtliche Schriften. Erster Theil, Welcher Den Ersten Theil von Der Kirchenpostill, Nemlich Die Auslegung Derer Evangelien Aus Alle So*, edited by Johann Georg Walch, Johann Justinus Gebauer, 1742, p. 34, https://martinluther.us/walch37.html. Accessed 12 December 2022.

other forms of property had already been acknowledged and protected by law at that point and no one thought to make up for the lack of protection regarding literary products (*International Copyright*, 19–20). Consequently, the belief formed that one could purchase the right to multiply and sell the content of a book by purchasing a copy, confusing the copy of a work with the property in the work itself (*International Copyright*, 21). Coincidentally, the value of literary property "consists chiefly in the right of multiplying the work," making it very easy to infringe upon this form of property (*International Copyright*, 21). The need for protection of literary property continually rises as "the cheaper [...] the means of multiplying become [...] the greater demand for books becomes" and the more frequently reprinting happens (*International Copyright*, 21). This is the reason Lieber appealed so strongly for a change in legislation at this specific moment in time – the law must change with the circumstances, and the international book market was quickly growing.

Lieber argues that legal protection for literary property which goes beyond existing copyright legislation is necessary to stop reprinting. Literary property would merely be acknowledged by such legislation, though, rather than created by it. Since literary property "is not material [and] cannot be grasped, or presented in bulk or size," it requires "more reflection and some power of abstraction to acknowledge it" but a government must nevertheless recognize the natural right of copyright (*International Copyright*, 22–29). Discussions surrounding the protection of literary property take place in other countries as well, Lieber points out, such as Britain and between the German states. He also refers to France's acknowledgement of literary property following the French revolution and claims that "all modern constitutions acknowledge [literary property]," a sweeping claim with no evidence to back it up (*International Copyright*, 25). In the German states, Lieber claims, "the 'rights of authors' are fully acknowledged as already existing" (*International Copyright*, 26). By situating the demand for literary property protection within a transnational context, Lieber adds validity and urgency to his demands. In doing so, he occasionally embellishes legislation in other countries to support his moral claims for literary property, glossing over the details of the actual laws to present a resonating narrative.

Lieber criticizes that the US frames books as regular objects of trade, wherefore they can be freely copied and reproduced in another country, causing economic and moral damage to authors (*International Copyright*, 26–28). Lieber disagrees with this legal framework. Instead, he believes there is "a difference between the book and the literary work or composition" (*International Copyright*, 31). The book belongs to the buyer, but the content of the work always remains the author's. The buyer of a physical book therefore does not purchase any rights to the literary work. To clarify, he refers to plagiarism, an act considered dishonorable by most: If there were no difference between buying a book and buying the work itself, Lieber posits, it would not be dishonorable to cut pieces from said book and present them as one's own work (*International Copyright*, 31). By referring to plagiarism as an example he aims to demonstrate that most people already understand the right an author has to the product of his intellectual labor – now the law must adapt to acknowledge that right as well. He then summarizes: "The right of the author's property lies in the composition, the *work*; this is the *product*, in which the author has invested his labor, skill, ingenuity and accumulated knowledge," even if the result is an immaterial product (*International Copyright*, 32). He continues:

> Thought is not marketable; but invested thought, ingenuity, calculation, combination, is daily brought to market. This literary *work* forms a separate independent product of its own, and is bona fide the author's own. It cannot belong to any one else. The author has truly and verily produced it; he is the owner; and he would not be the owner if he could not dispose of the work as he pleases (*International Copyright*, 33).

Consequently, the buyer of a book purchases the material book but not the work itself; the publisher merely buys the right to publish it but not the right to alter it (*International Copyright*, 33, 34, 37). The property right to the work itself remains with the author and "the ownership in a literary work is as clear, direct, real and sound as any existing, and more so than most others," Lieber claims (*International Copyright*, 34, 36). Thus, all literary works must be protected, "bad, foolish, good, on the general ground that they are property" (40).[41] The protection of literary works serves to "promote accumulation of property for the good of society and economy" and offers an incentive for authors to produce more works while providing for their families (*International Copyright*, 41–42). To Lieber, comprehensive copyright legislation would further the professionalization of authorship, educate members of society, and benefit the economy by facilitating trade. Since property is a natural right, copyright protection should not be limited in time – such a limitation is, according to Lieber, spoliation on part of the government (*International Copyright*, 43). This criticism includes domestic authors' as well as foreign authors' copyright.

Lieber's definition of literary property as a natural and essential right and his demands for unlimited copyright protection lay the groundwork for his

41 Lieber makes an exception for "flagrantly immoral or palpably injurious books" (40).

understanding of international copyright (*International Copyright*, 44). To him it is in accordance with civilization to "acknowledge rights beyond the limits of the state; that we acknowledge rights when we cannot acknowledge the citizen, but merely the man, in the interested individual" (*International Copyright*, 44). Lieber thinks beyond national boundaries and frames the right to property as a transnational right, a right not dependent on citizenship but merely on humanity. Literature, to Lieber, is a transnational property. That the work of a foreigner should not be granted copyright protection in the US is "a gross barbarous idea" to Lieber, an act of robbery not appropriate in civilized societies (*International Copyright*, 46). An author who produces a work through language has "an undeniable right, which civilization ought to deny no human being, to offer, directly or through some one authorized by him, his product in the best market, where it may obtain the highest price" (*International Copyright*, 47). International trade and markets offer benefits each producer must be able to enjoy, including authors, Lieber argues. Increased reward through international copyright would lead to increased literary production to the benefit of *all* societies, especially those who share a language and can thus exchange knowledge and aid civilization.

Currently, Lieber claims, the US not only hinders the progress of civilization and the production of literature, it engages in "literary piracy" (*International Copyright*, 49). Until an international copyright is introduced, the US robs foreign authors of the value of their works by allowing unauthorized hasty reprints to circulate freely (*International Copyright*, 50). Such an act is cruel for the author, who sees

> some one else who has no earthly claim upon him or the public, purposely mutilating or garbling [...] the work to which the author has staked his reputation and name, and to make which as perfect as his abilities would allow, he has spared neither time, labor, nor the sacrifice of money and many enjoyments, perhaps of health (*International Copyright*, 51).

A foreign author demanding protection of their work in the US asks nothing more "but what every human being has a right to claim, which you must grant him if he be your fellow-citizen, and which you ought to grant him because he is your fellow-man" (*International Copyright*, 52). To grant property protection is to recognize another's humanity, Lieber claims, and "the plainest justice to foreigners" (*International Copyright*, 52). Lieber harshly criticizes the US, suggesting that all civilized states – that is "[states of] mutual, candid acknowledgement of justice, fairness, liberty" – recognize international copyright and those that do not, exist in "a state of barbarity, of pilfer and plunder, meanness and violence" (*International Copyright*, 52–53). Lieber consequently excludes the US from the chorus of civilized nations and instead refers to international examples, naming Prussia and its *Prussian Copyright Act of* 1837 which "grants free and unconditional reciprocal international copyright" (*International Copyright*, 66). All authors, including US authors themselves suffer from the lack of copyright protection for foreign works, Lieber points out. Many nations grant copyright on a reciprocal basis only, thus denying US authors copyright protection in other nations and limiting their audience (*International Copyright*, 61). Publishers in the US are also less likely to publish American works if they have British literature cheaply and readily available, preventing the cultivation of a uniquely US-American national literature (*International Copyright*, 62–63). Such a national literature would contribute to the formation of the national character of the young republic. Thus, "[o]ur own protection then, as well as justice towards others, demand the passage of a law," Lieber argues (*International Copyright*, 64).

Lieber also values fair and reciprocal conduct between nations, characterized by "liberality and mutual respect" (*International Copyright*, 53). Only "[b]arbarous or degenerate nations" allow acts like "literary piracy" and Lieber demands the US decidedly position itself against such acts by recognizing and protecting the products of other nations' authors (*International Copyright*, 53). That the creator of a product enjoys "a proportionate share of those values which the consumer or those that desire the article give in exchange for it" is not only a matter of morality, it is "the principle which lies at the bottom of all industry, the moving power without which all interchange between men would be at the end" (*International Copyright*, 53). Thus, international copyright protection is a question of morality, of what is just and fair, but also a question of international cooperation, economic gain, and public access to error-free editions of books. Lieber ends his letter with a passionate plaidoyer for the introduction of international copyright, appealing directly to the citizens of the US when he asks: "Should we of all nations remain behind – we, who acknowledge no other master but Justice?" (*International Copyright*, 66). He appeals to the identity the US claims for itself, as a civilized country, demanding that "it is high time that we should now willingly follow the voice of civilization, of national honor, of conscience, of justice, fairness and righteousness" (*International Copyright*, 67).

6.1.2 Summary

Lieber discusses property in relation to several distinct categories within *On International Copyright*: The role of government in a state, the function of natural and positive law, and the rights and duties of citizenship. He also examines the role of morality in connection with civilization and progress, honor and justice, and nation's rights and duties in international relations. In this work, Lieber expands his understanding of property rights in literature, first asserted in the *Encyclopædia Americana* entries and then developed in *Manual of Political Ethics*. He now calls for tangible legal change, laying out his arguments in favor of comprehensive legal copyright protection, and focusing on the lack of international copyright protection in the US. Since, as he asserts, literary property is the purest form of property and exists by nature rather than government (*International Copyright*, 17), copyright protection should be exclusive, alienable, inheritable, internationally recognized, and reciprocal (*International Copyright*, 4, 5, 33). Lieber demands that domestic *and* foreign authors be granted unlimited copyright protection for their work, as unlimited property rights are acknowledged with regard to all other forms of property, domestic and foreign. Lieber believes that international copyright should be granted on the basis of human rights, as an inherent and natural right that precedes law, government, and society. It must therefore be extended to everyone, not just to citizens of one's own nation. Justice, fairness, and civilization demand legal protection of literary property, which Lieber frames as a transnational form of property. Comprehensive copyright legislation would protect national interests as well as international relations. It would also promote literary production, thus furthering economic growth and public education. The professionalization of authorship as well as the cultivation of a national literature are additional benefits that Lieber identifies.

In this extensive letter, the influences which shape Lieber's theory of literary property and copyright become more pronounced: Lieber refers to specific countries' copyright legislation as positive examples. He mentions England, where literary property was considered "property at common law," eliminating the need to protect it via a statute – until the *Statute of Anne* was passed in 1710. In France, Lieber writes, "one of the early acts of the first French Revolution [demanded] to acknowledge literary property on a comprehensive principle" (*International Copyright*, 25). The opinions brought forward in German states regarding the protection of literary property clearly influenced Lieber. Prussia's *Copyright Act of 1837* inspired him, as he frequently quotes from Julius Eduard Hitzig's commentary on the act. Lieber also cites the *Act of Union of the German Confederacy* of 1815, whose drafters proclaimed their intention to draw up "uniform decrees [...] respecting the protection of the rights of authors," officially recognizing the existence of authors' rights – rights that merely needed to be protected, not recognized (*International Copyright*, 26). The Leipzig book fair officially banned Austrian reprinters from attending, as Lieber reports (*International Copyright*, 23). Some German states have already established reciprocal copyright protection, significantly Prussia (*International Copyright*, 65, 66). Even the king of France, as Lieber claims, recently spoke of the necessity of implementing international copyright laws (*International Copyright*, 47). Evidently, Lieber considers copyright protection and legislation from a transnational and historic angle. He rejects the idea of nationally confined copyright legislation and instead demands a comprehensive and reciprocal network of copyright laws that could come about through international cooperation. US legislation did not allow such measures and thus Lieber looks towards Europe for inspiration. He cites laws and cases from other countries as positive examples. Rather than thinking locally, Lieber thinks transnationally. He combines his demands for property right protection with appeals for international cooperation in the name of justice and morality, and frames literature as a transnational property. He frames his arguments as an accessible narrative aimed at the public and at policy makers with the intention of mobilizing support for tangible policy change.

6.1.3 Reception

Once Lieber finished writing his letter on March 19, 1840, he sent the manuscript to William C. Preston to use during debates on international copyright in the senate.[42] He even had his close friend George S. Hillard send copies of *The Legal Observer* with additional information on copyright to Preston and Henry Clay, which Hillard forwarded writing "I sincerely hope they may be instrumental in promoting the interests of literary property."[43] Senator Preston agreed with Lieber's understanding of copyright as a natural and inherent right. Nevertheless, he sent a letter to Lieber on April 30, 1840, admitting that he had read and partially agreed with an opposing view: The abridged translation of Augustin-Charles Renouard's *Theory of the Rights of Authors* in *The American Jurist*, in which Renouard frames an author's right to his works as originating from positive rather than natural law.[44] Lieber had touched

42 Freidel, "Contribution," 203.

43 Hillard, George S. Letter to Francis Lieber. March 30, 1840. Francis Lieber papers. mssLI. Box 16, no. 31. LI1924. The Huntington. San Marino, CA.

44 Augustin Charles Renouard (1794–1878) was a lawyer and politician in France. His work on the rights of authors consists of the two books *Traité des Brevets d'Invention* (1825) and *Traité des Droit D'Auteurs* (1838–39). He proposed the legal implementation of authors' rights (droit d'auteur), but he did not frame these rights as property rights. He rather called for temporary printing monopolies, echoing the US understanding of copyright as an incentive for authors to create works and thus further the progress of science and art.

on Renouard's claims in his letter to Preston, expressing his disapproval of Renouard's dismissal of literary property as an inalienable right (*International Copyright*, 37).

In the first two parts of *Theory of the Rights of Authors*, Renouard compiled "all the facts, ancient as well as modern, which it has been possible for me to obtain, concerning the rights of authors" (*Traité*, 41). In the third part, subsequently summarized and published in the *American Jurist*, Renouard set out to draw conclusions from those facts in the form of propositions, which largely weigh the rights of the author against his duty towards society, to determine the best measures to balance both (*Traité*, 41). Renouard proposes that "[a]uthors have a right to profit by the produce of their works" but he does not believe that the right to derive profit from one's labor is a property right (*Traité*, 41, 42). Renouard argues that an author is

> the work of his own age and of former ages, as much at least as of his own proper genius ... the general domain has furnished him with the elements of the ideas which he has elaborated; that in restoring them to the civilization to which he is indebted for them, he acquits himself of a duty towards humanity, and pays to his contemporaries and to his descendants a debt of gratitude (*Traité*, 43).

An author is thus morally obliged to share the products of this intellectual exchange with the public. Once an author publishes a work, "[s]ociety acquires [...] a right to preserve the use of it" and the author receives influence, honor, and profit in exchange (*Traité*, 43). Any law addressing the rights of authors "cannot be good, but upon the double condition, that it neither sacrifices the right of authors to the public, nor the right of the public to that of authors," Renouard writes (*Traité*, 44). He rejects the notion of literary property (*Traité*, 48) because the works of science and literature are

> [a] novelty of combination in the result of thought ... thought, by its very essence, evades all exclusive appropriation ... When it passes into the minds which receive it, it does not cease to belong to the mind from which it emanates; like fire, it communicates and extends itself, without burning less brightly on its own hearth (*Traité*, 55).

See Augustin-Charles Renouard, *Traité Des Droits D'Auteurs, Dans La Littérature, Les Sciences et Les Beaux-Arts. Vol. I.* (Paris: Chez Jules Renouard &c., 1838). Hereafter abbreviated as *Traité I.* Augustin-Charles Renouard, *Traité Des Droits D'Auteurs, Dans La Littérature, Les Sciences et Les Beaux-Arts. Vol. II.* (Paris: Chez Jules Renouard &c., 1839). Hereafter abbreviated as *Traité II.*

Thought does not need to be limited through exclusive appropriation and is rather strengthened if shared. It is therefore not permissible to appropriate thought exclusively since such an act would hinder progress (*Traité*, 55–56). To Renouard, this also means that an author cannot pass the exclusive rights to their works on to their heirs because this would come as a detriment to society as a whole (*Traité*, 56–57).

Renouard emphasizes that by circulating thoughts and publishing a book, authors are "undertaking [...] a service towards society" (*Traité*, 65). The author thus has a right to be renumerated for that service, but not because they own their thoughts or expressions. Rather they are owed recompense for their service to the public – that is, following Renouard, an author's true right (*Traité*, 65). He argues that authors are chiefly laborers and they labor in exchange for rewards and "[t]he guaranty of an exclusive right of copy in the reproduction of a work is the best mode of renumeration on the part of society towards the author" (*Traité*, 69). A perpetual and transmissible privilege would evoke the same issues a property right would: Through the eradication of all competition the prices of books would increase. The books would be exposed to the risk of destruction because the right-holders could withhold new copies from the public. Such measures would hinder social progress and the propagation of ideas, decrease the fame and legacy of the author, and lead to the production of counterfeits as a reaction to a perpetual monopoly. Even a temporary privilege causes some of these issues, if only for a limited amount of time (*Traité*, 75–76). Thus, Renouard concludes that these consequences alone rule out "the dogma of literary property" as a "social evil" in practice and rather privilege the authors' rights system (*Traité*, 79–80). The publication of a book, he argues, is "a service rendered" and to confuse it with a property endangers the social and legal concept of perpetual, transmissible, and inviolable property (*Traité*, 81).

According to Renouard, an author's right "ought to exist for the life of the author, and for a certain period after his death," (*Traité*, 81). Additionally, Renouard recognizes that literary labor is very personal and thus an author should be awarded a high degree of control over their work. The author should therefore retain the right to modify and reissue the work and to control the intellectual communications with the public (*Traité*, 82). Since the life-span of an author is of an uncertain duration, the right to copy ought to be granted for a longer period of time to ensure that publishers can risk the financial investment necessary to publish a work. The family of an author should also profit from the work for some time following the author's death (*Traité*, 82–83). Renouard concludes his treatise by stating that he approves of the current legal system in France with regards to copyright. While incomplete, it is built on solid foundations and should not yield to the pressure to introduce a literary property right (*Traité*, 83).

Lieber summarizes Renouard's points in *On International Copyright*:

> [P]roperty cannot be predicated of thought, and consequently, the term Literary Property ought to be banished from the language of law [but nevertheless] the sole right of multiplication ought to be secured to the author for a limited time, on account of his merit, the advantage he bestows upon society (*International Copyright*, 37).

Lieber counters that property "can indeed not be predicated of thought" but that it "can be predicated of composition, of works" (*International Copyright*, 37–38). He calls Renouard's stance that the author "abandons all specific right respecting his composition" faulty (*International Copyright*, 37–38). Instead, he explains that property only becomes property if an exchangeable value can be attached to it and therefore an author must retain ownership of their work even when published – otherwise their property loses all value to them and is therefore not property (*International Copyright*, 38). Renouard claims that one loses rights of a work once published; Lieber criticizes that Renouard frames

> a composition [as] the property of the author so long as he chooses to keep it in his desk, but that he forfeits his ownership so soon as he publishes the composition, [it] is saying, this is your property, but the act itself of availing yourself of that property deprives you of it; which is absurd (*International Copyright*, 38–39).

Lieber also points out that predicating copyright on whether a work has "merit" is problematic for it evokes the question of "[w]ho would decide whether the majority of all books printed now a days are beneficial or the contrary?" (*International Copyright*, 39). Instead, all literary property has to be protected on the same grounds as any other property: "Because it is of essential importance to society that individual property should always be protected" (*International Copyright*, 39). In spite of Lieber's opposition to Renouard's standpoints, Preston found himself "greatly shaken" by Renouard's article.[45]

---

45 Renouard, Augustin-Charles. "Theory of the Rights of Authors." *American Jurist and Law Magazine from April 1838 to January 1843*, IV.43 (1843): 39–92; Freidel, "Contribution," 203.

Despite Preston's doubts, Lieber published his letter at his own expense, and the pamphlet gained national and international attention and support. As Thorvald Solberg and Friedrich Freidel claim, the pamphlet invigorated the interest in international copyright.[46] It was discussed in several newspapers and magazines and prompted a few letters of approval to be sent Lieber's way.[47] Editor J. T. Buckingham (1779–1861) reviewed Lieber's pamphlet in the *Boston Courier*. Buckingham first clarifies that with the review the paper does not "commit [itself] as an advocate of the doctrine of International Copy-Right. We are still […] opposed to the scheme of certain writers and politicians, who have petitioned our national legislature on this subject."[48] While this sounds like a direct criticism of Lieber's work, the review is partly favorable. Buckingham rejects Lieber's framing of literature as property but applauds his investigation of the origin of property and his demands of international cooperation and justice.

In July 1840, Gouverneur Kemble (1786–1875), representative from New York, sent Lieber a letter agreeing with his views on international copyright and offering to forward the pamphlet to others who might be interested.[49] Nathaniel Beverly Tucker (1784–1851), author and professor of law at William & Mary College in Williamsburg, Virginia, also sent Lieber a letter in 1840, thanking him for his "valuable work on copyright" and stating that "[t]o the few writers of this country the subject is one of personal interest."[50] Tucker followed up his letter a year later, ensuring Lieber that he would send "the President" the pamphlet on international copyright, likely referring to Thomas Roderick Dew (1802–1846), president of William & Mary College.[51] Tucker would also forward a summary of Lieber's demands along with the pamphlet,

> [a]s it will probably excite in him the wish to play the Maecenas [wealthy patron] for the protection of copyrights on both sides of the water from the pirates of editors and booksellers. The latter are bad enough – but the attempts

46 Freidel, "Contribution," 204; Solberg, "International Copyright," 9.

47 Freidel, "Contribution," 205.

48 Buckingham, J. T. "Lieber on International Copy-Right." Box 112, no. 6. LI475. The Huntington. San Marino, CA.

49 Kemble, Gouverneur (1786–1875). Letter to Francis Lieber. July 28, 1840. Francis Lieber papers. mssLI. Box 20, no. 62. LI2499. The Huntington. San Marino, CA.

50 Tucker, Nathaniel Beverly (1784–1851). Letter to Francis Lieber. October 22, 1840. Francis Lieber papers. mssLI. Box 67, no. 33. LI4428. The Huntington. San Marino, CA.

51 Tucker, Nathaniel Beverly (1784–1851). Letter to Francis Lieber. June 20, 1841. Francis Lieber papers. mssLI. Box 67, no. 35. LI4428. The Huntington. San Marino, CA.

> of the former to monopolize theft by adding half a dozen ill-considered notes to a foreign work, and taking out a copy-right, is a thousand times worse.[52]

Tucker even offered to discuss the pamphlet with President Dew "over a bottle of wine" in order to win him for the cause. Mitchell King (1783–1876), lawyer and judge from South Carolina, thanks Lieber for "[t]he copy of your excellent pamphlet on international copy right" in a letter from 1841.[53] Mitchell calls the pamphlet a "very interesting production" and the question of international copyright "a measure so obviously founded on everlasting justice." In October, Lieber wrote to Charles Sumner:

> Among the books and pamphlets which I received the last day I was in New York I found some numbers of the Allgemeine Press-Zeitung, published by [Julius Eduard] Hitzig. In them is an article on my Letter to Preston on International Copyright. It is the most favorable review of any writing of mine, I think which I have seen.[54]

The reviewer called Lieber's work precise, comprehensible, and surprising, noting that Lieber had "clearly developed the idea of intellectual property."[55] Lieber's work on international copyright had apparently reached the German states and been received favorably. This is not surprising, since Lieber's letter to Preston on international copyright was influenced by the *Prussian Law of Copyright* of 1837 (see chapter 3.2.2 and 6.1). Julius Eduard Hitzig, who edited the *Allgemeine Press-Zeitung*, had also published the commented version of the *Prussian Law of Copyright* which Lieber referred to during his own writing process (see chapter 6.1).

Evidently, Lieber's demands – though radically different from contemporaneous legislation – were received favorably by some authors and jurists, but not all reviews were supportive. On March 12, 1842, Lieber sent Charles Sumner a letter complaining about a review of his pamphlet in the *Southern*

52 Tucker, Nathaniel Beverly (1784–1851). Letter to Francis Lieber. June 20, 1841. Francis Lieber papers. mssLI. Box 67, no. 35. LI4428. The Huntington. San Marino, CA.

53 King, Mitchell (1783–1876). Letter to Francis Lieber. May 28, 1841. Francis Lieber papers. mssLI. Box 21, no. 15. LI2527. The Huntington. San Marino, CA.

54 Lieber, Francis. Letter to Charles Sumner. October 14, 1841. Francis Lieber papers. mssLI. Box 104, no. 7. N.n. The Huntington. San Marino, CA.

55 Lieber quotes the review in his letter to Sumner but the original is not enclosed. This quote must be Lieber's English translation from the German original.

Quarterly Review, written by an A. Everret.[56] Lieber describes the review as "so scurrilous, low and dirty a thing you can hardly conciene [sic]. The whole is an attack on the language. You know I do not defend it, although he makes a great deal even of misprints. The whole is run down in worst possible style." He laments that "[t]his slashing at me has now been going on for some time, for no other reason, although of course unavowed [sic], than that I am by birth a foreigner." Apparently, this was not the first negative review of his work, as Lieber argues that "the reviews [in the US] have never yet been liberal and fair toward me," while reviews published in the German states or France "express judgements which I do not desire better." In his letter, Lieber hints that "it is time for [...] some friend of mine to write a line or two, in the spirit of fairness" so that he should "rejoice therefore in seeing a word of comfort spoken for once." Lieber felt unfairly attacked for his style, as English was not his first language. Despite this criticism, Lieber did not feel that he had said all he could on the subject of property in *On International Copyright* and was not deterred from writing again on the subject. In 1841, a year after the publication of *On International Copyright*, Lieber expanded on and detailed his understanding of property in his new publication, *Essays on Property and Labor*.

6.2 *Essays on Property and Labor*, 1841

The collection titled *Essays on Property and Labor as Connected with Natural Law and the Constitution of Society* comprises 225 pages dedicated to Lieber's theory of the role of property and labor in society and proper government. Nevertheless, in the work Lieber largely reiterates what he had already outlined in his earlier works: He presents property as a timeless institution, a necessity and continuity throughout human history (*Essays*, 28). The urge to own property, he argues, is natural. It results from being human and is an expression of human individuality (*Essays*, 167–168, 182). Owning property comes with rights and with obligations but as an institution, it is indispensable for human progress and for civilization (*Essays*, 183). The protection of any form of property stabilizes society and promotes industry and peace (*Essays*, 16, 191).

Peter Becker argues that Lieber was prompted to publish this work by the depression of 1837 and by rising socialist tendencies. He posits that "Lieber

56 Lieber, Francis. Letter to Charles Sumner. March 12, 1842. Francis Lieber papers. OCLC 713642823. MS 5767. Manuscripts Division, South Caroliniana Library. Columbia, SC

wanted to make sure that property would be not at the mercy of the state, but would remain in private hands" because "Lieber believed that man's freedom could best be guaranteed through the acquisition of property."[57] Lieber himself details the genesis of *Essays on Labor and Property* in a letter to Charles Sumner in 1841. He writes:

> It was in the back room in my office in State Street where I used to hammer at my *Americana*, when one afternoon I happened to reflect upon the subject of Property more seriously than I had done before. I repeated my reflexion [sic] and arrived pretty much at Locke's theory, that is of the assimilation of our Ego with the matter around us, by imprinting our industry upon it. Not long after I found in a speech delivered by Mr Webster in Cincinnati these words: "No one can doubt, property is the creature of government and government the creature of the people. They can make and undo either."[58] There are the words so far as I remember them. I know the words: property is the creature of government were contained in his remarks. They struck me at once as very surprising, and continued reflexion [sic] showed me their unsoundness. You remember the letter I wrote you from New York relating to my meditations on property, sitting on the coach in Connecticut.[59] It then struck me for the first time very clearly that property is a necessary reflex of our individuality in the material world. When I came to the subject of property in my Senior Class, I told them I would give them two lectures upon the Right of Property, although not belonging to Political Economy. This obliged me to arrange my ideas more strictly. I put down the heads [sic] and began to write; the subject grew upon me, and, finally I was obliged fairly to wrestle with it and here is my little book. I meant simply to call it a tract, but the Harpers [publishing firm] would not hear of this.[60]

As Lieber describes in this letter to Sumner, the subject of property theory occupied him for years, at least since his work on the *Encyclopædia Americana*. Initially, he agreed with Locke's well-received theory of property as dependent on the investment of labor. He pondered the issue again when prompted by Webster's assertion that property is merely the creature of gov-

---

57 Becker, "Wissenschaftliche Leistungen," 4.

58 Lieber likely refers to lexicographer Noah Webster (1758–1843), a prominent copyright advocate. Lieber could also be referring to his son, Daniel Webster (1782–1852), senator of Massachusetts at the time and a personal acquaintance of Lieber.

59 These meditations are recorded in a letter Lieber sent Sumner on August 18, 1837, see chapter 5 (Lieber, *Life and Letters*, 119–120).

60 Lieber, Francis. Letter to Charles Sumner. September 15, 1841. Francis Lieber papers. mssLI. Box 104, no. 7. LI465c–d. The Huntington. San Marino, CA.

ernment and not a natural institution. In his letter to Sumner in 1837, Lieber presented property as "the realization or enactment of man's individuality" (*Life and Letters*, 119–120). He expanded on Locke's labor theory and blended it with notions expressed by Georg Wilhelm Friedrich Hegel in his personhood theory, which positioned property as a means for an individual's self-realization. In 1840, Lieber examined the subject publicly in *On International Copyright*, where he focused on literary property and emphasized the role of "personal, individual production" in the creation of property, combining his previous standpoints (*International Copyright*, 8). He portrayed property as contingent on both human individuality and investment of labor and argued that property preceded government, not vice versa (*International Copyright*, 11). A year later, in *Essays on Property and Labor* Lieber finally presented his completed theory of property.

6.2.1 Text Analysis

The 225-page volume published with Harper & Brothers contains an introduction by Reverend Alonzo Potter (1800–1865), professor of moral and intellectual philosophy at Union College and future bishop of Pennsylvania. Potter states that the theory of property is as of yet incomplete and continuously being developed by different writers as a fundamental right (*Essays*, III). With his work, Lieber thus joins notable authors such as Hobbes, Grotius, Pufendorf, Locke, Barbeyrac, Stewart and Parley, who investigate property's origin and the role it plays in society (*Essays*, IV–V).[61] Potter applauds Lieber for engaging the complexity of the issue of property rather than reducing it to "some single axiom of natural law" and for focusing on the current state of society rather than on the distant past (*Essays*, V). By proving that property existed before the creation of law or government, Lieber has done "an important service to philosophy," Potter claims (*Essays*, VI). He argues that Lieber's treatise will also help correct "bad legislation" (*Essays*, VII) and help protect property – and thus progress – further (*Essays*, VIII). Potter recognizes Lieber's role as an advocate for normative change and comments that with this work Lieber could indeed fuel social change and consequently, legal reform (*Essays*, XI).

Lieber himself positions his work as an introductory work on property, rather than a comprehensive one, and states that "[t]he subject of property

---

61 Hugo Grotius (1583–1645), Thomas Hobbes (1588–1679), Samuel Freiherr von Pufendorf (1632–1694), John Locke (1632–1704), John Barbeyrac (1674–1744), and William Paley (1743–1805).

and labour is one of great extent, and all its details of such moment to human society, that it would be impossible even merely to allude in these essays to every important point connected with it" (*Essays*, 15). He decided to write such an introductory work to make knowledge of property widely available and to educate a broad audience since "[e]very man who enjoys an active share in the government of his country is bound to endeavour, as far as lies in his power, to make himself acquainted with the elements of the society in which he lives" (*Essays*, 15). Education, to Lieber, is a means to mobilize the public and to effect legal change with regard to important legal issues. Property is one of these most essential issues, an institution which "calm[s], protect[s], and improve[s] mankind" as Lieber claims (*Essays*, 16). It is the desire to own property which encourages members of a society to work and to trade, and while property also causes "contention and crime," the protection of property is the foundation of a peaceful society (*Essays*, 16). Lieber props up his argument with references to the work of James Mackintosh (1765–1832),[62] to "ancient poets and prose," and to "[t]he Greeks, and before them the Egyptians and Hindoos, together with the Chinese" (*Essays*, 17–18). He aims to historicize and universalize the institution of property, to position it as a constant throughout human history and thus to legitimize it. Nevertheless, each society renegotiates property in relation to rights and duties and the social, political, and religious existence of its members (*Essays*, 18, 19, 21). Consequently, Lieber acknowledges that different societies implement property differently (*Essays*, 23).

Social, religious or political conditions at times impede the "inquiring spirit" of Western societies and corrupt property relations, leading to – in Lieber's opinion – wrong understandings of property (*Essays*, 21–24). As an example, Lieber criticizes Hugo Grotius' assertion that humans introduced private property intentionally and after careful consideration (*Essays*, 26). He argues that rather "the thing was before the word" and humans had no "conscious intention" of introducing property or an understanding of its purposes (*Essays*, 27, 28). Instead,

> [t]he origin of property can be referred to no fixed point of time. It grew up with man, as language, as government did. It was the necessary and unavoidable

62 Mackintosh, James. *A Discourse on the Study of the Law of Nature and Nations; Introductory to a Course of Lectures on the Science, to Be Commenced in Lincoln's Inn Hall, on Wednesday, Feb. 13, 1799, in Pursuance of an Order of the Honourable Society of Lincoln's Inn.* London, T. Cadell, Jun. and W. Daniels, 1799.

> effect of his physical and moral nature. The two first human beings could not but feel the import of Mine and Thine (*Essays*, 28).

The assertion that the first humans could not help accepting the importance of property as a structuring factor in their relations is noteworthy. By portraying property as natural and inherent to human nature, Lieber underlines his claim that literary property *must be* accepted and protected unconditionally by law and governments. Lieber emphasizes that property was not a conscious idea because he aims to position property as a force of nature, which has an inherent and unconditional right to exist in society. Nevertheless, the alleged timelessness of property as an institution leads some to understand the origins of property as "barbarous" and outdated. Lieber likely refers to understandings of property, whose proponents identify the continuity of private property as the root cause of social and political issues rather than a safeguard against them. Lieber instead argues that the continuity of property demonstrates that it stands the test of time since "[m]an acts according to the principles of his nature from the beginning, and to it he always returns, if, for a time, violence, blindness, or fanaticism force him away" (*Essays*, 29, 30).

After establishing the importance and inherent nature of property as an institution, Lieber presents his own definition of property: "Property is that which we own, and we own a thing if we have the exclusive disposal of it, or can exclusively use it for our purposes (use or abuse it)" (*Essays*, 33). Property is not to be confused with possession, which "means the mere fact of having a thing in our power, lawfully or not" (*Essays*, 34).[63] Property exists in all societies but it develops and becomes refined in accordance with civilization, which Lieber understands as man's continued progression towards his supposed true state of nature (*Essays*, 34). It can originate through peaceful appropriation or production, long and undisturbed possession, or forceable seizure (*Essays*, 35). Property is necessary for man's survival: Man must gather food, fashion arms, and provide shelter for his family's survival (*Essays*, 40–41). Thus, he must accumulate property through occupation and appropriation and through the production and exchange of his products (*Essays*, 54). But man does not merely want to survive, he wants to become civilized. Therefore, population must grow and production, accumulation, and exchange of resour-

63 Oddly, Lieber differentiates possession from property on the basis of lawfulness, contradicting his earlier assertion that property need not be acknowledged by law. Accordingly, possession should be defined as "having a thing in our power, which we *own* or not."

ces must increase because only with enough resources can man thrive (*Essays*, 41–42). Accordingly, man has an implicit right to property, Lieber argues:

> [I]f the Creator calls man into existence to live, and has destined mankind for civilization, he must, as an intelligent being, have furnished them with adequate means to support the one and to attain the other; and property, which is one of these adequate means, cannot, therefore, be unlawful (*Essays*, 44).

Here Lieber proposes a God-given right to property, a right given by divine design to ensure that man can survive and thrive. Lieber applies this right to all resources. While he does not mention literary property explicitly here, his statements also apply to literary property, the sale of which ensures the livelihood of a professional author and which must therefore be acknowledged by law. Production of property often requires the occupation of land and the appropriation of materials – literary property differs because it is created in the mind, as Lieber claims in earlier works. By writing ideas or stories down on paper or printing them in the form of a book, the author produces an exchangeable value through his labor.

Lieber argues that all men have the right but also the duty to occupy and appropriate in order to produce, accumulate, and exchange (*Essays*, 47–52, 54–62). Only the production, accumulation, and exchange of property can further civilization, he claims (*Essays*, 64). Governments exist to protect by law the property necessary for civilization, the desire for which is natural to the human race (*Essays*, 70–71). Law must not only protect the right to accumulate property but also the right to transfer it through grant, sale, and bequest. While the right to transfer property during one's lifetime is widely accepted, the right to transfer by bequest is not, Lieber claims (*Essays*, 79, 81). He rejects any criticism of transfer by bequest, stating that the laws of inheritance "are the effect, as well as a recognition, of the distinct and best feelings of man, and [...] operate essentially for the good of society" (*Essays*, 82). Inheritance has existed in all stages of humanity and develops in accordance with civilization, as does property, and is also founded on a natural principle (*Essays*, 84–85). The right to bequest accumulated property to his children motivates man to produce and be self-reliant, which in turn benefits society, Lieber claims. The absence of the right to bequest causes uncertainty, "retards civilization," interrupts family bonds, and prevents patriotism and community care, Lieber argues (*Essays*, 89). This argument corresponds to his criticism of copyright, which can only be bequeathed to the heirs of an author for a limited amount of time.

According to Lieber, it is the duty of the government to ensure the security of the property of its people. Poorly drafted laws or the absence of laws as well as the interference with property or free exchange can cause distrust in the government. Distrust in the government prevents capital from increasing and consequently population does not grow, civilization no longer advances, and no innovation takes place (*Essays*, 97–98). In *On International Copyright*, Lieber demonstrates this by using the example of copyright law: Due to the lack of comprehensive domestic copyright protection and international copyright legislation, authors cannot make a living by writing. Thus, they do not share their ideas with society and do not contribute to civilization – innovation, education, and social progress are inhibited.

In his defense of individual property Lieber rejects the idea of property held in common. With *Essays on Property and Labor* he aimed to rebut popular communist sentiments at the time, as he spelled out in a letter to Franz von Holtzendorff (1829–1889), a German jurist who shared Lieber's interest in penology. Lieber states that his intention had been to write

> against the Communists; at least they gave the motive for it. I refute the old arguments, that at first all things were given to all, and found the origin of property on appropriation and production with its consequent free disposition. Since then, I have added much in confirmation of my views, but no fundamental opinion is changed. I have constantly written against Communism, Jacobins, and Sans Culottes (*Life and Letters*, 416).

He believes that those who propagate a society without private property yearn for a blissful past, a golden age which never actually existed. He admits that much suffering in the world is caused by the inequality of property but argues that those who advocate for commonly-held property crave a state unexamined and impossible, a fantasy (*Essays*, 120). Lieber rejects current and historic examples of holding property in common as incoherent and dysfunctional, as obstacles to civilization (*Essays*, 154–161). While individual property comes with inequality, "it is but a minimum of the universal inequality of all things, and existing in all spheres of action," Lieber posits (*Essays*, 169). Since inequality exists in all areas of life and man cannot control all factors which influence equality, Lieber rejects searching for a different solution. Instead, he proposes that "[i]nequality of property is the will of the Creator; for individual property cannot exist without it, and individual property lies at the bottom of human advancement and civilization" (*Essays*, 173). As individual property is natural, it cannot be eradicated – any attempt to do so is futile and leads to more suffering (*Essays*, 174). Humans bypass circumstances in which they risk losing their individuality. They avoid situations

> in which [man] should be deprived of his natural and invaluable right to call the product of his own exertions, his own property; to accumulate as he chooses; to exchange it for what he desires, and to dispose of it for the benefit of his individual family, which bears his name, has been reared by himself, and for whom he collected it with toil and trouble (*Essays*, 182–83).

In his property, the result of his labor and investment, "[m]an yearns to see his individuality represented and reflected" (*Essays*, 183). This state of being is not acceptable and must be rectified because only if all property is safe and respected can man thrive in society and contribute to "physical or intellectual progress or existence" (*Essays*, 183). Only when individual property is secured can "general morality, manliness, and resolute activity stand and flourish" (*Essays*, 193). As Lieber clarifies in his earlier works, these conditions are not met for authors with regard to their literary property in the US at the time.

Lieber concludes this work with a call for more contentment with the general status quo in the US. He criticizes his fellow US-Americans for their "uniformity of discontent," claiming that

> [a] fretful uneasiness, a discontent unable calmly to enjoy these acknowledged blessings, and leading to a desire of changing real or supposed grievances by rash and extravagant schemes of sudden innovation, and not by gradual, and, therefore, sure improvements, pervade many large classes of our citizens (*Essays*, 195–196).

Lieber proposes that calm reflection is needed, an appreciation of things as they are. He condemns the tendency of his fellow countrymen to quickly adopt any "agitation or presumptuous theory started in foreign parts" (*Essays*, 209) and aims his criticism at labor unions and those who call for higher wages, better working conditions, and a more equal distribution of property (*Essays*, 199). While positioning himself as a neutral observer of the state of society, Lieber chastises those who call for more equality: He argues that everyone has their proper place in society, underlining his earlier argument of the permanence of inequality. He compares a "sound political community" to a forest with

> the greatest variety, from the overshadowing, broad oak and the towering tulip-tree, to the smallest blade and floweret, each striving upwards to the light of the

> sun, and, in doing so, developing its own peculiar individuality and destiny; no one interfering with the other, but all serving and aiding all; none degraded by the other, but all important in their own way, and forming, in their union only, that forest, without which none singly could exist or be what it is (*Essays*, 204).

Lieber proposes a model society in which everyone has a designated place where they serve their family and society best. It is a citizen's duty to work in the position where his talent benefits everyone – for some this will be physical work, for some intellectual (*Essays*, 204–206). If society thrives, the individual will thrive, he argues (*Essays*, 212–213). All riches accumulated by individuals will naturally be diffused and redistributed, benefiting everyone (*Essays*, 214). The free accumulation of property and capital, not regulated by law, promotes peace, liberty, and civilization, Lieber claims (*Essays*, 219–223). With his appeal, Lieber advocates on the one hand for free and unregulated accumulation of all property, on the other hand for comprehensive legal protection of the institution of private property in all its forms – including literary property. By framing private property as an inherently human institution, Lieber rejects all attempts to introduce a property framework focused on commonly-held property. This echoes his renunciation of literature as a resource that should be freely accessible to all. While he understands literature as a tool for education and the communication of ideas, he does not believe it should be common property, ready for everyone's use in the public domain. Rather, he believes it must be held privately by the author to be profitable – he clearly favors authors' rights to private property and the professionalization of authorship over the free availability of knowledge and ideas.

Lieber's appeal for private property was well received by his acquaintances. Simon Greenleaf sent Lieber a letter soon after publication, stating:

> The feature of your book on Property & Labor which struck me most strongly was the strong common sense & sound reason manifested in regard to the origin of property: – brushing away at a stroke the cobweb theories of previous tenancy in common, & of social compact. To me, who am by no means learned on this subject, though I have reflected a little, all the theories I had previously met with upon the original title to individual property appeared visionary & unsound: – but you have spoken directly to my understanding, & borne me along with you, my mind joyously assenting to each successive step in the induction. And this last remark I do not mean to confine to the origin of property, but apply it to the whole work. It is vigorous, & profound, yet exceedingly

> simple & plain. It is a book for the people. I wish it were in all the common school, social & society libraries in the country.[64]

Lieber must have been even more pleased by a later letter from Greenleaf, in which he states that Joseph Story fully approved of the work and that both "thought it by far the ablest treatise we had seen on that subject." Greenleaf even stated: "I constantly recommend it to my pupils, for whose use we have placed several copies in our Law Library."[65] Lieber had once again intertwined law and literature in his work and taken yet another step on his way to become a recognized authority on law in the US. He also managed to publish a work on property that was broadly received and had the potential to mobilize support from his audience for changes in property and copyright law.

The late 1830s and early 1840s were an immensely productive time for Lieber. He taught at South Carolina College, published several extensive works, exchanged countless letters with friends and colleagues in the US and in Europe, and he travelled to the North whenever possible. He also renewed his search for employment in the northern states but without success. In consequence, he grew increasingly bitter because he felt trapped in South Carolina. Lieber published fewer works during the mid- to late 1840s, though he continued to research and compile texts on various subjects. Notably, he collected notes and clippings on the topic of international copyright and eventually drafted a new copyright legislation for the United States, an unpublished source which has not yet been the subject of scholarly discussion.

6.3 Issue Conveyance, Advocacy, and Networking

During the early 1840s, Lieber remained avidly interested in the issue of copyright reform. As an issue entrepreneur, he not only published works framing his understanding of property and the importance of copyright as accessible narratives, he also lobbied members of Congress to influence copyright legislation more directly. Early in 1840, Lieber himself ran into issues with his own publishers when Marsh, Capen, Lyon & Webb in Boston published the first edition of Lieber's *Great Events, described by distinguished Historians, Chroni-*

64 Greenleaf, Simon. Letter to Francis Lieber. October 3, 1842. Francis Lieber papers. mssLI. Box 13, no. 65. LI1577. The Huntington. San Marino, CA.

65 Greenleaf, Simon. Letter to Francis Lieber. November 10, 1845. Francis Lieber papers. mssLI. Box 13, no. 66. LI1578. The Huntington. San Marino, CA.

clers, and other Writers.[66] Lieber designed this book as an instructive work for young people and eagerly collected and translated texts he considered inspiring.[67] The publishers printed 1,500 copies in the first edition, 1,000 of which were meant for school libraries. Contractually, Lieber was entitled to 10 percent of the $1,250 that the books were worth. The publishers had only agreed to publish the work under the condition that the manuscript was corrected, presumably to remove Germanisms. Lieber had to pay for the correction, as well as for the compilation of a glossary. All costs deducted, Lieber was entitled to $70.40, as his friend Hillard – who communicated with the publishers on-site – stated in a letter.[68] Soon after publication the publishers experienced financial difficulties and rejected Lieber's demand to print more copies of his work. They also did not pay Lieber what he considered a fair share of the profits. In November, Hillard warned Lieber: "You must not look for any more money from Marsh, Capen &co, for they have got none and never will have any."[69] Apparently, Lieber did not listen to his friend's advice and instead decided to sue the publishers. In December, Hillard sent another letter to Lieber and corrected him emphatically:

> But my dear, wise and learned friend. You have mistaken your rights and claims against Marsh, Capen &co.: and I am obliged to give you a lecture of attorney logic and practical common law knowledge which in this case must have more power than all that philosophical jurisprudence in which you are so much more revere than poor ignorant I. You have sold your M.S. to those gentlemen and they have agreed to pay you ten percent upon the retail price of every copy sold, and they have paid you that amount upon every volume published which sold or not, and can have no further claim upon them for any more money until a new edition is published. But you cannot compel them to publish any faster or any more than the public demands, nor can you compel them to dispose of their contract to another publisher who might sell more. In point of fact, Marsh, Capen &co. have become insolvent and all their property, and this among the rest, will be disposed of for the benefit of the creditors, and you will have the same rights against the person who takes it that you have against them, and no

66 Lieber, Francis. *Great Events, Described by Distinguished Historians, Chroniclers, and Other Writers, Published under the Sanction of the Board of Education of the State of Massachusetts*. Marsh, Capen, Lyon & Webb, 1840.

67 Schnurmann, *Sea*, 430–431.

68 Hillard, George Stillman. Letter to Francis Lieber. May 5, 1841. Francis Lieber papers. mssLI. Box 16, no. 32. LI1925. The Huntington. San Marino, CA.

69 Hillard, George Stillman. Letter to Francis Lieber. November 30, 1841. Francis Lieber papers. mssLI. Box 16, no. 33. LI1926. The Huntington. San Marino, CA.

> more. It is very possible that the Harpers would do better with the "Great Events" than they have done or can do, but the Harpers have not got and cannot get it and no power can give it to them except the voluntary consent of those who own the copyright and the plates. It may be a defect in our law that an author has no remedy against a publisher, to whom he sold his entire interest in a M.S. and who from lack of enterprise or capital cannot or does not supply the public with it up to the demand; but there can be no practical difficulty or a general rule because the impulse of self interest will [?] the publisher to act as the author desires. There I must beg of you to submit as patiently as you may to your lot in reference to this book for the law can do nothing for you. When the affairs of Marsh & co. are closed up we will see if any thing can be done with the person, whoever he may be, to whom the right of publishing the school library and the plates of it may be disposed.[70]

This fascinating passage is worth considering in its entirety, as it highlights Lieber's exact criticism of the state of copyright law in the US at the time: By signing a contract for publication with the publishers in Boston, Lieber had alienated all publication rights to his own manuscript to the publishers. While he disagreed with the publishers' decisions regarding the number of books and editions printed, he could not have a new edition printed by a different publisher. Marsh, Capen, Lyon & Webb owned, as Hillard pointed out, copyright and plates to Lieber's work. Lieber criticized copyright law accordingly: He asserted that an author ought to keep all rights to his literary property. While the author may sell the right to publish an edition of a work to a publisher, he should still be free to do with the literary work as he pleases – he retains his property rights. Hillard added insult to injury by explaining fundamental copyright law to Lieber, suggesting that while Lieber may engage in "all that philosophical jurisprudence," he knew less about actual copyright law than a studied lawyer. His critique highlights Lieber's primary sphere of activity: Lieber focused on morality, on what the law *ought to* permit or forbid. His concerns were of an ethical nature; he aimed to amend the law according to his understanding of right and wrong and to exert influence through his writing. It is thus not surprising that Lieber continued to criticize copyright law in the US and became more active in the political sphere, lobbying Congress to recognize the issue and change copyright legislation.

With his close friend Charles Sumner, at the time a practicing lawyer, Lieber exchanged many letters discussing his own works, legal questions, and poli-

70 Hillard, George Stillman. Letter to Francis Lieber. December 18, 1841. Francis Lieber papers. mssLI. Box 17, no. 34. LI1927. The Huntington. San Marino, CA.

tics. Between the years 1841 and 1843 Lieber and Sumner discussed the issue of copyright legislation in their letters. On April 1, 1841, Lieber asked Sumner whether he could send Lieber notes on the debate on a copyright bill in British Parliament, as well as an article reviewing and rejecting Thomas Babington Macaulay's (1800–1859) speech on copyright in parliament.[71] Apparently, Lieber closely followed Thomas Noon Talfourd's (1795–1854) attempts to secure an amendment of British copyright law (see also chapter 5.4). Talfourd demanded a post-mortem term of copyright for authors as well as legal security for foreign authors and their works in Britain but experienced fierce opposition, including the above mentioned speech delivered by Thomas Babington Macaulay in 1841.[72] Lieber also informs Sumner that he recently had a disagreement with William C. Preston. While Lieber argued "that Congress had no right whatever to impose the duty on authors to give copies to Congress, the Secretary of State, &c., because it was taking private property for public benefit without compensation," Preston disagreed. Evidently, Lieber stayed in contact with Preston and thus had the opportunity to discuss current copyright legislation with at least one member of Congress and to advocate for amendments to copyright law directly.

Lieber also followed other Congressional debates, such as those discussing whether to impose a tariff on foreign imported books. For Lieber, this issue was closely connected to the question of international copyright, as both issues concerned international cooperation, the transnational movement of books, and public access to knowledge. In June 1841, Lieber wrote to Sumner

> Mr. Preston wrote me about the tariff. He wants my views on the item of books. My view is simply this, that it is narrow, mean, and especially unbecoming for a free, striving, wealthy nation to impose taxes on books, maps, engravings, &c., that it greatly impedes its own onward march; and that, if publishers here must be protected, it would be over and above sufficient to say that all English books shall be duty-free one year after their publication, – until then, say, fifteen

71 Thomas Babington Macaulay, "Copyright. A Speech. Delivered in the House of Commons on the 5th of February 1841" in *The Miscellaneous Writings and Speeches of Lord Macauly* (London, New York: Longmans, Green, and Co, 1889), 609–618.

72 Ronan Deazley writes that Talfourd had brought his first copyright bill up to debate before the House of Commons in 1837. He aimed to "codify the various strands of existing copyright legislation within one statutory measure [...] he also proposed to put the issue of the rights of foreign authors [...] upon a legislative basis." His bill was rejected and Talfourd proposed four more bills in the following years. While the revised bills focused on domestic copyright issues, they each failed to pass the House of Commons (Deazley, "Copyright Amendment").

> per cent *ad valorem*, and not per weight, which is too silly a standard for the pecuniary value of a book (*Life and Letters*, 152–153).

Lieber frames the question of book tariffs as an issue of international relations. A "free, striving, wealthy nation" should not act in a "narrow, mean" way by hindering free trade. Such a tariff would impede the import of foreign books, thus limiting access to knowledge and obstructing the "onward march" of civilization. On July 8, 1841, Lieber sent Charles Sumner a letter commenting on the question whether imported books should be subject to tariffs. He stated that "[t]he tariff will not be touched this time; but it will next session, and Clay, Preston, Choate and a number of others will do all they can to carry my proposal, which is that all books [...] be free of duty" (for a more detailed examination of Lieber's stance on book tariffs, see chapter 7.2.2).[73] Evidently, Lieber did not only follow the debates in Congress focused on issues connected to literary property and international copyright closely. Rather, he continued to lobby members of Congress, including and besides Preston, in relation to relevant issues and aimed to influence the decisions made in Congress. He even claimed to have "some very fine materials, which convinced Mr Clay it seemed."[74]

In 1842 the popular British author Charles Dickens (1812–1870) visited the US and fueled interest in international copyright legislation. Dickens was another issue entrepreneur for international copyright and he convinced Washington Irving (1783–1859) and twenty-four other American authors to petition Congress and demand the passage of an international copyright law.[75] In "Charles Dickens and International Copyright," Lawrence Houtchens

73 Lieber, Francis. Letter to Charles Sumner. July 8, 1841. Francis Lieber papers. mssLI. Box 104, no. 7. N.n. The Huntington. San Marino, CA. This letter is a transcription by Mathilde Lieber.

74 Interestingly, this sentence is crossed out in the transcript of the letter by Mathilde Lieber. The question is whether Lieber also crossed out this sentence in the original. It is more likely that Mathilde crossed out the sentence from the transcript before handing it to Thomas Perry, who edited Lieber's *Life and Letters* following Lieber's death. Did Mathilde find this sentence boastful or did she try to cover up Lieber's direct exertion of influence on Preston and Clay?

75 Lawrence Houtchens includes a list of all signees in his article, as well as a copy of the unpublished petition. Lieber is not among these names, which is not surprising considering that Lieber lived in South Carolina, not New York. See Lawrence Houtchens, "Charles Dickens and International Copyright," *American Literature*, 13.1 (1941): 18–28, 19–20.

argues that style and argument of the petition suggest that Dickens drafted it himself.[76] In the petition, the signees state that

> Your petitioners are at a loss to perceive why literary property is not just as much entitled to protection as the productions of manual handicraft or labour. The toil of the author is as exhausting to the physical energies as the toil of the mechanic, and yet the foreign mechanic can transfer the products of his industry to his agent in this country and reap the benefit of their sale, while the foreign author may see his works pirated and mutilated, and sold for the advantage of another, and be unable to obtain redress.[77]

The petition echoes the same arguments brought forward by Lieber two years earlier. It speaks of literature as a property, which ought to be treated like any other form of property. The author is framed as a regular laborer who should be able to sell their works internationally. The reprint of foreign works is presented as a form of "piracy" against which authors cannot defend themselves. The similarities in argument between this petition, Lieber's pamphlet (see chapter 6.1), the petition of British authors presented by Clay in 1837 (see chapter 6), and Joel Barlow's letter to Elias Boudinot in 1783 (see chapter 3.2) demonstrate that a consistent discourse regarding literature as property had existed in the US for over half a century, which was clearly influenced both by British and early US-American concepts of literary property and copyright protection. Lieber and Dickens both reference this discourse in their efforts to bring about an international copyright in the US. Lieber certainly followed Dickens' efforts closely; he saved newspaper clippings of an article focused on Dickens' international copyright activism (see also chapter 5.4).[78]

Charles Dickens entrusted Henry Clay with the petition and noted in a letter to a friend: "When Clay retires, as he does this month, Preston will become the leader of the whig [sic] party. He so solemnly assures me that the international copyright shall and will be passed, that I almost begin to hope; and I shall be entitled to say, if it be, that I have brought it about."[79] Lieber and Dickens both positioned themselves as central figures of the reform movement for an international copyright, and both put their hopes in the same politicians, namely Henry Clay and William C. Preston. Henry Clay pre-

76 Houtchens, "Charles Dickens," 20.

77 Cited in Houtchens, "Charles Dickens," 20–21.

78 Dickens, Charles. *To the American People*, in *The Mercury*. May 17, 1842. Francis Lieber papers. mssLI. Box 92, no. 14. LI475. The Huntington. San Marino, CA.

79 Cited in Houtchens, "Charles Dickens," 19.

sented the petition to the House of Representatives on March 14, 1842.[80] From there it was referred to a committee under John P. Kennedy (1795–1870) from Maryland, himself an author.[81] While the House of Representatives entrusted the committee to consider whether amendments to the existing law of copyright were necessary, the committee did not issue a report on the subject.[82]

Lieber's contacts in Congress continued to inform him of the proceedings regarding international copyright. On January 1, 1843, almost a year after Clay presented the petition to Congress, Caleb Cushing, a Democrat from Massachusetts and member of the House committee on copyright formed in response to the petition by Dickens, Irving, and others, wrote to Lieber:

> The question of international copyright is gaining ground in Congress. A select committee on the subject was recently appointed on the motion of Mr. Kennedy of ML. and its jurisdiction enlarged my motion so as to embrace the whole subject of Copyright, then being other points in it which require revision in addition to its international relation.[83]

While the select committee did not bring about change to copyright legislation, this letter proves that Lieber continued to discuss international copyright with several members of Congress, both in the Senate and in the House of Representatives, using his large network to keep up to date on the subject and to receive insider information. The letter underpins his sustained interest and personal involvement in the topic. Lieber gathered information wherever he could, also observing attitudes among publishers. In September he wrote to Sumner:

> A stir is now making among the publishers here [in New York] to petition Congress for an international copyright. Lea & Blanchard even are for it; the Harpers will probably sign ~~it~~, certainly not oppose it. For once a ray of light on the horizon! I have written to Choate about it. He cannot do anything better than end for the present his Senatorial career by getting a law passed which if it shed no political luster upon its promoter will nevertheless be a real step for-

80 Solberg, *International Copyright*, 9.
81 Houtchens, "Charles Dickens," 19.
82 Solberg, *International Copyright*, 10.
83 Cushing, Caleb (1800–1879). Letter to Francis Lieber. January 1, 1843. Francis Lieber papers. mssLI. Box 10, no. 36. LI1190. The Huntington. San Marino, CA.

> ward and onward in the path of civilization and international good will. If you can, stir and promote.[84]

Lieber hoped to influence Rufus Choate (1799–1859), senator from Massachusetts and a correspondent of Lieber's, to promote international copyright legislation – a matter which Lieber considered a mainstay of national progress, international cooperation, and civilization. Three years after the publication of his pamphlet no law on international copyright had been passed, but Lieber remained focused on the issue, hoping to exert pressure through networking, lobbying, and correspondence. He also sent a letter to John S. Meehan, the librarian of Congress, asking a question regarding "Burke's Treatise on the Law of Copyright." Meehan could not answer Lieber's question but promised to

> place the title among others to be submitted for purchase; and, if I receive authority for the purpose from the Chief Justice of the U.S. Supreme Court, who is authorized by law to designate all works to be added to our Law collection, it will be a great satisfaction to me to procure it in good season for use at the approaching session of Congress.[85]

Apparently, Lieber recommended works on copyright to members of Congress, likely to influence the discussion in future sessions of Congress. His efforts in favor of international copyright did not go unnoticed. In 1843, Lieber received a letter from the "American Copy-right Club" in New York City, informing him that he had been "unanimously elected an associate member of the Club."[86] As issue entrepreneurs, the members aimed to "procure the enactment of such law or laws as shall place the literary relations of the United States and foreign countries, in reference to copy-right, on just, equitable, and proper grounds."[87] They offered to "receive any suggestions you may be able to make, to furnish you with such documents as it may issue, and to inform you, from time to time, of the progress of the cause."[88] The same year, the *Copy-*

84 Lieber, Francis. Letter to Charles Sumner. September 9, 1843. Francis Lieber papers. mssLI. Box 104, no. 7. N.n. The Huntington. San Marino, CA.

85 Meehan, John Silva (1790–1863). Letter to Francis Lieber. Francis Lieber papers. mssLI. Box 58, no. 13. LI2795. The Huntington. San Marino, CA.

86 Mathews, Cornelius. Letter to Francis Lieber. September 7, 1843. Francis Lieber papers. mssLI. Box 83, no. 5. LI134. The Huntington. San Marino, CA.

87 Mathews, Cornelius. Letter to Francis Lieber. September 7, 1843. Francis Lieber papers. mssLI. Box 83, no. 5. LI134. The Huntington. San Marino, CA.

88 Mathews, Cornelius. Letter to Francis Lieber. September 7, 1843. Francis Lieber papers. mssLI. Box 83, no. 5. LI134. The Huntington. San Marino, CA.

right Club published *An Address to the People of the United States, New York (1843)*, announcing its establishment. This address is a rich source which includes the names of members and associates of the cause, among them later secretary of state and friend of Lieber's, Hamilton Fish (1808–1893).[89] The letter encourages Lieber to form a copyright club in his own city "to co-operate with the 'American Copy-right Club', and to prepare to concentrate the action of the friends of the cause throughout the country, in such a manner as shall seem best calculated to insure its success." President of the club was William Cullen Bryant (1794–1878), poet and later a close friend of Lieber's in New York, who acted as pall-bearer at Lieber's funeral.[90] Lieber did not form his own copyright club in Columbia, SC – an undertaking unlikely to succeed in the small Southern town – but he kept the membership certificate.

On January 3, 1844, Charles J. Ingersoll (1782–1862), a Democrat from Pennsylvania, introduced a new bill focused on copyright to the House of Representatives. H.R. bill no. 9 was titled "A bill relating to copyright" and was drafted with the purpose of amending copyright law "to afford greater protection to literary works, music, and sculpture, and to the arts of design, engraving, modelling, pattern-making, and paper-staining."[91] This bill is interesting because it explicitly frames literature as property, resembling the early states' copyright statutes and Lieber's narrative. It states that

> the copyright in every book which shall, after the passing of this act, be published in the lifetime of its author, shall endure for the natural life of such author, and for the further term of seven years, commencing at the time of his death, and shall be the property of such author and his assigns.[92]

Interestingly, following the bill the copyright in a published book "shall be the property of the proprietor of the author's manuscript from which such book shall be first printed" (Sec. 3). The copyright thus belongs to the person who owns the manuscript – not necessarily to the author; the property is fully

89 An Address to the People of the United States, New York (1843), Primary Sources on Copyright (1450–1900), ed. L. Bently and and M. Kretschmer, www.copyrighthistory.org.

90 "The Late Dr. Lieber." Francis Lieber papers. mssLI. Box 87, no. 10. N.n. The Huntington. San Marino, CA.

91 H.R. 9 (Ingersoll Bill), Washington D.C. (1844), Primary Sources on Copyright (1450–1900), ed. L. Bently and and M. Kretschmer, www.copyrighthistory.org. Accessed 15 December 2022.

92 H.R. 9 (Ingersoll Bill), Washington D.C. (1844), Primary Sources on Copyright (1450–1900), ed. L. Bently and and M. Kretschmer, www.copyrighthistory.org. Accessed 15 December 2022.

alienable. The respective copyright is explicitly framed as transmissible personal property (Sec. 15). This conceptualization of copyright as property differs from Lieber's theory of literature as an *author's* property, a property right deriving from the investment of intellectual labor and a moral right deriving from the intimate connection between an author and the work. Lieber argues that there is a difference between the property of the individual book, the ownership of a manuscript, and the copyright to a work (*International Copyright*, 6). Therefore, the right to the work cannot pass to the owner of a manuscript, if he is not the author of said manuscript. Additionally, Ingersoll's bill explicitly denies copyright to anyone who is not a citizen or *bona fide* resident of the United States (Sec. 19), rejecting international copyright protection entirely. Ingersoll's bill did not understand property the same way Lieber did, but it significantly diverged from existing legislation and attempted to codify copyright as a property. Unsurprisingly, the bill was referred to a special committee but not discussed again.

The initial interest in international copyright legislation died down quickly despite the combined efforts of Lieber, Dickens, Clay, and Preston, and Lieber felt defeated. In 1842 he sent a letter to George S. Hillard, lamenting:

> Would that my pamphlet on International Copyright had done some practical good! [...] Here is a Benjamin writing all the time outrageously against it. Peter Parley and other pirates hold meetings and vote their plunder righteous, and not a voice of the prominent is heard; so that, in fact, none but their personal friends know their opinion. This is not right, not fair. It is a question of national honor, and we have not overmuch just now of that article to trifle with it in any shape. I know they do not wish to be disturbed in their literary ease, in their bookish comfort; but our luxury is not the question in this world when morality and honor are at stake. I do not think that Boston – the most literary place in the United States by a great many odds – does in this matter what it ought to do (*Life and Letters*, 169).

For Lieber, the issue of literary property and international copyright was not of fleeting interest. He understood international copyright as interwoven with questions of national honor and international cooperation, with morality and civility. International copyright was representative of the larger issue of personal rights and property, of the question of how countries should treat each other in an increasingly globalized world. Consequently, Lieber did not stop advocating for international copyright legislation. While he did not publish another written work on international copyright, Lieber continued to mobilize support through networking, speeches, and even drafted his own version of a federal international copyright law.

6.4 A New Copyright Law for the United States?

Lieber's draft for a "new copyright law for the United States" has not yet been discussed in any other scholarly work.[93] It is hidden away at the Huntington's archives, in a cluttered folder of collected newspaper clippings and notes focused on copyright. The draft itself has no date; it appears to be a fair copy. The enclosed notes do not only showcase the catalogue of national and international sources Lieber referred to during the writing process, they also narrow down the timeframe for the possible date of origin. The oldest source is from 1837, the newest from 1850; the bulk of the clippings is from the early 1840s. We can thus assume that the draft dates back to the period between the early 1840s and 1850, most likely to the year 1842.[94] The clippings stem from different newspapers, domestic and foreign, showcasing the breadth of Lieber's research.

The earliest source, dated May 22, 1837, is an article from *Galignani's Messenger*, an English-language newspaper from Paris, France.[95] Titled "House of Commons, May 18. Law of Copyright," the article offers a full transcript of a speech in favor of consolidating the law relating to copyright and of extending the term of duration, delivered by Sergeant Thomas Noon Talfourd (1795–1854) in the British House of Commons (see also chapter 5.3).[96] Talfourd begged leave for the introduction of a bill "to consolidate and amend the

93 Lieber, Francis. A Draught of a new copyright law for the United States. Approx. 1840–1850. Francis Lieber papers. mssLI. Box 92, no. 14. LI475. The Huntington. San Marino, CA.

94 There are no sources from after 1842 until 1849. Since Lieber focused on international copyright most avidly between 1837 and 1842, it is possible that he devised the draft in 1842 and merely added two clippings in November 1850. This seems to be the most likely scenario since Lieber did not publish on copyright during the mid- to late 1840s – he likely drew up his draft shortly after writing and publishing *On International Copyright* and *Essays on Property and Labor*. Presumably, he wanted to follow up his criticism of international copyright legislation expressed in these works with an actual suggestion for new legislation. Why Lieber never actually published the draft cannot be said for certain.

95 *Galignani's Messenger*. House of Commons, May 18. Law of Copyright. May 22, 1837. Francis Lieber papers. mssLI. Box 92, no. 14. LI475. The Huntington. San Marino, CA.

96 A transcript of the speech is available here: Talfourd, Thomas. "Law of Copyright." *Commons Sitting 18 May 1837*. Hansard 1803–2005, UK Parliament. https://api.parliament.uk/historic-hansard/commons/1837/may/18/law-of-copyright. Accessed 8 February 2023.

laws relating to property in the nature of copyright in books, musical compositions, acted dramas, pictures, and engravings, to provide remedies for the violation thereof, and to extend the term of its duration." He also advocated for "acknowledging the rights of foreigners to copyright in this country and of claiming it from them for ourselves in return." Talfourd argued that a precedent for the recognition of international copyright already existed in Britain due to a recent decision on musical copyright by judge Abinger.[97] Consequently, British courts should move to protect the rights of foreigners against infringement and thus "se[t] an example which France, Prussia, America, and Germany are prepared to follow." Thomas Spring-Rice (1790–1866), chancellor of the exchequer, added that Talfourd "had brought the subject forward at a most opportune period, inasmuch as that other brother of the English family – for so he must ever describe the nation on the other side of the Atlantic, had already given it some attention." He pointed out that "[the question of international copyright] had been brought under the consideration of the American Congress by a report drawn up by one of its most eminent statesmen, Mr. Clay." This clipping is likely only one of many articles Lieber read on proposals for international copyright legislation in Britain. It illustrates that he closely followed the proceedings in other countries, especially in Britain, the German states, and France, and incorporated these transnational influences into his own understanding of international copyright.

Fittingly, the next clipping is titled "Copyright in Prussia," also from *Galignani's Messenger* and dated January 2, 1838.[98] The article details the new copyright law recently passed in Prussia, the same law Lieber translated for *The Law Reporter* a year later. The article uses some of the same rhetoric Lieber adopts, speaking of "pirated copies" rather than of reprints. Literary property as a concept is not mentioned in the article, though the preamble of the original German law speaks of the authors' property in their works.[99] Most relevant to

---

Talfourd reintroduced the bill in 1839, 1840, and 1841. He was not a member of Parliament when a modified version of the bill became law in 1842.

97 James Scarlett (1769–1844), 1st Baron of Abinger and Lord Chief Baron of the Exchequer (1834–1844).

98 *Galignani's Messenger*. Copyright in Prussia. January 2, 1838. Francis Lieber papers. mssLI. Box 92, no. 14. LI475. The Huntington. San Marino, CA. The title, date, and source of the article were added in Lieber's handwriting.

99 "Damit dem Eigenthum an den Werken der Wissenschaft und Kunst der erforderliche Schutz gegen Nachdruck und Nachbildung gesichert werde [...]," see Hitzig, Julius Eduard. *Das königl. preußische Gesetz vom 11. Juni 1837. Zum Schutze des Eigenthums an Werken der Wissenschaft und Kunst gegen Nachdruck und Nachbildung dargestellt in seinem Entstehen und erläutert durch Dr. Julius Eduard Hitzig*. Ferdinand Dümmler, 1838, p. 47.

Lieber, the article closes by stating that "this law is applicable to works published in a foreign state, in so far as the rights established in that state are conferred equally by the laws of the said state to works published in Prussia." Lieber also favored such a reciprocal relationship between states.[100] Clearly, Lieber kept up to date with the proceedings of copyright in his home state Prussia, but he also monitored changes to copyright legislation in other countries. Another clipping reads:

> The King of Naples and the Grand Duke of Tuscany have acceded to the treaty recently concluded between Austria and Sardinia, for the protection of literary property. The Court of Rome has been applied to, and has declared that it will take the matter into immediate consideration.[101]

The mention of literary property certainly interested Lieber, especially with regard to Austria, which Lieber frequently used as a negative example with regard to reprinting (see chapter 4.2 and 4.3).[102] The treaty between Austria and Sardinia is indeed compelling, as it constitutes the first international copyright treaty a German-speaking country participated in.[103] Sardinia prompted the treaty to resolve reprinting conflicts between Sardinian and Austrian publishers. The treaty was later included in domestic Sardinian leg-

---

100 As stated in chapter 2.2.2, the final paragraph of the *Prussian Copyright Act* was drafted to implement reciprocal copyright between the different states of the German Confederation, though Lieber usually claims it granted a general reciprocal copyright.

101 Curant of Ealigniani. International Copyright. August 19, 1840. Francis Lieber papers. mssLI. Box 92, no. 14. LI475. The Huntington. San Marino, CA. The title, date, and source of the article were added in Lieber's handwriting.

102 See for example Lieber, Francis. "Copyright." *Encyclopædia Americana. A Popular Dictionary of Arts, Sciences, Literature, History, Politics and Biography. Vol. III.* (Philadelphia: Carey and Lea, 1830), 527–529, 528.

103 Original title: *Vertrag zwischen Seiner Majestät dem Kaiser von Oesterreich und Seiner Majestät dem König von Sardinien zur Sicherstellung der Eigenthumsrechte hinsichtlich der in Ihren beiderseitigen Staaten erscheinenden litterarischen und artistischen Werke. Abgeschlossen zu Wien den 22. Mai 1840, und in den Ratificationen ausgewechselt ebendaselbst den 10. Junius 1840.* Available at: *Bilateral Treaty between Austria and Sardinia, Vienna (1840)*, Primary Sources on Copyright (1450–1900), ed. L. Bently and and M. Kretschmer, https://www.copyrighthistory.org/cam/tools/request/showRecord.php?id=record_d_1840. Accessed 16 April 2024. A few years later, in 1846, Prussia and Great Britain entered into a bilateral international copyright treaty, making Prussia the second German-speaking state to enter into such a reciprocal treaty, see *Bilateral Treaty between Prussia and Britain (1846)*, Primary Sources on Copyright (1450–1900), ed. L. Bently and and M. Kretschmer, www.copyrighthistory.org. Accessed 16 April 2024.

islation and incorporated into the *Austrian Copyright Act of 1846*.[104] A treaty recognizing property rights to literature was noteworthy to Lieber, especially since the act secured authors lifelong property rights to their works in both states. Such a bilateral treaty may well have acted as inspiration for Lieber's draft for new copyright legislation.

Lieber also kept sources on US copyright, for example entries from *The American Almanac and Repository of Useful Knowledge, For the Year 1840*. Lieber was enthusiastic about data and kept statistics on many different topics. From the *American Almanac* he saved an entry on "Produce of Copy-Right," which breaks down the earnings of different English authors from their copyright.[105] He also cut out an entry on "International Copyright," which offers an abstract of the British *Act for securing to Authors, in certain Cases, the Benefit of International Copyright*, passed on July 31, 1838.[106] The act declared it lawful to secure to authors the sole liberty of printing and reprinting works in Great Britain and Ireland, even if they had previously been published in foreign countries – as long as said foreign countries also grant protection to British works. Copyright legislation was avidly discussed in Great Britain at the time; Thomas Talfourd reintroduced his international copyright bill to Parliament in 1841 and Lieber followed the debates. Another clipping from *Galignani's Messenger* reports on the proceedings of the British House of Commons on February 5, 1841, including a summary of the abovementioned exchange between Thomas Noon Talfourd and Thomas Babington Macauly.[107] Three other clippings detail the developments in Britain: One article without source and an article from *Galignani's Messenger* report on the

---

104 Friedemann Kawohl, "Commentary on the Bilateral Treaty between Austria and Sardinia (1840)" in *Primary Sources on Copyright (1450–1900)*, ed. Lionel Bently and Martin Kretschmer (Copyrighthistory.org, 2008); Full title: *Gesetz zum Schutze des literarischen und artistischen Eigenthumes gegen unbefugte Veröffentlichung, Nachdruck und Nachbildung*. Available at: Austrian Copyright Act (1846), Primary Sources on Copyright (1450–1900), ed. L. Bently and and M. Kretschmer, https://www.copyrighthistory.org/cam/tools/request/showRecord.php?id=record_d_1846b. Accessed 16 April 2024.

105 "Produce of Copy-Right." *The American Almanac and Repository of Useful Knowledge, For the Year 1840*, ed. David H. Williams (Boston: Charles C. Little and James Brown, 1840), 100–102.

106 "International Copyright." *The American Almanac and Repository of Useful Knowledge, For the Year 1840*, David H. Williams, Boston, Massachusetts, 1840, p. 102. Full title of the act: International Copyright Act, London (1838), Primary Sources on Copyright (1450–1900), ed. L. Bently and and M. Kretschmer, https://www.copyrighthistory.org/cam/tools/request/showRecord.php?id=record_uk_1838. Accessed 16 April 2024.

107 *Galignani's Messenger*. House of Commons, Feb. 5. No date. Francis Lieber papers. mssLI. Box 92, no. 14. LI475. The Huntington. San Marino, CA. See also: Thomas Babington Macaulay, "Copyright. A Speech. Delivered in the House of Commons on the 5th of

debates about the copyright bill on April 6, 1842; an article from *The Spectator* also details the continued debates between Talfourd and Macauly.[108] An article from *The Mercury* includes a transcript of Charles Dickens' letter to the American people, advocating for an international copyright treaty between the US and Great Britain (see also chapter 5.3).[109] Dickens writes that "the question of International Copyright can only be viewed by enlightened Americans – first, as affecting the interests of American authors – secondly, as influencing those of the American public." Lieber certainly considered himself an "enlightened American" and approved of Dickens' call for an international copyright – even if Dickens did not frame it as a matter of property rights. An article titled "The Rights of Inventors" from *The Spectator* of November 16, 1850, concludes Lieber's collection of articles on British copyright law.[110]

This small collection of newspaper articles might have been much more extensive. Considering that all articles are loose leaf sheets, more may have easily been lost in Lieber's vast compilation. Nevertheless, they account for Lieber's avid interest in international copyright legislation in other countries. This collection corroborates the thesis that Lieber took inspiration from several other countries, especially from Great Britain, the German states including Austria, and France. He considered carefully and eventually incorporated these transnational influences into his own understanding of literary property and international copyright legislation. Likely, the examples from other countries also shaped his own draft for a new international copyright. While Lieber clearly and repeatedly expressed his criticism of the lack of international copyright legislation in the entries of the *Encyclopædia Americana,* in *On International Copyright,* and in *Essays On Property and Labor,* in his draft for a new international copyright he condenses his critique into proactive suggestions. It is thus a highly valuable source which showcases both Lieber's critique and his suggestions for a solution. In the draft, Lieber also applies his moral considerations to actual legislation, namely section 8 of the US constitution.[111]

February 1841." *The Miscellaneous Writings and Speeches of Lord Macauly,* (London, New York: Longmans, Green, and Co, 1889), 609–618

108 Francis Lieber papers. mssLI. Box 92, no. 14. LI475. The Huntington. San Marino, CA.

109 Dickens, Charles. *To the American People,* in *The Mercury*. May 17, 1842. Francis Lieber papers. mssLI. Box 92, no. 14. LI475. The Huntington. San Marino, CA.

110 "The Rights of Inventors." November 16, 1850. Francis Lieber papers. mssLI. Box 92, no. 14. LI475. The Huntington. San Marino, CA.

111 See for example: "Constitution of the United States." *United States Senate,* Secretary of the Senate, 21 Jan. 2020, www.senate.gov/civics/constitution_item/constitution.htm. Accessed 8 Feb. 2023.

Lieber titles the piece "A Draught of a new copyright law for the United States" (for a full transcript of Lieber's draft, see Appendix).[112] The handwritten document includes several additions and corrections, emphasizing its nature as a draft rather than a finalized article ready for distribution. The draft begins with the popular quote from article 1, section 8 of the US Constitution, which grants Congress the power "To promote the Progress of Science and useful Arts, by securing for limited Times to Authors and Inventors the exclusive Right to their respective Writings and Discoveries." Following this provision, the *Copyright Act of 1790* was passed. This act is based in large parts on the British 1710 *Statute of Anne*, as Oren asserts in his "Commentary on the Copyright Act 1790."[113] The drafters of the 1790 act took paragraphs verbatim from the *Statute of Anne*, either directly from the statute's text or from original states' statutes citing the *Statute of Anne* (see chapter 3.1.1 and 3.1.2). An Anglo-American authorship-based copyright is the result. But Lieber dissociates himself from this Anglo-American copyright framework: By quoting the constitutional provision, which enables Congress to protect works of science and useful art for a limited time period, rather than the resultant *Copyright Act of 1790* Lieber distances himself from the 1790 act. He indicates that he does not wish to amend the 1790 act; instead, he offers an alternative, which derives its authority from the same constitutional clause. Lieber uses the *Prussian Law of Copyright of 1837* as a template, introducing continental-European understandings of authors' rights to the US (see chapter 3.2.2). Throughout his draft, Lieber closely follows his own translation of the *Prussian Law of Copyright of 1837*, published in *The Law Reporter* in 1839, occasionally directly quoting it. Periodically, Lieber expands the Prussian template to implement even stricter protection of authors' rights.

Lieber opens his draft by stating that

> The author of a literary work or composition, his heirs or assignees, or those who derive their authority *in writing* of reprinting such work or composition already published, or of causing it to be multiplied in any mechanical way or by representing it on the stage from him or them, or of causing it to be multiplied

112 Lieber, Francis. A draught of a new copyright law for the United States. Approx. 1840–1850. Francis Lieber papers. mssLI. Box 92, no. 14. LI475. The Huntington. San Marino, CA. The word "draught" means "draft."

113 Oren Bracha "Commentary on the Copyright Act 1790" in *Primary Sources on Copyright (1450–1900)*, ed. Lionel Bently and Martin Kretschmer (Copyrighthistory.org, 2008).

in any mechanical way or by representing it on the stage from him or them, are the only persons lawfully entitled of doing so.[114]

He grants authors or their heirs or assignees the exclusive right to print or multiply their literary work. Anyone who reprints a work must have the author's permission in writing. This need for written permission is emphasized several times throughout the draft, as Lieber values the protection of authors' rights highly. Significantly, he does not speak of a property right to literature, as he does in his other works, but rather of an exclusive copyright. He declares any violation of this exclusive copyright through reprinting without permission "unlawful and a punishable offence."[115] It is noteworthy that Lieber does not adopt the term "piratical reprinting" used in his translation of the *Prussian Law of Copyright*. Evidently, he mitigates his rhetoric in this text because of its intended purpose as a legal text. This is likely also the reason Lieber chose to omit the explicit framing of literature as property in this text – he aimed to appeal to a large audience and was therefore willing to compromise. While the concept of literary property could be found in the states' statutes and later in the Ingersoll bill (see chapter 6.3), it was not commonly accepted. To mobilize broad support for his goal of comprehensive protection of authors, Lieber merely implied the framing of literature as property. Mostly he presented a more accessible narrative of copyright and focused on the issue of international copyright protection, rather than literary property.

In his draft, Lieber extends protection against nonconsensual reprinting or performance to all forms of written works, including stage plays, manuscripts, letters, sermons, lectures, orations, discourses, and abridgements. He follows §3 of the *Prussian Law of Copyright* by pointing out that the lawful possession of a manuscript does not entitle the owner to publish the manuscript or to perform the play – owning a manuscript does not mean owning the content of the manuscript, the literary work itself.[116] The buyer merely owns the right to the physical object, not to the work it is the result of. The author retains the

114 Lieber, Francis. A Draught of a new copyright law for the United States. Approx. 1840–1850. Francis Lieber papers. mssLI. Box 92, no. 14. LI475. The Huntington. San Marino, CA. Here, Lieber echoes section I. of his translation of the *Prussian Law of Copyright.*

115 Lieber, Francis. A Draught of a new copyright law for the United States. Approx. 1840–1850. Francis Lieber papers. mssLI. Box 92, no. 14. LI475. The Huntington. San Marino, CA. Here, Lieber echoes section II. of his translation of the *Prussian Law of Copyright.*

116 All references follow the version of the Prussian Law of Copyright published in the official collection of law texts from 1837, see "Gesetz zum Schutze des Eigenthums an Werken der Wissenschaft und Kunst gegen Nachdruck und Nachbildung. Vom 11. Juni

exclusive right to copy, print, and publish his work, even after selling the physical manuscript.[117] While he does not spell it out explicitly, Lieber frames authors' rights as extensive property rights rather than as exclusive copyrights. Thus, he actually adheres to the ideas presented in his other works, though not categorically. Lieber presents certain exceptions to these property rights: It remains lawful to publish "speeches delivered in any official capacity, or before political meetings [...] and [...] all official documents, unless their publication be especially prohibited, and of reports of general interest, and not strictly scientific." Evidently, he privileges public interest and political participation over the rights of the authors of such speeches. Likely he also did not believe that anyone should financially profit from the sale of political speeches. Reprinting newspaper articles is also lawful according to Lieber's draft, to promote public interest and to quickly distribute important news. To quote single passages verbally or to include essays and poems in "critical and literary-historical works, or in collections for the use of schools" is also lawful for educational and scientific purposes.

To translate a published work is lawful, unless the work was originally published in several languages, including the language of the new translation. In that case, publishing another translation would be illegal. Lieber also states that it is "not lawful to publish an English translation of a work, issued by its author in a dead language [...] nor is it lawful to publish an unauthorized translation in a dead language, of a work or manuscript written in a living one." These provisions have largely been adopted from §4, section 3a. and 3b. of the *Prussian Law of Copyright*. Lieber does not explain why the translation of a work into a different language should be legal, while the translation of a work into a dead language or vice versa should be illegal. Julius Eduard Hitzig's commentary on the *Prussian Law of Copyright* offers a possible explanation: A translation is not usually a reprint of a work but rather a new work. The translator has a literary property in the translation, not the work itself. Therefore, multiple translations into the same language would be legal – they would be considered different works, unless the second translator plagiarizes the first. Hitzig argues that a translation of a work usually targets a different national audience and therefore rarely competes directly with the original work (*Preußisches Gesetz*, 57–58). If a work was initially published in a dead language, a German translation published in the German states would target

1837." *Gesetz-Sammlung für die königlichen preußischen Staaten 1837*, (Berlin: Gesetz-Sammlungs-Debits- und Zeitungs-Kontoir, 1838), 165–171.

117 Lieber grants an exception, if the manuscript is older than a hundred years or if no known author exists.

the same market as the original and should be considered a reprint and thus be made illegal, Hitzig explains.[118] Additionally, an author might have published a work in a dead language to restrict access to the work to a smaller circle of readers. The law should thus protect the author's wishes, Hitzig states. It is likely that Lieber adopted these provisions in his draft because protecting an author's control over their work was important to Lieber.[119]

In a similar vein, Lieber emphasizes that "[i]t is not necessary to state in any part of a publication, that the copyright has been secured, or to quote this present Act, or any other words for that purpose, in order to secure for the said publication all the rights acknowledged and granted by this Act." Lieber never agreed with conditional copyright in the US. In his understanding, copyright protection must be granted automatically and to all works. To require the author to undertake considerable efforts and costs to secure the copyright to their works seemed unfair to Lieber and he had previously criticized these requirements implemented by the 1802 amendment to the *Copyright Act of 1790* (see chapter 6.1).[120] In his draft Lieber reversed the conditions: Authors

---

118 "Dead language" here mostly refers to Latin and ancient Greek.

119 The fact that translations were not conceptualized as a reprint but rather as a new work, a work of authorial property – "schriftstellerisches Eigenthum," as Hitzig claims (*Preußisches Gesetz* 57) – is interesting to note. Lieber himself clearly agreed: In 1832 and 1833, Lieber translated Alexis de Tocqueville's and Gustave de Beaumont's treatise on the penitentiary system in the United States into English. Lieber had met de Tocqueville and de Beaumont during their stay in the US and had afterwards asked both to have their work translated into English. De Toqceville and Beaumont asked Lieber to write the translation and Lieber eagerly agreed. He not only translated the work but changed its content, writing in a preface to the work that "A few of the statements of the authors I have thought to be erroneous, and I have not omitted to add in a note what I hold to be correct" (cited in Schnurmann, *Brücken*, 355). As Claudia Schnurmann also points out, Lieber considered the translation his own original work, rather than a mere act of copying. Previously, translation had often been framed as undemanding work performed by women within one's own family. Lieber understood the act of translation as an act of creation, stating in a letter to Mittermaier that he had added many comments and references to other works during translation. He also promised to send Mittermaier a copy of "my work" or "my labor" ("meiner Arbeit")," claiming ownership of the translation (cited after Schnurmann, *Brücken*, 355–356). Lieber's complete name is printed prominently on the title page of the work, emphasized through design elements, while the first names of de Tocqueville and de Beaumont are shortened to one initial (Schnurmann, *Brücken*, 356). The translation was published as: Lieber, Francis. *On the Penitentiary System in the United States and its Application in France; with an Appendix on Penal Colonies, and also Statistical Notes. By G. De Beaumont and A. De Tocqueville, Councellors in the Royal Court of Paris, and members of the Historical Society of Pennsylvania. Translated from the French, with an introduction, notes and addition by Francis Lieber.* Philadelphia 1833.

120 1802 Amendment (1802), Primary Sources on Copyright (1450–1900), ed. L. Bently and and M. Kretschmer, www.copyrighthistory.org. 23 February 23, 2023.

may print "Copyright waived" on a work's title or back page if they do not claim an exclusive copyright. This reversal grants the author control over the copyright rather than predicating the copyright on certain conditions and making the author dependent on the approval of the government. Following Lieber's unconditional copyright law even anonymous authors retain copyright. Consequently, the copyright afforded by Lieber's draft is automatically granted to the author and lasts for a lifetime, similarly to the provisions in §5 of the *Prussian Law of Copyright*. Thus, the copyright an author enjoys is akin to a property right in many – but not all – aspects: While the right is unconditional, lifelong, and can be transmitted to heirs and successors, they can only enjoy that protection for "thirty successive years [...] from the day of his death, provided always that the time of the author's life after the publication of his work, and the thirty years, after his death, be not less than sixty years." The assertion that the copyright must always be granted for at least sixty years goes beyond even the period secured by §6 of the *Prussian Law of Copyright*. In the US the original *Copyright Act of 1790* had been amended in 1831 and now granted an exclusive copyright to the author for twenty-eight years; a surviving author or his widow or children could renew the copyright for fourteen additional years.[121] Lieber thus advocated for a significantly longer period of copyright protection in his draft. He effectively extended the term even more by stating that "[e]very lawful new edition of a work, issued within the time during which the preceding edition was entitled to protection, according to the present Act, is considered [...] a new work and entitled to all its protection." This provision does not come from the *Prussian Law of Copyright* and goes well beyond the protections granted by the Prussian template.[122]

Unlike US copyright law, which refers to maps and charts along with – and even before – books, Lieber mentions maps and charts as an afterthought. They enjoy similar protection to written works but "the publication of copies on a reduced or enlarged scale shall be lawful," Lieber writes. It becomes apparent that Lieber is less interested in and experienced with the protection of other artistic works: While he mentions engravings, woodcuts, and sculptures, they are dealt with quickly. The *Prussian Law of Copyright* goes into

121 Copyright Act, Washington D.C. (1831), Primary Sources on Copyright (1450–1900), ed. L. Bently and and M. Kretschmer, www.copyrighthistory.org. Accessed 23 February 2023.

122 Copyright can be granted to institutions, such as academies, universities, learned and lawful societies but for a different amount of time, which Lieber does not specify in his draft. In the Prussian template institutions are entitled to copyright protection for thirty years. For works published in several volumes, such as lexicons, the period of protection is counted starting with completion of the series. For works published continuously, the period is counted for each separate volume.

more detail concerning drawings, works of fine art, and plastics, but Lieber disregards these parts of his template, demonstrating again that his interest lies in written works. Regarding musical compositions, Lieber simply inserts a cutout from section XIX. and XX. of his own translation of the *Prussian Law of Copyright*. He also seems out of his depth once penalties and fines are discussed; he copies several columns (sections X.–XVII.) from his translation of the *Prussian Law of Copyright* rather than drafting original penalties. This highlights two things: Firstly, the *Prussian Law of Copyright* was clearly Lieber's greatest inspiration for his own draft; secondly, Lieber cared more about the moral questions of reprinting than the actual legal consequences. He liked to discuss what was right and ethical or wrong and piratical; he did not like to focus on legal processes or to determine punishments. Lieber was not a lawyer and had no experience drafting laws; he was interested in jurisprudence, in the philosophical examination of the issue.

On the last pages of his draft, Lieber returns to the issues most important to him. He writes that "[t]he present Act extends the same protection to works which have first been published in foreign states, provided their respective governments grant all the rights secured by them for works first published there, likewise to works first published in the U. States." This short sentence implements the international copyright Lieber had demanded for years. Interestingly, he suggests a reciprocal copyright, only granted to authors in those states that grant protection to US authors. This contradicts Lieber's earlier calls for an international copyright for *all* authors, as expressed in his *Encyclopædia Americana* entries and in *On International Copyright* (see chapters 4.2, 4.3 and 6.1). While he once stated that only "[b]arbarous or degenerate nations" allow acts like "literary piracy" and consequently demanded that the US decidedly protect the production of all foreign authors, that protection is contingent on reciprocity in his draft. But Lieber makes explicit two other aspects he values greatly: Copyright protection is granted to all US residents, not just to citizens. While this point is not made in the Prussian template, it is, in fact, already included in the *Copyright Act of 1790*. Lieber also emphasizes that authors can transfer the right of publication and distribution of their works for a limited space or time, allowing authors to publish editions of the same work through different publishers. In his last sentence Lieber states that it is not permitted to assume the name of a living author when publishing a composition, leaving the actual punishment blank.

While Lieber evidently used the *Prussian Copyright Act of 1837* as a template, he intended for his draft of a new international copyright to be an alternative to the US *Copyright Act of 1790* and the following amendments. Consequently, Lieber's draft differs significantly from the existing US copyright.

It introduces a hybrid model, combining continental-European – especially Prussian – ideas of strong authors' rights with the existing Anglo-American model of exclusive authorship-based copyright. He implements a reciprocal copyright for foreign authors, a provision not yet available in the US, as well as non-conditional copyright for all US authors. The draft grants foreign authors copyright if they are citizens of a nation which grants copyright to authors from the US. Notably, Lieber avoids calling an author's right to a written work a property right in this draft. Instead, he adheres to the copyright model present in the US, but combines it with extensive authors' rights, including lifelong copyright protection, transmissibility, free power of disposition, and a clear distinction between the ownership of the physical object, the manuscript, and the intellectual work. Considering Lieber's explicit calls for comprehensive and perpetual property-based copyright in his other works, his draft appears as a compromise intended to amend but not completely change existing copyright regulation. Likely, the transformation of his moral claims into legislation is responsible for this mitigation of demands – moral demands did not translate quite as forcefully into legal provisions.

The draft is not mentioned in Lieber's correspondence, presumably because he did not share this draft with his usual contacts. This suggests that Lieber realized that *writing laws* was not his area of expertise. He was skilled in other areas and had an aptitude for curating appealing narratives and writing passionate, even moralizing speeches. He had the ability to convince people of his own point of view, to set idealistic goals and to lay out visions of a better future. At heart, Lieber was an educator. By painting a picture of continued social progress and "civilization," Lieber appealed to the ideas people had about themselves and about the society they wished to be part of, with the goal to educate them and mobilize them for his cause. He published his works to communicate his own understanding of an ideal society and the rights and duties that come with citizenship. The unpublished draft for a new copyright law for the United States appears to be a personal exercise, a reflection on current legislation, necessary changes, and a vision for a better future. While Lieber evidently did not feel that he could educate his fellow citizens through a legal draft, he dedicated much time and labor to his new work, *On Civil Liberty and Self-Government*, which would become his most influential monograph.[123]

---

123 Lieber's *Code 100* is likely his most influential work but *On Civil Liberty and Self-Government* is his most influential and well-received monograph.

CHAPTER 7

The 1850s and Beyond: Lieber's later Advocacy

In 1848, current events shifted Lieber's focus towards Europe and the incipient German revolutionary movement occupied his mind. Claudia Schnurmann argues that Lieber initially rejected the earliest revolutionary efforts in France and Italy as communist acts doomed to fail. In a letter to Henry Wadsworth Longfellow, Lieber lamented that "people always will consider a kingless government on that account alone, a republic."[1] Schnurmann attributes Lieber's early criticism of the revolution in Europe to a general distrust of France and of democratic movements without proper leadership and constitutional protection. As soon as the revolutionary spirit spread to the German Confederation, Lieber was no longer skeptical. A sense of agitation rippled through the German community in the US and Lieber was eager to travel to the German states to participate in the revolution. Schnurmann argues that Lieber was convinced he could bring about actual change in his home country if he were only there in person, and that he had high hopes for a possible future in a "new" Germany.[2] As a German who had left his home country due to political persecution, he desired to see things finally change (see chapter 4). He felt he needed to be on the ground in the German states to help dismantle the traditional autocratic government and establish Republican institutions.

When Lieber traveled across the Atlantic to Europe in June 1848, some US newspapers reported on his journey. His friends and other Germans in the US expected him to "establish liberal institutions" in Europe.[3] However, once Lieber arrived in the German states, he was bitterly disappointed to find that the members of the national assembly in Frankfurt had by no means fully committed to the Republican principles he valued so much. He positioned himself as an educator on the parliamentarian and republican principles of US political praxis, a stance Claudia Schnurmann characterizes as paternalistic. While Lieber was well connected in the German states, no one had been eagerly awaiting his input and no job opportunities revealed themselves.[4] The prevalent lack of experience with republican principles and "of all political culture [in the German states]," as Lieber wrote to his wife Mathilde,

1 Cited in Schnurmann, *Brücken*, 395.
2 Schnurmann, *Brücken*, 395–397.
3 Cited in Schnurmann, *Brücken*, 403.
4 Schnurmann, *Brücken*, 404–405.

 | HTTPS://DOI.ORG/10.1515/9783112239407-007

prompted the realization that he had become "considerably un-germanized" and he longed to be back in America to which "belongs [...] my soul."[5] His last hopes for a diplomatic position as minister of the German states to the US were finally disappointed in the fall of 1848 and Lieber returned to the US, even before the revolution failed with the dissolution of the Frankfurt National Assembly in 1849.[6]

Disappointed by the outcome of the revolution in the German states, Lieber focused on the development and protection of liberty in his work *Civil Liberty and Self-Government*.[7] The monograph was published in two extensive volumes in 1853 and became arguably his most popular work. It was well-received in the field of political science and used as a textbook in high schools and colleges. Even Yale College adopted the work as a textbook for students as a friend points out in a letter to Lieber.[8] In "Lieber's Place in History," Peter Becker argues that *Civil Liberty and Self-Government* was Lieber's only financial success.[9] Lieber worked on this book for a long time, accumulating several folders of notes for the first and second edition, which are now preserved in the archives of The Huntington.[10] Also preserved is an entire box of reviews of *Civil Liberty and Self-Government*, which Lieber carefully cut out and collected.[11] He also circulated the work among his friends in the US. Henry Wadsworth Longfellow (1807–1882) praised the work in a letter to Lieber, writing "[the book] seems to me admirable, full of ripeness and wisdom, very strong and very suggesting. This is a lore in which you very well know, I am not learned; but your book stirs me and makes me think,

---

5 Cited in Schnurmann, *Brücken*, 406.

6 Schnurmann, *Brücken*, 410–412.

7 Francis Lieber, *On Civil Liberty and Self-Government. Vol. I.* (Philadelphia: Lippincott, Grambo and Co., 1853). Hereafter abbrieviated as *Civil Liberty I*. Francis Lieber, *On Civil Liberty and Self-Government. Vol. II.* (Philadelphia: Lippincott, Grambo and Co., 1853). Hereafter abbreviated as *Civil Liberty II*.

8 Tyler, Samuel to Francis Lieber. April 30, 1856. Francis Lieber papers. SCL-MS-0324. ALS 5767. Manuscript Division, South Caroliniana Library. Columbia, SC. Yale College is now Yale University. This letter is a copy of the original.

9 Becker, "Prologue," 5.

10 Francis Lieber. On Civil Liberty and Self-Government: Notes and Clippings. 1837–1858. Francis Lieber papers. mssLI. Box 75, no. 10. Box 76, no. 1. Box 76, no. 2. Box 76, no. 3. Box 76, no. 4. LI50. The Huntington. San Marino, CA.

11 Civil Liberty: Reviews only. 1857–1859. Francis Lieber papers. mssLI. Box 76, no. 5. LI50. The Huntington. San Marino, CA.

and puts a new spoke [sic] into my brain."[12] Lieber also sent the work to friends in Europe, clearly with the intention to make it known there.

In the book Lieber discusses European institutions and understandings of liberty, and references current events in Europe. Lieber asked Alexis de Tocqueville (1805–1859), whom he quotes several times in the work, to present the book to "the institute," meaning the *Institut de France* – but only if his views should be welcome there.[13] Apparently, Lieber was unsure whether his discussion of "Gallican liberty" in opposition to "Anglican liberty" would be well received in France. Lieber also wrote to Mittermaier in 1854 that he aimed to have this work translated into German but had "no hope that any censorship would permit it to pass."[14] Mittermaier initially declined to write a translation of the work but offered to write "a detailed account" and publish it in his own periodical.[15] Later he changed his mind and translated the entire second edition into German. Lieber was elated and sent Mittermaier a cheerful letter in 1860, stating that he had found two copies of Mittermaier's translation in a bookstore and that he was "grateful for the pleasure of seeing my work translated into my own language."[16]

---

12 Longfellow, Henry. Letter to Francis Lieber. June 1, 1854. Francis Lieber papers. SCL-MS-0324. ALS 5767. Manuscripts Division, South Caroliniana Library. Columbia, SC. This letter is a copy of the original.

13 Lieber, Francis. Letter to Alexis de Tocqueville. March 12, 1854. Francis Lieber papers. mssLI. Box 105, no. 1. FAC 464, no. 2. The Huntington. San Marino, CA.

14 Lieber, Francis. Letter to C. J. A. Mittermaier. March 10, 1854. Francis Lieber papers. mssLI. Box 39, no. 50. The Huntington. San Marino, CA. Lieber likely tried to profit from Mittermaier's reputation by having the popular jurist translate his work, rather than translating it himself.

15 Mittermaier, C. J. A. Letter to Francis Lieber. February 8, 1854. Francis Lieber papers. SCL-MS-0324. ALS 5767. Manuscripts Division, South Caroliniana Library. Columbia, SC. This letter is a translation of the original. Mittermaier published his article "Freiheit und Selbstregierung in England und Nordamerika" in *Kritische Zeitschrift für Rechtswissenschaft und Gesetzgebung des Auslandes*, 26 (1854). Mittermaier was one of the editors of the journal, which focused on legal studies and legislation abroad.

16 Lieber, Francis. Letter to C. J. A. Mittermaier. December 29, 1860. Francis Lieber papers. mssLI. Box 39, no. 57. The Huntington. San Marino, CA. This letter is a copy of the original. The translation was published as *Ueber Bürgerliche Freiheit und Selbstverwaltung von Dr. Franz Lieber*. (Heidelberg: Akademische Verlagshandlung von J. C. B. Mohr, 1860).

7.1 *Civil Liberty and Self-Government*, 1853

The experiences during his recent journey to Europe and his disappointment about the failed revolution in Germany inspired Lieber to lay down his understanding of the importance of civil liberty and self-government in writing. He was also prompted by the secession efforts in the US, which he rejected outright, and by Napoleon III.'s victory in the elections in France.[17] In *Civil Liberty and Self-Government,* Lieber examines the origins and features of liberty within a civil society and how to implement and protect liberty in a federal system. Here, Lieber again assumes his now well-established role as an educator on the rights and duties of the citizens of a republic. He gives a historiographic account of the development of liberty as a prerequisite of a proper state, maintained by civil institutions and self-governance through the people. The protection of private property is among the guarantees of civil liberty Lieber discusses in this work.

Civil Liberty and Self-Government was Lieber's urgent appeal to the citizens of the US, in which he calls on them not to take their liberties for granted and instead to actively protect them. "[Y]our duties are proportionate to the blessings you are enjoying," he writes, "[t]he period we live in, our country's position and youth, our abundance of land, our descent, and our freedom – all call upon us, and warn us" (*Civil Liberty I*, VIII–IX). Civil liberty is difficult to define, Lieber points out, but it can be described as

> a high degree of mutually guaranteed protection against interference with the interests and rights, held dear and important by large classes of civilized men or by all the members of a state, together with an effectual share in the making and administration of the laws as the best apparatus to secure that protection, and constituting the most dignified government of men who are conscious of their rights and of the destiny of liberty. (*Civil Liberty I*, 34)

Everyone desires freedom of action but civil liberty recognizes that "we should grant the same civil liberty to others which we claim for ourselves" and that liberty must necessarily be relative and limited (*Civil Liberty I*, 35, 48). In order to establish civil liberty, the government must protect its citizens against interference wherever necessary. This becomes possible through a number of guarantees and checks, ensuring comprehensive individual rights and making self-government possible (*Civil Liberty I*, 320). Self-government, then, is "[t]he highest ethical and social production of which man, with his insepara-

17 Becker, "Prologue," 5.

ble moral, jural, aesthetic and religious attributes is capable" (*Civil Liberty I*, 36). It consists of

> the independence of the whole political society, in a national representative government and local-self-government, which implies that even general laws and impulses are carried out and realized, as far as possible, by citizens who, by receiving an office, be it by election or appointment, essentially remain citizens, and do not become members of a hierarchy of placement [...] that there be an organism to elaborate and ascertain public opinion, and that, when known, it shall pass into law, and, plainly, rule the rulers; that government interfere as an exception, and not as a rule; and that, on the other hand, self-government neither means self-absolutism, nor absence of rule, but that, on the contrary, liberty requires true government. (*Civil Liberty I*, 320–322)

The protection of individual property is a core principle of civil liberty and the government must therefore guarantee "unrestrained action in producing and exchanging, the prohibition of all unfair monopolies, commercial freedom, and [...] that no property shall be taken except in the course of law" (*Civil Liberty I*, 122). While the government must interfere only when absolutely necessary, Lieber designates property an exception. Civil liberty consists of "guarantees (and corresponding checks) of those rights which experience has proved to be most exposed to interference, and which men hold dearest and most important" (*Civil Liberty I*, 54). Property is one value both central to the human experience and prone to interference, as Lieber criticized at length in his past works. Over a decade had now passed since Lieber published *On International Copyright* in 1840 and copyright protection was still limited to US citizens or residents. Literature was not protected as a property either, as Lieber had repeatedly demanded. These issues had still not been put on the political agenda and his frustration is reflected in this work:

> Every single subject here mentioned, monopolies, freedom of trading, freedom of home production, freedom of exchange, possession of property, taxation and confiscation – each one has a long history, full of struggles against error and government interference, running through many centuries and even a thousand years [...] Each shows the continued course of gradually, though very slowly, expanding freedom. Nor has this history of development reached its close. (*Civil Liberty I*, 126)

Lieber positions property and its protection as a core value of civil liberty. This position corresponds to his arguments on literary property expressed in his former works: He understands the lack of comprehensive protection of literary property as a failure on part of the government, which does not protect the liberties of its citizens and of all authors, even though their works in turn promote progress and constitute an important part of national identity. While discussions of property are not as prominent in this treatise as they were in Lieber's former works, the framing of property as a core principle of civil liberty and self-government emphasizes that Lieber did not engage with the issues of copyright and literary property protection for financial gain or his personal success as an author. The protection of literature as property is, to him, deeply interwoven with political values and aspirations. He positions property as a pillar of each functioning state and as a core right of every citizen. Only if all forms of property, including literature, are protected, can a citizen enjoy true liberty. When considered within the context of *Civil Liberty and Self-Government*, Lieber's discussion of the protection of literature as property goes beyond technical discussions of laws – it touches upon the very foundations of the US state and citizenship and informs his understanding of liberty and government.

7.1.1 Reception

Lieber, who was proud of his work, collected many reviews which now offer insight into the contemporary reception of *Civil Liberty and Self-Government* and Lieber's stance in US society.[18] The *Southern Literary Messenger* remarks on the fact that "the most elaborate and philosophical treatises upon our republican system, at least in our day, should have been the production of two men – not only of foreign birth, but of foreign political education – Lieber and De Tocqueville."[19] While this article highlights Lieber's foreignness, *De Bow's Review* explicitly positions Lieber as an American writer and states that "[t]he name of Francis Lieber stands out in bold relief among those of the greatest of American authors, and his works occupy the front rank among the standard literary productions of our country."[20] The *Saturday Gazette* even characterizes the work as thoroughly American, stating it is "the most

18 It is important to bear in mind that Lieber likely kept the favorable reviews and might have discarded less favorable ones. Therefore, this collection of reviews is by no means representative of all opinions on the work; it merely highlights encouraging and agreeable responses.

19 "Lieber's Civil Liberty and Self-Government," *Southern Literary Messenger*, 19.12 (1853): 713–721. http://quod.lib.umich.edu/m/moajrnl/acf2679.0019.012/717.

20 "Civil Liberty and Self-Government. By Francis Lieber, LL.D." *De Bow's Review and industrial Resources, Statistics, etc.*, xv (1853): 646–647.

thorough, most original, and most soundly American political treatise yet published."[21] The *Boston Daily Courier*, on the other hand, could not help but mention that

> Dr. Lieber has never learned to write easy and idiomatic English, though he often hits upon rich and significant expressions. His discussions and conclusions are those of a sound and practical English or American statesman and jurist, but they are frequently presented in those long and involved sentences in the midst of which the student of German is so often hopelessly bogged.[22]

In England the work was also well received, as showcased by a newspaper clipping Lieber kept: In a letter to the editor titled "What they think of Dr. Lieber in Old England" someone using the pseudonym "A Carolinian" points out that the English historian and jurist Edward S. Creasy positions Lieber as one of the "great political writers of the United States," alongside judges Kent and Story.[23] Lieber clearly improved his standing as a writer in the field of political science and cultivated a prominent position in US intellectual culture. James Farr claims that Lieber contributed greatly to the establishment of political science in the US with this work because his "analysis of politics was sustained, without much admixture of duties, ethics, or morals; that is, as a text, it had broken free of the formal mold of moral philosophy altogether. It was also secular, urbane, and cosmopolitan."[24] The protection of literature as transnational property was no longer at the forefront of Lieber's writing; nevertheless, as a central value it continued to be foundational for his thinking. Lieber's main concern, throughout all his works, is an idealistic one: He investigates how to create the perfect society with an optimal political system and appropriately aligned laws. Property as an institution and the protection of literature as property remained central to his outline of an ideal system for human flourishing and its importance as an issue of concern for Lieber can therefore not be overstated – even if not discussed in detail in each specific work, his notions on property, literary property and international copyright

---

21 Cited in Walker, John. *A Key to the Classical Pronunciation of Greek, Latin, and Scripture Proper Names* (Philadelphia: J. B. Lippincott & Co, 1857), 116.

22 "Dr. Lieber's New Book." *Boston Daily Courier*, January 13, 1854. Francis Lieber papers. mssLI. Box 86, no. 8. The Huntington. San Marino, CA.

23 A Carolinian. "What they think of Dr. Lieber in Old England." No date. Francis Lieber papers. mssLI. Box 86, no. 8. The Huntington. San Marino, CA. It is possible that Lieber himself sent this letter to the editor under a pseudonym.

24 Farr, "Moral Philosophy," 121.

appear repeatedly in other areas of his work and he continued his activism as an issue entrepreneur.

Also in 1853, Secretary of State Edward Everett (1794–1865) negotiated a treaty on international copyright with Great Britain. Thorval Solberg claims that the impetus for the negotiation of this treaty had originally come from five New York City publishing firms, among them G. P. Putnam & Co, vocal opponents of international copyright. These publishing firms reached out to Everett with a list of aspects they deemed relevant to the passage of an international copyright treaty, including registration of a work with a district court and manufacture of the work in the US.[25] The treaty outlined a reciprocal relationship between Great Britain and the US, providing that authors entitled to copyright in one country would be entitled to copyright in the other, on the same terms and for the same time period. Should a work be pirated in one country, the author would therefore be entitled to the same legal redress in both countries. Congress referred the treaty to the Committee on Foreign Relations under senator James Mason (1798–1871). Eventually, the Senate tabled the treaty and never reconsidered it. As Thorvald Solberg summarizes, opponents of international copyright presented a dozen petitions against Everett's proposed copyright treaty. Senator James Cooper (1810–1863) even sent a letter to publisher Henry C. Carey, asking Carey to weigh in on the matter of international copyright – Carey published his answer in the aforementioned pamphlet titled *Letters on International Copyright* (1853), which became very popular among opponents of international copyright at the time.[26] The copyright debate continued and while he focused on other issues, Lieber followed the Congressional proceedings closely while he lived in South Carolina.

7.2 Frame Bridges to Other Issues

While he worked at South Carolina College, Lieber felt he could not voice his disapproval of slavery without risking his job as well as his personal safety,[27]

25 Solberg, "International Copyright," 13.

26 Solberg, "International Copyright," 13.

27 Lieber did not publicly disavow slavery while he worked at South Carolina College. Actually, he had slaves working in his own household. He disclosed his dislike of slavery in many letters to friends in the North but was afraid to lose his professorship in South Carolina or risk his family's safety should he be too vocal in his criticism of slavery. One of his friends in particular, Charles Sumner, openly criticized Lieber for not disavowing slavery publicly and they did not speak for years following. Lieber's silence on (rather than open support of) the institution of slavery might have cost him the South Carolina

and only did so in letters to his friends in the North, whom he missed dearly.[28] Even after twelve years living in the South, Lieber still proclaimed: "How *verpfuscht* [messed up] my life has been and is!" (*Life and Letters*, 212). Nevertheless, Lieber produced some of his most prominent works during his twenty-one years in Columbia, SC. He cultivated his research in various areas, such as penology, property, international copyright, hermeneutics, and political ethics, through his correspondence with other scholars. Via letters he ordered books, newspapers, and articles from his friends in the North as well as in Europe, and frequently left Columbia for business trips to the North. Francis and Mathilde Lieber also raised three sons – their only daughter had died in 1833 – and one of them, Oscar, would grow up to love the South passionately.

In 1855, after years of dispute between Lieber and his colleagues as well as with the Board of Trustees at South Carolina College, Lieber resigned from his post. He felt the Board of Trustees had passed him over for the position as president of South Carolina College. Instead, they elected Charles F. McCay (1810–1889) whose capacities, according to Lieber, "were wholly unknown to the Trustees and who has been connected with our institution a short time only."[29] Lieber himself was "thoroughly known to the Trustees, and preferring an unknown person to me was, therefore, virtually saying to me: You shall not expect anything at our hands, do for the College what you may."[30] In 1856, he finally received an offer from Columbia College (today Columbia University) and moved to 48, East 34th Street, New York City on August 1, 1857 (*Life and Letters*, 293). Lieber was glad to be back in the North, though he was saddened by his son Oscar's decision to remain in the South.

College presidency in 1855 and he resigned his post a day after the trustee board's decision (Becker, "Prologue," 4–6).

28 Lieber missed his friends dearly, as demonstrated in this letter to Hillard: "[A]ll such remarks as yours only tell me again and again what, alas! I know but too well, that I live in barren loneliness. The regulative and corrective, which a man finds in that friendship which unites intelligence with sincere affection, is denied to me, who, nevertheless, would make so good a use of it [...]" (Lieber to G. S. Hillard, November 30, 1839, quoted in Lieber, *Life and Letters*, 142). It is largely thanks to Lieber's prolonged "exile" in the South that so many lengthy letters to his friends survived.

29 Lieber, Francis. Lieber's reasons for his resignation from the South Carolina College. December 1855. Francis Lieber papers. mssLI. Box 88, no. 15. LI144. The Huntington. San Marino, CA.

30 Lieber, Francis. Lieber's reasons for his resignation from the South Carolina College. December 1855. Francis Lieber papers. mssLI. Box 88, no. 15. LI144. The Huntington. San Marino, CA.

While the 1830s and 1840s were a period of isolated literary production for Lieber, the 1850s ushered in a period of change. He was unanimously elected as professor of history and political science and took up his duties at Columbia College in September 1857 (*Life and Letters*, 294). His relocation constituted a caesura in his intellectual activities and production. He settled into his role as a pioneer in the field of political science, having requested that title for himself – Columbia College had offered him the professorship for history and political economy but Lieber requested a title change (*Life and Letters*, 295). He had also been awarded the honorary degree of doctor of law by Harvard University, reinforcing his stance as an authority on the study of law.[31] Lieber remained interested in the political and social proceedings in the German states, but continued his efforts to be recognized as an expert on US political economy and law. Claudia Schnurmann claims that he increasingly focused on his role as college professor, father, relative and friend, looking for close connections with his fellow countrymen – especially in confrontation with increasing efforts for secession in the South.[32] Nevertheless, archival sources highlight that he continued to be an issue entrepreneur for literary property and international copyright. He increasingly built frame bridges with other issues to convey his narrative to his contacts, legislators, and the public. The most prominent issues he referred to in connection with literary property and international copyright were slavery, book tariffs, free trade, and international law and cooperation.

7.2.1 Slavery, Property, and Copyright

Lieber remained preoccupied with the subject area of literary property, copyright, and the book trade, as evidenced by a speech he wrote for the Complimentary Fruit Festival at the New York Crystal Palace in 1855, hosted by the *New York Book Publishers' Association to Authors and Booksellers*.[33] Lieber saved a printed version of this speech, published in the *American Publishers' Circular and Literary Gazette*, in his personal documents.[34] The *New York Publishers' Association* invited Lieber but he could not attend personally. In

---

31 Sparks, Jared. Letter to Francis Lieber. October 4, 1850. Francis Lieber papers. OCLC 713642823. MS 5767. Manuscripts Division, South Caroliniana Library. Columbia, SC.

32 Schnurmann, *Brücken*, 445.

33 Lieber, Francis. "Complimentary Fruit Festival of the New York Book Publishers' Association to Authors and Booksellers, at the Crystal Palace, September 27, 1855." Francis Lieber papers. mssLI. Box 108, no. 14. The Huntington. San Marino, CA.

34 Lieber, Francis. "Speech Written for the Complimentary Fruit Festival." *American Publishers' Circular and Literary Gazette*, I, no. V, 29 Sept. 1855, p. 76.

his printed speech he expresses his appreciation for the festival that provided "an opportunity of closer contact to all engaged in the great economy of literature." He calls for increased "sympathy and cordial contact among the laborers" in the "vineyards, and fields, and gardens, and copses [sic], and prairies of literature." He speaks in favor of a division of labor, not a division of laborers. The "Law and Literature" of nations, he writes, are "[t]he greatest monuments that noble nations can erect in honor of themselves" and he welcomes any measure in service of the advancement of literature. As Lieber did in his previous works – which were likely the reason he was invited to speak at the Fruit Festival – he intertwines law, literature, and politics in his speech. He highlights the central role authors play in the progress of civilization and encourages the comprehensive protection and promotion of a national literature. Lieber references the diverse selection of fruits present at the festival and calls for a national literature just as diverse. This is not without reason – in the last paragraph of his speech Lieber transitions into a call for national unity despite differences, prompted by the simmering tensions between the free and the slave-holding states.[35]

The discussions surrounding slavery in the United States concerned Lieber greatly during the 1850s and 1860s. His interest in literature as a form of property and the author as proprietor was inextricably linked with the discourse regarding slavery – the forced propertization of humans. Because they were denied legal personhood, enslaved authors in the US could not claim literary property in their work. This posed a challenge to Lieber's stance that all authors should have perpetual and unlimited property rights in their written works. Lieber does not address this tension in his works on literary property, likely purposefully avoiding the subject. Some authors addressed the issue of slavery and property ownership in their contemporary works, most prominently Harriet Beecher Stowe in *Uncle Tom's Cabin*.[36]

---

35 A year earlier, in 1854, Congress had passed the Kansas-Nebraska Act, which determined that in new territories popular vote should determine whether slavery would be allowed. This act prompted political conflicts in Kansas and Missouri and culminated in a period of violent clashes between anti- and pro-slavery advocates from 1855 to 1861, often referred to as "Bleeding Kansas." See for example Watts, Dale. "How Bloody was Bleeding Kansas? Political Killings in Kansas Territory, 1854–1861." *Kansas History*, 18.2 (Summer 1995): 116–129.

36 In his work on race, copyright, and possessive investments in US literature, Cedric Essi further analyzes the intricate relationship between slavery, authorship, and literary property within the racialized property regime of antebellum America. He highlights how authors dispossessed of their legal personhood were denied a copyright in their own works and how their labor was taken advantage of by the book industry, but he also emphasizes how these writers in turn used authorship to assert their existence as a

When Harriet Beecher Stowe published *Uncle Tom's Cabin* in 1852, the discussion of slavery and property in literature became more prominent. In "Who owns *Uncle Tom's Cabin*? Literature as Cultural Property," Peter Schneck argues that the immense success of Stowe's novel also positioned it at the center of debates surrounding international copyright protection and literary property.[37] Its success also contributed to the "change in the perception of literary property and copyright that increasingly centered on the interest and the rights of the author as original creator and proprietor of the literary work."[38] Schneck interrogates ownership of *Uncle Tom's Cabin* by examining both ideas of property and ownership *in* the text and ownership and protection *of* the text, contextualizing Stowe's efforts for authorial control. He also argues that by the end of the nineteenth century, Stowe's work became a "collective form of cultural property as an exemplary literary achievement of nineteenth-century American culture."[39]

Stowe's novel also stood at the center of the case *Stowe v. Thomas* in 1853, after a German translation of *Uncle Tom's Cabin* was sold in the US without Stowe's permission. As Peter Schneck points out, Stowe's lawyers did not pursue an economic strategy centered on possible monetary losses caused by the publication of an unauthorized translation of the text – instead, they presented an argument centered on the natural and inherent right Stowe had to her creation.[40] They asserted Stowe's "moral absolute rights [as] the 'author-creator,'" a romantic notion nonetheless rejected by the court, which instead argued that "author's right 'consists only in a right of copy'."[41] This decision highlights two opposing understandings of property: Stowe's lawyers insisted on the author's right to her "incorporeal property," while the court ruled "that Stowe's rights as an author are limited precisely by the physical object, the copy" and translations of her work therefore did not infringe on her prop-

---

person. Essi also outlines the role enslaved authors and the antebellum slave narrative as a genre played in the formation of a US literature and its popularity in other countries, especially in Germany. As he shows, literary property in antebellum America cannot be discussed without discussing slavery as a racialized property regime, see Essi, Cedric. "Black Copyright. The Slave's Narrative as Literary Property." Unsettling Law. Annual Conference of the Association for the Study of Law, Culture and the Humanities. June 16, 2022. Emory Law School, Atlanta. Paper presentation.

37 Peter Schneck, "Who Owns Uncle Tom's Cabin? Literature as Cultural Property" in *Copyrighting Creativity: Creative Values, Cultural Heritage Institutions and Systems of Intellectual Property*, ed. Helle Porsdam (London: Routledge, 2015), 129–150.

38 Schneck, "Uncle Tom's Cabin," 137.

39 Schneck, "Uncle Tom's Cabin," 132.

40 Schneck, "Uncle Tom's Cabin," 137.

41 Schneck, "Uncle Tom's Cabin," 138.

erty.[42] For many, Stowe's claim of extended property rights stood in opposition to her criticism of slavery, transforming the question of literary property into a moral one. Some criticized her rejection of a settlement offer as well as the fact that her own translation seemed to be inferior to the translation in question.[43] Consequently, as Schneck argues, the debate on international copyright and literary property became intertwined with the abolitionist debate on slavery and property:

> [T]he conjunction of the two debates in the overall rhetoric of possession and ownership that framed existing notions about property as absolute dominion versus a bundle of rights, also effectively harmed the position of American authors and publishers in favour of extended international copyright protection.[44]

Advocating for literary property and international copyright now meant taking a stance on slavery.[45]

Francis Lieber also read *Uncle Tom's Cabin* and even prepared a review of Stowe's work in 1853, but did not end up publishing it.[46] In the draft for the review, Lieber affirms Stowe's portrayal of slavery, writing "I know all the facts in the book to be true; I could give many additional facts – painful in the last degree."[47] He also criticizes the work because while it portrays some of the horrors of slavery and fugitive slave law, it does not offer any thoughts on "what ought to be done towards extinction of slavery." Interestingly, Lieber's examination of *Uncle Tom's Cabin* leads him to reflect on his own day-to-day observations of slavery in South Carolina:

---

42 Schneck, "Uncle Tom's Cabin," 138.

43 Schneck, "Uncle Tom's Cabin," 139.

44 Schneck, "Uncle Tom's Cabin," 140.

45 Schneck, "Uncle Tom's Cabin," 140.

46 Lieber, Francis. "Uncle Tom: A Review of Mrs. Stowe's Book." No date. Francis Lieber papers. mssLI. Box 4, no. 7. LI496. The Huntington. San Marino, CA.

47 Lieber's insistence on the "facts" portrayed in Stowe's fictional work hints at the lack of clear separation between fact and fiction in the discussion of this work. This is evidenced also, for example, by a reference Lieber makes to a statement by the *London Spectator*, which Lieber paraphrases as follows in his review: "The saying of the *London Spectator* that *a system which could produce such a saint would not be so bad*, is utterly fallacious" [emphasis added]. Apart from the obvious inaccuracy of the *London Spectator*'s statement, it also dangerously confuses the harsh reality of the system of chattel slavery with Stowe's fictional portrayal of slavery and of Uncle Tom as a character.

> Day before yester-day I saw, at 10 oclock A M [sic] in main street, Columbia S.C. a man on horseback. He held a rope, which was around the neck of a negro, whose hands were tied behind. The rope which tied his hands also passed round the neck of a little boy behind him – perhaps 12 years old. The hands of the latter were also lashed behind. And thus they proceeded (the negro bare footed, in the middle of the street in the mud.) Were they run-aways? Perhaps they were taken from their families, and fear that their yearning haste would make them run-aways, led to the lashing. Oh God of mercy! Some years ago a fellow came here who erected a pen, as it were, some few miles from Columbia, into which he put all the children he could pick up, for a southern market. Preston told me of it, with utmost indignation. But then, there the matter stops, I mean the indignation. A black man in Columbia married a black girl. They loved each other much. The man was most gayed. His master owed, besides, a debt to Dr. Toland, and wished to pay it. So, with the consent of the master, Bellinger told the negro to come to him for a task. The moment he appeared he was hand-cuffed & and run off to Alabama, with leave taking &c, where Bellinger sold him. The negro has occasionally written to his wife. Lately he wrote that he despairs of ever coming back and advises her to marry again. The woman is in consequence so ill that serious doubts about her health are entertained.[48]

Lieber even claims that he bought Gzaesa, an enslaved woman, so she would not be traded and thus forcefully separated from her husband, Titus. It is indisputable that Lieber had slaves working in his household in South Carolina – Claudia Schnurmann states that the Lieber family owned slaves, while Aviam Soifer and Paul D. Carrington argue that Lieber "leased" them.[49] Either way, Lieber participated in the system of slavery, even though he reflected critically on the relationship between slavery and property while he still lived in South Carolina. He rejected the propertization of humans as slaves by asserting that "Man cannot become a thing" in a letter as early as 1837 (*Life and Letters*, 121). Nevertheless, he did not openly discuss his abolitionist ideas until he left South Carolina in 1856, only sharing his beliefs with friends in the North or in his private notes. This is likely also the reason Lieber did not end up publishing his review of *Uncle Tom's Cabin*.

While Lieber emphasizes the suffering of the humans enslaved in this review, he also laments the hypocrisy of slaveholding states. Lieber states

48 Lieber, Francis. "Uncle Tom: A Review of Mrs. Stowe's Book." No date. Francis Lieber papers. mssLI. Box 4, no. 7. LI496. The Huntington. San Marino, CA.

49 Carrington, "The Theme," 367; Soifer, "Facts," 2319; Schnurmann, *Brücken*, 234.

that "Could I mount the scaffold for the abolition of slavery I would do it tomorrow," but he felt unable to adopt an abolitionist position in a slave-holding state, fearing for his reputation, his position at South Carolina College, and his safety. Senator and avid abolitionist Charles Sumner even accused Lieber of being "the apologist of slavery" after Lieber had asked him to stop sending him abolitionist material to South Carolina. Lieber feared retribution by his fellow citizens in South Carolina should anyone see these letters – or should Sumner leak Lieber's letters to the press.[50] When Lieber unsuccessfully campaigned to become president of South Carolina College in 1855, he suspected that a private admission of support for the Republican party cost him the position.[51] After Charles Sumner was violently attacked and severely injured by pro-slavery advocate Preston Brooks (1819–1857) in 1856, Lieber – who had now severed ties with South Carolina College – "assumed a violent stand against slavery," as Freidel writes. After he moved to New York City in 1857 and assumed his position at Columbia College, Lieber began to publicly denounce slavery and the secession efforts in slave-holding states.[52] Lieber's improved position in the big northern city of New York enabled him to conduct his activism directly, in his university lectures, through public speeches and through participation in the events of interest groups. He used this platform to speak against secession, slavery, and in favor of copyright and free trade.

Even during the years in which the Civil War loomed, Lieber did not abandon the issue of international copyright regulation and followed debates in Congress. On January 18, 1858, representative Edward J. Morris (1815–1881) presented House bill no. 82 on international copyright to Congress. After the bill was referred to the Joint Committee on the Library and no further action was taken, Morris reintroduced the bill on February 15, 1860, as House bill no 32, "A Bill to Provide for an International Copyright Law." As the second international copyright bill introduced to Congress, it was designed to amend the *Copyright Act of 1831* to extend copyright provisions to persons who were not

50 Freidel, "Slavery," 89.

51 The Republican Party opposed an expansion of slavery in the US, a sentiment contrary to the position held by many citizens in the slave-holding state of South Carolina.

52 In 1864, prompted by the secession of the Confederate States of America, Lieber worked on a new draft of the articles of the Constitution, proposing seven new articles. These included a mandatory "plenary allegiance" to the US government of all native and naturalized citizens, a definition of treason against the US and the crime of sedition, the complete and permanent abolishment of slavery, and the definition of slave trade as "piracy." Lieber, Francis. A Draft for the proposed XIII-XIX Articles of the Constitution. March 15, 1864. Francis Lieber papers. mssLI. Box 1, no. 19. LI3637. The Huntington. San Marino, CA; Freidel, "Slavery," 91–92.

citizens of the US and their families. Congress referred the bill to the Committee on Foreign Affairs, but no action was taken.[53] The topic apparently did not find much interest among the majority in Congress and the rising tensions between free states and slave-holding states and the threat of secession absorbed much attention in Congress. The threat of a Civil War occupied Lieber professionally and personally: While he stood firmly against secession, his son Oscar remained in South Carolina and eventually enlisted with the Confederate States Army. The conflict and following Civil War, which shook the very foundations of the United States, concerned Lieber greatly and he engaged with it in terms of political ethics and institutional law. It remained at the forefront of his mind for much of his remaining life and dominated his intellectual activities, resulting in his most prominent work, the *Lieber Code*.[54] Nevertheless, the protection of literary property through international copyright, especially in connection with book tariffs, free trade, anti-protectionism, and international law and cooperation, remained of interest to Lieber. While he did not publish on the topic anymore, he closely followed any proceedings in Congress and engaged in activism and public outreach.

7.2.2 Book Tariffs and Free Trade Activism

Lieber rarely discussed book tariffs in his earlier works, but he began connecting the demand for comprehensive international copyright legislation with the effort for the eradication of book tariffs in the 1850s. In 1852, he sent a letter to the editor of the *South Carolinian*, referencing an article the newspaper copied from *The Register* in Winnsboro. The author of the article in *The Register* had criticized Lieber's statement "that the absence of an international copyright between the United States and England is a shame to us."[55] Lieber responds that he does not "wish to enter into a discussion of this subject – at least not at present. One battle at a time is always enough." Interestingly, he states that the current battle is the "fight for *free books*." Only when books are free, Lieber argues, "will [it] be time to see what is to be done next." Apparently, Lieber temporarily focused his efforts on an issue related to the subject of international copyright – he connects international copyright with the

53 Solberg, *International Copyright*, 13.

54 *Instructions for the Government of Armies of the United States in the Field, prepared by Francis Lieber, LL.D., Originally Issued As General Orders No. 100, Adjudant General's Office, 1863* (Washington: Government Printing Office, 1898).

55 Lieber, Francis. "For the South Carolinian. International Copyright." No date. Francis Lieber papers. mssLI. Box 109, no. 9. LI5022. The Huntington. San Marino, CA.

effort for the eradication of tariffs on imported books, framing them as similar and interrelated issues.[56]

Lieber kept this letter to the editor in a scrapbook from 1852, along with another letter he wrote to the editor of the *South Carolinian*, titled "Our Tariff on Foreign Books."[57] In this letter Lieber details his views on book tariffs, claiming that the subject of duties on foreign books "does not seem to have attracted any attention adequate to its importance," highlighting again the significance of public attention and broad mobilization in a civil society. Tariffs on imported goods were designed to generate federal income, to promote domestic production, and to decrease foreign competition by increasing the prices on imported goods. Foreign books as imported goods were also subject to tariffs. While Lieber promoted copyright protection for foreign books, he rejected taxes on imported books. In this letter he spells out his reasoning: A book, he writes, "is the intellect enshrined in board and paper" and "the import of intellect" should not be taxed. Firstly, because it is impractical and difficult to realize; secondly, because labor and skill is imported – and welcomed – all the time through the process of migration, and thirdly, because "a free and intellectual nation" should not restrict access to the products of intellectual labor through taxes. "Turn the question whichever way you please," Lieber writes, "it is pitiful, and nothing less, that a nation so proud of freedom and its love of knowledge taxes foreign books." He argues that the revenue generated by tariffs is neglectable but the damage of erecting financial barriers against the import of intellect is considerable. "A love of knowledge and respect for intellect" render books, the "holy missionaries of knowledge and civilization," "intaxable [sic]" in Lieber's mind.

While Lieber appeals to idealistic notions in his framing of the issue, he also has practical concerns: He fears that those who need foreign books for study

---

56 Though Lieber claims that he does not want to discuss international copyright, he nevertheless makes two claims in his letter: Firstly, he points out that the arguments against international copyright are the same arguments originally raised against copyright in England when the *Statute of Anne* was passed, and lately raised against Thomas Noon Talfourd's (1795–1854) attempts to secure an amendment of British copyright law in 1837. He places these arguments in a long tradition of arguments directed against the proper protection of private property, dating back to the Middle Ages. Secondly, he offers for reflection "that an American, no matter where he be, can take out a copyright in England; but an Englishman cannot take out a copyright in the United States unless he resides here, and has declared his intention to become a citizen." Lieber, Francis. "For the South Carolinian. International Copyright." No date. Francis Lieber papers. mssLI. Box 109, no. 9. LI5022. The Huntington. San Marino, CA.

57 Lieber, Francis. "For the South Carolinian. Our Tariff on Foreign Books." No date. Francis Lieber papers. mssLI. Box 109, no. 9. LI5022. The Huntington. San Marino, CA.

and work, including himself, can no longer afford them due to high tariffs. The United States are "not over-blest [sic] with books," he writes, "and Congress ought to facilitate in all possible ways their importation, and not impede it."[58] Lieber demands that foreign books be made duty free for everyone, as they already are for public educational institutions. While he does not discuss the subject of international copyright law directly, he addresses many related concerns in this article. The same arguments that he presents in favor of an international copyright law, he presents as reasons against a tariff on foreign books: Civilized nations should protect intellectual production and guarantee access to knowledge in order to facilitate knowledge exchange and increase respectful international cooperation. The prices of books may be increased by the cost of copyright to enable authors to make a living from writing and thus incentivize the production of original and creative works, but they must not be escalated further through additional tariff payments – especially if authors do not benefit from them financially. A balance must be struck between financially supporting authors and ensuring access to knowledge through low book prices. Both arguments are rooted in the same understanding of books and the knowledge they transport as key elements of civilized societies with responsible citizens. In Lieber's opinion it is the duty of all governments to protect the author as a pioneer of civilization and the book as the means of conveyance.

Lieber remained interested in the subject of book tariffs in the US and in England.[59] In another newspaper clipping from his personal collection Lieber still discusses book tariffs over a decade later. The clipping is from a letter Lieber wrote to the *Daily Globe*, printed in the newspaper on July 6, 1866.[60] In the letter, Lieber refers to a new tariff bill and its regulation of the import of books, which he claims contains "grave inconsistencies." He states that he

---

58 Lieber, Francis. "For the South Carolinian. Our Tariff on Foreign Books." No date. Francis Lieber papers. mssLI. Box 109, no. 9. LI5022. The Huntington. San Marino, CA. Interestingly, this argument stands in direct opposition to another argument often brought forward in support of international copyright: Proponents often claimed that only a copyright on imported books could limit reprinting and the reliance on cheap foreign works, and instead shift focus to the national book market and support domestic authors.

59 Lieber kept a newspaper clipping someone addressed to him in handwriting; it contains a highlighted section reading the following: "No books whatever, reprinted abroad from original British publications, are allowed to be imported, except when the copyright has expired. Prohibition not to take place unless notice of copyright and date of its expiration be given to commissioners of customs." Evidently, Lieber followed the discussion in England as well. No author. "Abstract of the New Tariff Bill." No date. Francis Lieber papers. mssLI. Box 112, no. 1. No LI number. The Huntington. San Marino, CA.

60 Lieber, Francis. Article in the *Daily Globe*. July 6, 1866. Francis Lieber papers. mssLI. Box 112, no. 14. No LI number. The Huntington. San Marino, CA.

"hasten[s] to point them out [...] when there may yet be time to propose some changes." Presumably, Lieber sent this letter to an acquaintance of his, probably a politician, and had it printed in the *Daily Globe* afterwards. He hoped that his criticisms might actually influence the bill if he sent them both to a legislator and shared them with the public to exert pressure and educate. He reiterates a point he first made years earlier: A duty of 25 percent on all imported books "makes it nearly impossible for all those persons who stand in real need of foreign books, as well as of American productions, to obtain them for their libraries." Fewer books would be imported as a result, actually diminishing the monetary benefits to the state. He also highlights that scholars would be at a disadvantage because they can rarely afford to pay the duty; a tariff on books "would work positive exclusion for all the real laborers in the vineyard of knowledge." Learned men are "the servants of the public" and must thus be protected, Lieber argues. Everyone else, he claims, would also "forego the advantage of having presented to them the results of the laborious and lifelong study of foreign scholars," impeding knowledge exchange and education. But exchange of knowledge between nations is crucial to civilization and

> [c]ivilization is a church universal; like our religion it is for all; and civilization advances only in that degree in which one generation or one country seizes upon the stock of skill or knowledge acquired by another and infuses it into its own life. All give and all take; and above all other things, books are the bridges over which civilization travels from one country or region to another, and from one generation to another. Whatever is done to impede the free exchange of books materially impedes the progress of our kind.[61]

In this letter Lieber also actively connects the lack of international copyright with book tariffs when he criticizes US publishers who advocate for high book tariffs. Many publishers in the US claimed that producing books in England was much cheaper and a duty on imported books was necessary to protect them from foreign competition. Lieber argues that "the advantage which they derive from reprinting English books without paying anything for the copyright" is great enough to balance out this perceived disadvantage. This, of course, is a rather short-sighted argument since Lieber remained in favor of copyright payments on foreign books – the advantage would thus dissipate, if a copyright payment were allotted. Lieber's statement here rather highlights a certain cynicism, likely a result of years of futile activism.

61 Lieber, Francis. Article in the *Daily Globe*. July 6, 1866. Francis Lieber papers. mssLI. Box 112, no. 14. No LI number. The Huntington. San Marino, CA.

More broadly speaking, Francis Lieber was an advocate of free trade in general and, as Martin Thayer claims, Lieber published many pamphlets and articles supporting unrestricted trade.[62] In a letter to the *Palmetto States Banner* written under the pseudonym "Columbiensis" from December 1, 1846, Lieber severely attacks Henry Clay's (1777–1852) position that free trade "has brought in its train disaster and ruin to every Nation that has had the temerity to try it."[63] While Lieber and Clay were allies in their fight for an international copyright, Lieber disagreed with Clay with regard to free trade. He argues that free trade is necessary to help nations flourish and to cultivate good relationships with neighboring countries. The demand for international cooperation and mutual respect between civilized nations again plays a central role in Lieber's issue framing here, emphasizing the connections he drew in his narrative between activism for international copyright, for free trade, and against book tariffs. His stance reflects a common position and rhetoric at the time, as Adrian Johns points out in *Piracy. The Intellectual Property Wars from Gutenberg to Gates*. Johns argues that the debate over literature as property and the need for international copyright protection was often portrayed by both sides as "a struggle for the soul of the republic."[64] This struggle, he states, would soon

> metastasize into a conflict over fundamentals: protection versus free trade, manufacturing versus commerce, democracy versus oligarchy, Philadelphia versus New York. It would address central questions of modern culture as that culture came into being. What was knowledge, and how were its development, transmission, and storage best secured?[65]

Of the opponents of international copyright and free trade, Henry Charles Carey was likely the most influential figure. Carey's stance reflected the position of many publishers at the time and as the son of publisher Mathew Carey, "[Henry] enjoyed deeper familiarity with the world of publishing, in all prob-

62 Martin Russell Thayer, "Biographical Discourse by Hon. M. R. Thayer" in *The Miscellaneous Writings of Francis Lieber. I. Reminiscences, Addresses, and Essays*, ed. Daniel C. Gilman (Philadelphia: J. B. Lippincott & Co., 1881), 13–44, 40.

63 Columbiensis. "Temerity." December 1, 1846. Francis Lieber papers. mssLI. Box 87, no. 8. No LI number. The Huntington. San Marino, CA. The scrapbook containing the letter bears the title "Newspaper Slips containing Communications by myself, Columbiensis &c," giving certainty to the claim that Lieber wrote the letter himself.

64 Johns, *Piracy*, 308.

65 Johns, *Piracy*, 309.

ability, than any American contemporary [...] He knew the culture of reprinting so intimately because he was largely responsible for its existence," as Johns argues.[66] In his works Carey represented a protectionist ideology and criticized calls for international copyright protection and the dominant free trade ideology.[67] For Carey, the question of copyright was one of centralization versus civilization. He feared increasing centralization of the book trade in the large cities where most publishing houses were located and consequently an "erosion of intellectual quality" in the US, as Johns summarizes in his analysis of Carey's work.[68] Decentralization, Carey argued, led to a wider distribution of cheaper books outside of larger cities and enabled every citizen to be a reader, thus improving the country and furthering innovation. He identified the British system of centralization of the book trade in London as the problem, not reprinting in the US – such centralization would halt and endanger civilization, he claimed.[69] Carey also rejected the understanding of literature as property, claiming that "positive knowledge rested in facts, and in facts there could be no property."[70] Writers repurposed the ideas of others rather than generating new knowledge, Carey claimed, and thus they should receive remuneration but no property rights to their published works.[71] As an opponent of slavery, Carey also introduced abolitionist rhetoric into his argument, contending that knowledge should be free for all and that "[u]niversal copyrights [...] were a relic of the ideology of slave owners."[72] Lieber and Carey agreed on the central social role of knowledge, but they fundamentally disagreed on how to protect and further knowledge, leading to opposing stances on copyright protection, literature as property, free trade, and import tariffs.

Lieber remained an avid and lifelong opponent of book tariffs and proponent of free trade, as proven by an address he delivered at a convention of the *Advocates of Free Trade* in 1868, a few years before his death. The convention invited "those who, without diction of sect or party, are in favor of abandoning the principle of protection by tariff and imposing taxes for revenue only."[73] In his speech, Lieber reportedly focused on the causes of the US' rapid progress.

66 Johns, *Piracy*, 309.

67 Johns, *Piracy*, 311, 320. Carey's works included *Letters on International Copyright* (1853) and *The International Copyright Question Considered* (1872).

68 Johns, *Piracy*, 322.

69 Johns, *Piracy*, 320–321.

70 Cited in Johns, *Piracy*, 323–324.

71 Johns, *Piracy*, 324.

72 Cited in Johns, *Piracy*, 324.

73 No author. ""Convention of the Advocates of Free Trade. Addresses by Dr. Francis Lieber, Rev. Dr. Leavitt, Prof. Perry and Others. Resolutions Adopted Relative to Revenue Reform." May 13, 1868. Francis Lieber papers. mssLI. Box 99, no. 4. LI305. The Hunting-

He deems it "common sense" that prosperity "demands that there should be perfectly unshackled exchange within a country." Consequently, he claims, external trade must also be unregulated to flourish. Lieber again resorts to familiar rhetoric, claiming that "[e]verything, indeed, in this life, depends first of all on exchange; and all obstruction of exchange is an offence against humanity." Free exchange, in his understanding, leads to greater wealth and greater wealth aids civilization. Civilization is the goal all nations should strive towards and Lieber emphasizes "the all-pervading inter-dependence of men" and nations, who must produce more and rely on exchange to generate enough wealth for "the progress of man." Protection to Lieber is "a misnomer for obstruction or privation" in the case of tariffs. Surprisingly though, he does not reject all tariffs outright. Rather, he calls for a "revenue tariff," meaning a duty on foreign articles which both generates revenue for the government to alleviate public debt and is cheap enough not to impede import. This would be "a truly protective tariff, that is protective of the interests of the consumer" who could still afford imported articles, especially those which could not be produced at a comparably cheap price domestically.

Interestingly, Lieber's advocacy for free trade and against book tariffs constituted a constant challenge for his role as an issue entrepreneur for international copyright: On the one hand he considered "obstraction [sic] of exchange [...] an offence against humanity" and called protective measures in trade "obstruction or privation."[74] On the other hand, he lobbied for comprehensive and international copyright as a tool to protect authors, curtail the import of foreign literature, and end reprinting. He called for the support of domestic authors and the promotion of a national literature, but at the same time he demanded low or no tariffs to be paid on imported books. While Lieber advocated for unobstructed knowledge exchange in his speech, he did not actually envision entirely free trade, which could also include unrestricted reprinting. Rather, he was in favor of regulated trade and copyright measures. In his efforts as an issue entrepreneur to cultivate an accessible narrative to mobilize support, Lieber struggled to avoid the common pitfalls of issue framing:[75] He ran the risk of oversimplifying the issue in his efforts at conveyance. The bold state-

---

ton. San Marino, CA. Day and month are penciled in; where the article was published is unclear since the source consists of a clipping.

74 No author. "Convention of the Advocates of Free Trade. Addresses by Dr. Francis Lieber, Rev. Dr. Leavitt, Prof. Perry and Others. Resolutions Adopted Relative to Revenue Reform." May 13, 1868. Francis Lieber papers. mssLI. Box 99, no. 4. LI305. The Huntington. San Marino, CA. Day and month are penciled in; where the article was published is unclear, since the source consists of a clipping.

75 Kingston, *Fully Human*, 206, 212.

ments in his value-based narrative suggest clear-cut rights and wrongs but while building frame bridges between the issues, Lieber downplays their complexity and ignores their contradictions.

7.2.3 International Law and Cooperation

The outbreak of the American Civil War in 1861 coincided with Lieber's rising popularity in other areas of public life: As Lewis Harley points out in his extensive treatise on Lieber's life and work, Lieber had gained renown as a political scientist and publicist and shifted his focus to the subject of international law.[76] In 1850, while he still resided in South Carolina, Lieber had been awarded an honorary degree of doctor of law "as a token of the high respect entertained by [the corporation and overseers of Harvard University] for [his] character, learning, and eminent success in the cultivation of letters."[77] In 1860, Lieber transferred to the law faculty at Columbia College as professor of constitutional history and political philosophy.[78] While not a studied jurist, Lieber had become a recognized expert in the field of law.

During the Civil War Lieber actively supported the North by printing pamphlets and authoring newspaper articles. Though he was deeply saddened by the division of the country he so passionately loved, he believed the war necessary and just. He hoped that through the war, more union and nationalization would become possible and that the institution of slavery would disappear completely (*Life and Letters*, 320). Lieber was even more saddened by the fact that his son Oscar was a passionate supporter of the South and had enlisted with the Confederate States Army. Oscar died of injuries sustained while fighting for the Confederate States Army in 1862, while his brothers Hamilton and Guido Norman fought with the Union Army.[79] Francis Lieber continued his activities as professor, author, and publicist while grieving the loss of his son and dealing with health issues. Still, he acted as an advisor to the Lincoln, the Johnson, and the Grant administrations.[80] In 1861 Lieber lectured on the law and usages of war and in 1862, Lieber sent a letter to General Henry Halleck (1815–1872), general-in-chief of the Union Army, writing: "Ever since the beginning of our present War, it has appeared clearer and clearer to me, that the President ought to issue a set of rules and definitions providing for the

---

76 Harley, *Francis Lieber*, 97.

77 Sparks, Jared. Letter to Francis Lieber. October 4, 1850. Francis Lieber papers. OCLC 713642823. MS 5767. Manuscripts Division, South Caroliniana Library. Columbia, SC.

78 Schnurmann, *Brücken*, 150.

79 Schnurmann, *Brücken*, 150.

80 Schnurmann, *Brücken*, 151.

most urgent issues occurring under the Law and usages of War, and on which our Articles of War are silent."[81] Halleck initially brushed Lieber off but eventually called a committee on the issue; Lieber served as chair of the committee in Washington, DC. The results of the committee were published as *Code 100: Instructions for the Government of the Armies of the United States in the Field*, also known as the *Lieber Code*, on April 24, 1863. The *Lieber Code* was signed by Abraham Lincoln and issued orders for soldiers concerning their conduct in times of war.[82] The *Code 100* is still discussed by historians and legal scholars today.[83] Claudia Schnurmann praises the work as an impressive "Atlantic synthesis" of Lieber's own theories, military experience, US legal texts, European classics and international law texts, while at the same time rejecting Lieber's claim of originality for the work.[84] She also points out that, along with the *Encyclopædia Americana*, the *Code 100* was Lieber's most prominent work and remains influential to this day.[85] Schnurmann argues that the *Code 100* resulted from a combination of Lieber's political and legal expertise, his personal experiences as a prisoner of war in 1815, the grave injury sustained by his son Hamilton and the death of his son Oscar during the Civil War. It was also a response to the rumors that soldiers of the Confederate Army mistreated and even tortured civilians and prisoners of war. In 157 articles, the *Code 100* outlines a legal framework for conduct during a war and gives instructions regarding the conduct of troops in the field and the treatment of civilians and prisoners of war.[86]

The laws of war were but one of the many aspects of international law and cooperation Lieber became interested in. As he wrote in a letter to Secretary of State William H. Seward in 1865, Lieber favored an "international spirit of peace" and envisioned "an increasing and widening family of nations, bound

---

81 Cited after Schnurmann, *Brücken*, 154–155.

82 This code is still part of the standard instructions in the US military. It guided the conduct of US troops during the occupation of Germany during and following the Second World War (Becker, "Prologue," 6).

83 In *Brücken aus Papier* Claudia Schnurmann outlines the genesis of the *Code 100* and the reception of the work through Lieber's correspondence. She also traces possible influences on the work and its legacy in public life as well as in Lieber's own personal life (437–465).

84 "Anders wie von ihm öffentlich dargestellt, schöpfte er das Wissen für die Produktion des *Code 100* nicht gänzlich aus dem eigenen Hirnschmalz, sondern fabrizierte eine eindrucksvolle atlantische Synthese" (Schnurmann, *Brücken*, 456).

85 Schnurmann, *Brücken*, 151.

86 Schnurmann, *Brücken*, 451.

together by the great law of nations."[87] Through international arbitration any conflicts bound to happen in close contact between nations could lend "reason, fairness and submission to justice, for defying power or revengeful irritation." It is likely that Lieber's lifelong criticism of the lack of an international copyright and the resulting political conflicts between the US and other countries informed his interest in international law and arbitration. He also exchanged ideas with Charles Sumner and Johann Caspar Bluntschli (1808–1881) in Heidelberg regarding an international code and an international congress on the rights of nations (*Life and Letters*, 362).[88] Lieber was even in favor of an international monetary unit – meaning that "the world should adopt the dollar" – and any measure that would lead to more uniformity in "the great commonwealth of nations" (*Life and Letters*, 374). Yet it is important to emphasize that Lieber only included members of – in his words – "our Cis-Caucasian race" in his idea of an international commonwealth of nations (*Life and Letters*, 423). Charles Robson claims that Lieber believed the "Caucasian race" superior to other races, though not on the basis of blood but rather, as Lieber writes himself, due to "certain conditions of geographic and chronological position, of intellectual succession," and of intellectual and cultural heritage – a stance Lieber later softened during the Civil War.[89] Lieber also rejected the idea that Black and white people could share a common ancestry and while he advocated for abolition during the Civil War, he accepted the genocide of Indigenous people in the US and favored immigration restrictions for non-white people.[90] In many ways Lieber advocated for a radical vision of global unity; he dreamed of a united global community with shared laws, free

---

87 Lieber, Francis. "International Arbitration. A Letter to Hon. William H. Seward, Secretary of State, by Francis Lieber." September 17, 1865. Francis Lieber papers. mssLI. Box 112, no. 10. No LI no. The Huntington. San Marino, CA.

88 See also Lieber, Francis. Letter to Charles Sumner. May 25, 1866. Francis Lieber papers. mssLI. Box 104, no. 8. No LI no. The Huntington. San Marino, CA; Lieber, Francis. Letter to Charles Sumner. December 16, 1866. Francis Lieber papers. mssLI. Box 104, no. 8. No LI no. The Huntington. San Marino, CA.

89 Robson, "Nationalism," 58–59.

90 Robson, "Nationalism," 58. As late as 1868 Lieber wrote the following to Bluntschli: "I am not in favor of universal suffrage though for a very extensive one; nor do I agree with you that the white race must lead every other race to civilization. That may be the case for the present; but I believe that the white race will eventually absorb and sweep away all others, at least in this country. We always speak of the extinction of a race as if we were talking of the murder of an individual, while the question is merely the non-renewing and non-regenerating. The fighting and slaying the Indian is terrible to me; but their gradual extinction I consider desirable, and the quicker the better" (Lieber, *Life and Letters*, 384–385). Genocide is the deliberate destruction of a group, e.g., a racial group, through measures including but not limited to killing members of that group. It also

trade, and mutual exchange of knowledge. At the same time, though his understanding of the differences between races softened over time, his vision of a global commonwealth did not include all people equally.

7.3 International Copyright Activism: The Final Years

Once the Civil War ended, Lieber helped to organize and archive confiscated Confederation papers.[91] He also continued to position himself as an expert on international law and in 1866 he stated to his wife that "the oldest brother of General Sherman, a lawyer here, asked me whether I felt at liberty to become one of the lawyers in a case before the Secretary of the Treasury for the recovery of capital and interest" (*Life and Letters*, 366). He had political aspirations and would have liked to serve as a member of the Republican party, yet he felt that

> in this world of ours a man must have or represent power – power of some sort – authority, or money, or land, or party, or sect, or profession, or recklessness, or loud mediocrity – to elbow through and succeed. I have none of these elements of power. So be it.[92]

Lieber's activism for international law and cooperation, for free trade and against book tariffs complemented his activism in favor of international copyright protection, which he continued during the 1860s. Lieber attempted to direct the Senate's attention towards international copyright with the help of his friends. Lieber's strained relationship with Charles Sumner improved after Lieber had relocated to New York City and positioned himself against slavery. In 1866, Lieber sent a letter to Sumner in his function as chair of the Senate Foreign Relations Committee.[93] Lieber stated that the subject of international copyright "requires serious attention" and asked Sumner to hand an article on tariffs on foreign books to "the Senator or Representative most likely to occupy himself earnestly with a possible copy-right treaty and with a revision of the

---

includes measures such as the preventing of regeneration through reproduction – exactly the measures Lieber mentions here.

91 Schnurmann, *Brücken*, 151.

92 Lieber, Francis. Letter to Andrew D. White. April 13, 1867. Francis Lieber papers. mssLI. Box 104, no. 10. No LI number. The Huntington. San Marino, CA.

93 Lieber, Francis. Letter to Charles Sumner. January 1866. Francis Lieber papers. mssLI. Box 104, no. 8. No LI no. The Huntington. San Marino, CA. This is a transcript of the original letter.

uncouth portion of our tariff which relates to the importation of foreign books." Lieber also inquired whether Sumner could establish contact between himself and anyone interested in the subject; he had previously tried to reach out to general Nathaniel Banks (1816–1894) but "somehow, [did] not have his ear." A few weeks later, in March 1866 Lieber wrote to Sumner again and seemed rather upset:

> I observe that you have presented a petition for an international copyright act, and that it has been referred to the Committee on Foreign Affairs, of which you are chairman. This is the first I hear of this petition. No one has presented it to me for signature […] You know that long ago, I published a pamphlet on international copyright […] and you recollect that I have repeatedly written to you and conversed with you on this subject […] The protection of authors and publishers by international copyright is nothing more than the protection granted in our great family of civilized nations to property's producer and owner.[94]

A part of the transcript is missing, but Lieber ends his letter by stating that the Committee should know that "the absence of my name from that petition is not owing to any disagreement of mine with its substance." On February 19, 1866, Edwin D. Morgan (1811–1883), senator from New York, handed over a petition of New York citizens to the Senate, who demanded the enactment of an international copyright law. During March and April Charles Sumner presented eleven additional petitions for international copyright, including one signed by William Cullen Bryant (1794–1878) and one signed by Henry Longfellow (1807–1882). They were referred to the Committee on Foreign Affairs but eventually discharged without result.[95] Clearly, Lieber felt he should have been offered a chance to review and sign the first petition – either Senator Morgan should have approached him directly or Sumner should have involved him, knowing how much he cared about the topic. Lieber's anger also underpins the assumption that Lieber was previously involved in the introduction of petitions to Congress and still considered himself an authority on the subject of international copyright. That Sumner and Morgan apparently did not share this view and did not recognize Lieber as an issue entrepreneur hurt him deeply; he bristled at the thought that all members of the Senate and

---

94 Lieber, Francis. Letter to Charles Sumner. March 3, 1866. Francis Lieber papers. mssLI. Box 104, no. 8. No LI no. The Huntington. San Marino, CA. This is a transcript of the original letter.

95 Solberg, *International Copyright*, 14.

the Committee on Foreign Affairs could see that he had been passed over. While Lieber's legacy proves his continued examination and activism in favor of international copyright legislation, it seems he struggled to stay involved in the actual proceedings in Congress during his later years.

Nevertheless, Lieber did not lose interest in the issue of international copyright and continued to call for reform, as proven by a speech he delivered at a meeting of *The Copyright Association for the Protection and Advancement of Literature and Art* in 1868, only four years before his death.[96] Supporters of international copyright convened on January 30, 1868 in New York City to strategize how to best lobby Congress and mobilize public support. They appointed a committee of five to outline how civil activism could encourage the implementation of an international copyright in the US.[97] In their initial meeting, they considered whether a treaty or an act of Congress would be the better measure to implement international copyright and decided to procure necessary information from Senator Charles Sumner in Washington. Sumner replied:

> There are two ways of dealing with the question of International Copyright; one is by the treaty power, and the other is by reciprocal legislation. I have always thought that the former was the easiest; but at the present moment the House of Representatives is not disposed to concede much to the treaty power. Mr. Everett, while Secretary of State, negotiated a treaty on this subject with Great Britain, which was submitted to the Senate, reported by the Committee on Foreign Relations, considered in the Senate, and finally left on the table, without any definite vote. I shall send you a copy of this treaty, which, I believe, has never seen the light. I have always been in favor of an International Copyright, as justice to authors and a new stage in the unity of nations. Perhaps the condition of public affairs at this time, the pre-occupation of the public mind, the imminence of the Presidential Election, and also the alienation from England, may present temporary obstacles. But I am sanguine that at the least the victory

---

96 *International Copyright. Meeting of Authors and Publishers* (New York: International Copyright Association, 1868). Hereafter abbreviated as *Meeting*. Throughout the work, the *Copyright Association* uses the names "International Copyright Association," "Copyright Association," and "The Copyright Association for the Protection and Advancement of Literature and Art" interchangeably. The publisher of this volume is the *International Copyright Association*; therefore, the association will be referred to as *International Copyright Association* throughout this subchapter.

97 The committee consisted of George P. Putnam (1814–1872), S. Irenæus Prime (1812–1885), Henry Ivision (no date of birth and death), James Parton (1822–1891), and Egbert Hazard (no date of birth and death).

will be won. If authors should have a copyright, they should have it everywhere within the limits of civilization. (*Meeting*, 15–16)[98]

This short response by Sumner is a highly interesting source as it concisely summarizes some of the obstacles to international copyright legislation during the three decades directly preceding the passing of the *International Copyright Act of 1891*.

The committee's report also refers to the recent international copyright report John Baldwin, chairman of the Library Committee, presented to the House of Representatives on February 21, 1868, along with a new international copyright bill – the third one presented to Congress. The bill proposes that foreign authors of books first published abroad should be granted the same copyrights granted to citizens of the US, provided that the country of first publication grants US authors equal rights. While this bill was much discussed by the public, Congress took no action on Baldwin's report or bill.[99] Lieber followed this bill closely; only a week after its introduction he wrote to his friend Johann Caspar Bluntschli in Heidelberg: "An attempt is making in Congress to pass a law on international copyright. Many years ago I wrote a small pamphlet on the subject" (*Life and Letters*, 380). The members of the *International Copyright Association* reached out to the Library Committee and were assured that the bill would be "as satisfactory to parties immediately concerned as justice will permit" (cited after *Meeting*, 17). The Library Committee wished to "accomplish the object with as little disturbance to the established system, and with as little inconvenience to the book-trade and public, as possible," demonstrating how the lobbying of the book industry as well as public opinion heavily influenced the discussions of international copyright in Congress (cited after *Meeting*, 17). The *International Copyright Association* decided to become active and resolve a number of measures meant to reflect further on the subject while the bill was considered by Congress.

The committee then invited everyone interested in the subject of international copyright through a circular titled "JUSTICE TO AUTHORS AND ARTISTS" (*Meeting*, 5). Attached to the circular was a memorial, for which the recipients were asked to sign and to procure further signatures. On April 9, 1868, "authors, artists, publishers, and others wishing to consider the question of International Copyright" convened in the Halls of the *Historical*

98 For more details on Everett's treaty, see chapter 7.1.

99 Solberg, *International Copyright*, 14–16. The bill proposes additional provisions, e.g., that the books must be manufactured in the US, sold by citizens of the US, and registered with the clerk's office of a district court in the US.

Society in New York City. The members met to "concert measures for securing the early establishment of an International Copyright system among all the civilized nations on earth," an approach in accordance with Lieber's efforts for international law and cooperation (*Meeting*, 5). Lieber had found an active network of issue entrepreneurs, who framed the issue of international copyright in similar terms and proposed their own narratives to address legislators and mobilize support for the cause. He served as vice-president of the *International Copyright Association* under chairmen and publisher George P. Putnam (1814–1872) and William Cullen Bryant (1794–1878), author and lawyer. The speeches delivered during this meeting were later printed with the explicit purpose of drawing the attention "not only of journalists and speakers who make public opinion, but of the national representatives at Washington, by whose act alone can the United States be set right upon the question before the world" (*Meeting*, 3).

Before the speeches were delivered, the members of the *International Copyright Association* passed different agreements: They resolved that authors should have "legal right to permit, forbid, and control, absolutely and everywhere on earth, the multiplication and sale of copies of their works"; that the government must protect "the property and rights of its citizens, wherever in the world those rights may be infringed"; that since European countries have long since shown willingness to enter into reciprocal copyright agreements, "we are, as a people, in fault for not having long ago responded to their desire"; that a just system of copyright protection would render publishing "more stable, safe, and legitimate […] extensive and profitable, to the advantage of all"; that an international copyright system would increase the number of good and cheap books on the market; and that the Baldwin Bill was "substantially wise and right" (*Meeting*, 17). Remarkably, these agreements call for an absolute protection of literature as property on the basis of justice and morality, adopting a similar framing as Lieber did. This narrative reflects the opinions and standpoints Lieber voiced as early as 1830 in his *Encyclopædia Americana* entry on copyright ("Copyright," 527–529). The agreements also echo an understanding of literature as property that mirrors the sentiments of the early state statutes, rather than the prevailing understanding of copyright as a temporary printing monopoly designed to encourage the progress of science and art, as stated in Art. 1, § 8, cl. 8 of the Constitution.[100] Lieber's speech followed after the passage of resolutions at the meeting and he echoed these notions – and

---

100 The Constitutional Copyright Clause, Philadelphia, Pennsylvania (1789), Primary Sources on Copyright (1450–1900), ed. L. Bently and and M. Kretschmer, www.copyrighthistory.org. Accessed 16 November 2022.

the same standpoints he had presented in 1830 – in his last preserved public statement on international copyright.

Lieber gave his speech in person in front of the other members of the *International Copyright Association*. In this speech, Lieber expresses his agreement with the resolutions and opinions presented at the meeting. He refers to his experience as a long-term issue entrepreneur by pointing out that the current objections voiced against international copyright "are the self-same objections which have been made each time the subject has been before Congress, and when International Copyright was first discussed in Europe" ("Speech," 20). He highlights the continuity of the present debate and sets it in relation to debates in Europe, positioning himself again as a transnational expert. Lieber offers a brief overview of the previous political efforts by Edward Everett, Henry Clay, William C. Preston, and Washington Irving to introduce an international copyright regulation. In doing so, Lieber situates the current efforts within their historical context and calls attention to the persistence of these issue entrepreneurs in their efforts to bring about legal change. These efforts were often endorsed by "most of our conspicuous publishing houses," Lieber claims, emphasizing the agreement between authors and publishers to lend further credibility to the demands ("Speech," 20).

Lieber also references the European – and especially German – roots of his contemplations on the topic, as well as his belief that an international copyright would be a "move in the progress of civilization" ("Speech," 20). These allusions towards parallels with European proceedings recall Lieber's earliest works on the topic, including his entries in the *Encyclopædia Americana* and *On International Copyright* (see chapters 4.2 and 4.3). To imbue his position with historic significance and extend his narrative framing, he details the history of copyright law advocacy between the German states during the late eighteenth and the nineteenth century, writing that "an International Copyright between the German States came loudly to be called for [...] Prussia took the initiative" ("Speech," 20–21). He details the involvement of his acquaintance Julius Eduard Hitzig, likely to lend more credibility to his depictions of the proceedings in the German states. By referring to another German issue entrepreneur, Lieber also highlights the transnational interconnectedness of these efforts. In a rhetoric move, which he also used in the *Encyclopædia Americana*, Lieber presents Austria as a "pirate nation," much like the US, and as the enemy in his narrative of international copyright advocacy. The purpose here is clear: Lieber compares the US to Austria, positioning the republic as the villain of the copyright story, and uses colorful imagery to describe reprinting when he points out that "[t]he writers against the proposed International Copyright used then the reasons in favor of bibliopolic buccaneering, which are used now" ("Speech," 21).[101] These reasons, he details, are two-fold: Firstly, "[i]t is maintained that there is no such thing as literary property" and it is instead rejected as "an arbitrary creature of the law" ("Speech," 21). Secondly, the arguments in favor of the expediency and cheapness of piratical reprinting outweigh the concern for proper copyright regulation ("Speech," 21). Over decades, the justifications for reprinting have not changed, Lieber claims, and they are similar in different countries, even if these countries are an ocean apart.

Lieber then points out that the second argument in favor of expediency and cheapness can only exist because the first argument is accepted at face value: If literary property were accepted as a "real property," reprinting books would clearly be theft ("Speech," 21). Lieber uses an appeal to morality in his narrative when he states: "Right and wrong are not defined or confined by the blue or red colors of political demarcations on the map" ("Speech," 21). For Lieber, international copyright regulation is still a moral necessity in 1868 and he seeks to amend the law in correspondence with his moral understanding of right and wrong: An author has a property right in their own works, therefore copying it without permission should be illegal. Since it is morally wrong, he argues, it must be legally wrong – the law must be amended to express the norm. Here the reason for his advocacy as an issue entrepreneur can be identified: Lieber understands morality as a sign of civilization and believes that moral rights and wrongs should be reflected in the laws of any progressive society. To Lieber, there are very clear rights and wrongs with regard to morality in a civilized nation and he positions himself as an expert when he claims: "[A]llow a teach [sic] of the law of nations to say that it is one of the characteristics of our progressive civilization, that as it advances, it takes more and more from the meaning of the colors of the map, reducing them more and more to a political meaning alone" ("Speech," 21). For Lieber it is clear that questions of morality, of right or wrong, are not questions of political partisanship – all members of a progressive society should agree on and adhere to what is morally right.

Lieber then refers back to an argument he also made forty years ago: He still argues that there is, in fact, a literary property which existed prior to and independent of laws and government – a transnational property in literature that exists beyond national borders ("Speech," 21). He claims that humans instinctively know of property and

101 The adjective "bibliopolic" refers to booksellers, or "bibliopoles."

> every human being is as conscious as of his own identity, that if he appropriates what belongs to no one [...] and if he produces a new thing [...] this appropriation, or this product, is verily his own; that he can do with it what he likes, and that every one [sic] who in turn attempts to appropriate it without the process of exchange, is an intruder, a robber, and the attempt will not only be resisted but resented. The whole right of property, however developed and ramified in a code of laws it may be, rests on this primordial consciousness of mine and thine – on appropriation and production; and I now appeal to the *intuitive conviction* of every living man to say whether a literary work [...] is not a *production* in the fullest sense of the word [...] and whether anyone has a right to meddle with this property by production. ("Speech," 21–22)

This passage summarizes Lieber's unchanged narrative of literary property: It is the "purest" form of property, and it becomes property through the process of production. Property is a pre-legal and pre-governmental natural law institution which exists through the intuition of each person and is therefore *simply right* ("Speech," 22). Literary property needs no law to define it or call it into existence – but it needs to be legally recognized to be protected. While opponents of literary property may say there can be no property in a literary work since it consists of ideas "which were common property, gathered, strung together," Lieber argues that the property in literary works does not consist of the ideas but of their expression. The expression of an idea in a literary work is *produced* through the combination of labor with the common idea – just like a farmer does not produce the seed he sows but nevertheless has a property in the harvest he *produces*. Lieber strongly emphasizes the idea-expression dichotomy as well as Locke's labor theory of property.

Lieber then specifies his belief that the existence of a right to literary property by natural law has long been accepted as the norm – this is proven, he claims, by the fact that "our law and the municipal law of every civilized country acknowledge and protect [literary property] naturally" through copyright law ("Speech," 22). Since domestic works are protected by copyright law, it should logically follow that literary property should be protected internationally, "as all righteous property is" ("Speech," 22). While Lieber offers the astute observation that it seems illogical to protect literary works domestically but not internationally, he also confuses – or intentionally equates – the protection of literature as property and the protection of literature through copyright. The domestic protection of a work through copyright serves to ensure a temporary monopoly on printing in order to offer a financial incentive to authors to produce – but this is by no means a recognition of a (natural) property right in literature. Lieber equates the two in his narrative to further his argument and convince his listeners.[102] But he also calls for much more profound changes to copyright law than merely the implementation of an international copyright, as he did in his recent, more moderate works, such as *A Draught of a New Copyright Law for the United States* (see chapter 6.4). In the company of a network of equally-minded activists he returns to demanding the protection of literature as a transnational form of property.

As he continues his speech, Lieber incorporates appeals for international cooperation and shared legal conventions and sets them in relation to the issue of international copyright protection. He states that "the whole law of nations has made its greatest strides only in recent times" and that "the great law of good neighborhood" demands that one state should respect the property protected in another state – literature should be protected as a transnational form of property that exists beyond national borders ("Speech," 23). Other countries outside the US have already accepted this and there are, as Lieber argues, treaties between German states, France, England, and Italy to protect copyright. Resorting to rhetoric familiar from *On International Copyright* (see chapter 6.1), Lieber asks: "Why should we lag behind? We, whose boast it is to honor and protect human rights with eager jealousy, should we, of all leading nations, disregard the right of property because the owner is a foreigner?" ("Speech," 23). Here Lieber refers to the national narrative of the US as a global leader in matters of fairness, progress, civilization, and human rights, in order to appeal to the patriotic pride of his fellow Americans ("Speech," 23). He also addresses legislators in the US government when he claims that that the US owes it to the citizens to adhere to the high standards set for a model nation. In turn, each citizen owes it to the country to promote the passing of an international copyright bill ("Speech," 23). Lieber concludes his speech by highlighting that an international copyright would not be passed to protect "foreign authors as the poor benefactors" since "the enervating trash [meaning imported foreign books] which we receive is boundless" ("Speech," 24). Rather, property must be protected regardless of "the degree of direct good it does" and should be accepted as a measure of reciprocity, "as a thing due to us" as a nation ("Speech," 24).

Though many years have passed, Lieber's statements in this speech echo the opinions he expressed in his earlier works, such as the *Encyclopædia Amer-*

102 While he gave his speech in front of the members of the *International Copyright Association*, the intended audience of the speech were likely not the association's members but those who would read the printed version of the speech later on. There was evidently no need to convince those who already joined the association, they were all already entrepreneurs for the issue of international copyright and according to the agreements, they already shared Lieber's understanding of literature as property.

icana entries, *On International Copyright*, and *A Draught of a New Copyright Law for the United States*. He classifies the issue of international copyright as an issue of property rights more so than copyright: Literary property exists by natural law, which precedes government and positive law. Property must merely be *protected* by the government, but it exists in its own right. Regardless of political differences or national borders, protecting literary property is a moral objective. The US, Lieber demands, should respect its neighbors and hold itself to a higher standard than enabling "literary piracy." Thus, the US must reciprocate rights and protections granted to US authors by other countries and live up to its own understanding as a global leader in matters of progress and civilization. In his speech, Lieber also recounts the political efforts by different politicians to bring about changes in copyright legislation, offering a sense of continuity regarding the struggle for international copyright. He places the present efforts for international copyright in the US in the tradition of earlier European efforts, referencing German accomplishments and European reciprocal treaties. In his speech, he appeals to Congress, politicians, and citizens directly, reminding everyone of their shared duty to strive for progress, civilization, and the protection of literature as transnational property.

Lieber's speech was published in a volume along with four other speeches and fifteen letters of support. Added to the volume was the constitution of the *International Copyright Association*, adopted at a later meeting on May 4, 1868, and a petition addressed to the Senate and the House of Representatives of the United States, along with 153 collected signatures. The expressed goal of the association, laid down in its constitution, was to "promote, by all legitimate means, the enactment of a just and suitable International Copyright Law, for the benefit of authors and artists in all parts of the world" (*Meeting*, 41). The petition to Congress is short and concise, it reads:

> We, the undersigned, concerned in the production, manufacture, and sale of Books, Periodicals, Designs, and Objects of Art, request the early attention of your honorable bodies to the subject of International Copyright. We respectfully solicit the passage of a Bill such as, in the judgement of the Congress, may best secure the rights of Authors, Artists, and Designers to control and derive profit from the multiplication of copies of their works in countries other than their own. (*Meeting*, 42)

This petition carefully avoids framing literature as property and is thus less radical than the resolutions of the *International Copyright Association*. This is likely to garner more support for the petition and to heighten its chances of success in Congress. The petition, along with the names of the undersigned, also reflects a change taking place in the second half of the nineteenth century: Different agents involved in the book trade combined their efforts. Authors, printers, and publishers joined forces in their activism for an international copyright. While not all printers and publishers agreed with these demands,[103] there are many artists, publishers, booksellers, editors, journalists, an engraver, several "commercial advertisers," and an employee of the entertainment agency "American Literary Bureau" amongst those who signed the petition (*Meeting*, 42–46).

Unsurprisingly, the petition remained unsuccessful. Francis Lieber's speech at the meeting of the *International Copyright Association* in 1868 was his last public statement on the issue – that is, the last public statement preserved in the archives. Nevertheless, Lieber did not let the subject rest and instead continued lobbying, as evidenced by a letter he sent to Secretary of State Hamilton Fish (1808–1893) on April 25, 1871. He writes: "When a few minutes ago I was searching for a pamphlet, my letter to William C. Preston on International Copyright fell into my hands. A thought flashed through my mind, – or rather a pang shot through my heart. Could that subject [...] have been settled by the High Commission?" (*Life and Letters*, 410). Lieber felt disheartened by Congress's repeated refusals to take action when presented with an international copyright bill. He searched for alternatives ways to implement an international copyright and turned towards the American-British Joint High Commission, coordinated by Fish and others and held to settle disputes between Great Britain and the US. In his letter, Lieber attempts to convince Fish that international copyright is an issue important enough to be settled by the High Commission.[104] He echoes Sumner's claim that "this subject ought to be settled by treaty rather than in any other way" (*Life and Letters*, 410). He then prompts Fish to read *On International Copyright*, which can be found in the Library of Congress. Remarkably, Lieber writes "It was published in 1840, so it is like the work of quite another person," even though the points presented in it mirror, as shown above, his standpoints towards the end of his life (*Life and Letters*,

103 Most prominently, publisher Henry Charles Carey (1793–1879) published his extensive rejection of international copyright in the form of letters, mimicking Lieber's *On International Copyright*.

104 The High Commission drafted the *Treaty of Washington*; signed on May 8, 1781. Details of the proceedings of the High Commission can be accessed here: United States Government Printing Office. "Papers Relating to the Foreign Relations of the United States, Transmitted to Congress, With the Annual Message of the President, December 1, 1873." *U.S. Department of State*, history.state.gov/historicaldocuments/frus1873p2v3. Accessed 20 July 2023.

410). Lieber asks Fish to promote international copyright regulation, explicitly characterizing it as an aspect of the modern law of nations (410). Merely three days later, on April 28, 1871, Lieber writes a letter to judge Martin Russel Thayer (1819–1906), commenting on the proceedings of the High Commission. He writes: "I have heard no rumor of the High Commission having adopted Bluntschli's views, nor do I believe it. If I had been asked, I should have tried to draw international copyright, and emigration and immigration, within the treaty" (*Life and Letters*, 410–411). Lieber also brings up *On International Copyright* in this letter, asking Thayer:

> Have you ever read my letter to Senator Preston, published in 1840, on International Copyright? I glanced at it a few days ago, and was very much pleased. You smile at this observation? I once stood with the famous Mrs. Herz [...] when she was quite old, before her own portrait, taken when she was young. She looked silently at the picture for some time, and then said, "She was very beautiful!". (*Life and Letters*, 410–411)[105]

This statement to Thayer constitutes Lieber's last preserved statement on international copyright and Lieber's analogy beautifully demonstrates that his views on international copyright remained consistent throughout his life: Even after three decades, Lieber still stood behind *On International Copyright* and admired his most passionate defense of literary property. Lieber died on October 2, 1872, in his flat in New York City of a heart attack.[106] He should not live to witness the passing of the first US international copyright act in 1891. While Lieber certainly would not have agreed with the provisions of the act, which did not adopt Lieber's framing of literature as property, he would have been pleased to see the fruits of his decade-long activism.

Others picked up where Lieber left off: A few years before Lieber's death James Parton published an article on international copyright in *The Atlantic Monthly*, in which he focuses on Harriet Beecher Stowe's *Uncle Tom's Cabin* to criticize US national and international copyright law.[107] Parton castigates that despite the immense success of the work in the US and abroad Stowe did not receive a fair share of the profits – due to the lack of reciprocal copyright relations she earned no money from sales abroad.[108] He uses this case to

---

105 Henriette Herz (1764–1847) was a popular writer and acquaintance in Lieber's youth.

106 Martin Russell Thayer, *The Life, Character, and Writings of Francis Lieber. A Discourse Delivered before the Historical Society of Pennsylvania, January 13, 1873* (Philadelphia: Collins, 1873), 33.

107 Parton, James, "International Copyright," *The Atlantic Monthly* 20 (1867): 430–451.

108 Parton, "International Copyright," 433.

show the "cruel and shameful indifference with regard to the rights of authors, native and foreign" and highlights the harm done to the publishing business, American literature at large, and the national honor to demand the complete protection of literary works and of the rights of authors.[109]

A few years after Lieber died, Eaton S. Drone published *A Treatise on the Law of Property in Intellectual Productions in Great Britain and the United States* in 1879, the most comprehensive legal treatise on copyright law yet.[110] Drone dedicates over 800 pages to intellectual property and frames copyright as literary property. He summarizes the origin and nature as well as the history of literary property in England and the US and even connects his understanding of literature as property to the current calls for international copyright protection (*Law of Property*, 92–96). "This country is put to shame by the legislation of England and other foreign nations on [international copyright]," he writes, highlighting the moral aspect of his demands. He echoes Lieber when he demands that the United States should open its gates "wide to the authors of all tongues, all races, all creeds. All countries should be one for noble men who labor [...] for the advancement of knowledge and truth" (*Law of Property*, 95–96).

Pastor Henry van Dyke (1852–1933) published the sermon *The National Sin of Literary Piracy* in 1888.[111] Van Dyke was pastor at Brick Presbyterian Church in New York City, an author, and later a professor of English literature and US ambassador in Europe. He approached the subject of copyright from a religious perspective, ordaining it a sin committed by the entire nation and a moral failure by the American people (*National Sin*, 5). Nations are judged by God on whether they are "true and just and upright in all their dealings," and "literary piracy" does not, Van Dyke claims, adhere to the law of God (*National Sin*, 22). Included along with the sermon is a letter on behalf of the *International Copyright Association*, whose members continued their activism. Van Dyke urged everyone to circulate the sermon, to join the association, and to contact their senators and representatives to appeal for copyright reform (*National Sin*, 25).

Others, such as Richard Rogers Bowker (1848–1933) heralded the beginnings of today's copyright scholarship: Bowker published *Copyright. Its Law and its Literature* in 1886, in which he analyzed the "principles, history, and

---

109 Parton, "International Copyright," 433, 438–439, 451.

110 Eaton S. Drone, *A Treatise on the Law of Property in Intellectual Productions in Great Britain and the United States* (Boston: Little, Brown, and Company, 1879). Hereafter abbreviated as *Law of Property*.

111 Henry Van Dyke, *The National Sin of Literary Piracy* (New York: Charles Scribner's Sons, 1888). Hereafter abbreviated as *National Sin*.

present law of copyright, domestic and international."[112] He draws on legal treatises on copyright, bills, reports of Congress, and various other sources. The work also includes a collection of articles on copyright in England in the US, as well as copies of the copyright statutes of Great Britain and the US. The appendix contains a bibliography of literary property, written by Thorvald Solberg (1852–1949), US Register of Copyright. Solberg gives an overview of the history of copyright and the scope of copyright law towards the end of the nineteenth century, along with his comprehensive international bibliography of literary property, spanning sixty pages. Interestingly, despite his decade-long activism, Lieber is not included in the bibliography.

7.4 Epilogue: "An American of Americans […]"

While Lieber had become "the most renowned American law teacher" by 1872,[113] and was praised as the "father of political science,"[114] he remained less acknowledged and included by the literary and political elites of the Eastern cities than he would have liked. He did not receive a position at Harvard or Cambridge, or as a diplomat for the US government. Neither did he receive a permanent position as president of Columbia College in South Carolina, where he worked for three decades. Schnurmann reasons that this might have been because he was an immigrant – one who spoke with a heavy German accent – and due to his jovial demeanor.[115] Soifer claims that Lieber was "crusty, egocentric, and often desperate to ingratiate himself, while also con-

112 R. R. Bowker, *Copyright. Its Law and Its Literature* (New York: Sampson Low, Marston, Searle & Rivington, 1886), 1.

113 Since 1860 Lieber was affiliated with the law school at Columbia and seen as an expert on international law. Paul D. Carrington also argues that while Lieber was not a trained lawyer, academic credentials had little meaning during his life time. While historians tended to value those credentials very much and therefore largely ignored Lieber's legal writings, "professional status as a lawyer was loosely worn, more as a tool than as an ornament" in Lieber's time, as Carrington proposes. He believes Lieber played a major role in early legal sciences, despite lacking the official title and "technocratic skill" of a lawyer (Carrington, "The Theme," 356–358).

114 Weiss, "Americanization," 273.

115 Schnurmann, Brücken, 12. Lieber considered himself a US-American and favored assimilation (Weiss, "Americanization," 283). He lamented that he continued "to be called a foreigner, although I have been an American citizen for a much longer time than it takes to be born here and arrive at the age of voting; although I have nursed and nurtured young Americans for many years, and have instructed them in their own Constitution, in politics, and public law; although my whole name – the little I have of it – is exclusively American, and my children were all born this side of the water which divides republi-

stantly compelled to flaunt his learning" and consequently his "social and intellectual successes tended to exceed his professional and financial ones."[116] Despite Lieber's attempts to advertise his works in Europe, they were often criticized and rejected there.[117] Still, he considered himself one of the most influential "historico-philosophical publicists," alongside Alexis de Tocqueville and Charles-Louis de Secondat, Baron de La Brède et de Montesquieu. His works, he believed, "belon[g] to the list which begins with Aristotle, and in which we find the names of Thomas Moore, Hobbes, Hugo Grotius, Puffendorf [sic]" – a notion occasionally echoed by the domestic press but rejected by many scholars.[118] German-Americans often presented Lieber as a paragon of integration and assimilation. He served as an "Identifikationsfigur" (a figure of identification) for German migrants in the US and as a mediator between the "old world" and the "new world."[119]

After Francis Lieber's death his wife Mathilde, who survived him by eighteen years, managed his estate, cultivated his public persona, and collected many of the dedications to and obituaries for Francis Lieber. The writers of these obituaries remember Lieber in his various different functions – as a scholar, an educator, a member of the republic of letters, as an American and as a German in America. Examining these dedications and obituaries allows for a closer look at Lieber's legacy and the reception of his work in the US and in the German states and the German Empire. While obituaries often overemphasize the successes of the deceased and magnify the impact of their works, they are nevertheless valuable sources that help trace the influence a person had on others – if taken with a grain of salt.

A few days after Lieber's passing, *The College Courant*, a weekly journal focused on college interests, science, and literature, printed a two-page obituary, which summarizes Lieber's various functions in US society.[120] The anonymous author points out Lieber's popularity as a scholar, a publicist, and a

---

canism from monarchy. I am an American by choice; others are so by chance" (Lieber, *Life and Letters*, 248).

116 Soifer, "Facts," 2307, 2319.

117 Schnurmann, *Brücken*, 20.

118 Schnurmann, *Brücken*, 21. As Claudia Schnurmann points out, some of Lieber's contemporaries shared his opinion and in 1853 *The Daily South Carolinian* proclaimed that "[t]he author's name is of itself sufficient to give character to the work as that of one who is in the world of humanity what Humboldt is in the world of nature." "Dr. Leiber's [sic] Work." The Daily South Carolinian, 30 Dec. 1853 (cited in Schnurmann, *Brücken*, 21). Notably, the newspaper still misspelled his last name.

119 Schnurmann, *Brücken*, 15–16.

120 "Dr. Francis Lieber," *The College Courant*, 11.14 (1872): 160–161, 161. Hereafter abbreviated as "Dr. Francis Lieber."

networker ("Dr. Francis Lieber," 160). They refer to his numerous writings on ethics, law, and political history, political morals, political economy, and political philosophy, and compliment his liberal stance on the important movements of his time ("Dr. Francis Lieber," 160). They also remark on his "boldness and independence [and] extraordinary industry" and emphasize that Lieber was "no compiler of other men's opinions either, but on all the subjects upon which he wrote he was an original thinker, who could seize upon the strong points of an argument, arrange them logically and state them clearly" ("Dr. Francis Lieber," 161). While the author attests to Lieber's independence and originality, they also point out that Lieber was at the same time "very fond of public notice" and aimed to be recognized by other scholars, journals, and newspapers ("Dr. Francis Lieber," 160). Another newspaper clipping from an unidentified journal, likely dating back to before Lieber's death, even claimed that

> [n]o one can estimate the benefit which would result to the intellectual wealth of the United States, if all our citizens could be made to "read, mark, learn and inwardly digest" three great works – the Manual of Political Ethics, the Manual of Legal and Political Hermeneutics, and the profound yet transparent treatise on Civil Liberty and Self-Government. The greatest legal authorities of which our country could even boast, have expressed their admiration of the writings of Lieber in the strongest terms.[121]

Lieber had certainly carved out his niche as a political scientist and as an authority on law, establishing and cultivating the field of political science in the US.

Nevertheless, Lieber's literary oeuvre and his position as a scholar were also criticized. One author calls *Manual of Political Ethics*

> the work in which [Lieber's] defects, or rather shortcomings, are most conspicuous. Its substantial merits are very high, but in matters of form, style and construction it is deficient [...] He is at needless pains to argue undisputed propositions, and states obvious truths at unnecessary lengths.[122]

---

121 No author. Article for the *Pennsylvania Enquirer*. No title. No date. Francis Lieber papers. mssLI. Box 86, no. 9. No LI number. The Huntington. San Marino, CA. The source is dated 1857 in pencil.

122 No author. Article in unknown newspaper. No title. No date. Francis Lieber papers. mssLI. Box 86, no. 9. No LI number. The Huntington. San Marino, CA.

The author also states that "Dr. Lieber never became a finished and graceful writer" in his second language, English, and that they doubt "if Dr. Lieber was a good writer, even in his own language." In an article in *The Nation*, published a decade after Lieber's death, an unknown author writes that Lieber's work lacks both system and originality. Lieber was, according to this article, a practical reformer, not a theorist. The author, who claims to have access to Lieber's private correspondence, also criticizes that "toward the close of his life (he has been so often applied to for advice and instruction) he got into the way of volunteering it somewhat unnecessarily on every variety of subject, and in all quarters."[123] An earlier article from *The Nation*, on the other hand, remarked on Lieber's practicality and set it in relation to Lieber's common sense and honesty, which enabled him to "reach political truths which rest upon a sure and solid foundation." The author also compliments Lieber's ability to explain things by illustration, stating that "throughout his volumes, what was new and obscure, or difficult, is made at once palpable by some homely image, or by a felicitous reference to some historical anecdote or incident."[124] The author emphasizes Lieber's ability to convey things to an audience, highlighting his prominent role as an educator and an advocate for legal reform.

During his lifetime, Lieber was already recognized as a passionate educator of American youth. The *Pennsylvania Enquirer* wrote in 1857 that "America owes a large debt to Lieber; for [...] perhaps no man, living or dead has decidedly and instrumentally instructed so many of our countrymen in the laws of sciences, the principles of philosophy, the canons of ethics, and the institutes of political economy."[125] *The Cap and Gown*, the newspaper of Columbia College, dedicated three pages to an obituary for Lieber.[126] The author, a former student of Lieber, praises him "chiefly as an educator of the youth" ("Francis Lieber," 1).[127] He writes of Lieber's

---

123 No author. "Francis Lieber." Article in *The Nation*. January 18, 1883. Francis Lieber papers. mssLI. Box 86, no. 9. No LI number. The Huntington. San Marino, CA.

124 No author. No title. Article in *The Nation*. Francis Lieber papers. mssLI. Box 87, no. 10. No LI number. The Huntington. San Marino, CA. The source is dated to October 1872 in pencil.

125 No author. Article for the *Pennsylvania Enquirer*. No title. No date. Francis Lieber papers. mssLI. Box 86, no. 9. No LI number. The Huntington. San Marino, CA. The source is dated to 1857 in pencil.

126 "Francis Lieber," *The Cap and Gown* 5.1 (1872): 1–3. Hereafter abbreviated as "Francis Lieber."

127 The article also contains a long list of Lieber's publications, as well as resolutions of the *Alumni Association of Columbia College*, in which they outline the importance of Lieber to Columbia College and its alumni.

> genuine pleasure he took in assisting earnest students in their researches; of his delight in the companionship of young people; of the heartiness with which he entered into the sports of children; of the never-failing goodness of heart and geniality of disposition which were manifest in the circle of his family and friends. ("Francis Lieber," 3)

Many felt that Lieber did a great service to his chosen home country by educating generations of students. Lewis R. Harley emphasizes Lieber's service to the US and the German states alike in his treatise on Lieber's life and political philosophy, and writes that he "enriched [his] fatherland, as well as America, with his great productions on civil liberty."[128] Through his role as an educator Lieber passed on knowledge about the German states to his American students, installing deeper respect for German culture in the US and "thus, Germany has been well repaid for her contributions to our civilization," Harley writes.[129]

As a German and a US citizen, Lieber played a central role in the intellectual exchange between the two countries and in the transfer of German knowledge to the US. An article in *The Library Docket* argues that Lieber will be remembered by historians because

> his writings mark an epoch in our literature, as having been the first to open communications between the American mind and that of the Continent of Europe, entirely independent of those English channels through which our writers and students had previously drawn their knowledge of European thought.[130]

The article also credits Lieber with transporting US legal and political thought to Europe through his works, which were, the article claims, the first American books to be well-received by influential jurists in the German states. *The Illustrated Family Friend* stated as early as 1851 that "Francis Lieber, we believe, has a higher celebrity in the republic of Letters, than any other man in the United States."[131] The *Vermont Chronicle* also praises Lieber's ability to combine "the thorough scientific discipline of his native country with the practical insight of

---

128 Harley, *Francis Lieber*, viii.

129 Harley, *Francis Lieber*, viii.

130 No author. Article for *The Library Docket*. No title. No date. Francis Lieber papers. mssLI. Box 86, no. 8. No LI number. The Huntington. San Marino, CA. The source mentions a new edition of Lieber's *Legal and Political Hermeneutics*, which was published in 1880.

131 *The Illustrated Family Friend*. "Francis Lieber, L.L.D." December 6, 1851. Box 86, no. 9. No LI number. The Huntington. San Marino, CA.

his adopted country."[132] In a review of Lieber's posthumously published *Miscellaneous Writings*, Lieber is portrayed as "a German plant on American soil, [who] combined in himself much that is best in the intellectual character of both peoples."[133]

The College Courant once emphasized Lieber's "thorough Americanization" and praised him as "an American of Americans," "a master of our political system and one of its most ardent admirers, as well as a patriot in the best and truest sense of the word" ("Dr. Francis Lieber," 161). While he could not bring about broad acceptance of literature as transnational property and did not live to see the implementation of an international copyright in the US, Lieber nevertheless reached his goal to make a home in America and to become a respected citizen, reformer, and authority on history, politics, and law.

132 No author. Article for the *Vermont Chronicle*. No title. No date. Francis Lieber papers. mssLI. Box 86, no. 9. No LI number. The Huntington. San Marino, CA.

133 No author. Article reviewing *The Miscellaneous Writings of Francis Lieber*, edited and published by Daniel C. Gilman in 1881. No title. No date. Francis Lieber papers. mssLI. Box 86, no. 9. No LI number. The Huntington. San Marino, CA.

CHAPTER 8

Conclusion

A century after the first *Copyright Act of 1790*, the United States Congress extended limited copyright protection to foreign authors and passed the *International Copyright Act of 1891*.[1] The act took effect on July 1, 1891, almost twenty years after Francis Lieber's death. The bill was sponsored by Senator Jonathan Chace (1829–1917) from Rhode Island and became known as the *Chace Act*. Foreign authors who did not reside in the US could now register their works for copyright protection within the US. Following the *Chace Act*, the author of a work had "upon complying with the provisions of this chapter [...] the sole liberty of printing, reprinting, publishing, completing, copying, executing, finishing, and vending the same," as well as the liberty to dramatize the work or produce translations for a term of twenty-eight years.[2] This copyright was contingent upon proper registration at the office of the Librarian of Congress and payment of a fee. During the copyright term, all editions of a copyrighted work sold in the US had to be printed from plates produced within the country and the import of other editions was strictly prohibited. Once foreign authors registered their work according to these provisions, reprinting these works became illegal in the US. The provisions of the act only applied to citizens of foreign states or jurisdictions which

> permi[t] to citizens of the United States of America the benefit of copyright on substantially the same basis as its own citizens; or when such foreign state or nation is a party to an international agreement which provides for reciprocity in the granting of copyright.

The president of the US determined through proclamations whether these conditions were fulfilled. Initially, copyright protection was extended to Bel-

1 *An Act to amend title sixty, chapter three, of the Revised Statutes of the United States, relating to copyrights*, passed on March 3, 1891, by the 51st Congress. It was signed into law by President Benjamin Harrison and took effect on July 1, 1891. See *International Copyright Act* (*The Chace Act*), Washington D.C. (1891), Primary Sources on Copyright (1450–1900), ed. L. Bently and and M. Kretschmer, http://www.copyrighthistory.org. Accessed 24 April 2024.

2 Authors, their surviving spouse or their children could record the title again for another fourteen years.

 | HTTPS://DOI.ORG/10.1515/9783112239407-008

gium, France, Switzerland, Great Britain and British colonies, and a proclamation to the German Empire followed in 1892.

With the *Chace Act* a conditional and reciprocal international copyright came into force in the US and reprinting of foreign works was significantly curtailed. Despite its limitations the act represented a legal caesura in the US: After a century of advocacy by many different issue entrepreneurs, the US renounced reprinting and the exploitation of foreign authors and their works. As a life-long entrepreneur for the issues of international copyright and literary property protection, Lieber significantly contributed to the mobilization of support for the cause. The final legal reform of the copyright system was the result of the cumulative effort of a network of well-connected issue entrepreneurs in the US and in Great Britain. Each issue entrepreneur offered a unique perspective on the issue, told their own narrative of copyright protection, and contributed in different ways to the final legal adjustments.

Initially, issue entrepreneurs like Lieber were those closely involved in the literary industry: As authors or publishers they were personally affected by the common practice of reprinting in the US. Authors criticized their mistreatment and the devaluation of the profession of authorship. They demanded the possibility of making a living through writing and highlighted their contribution to public education, social progress, and the nation-building process. Publishers rejected the unfair competition illegal reprinting had introduced to the literary market in the US; some criticized the treatment of authors they respected and worked with. Authors and publishers in the US and in Great Britain were the first to identify the issue of reprinting and to attribute it to the lack of comprehensive domestic copyright protection and of international copyright legislation in the US. They reached out to others affected and connected over a shared problem. By building networks within the country and across the Atlantic they were able to exchange opinions and knowledge, to discuss, and to support each other in their advocacy. Within their networks they sketched the theoretical foundation for the issue and outlined their rationale and their demands. Not all issue entrepreneurs shared the same reasons, nor did they always agree on their methods and demands. On the one hand, the initial lack of joint demands and a united front impeded their activism and made it more difficult for outsiders to understand the issue. On the other hand, the diversity of opinions also highlighted the complexity of the issue and offered many points of connection for outsiders.

Throughout the following decades, issue entrepreneurs like Lieber tried out different ways to frame the issue in their attempts to reach others; their discussions laid the foundation for diverse framings of the issue. Direct appeals to their honor did not stop reprinters, neither did shaming them. Issue entrepreneurs therefore settled on the common goal of bringing about legal change through a reform of copyright law. Consequently, they needed a compelling argument to garner broad public support and to convince legislators – a narrative framing of the story of copyright that would catch the attention of others. With their individual narratives of the wrongs of reprinting and the injustices of the current copyright regime, they increasingly turned outward in their attempts to reach others, to interest them in the issue, and to mobilize support for their cause. They conveyed the issue in an appealing and understandable way in letters, speeches, petitions, and newspaper articles. By connecting the issue to existing social norms and values, such as the self-conception of the US as an honorable and just nation, they integrated the issue into the normative understanding of the public. They also built frame bridges to other issues, such as education, social progress, and economic well-being to reach more people and bring about normative change within society. Issue entrepreneurs also began organizing in associations dedicated to the issue of international copyright, such as the *Copyright Association for the Protection and Advancement of Literature and Art* and the *American Copyright League*. In these associations diverse actors, including authors, journalists, printers, typesetters, and publishers, combined their efforts to reach more people and to increase their influence.

Over the course of the nineteenth century, more US-Americans began to support the issue of international copyright; public opinion shifted in favor of more comprehensive protection for foreign authors. Issue entrepreneurs then turned towards politics and began lobbying legislators to bring about actual legal change. They expanded their networks by reaching out to politicians sympathetic to the cause, adding political expertise to their demands. Legislators like Henry Clay, William C. Preston, Charles J. Ingersoll, and finally Jonathan Chace introduced international copyright bills to Congress and thus translated the narratives of the issue entrepreneurs into legislation. It took many attempts and decades of lobbying by the increasingly organized network of issue entrepreneurs to convince Congress: Only through a century-long process of issue identification, narrative framing, issue conveyance, public mobilization, and lobbying could issue entrepreneurs finally convince Congress to change the law. Though it did not meet all the demands of the different issue entrepreneurs, the *International Copyright Act of 1891* codified international copyright protection in the US and represented at least a compromise; a step away from reprinting and towards copyright protection for all authors.

Within this network of diverse issue entrepreneurs, all with different motivations and individual narrative framing, Francis Lieber was certainly an influential entrepreneur who contributed a unique transnational perspective. He migrated to the US in 1827, alone and in pursuit of opportunities not offered to him in Prussia. With the help of influential friends and through ceaseless work, persistence, and a talent for being in the right place at the right time, Lieber became a prominent personality in US politics and academia. When he died in 1872, he had become a nationally and internationally renowned author and the first professor of political science in the US. Among his many legal and political interests, the matter of copyright and literary property remained a notable one: Lieber closely observed the debates surrounding the introduction of domestic and international copyright in the US and contributed from his transnational point of view, characterized by the integration of different legal understandings. As an author, publicist, and editor, Lieber gained national and international renown and established a vast network of prominent political and legal contacts in the US and in Europe. Lieber evolved into a central figure of the legal and political reform movement in the US and he supplemented these discourses through written works, lobbying, and exchange and cooperation within his network.

As a German migrant and a citizen of the US, he became an issue entrepreneur with an uncommon perspective. In his narrative framing of the issues of international copyright and literary property, he assumed the role of a transnational mediator and translator, conveying Prussian and European ideas about authorship and literary property as a form of legal and political participation to the US. He combined Prussian and US-American political, legal, and cultural notions of authorship and property and integrated them into a transnational framework, cultivating his own understanding of literature as a transnational form of property and international copyright as the legal tool to protect literary property. He (re-)introduced a sweeping conceptualization of literature as a form of property to the US, which added a new dimension to the discourse. His understanding arose from decades of research and examination of the issue and evolved throughout his life. His advocacy was not merely a brief and opportunistic engagement with the issue. Instead, he significantly contributed to the recognition of authorship as a form of political participation and to the appreciation of the social and political function of literature. As an entrepreneur Lieber intertwined the issues with his foundational understanding of the duties and rights of citizens, the role and responsibilities of the government, the function of law, the importance of international respect and cooperation, and the significance of authorship and literature to progress, civilization, and national identity.

Lieber used his published works as a way to assert and disseminate his standpoints, to influence public debates, mobilize support, appeal to legislators, and to bring about normative and legal change. As an author he was appreciated both in his home, the German states, and in his chosen home, the US. His ability to understand both legal and political spheres and to combine this knowledge in a productive way distinguished Lieber from many other issue entrepreneurs. His works and the notions they transported about literary property and international copyright demonstrate the nuances of the discourse in the US. Current copyright research is often limited to the analysis of the national discourse or focuses only on the Anglo-American sphere. The analysis of Lieber's works and his contribution to the US discourse expands this perspective by highlighting the presence of German influences and adding a comparative perspective. As Lieber's advocacy shows, the continental-European understanding of authors' rights and the Anglo-American copyright regime were not diametrically opposed during the nineteenth century, though research like Peter Baldwin's *The Copyright Wars* often perpetuates this juxtaposition. The examination of the advocacy network that Lieber was part of disproves the notion that US-American understanding of copyright developed detached from continental-European understandings of authors' rights and natural law. Rather, Lieber's works illustrate the integrative legal discourse in the US and its transnational dimension.

Using the model of issue emergence during the analysis made it possible to follow the entire life cycle of the issue of international copyright in the US during the nineteenth century. Lieber participated in this process of issue emergence: From the initial identification of the issue, over the narrative framing and conveyance of the issue, to inducing normative change and mobilizing support, putting the issue on the political agenda, and lobbying legislators. By analyzing Lieber's oeuvre and his advocacy through the lens of issue emergence, it was possible to map out his contribution to the international copyright debate in the US, to carve out his narrative of literary property, and to position him within a network of issue entrepreneurs working towards a shared goal. By understanding Lieber as an issue entrepreneur, this work explored his distinct narrative framing and the diverse channels he used to convey his narrative both to the public and to legislators. The interconnectedness of the issue entrepreneurs illustrates that both individual contributors like Lieber and the collective advocacy by all actors brought about legal change. Lieber was part of a bigger reform movement, whose participants reframed the issue of international copyright and prefigured the emergence of the concept of intellectual property.

This analysis of Lieber's contribution also confirmed the influence of continental-European concepts of literature as property and of authors' rights on the US copyright debate. Lieber's integration of these notions into his narrative framework highlights the transnational dimension of the debate. The continental-European understanding of natural rights and authors' rights and the Anglo-American understanding of copyright as a temporary monopoly on reprinting to encourage literary production were not entirely detached from each other. Rather, an exchange was enabled by actors like Lieber. As an issue entrepreneur, Lieber amalgamated both understandings in his work and curated his distinct narrative of literature as transnational property, in which he even integrated earlier notions from the state statutes. He introduced this narrative to the US cultural, legal, and political debate on copyright through his writings, lobbying, and public outreach.

Lieber's understanding and narrative framing of, as well as his demands for the issues of literary property and international copyright evolved throughout his life, as the analysis of his writings and correspondence confirmed. They developed in confrontation with other countries' legislation, with the current state of the debate and legal changes in the US, in exchange with other issue entrepreneurs, and in opposition to the counter narratives offered by opponents of the cause. While Lieber's contribution to the copyright debate is often reduced to his work *On International Copyright*, this evolution is visible in many of his works and in his correspondence, his lobbying activities, private reflections, and public statements. His advocacy for these issues cannot be minimized to a single moment: This analysis proves a prolonged engagement with the issues, which informs his general body of work.

The entries on copyright and literary property in the *Encyclopædia Americana* constitute Lieber's seminal work on these issues and his debut as an issue entrepreneur. Through international comparison he identified copyright legislation as an issue, outlined his initial criticisms, established the theoretical underpinnings of his critique, and spelled out his demands. He reached out to others who might hold similar opinions through his publication. He also aimed to convince the public and mobilize support for his demands, as comprehensive copyright protection was not a popular position. Lieber's focus was on copyright, not yet on international copyright specifically, and as a Prussian who had only recently migrated to the US, he was clearly inspired by continental-European notions of authors' rights. His argument consisted of three distinct aspects: Firstly, he argued that literature is a form of property and that copyright should be treated as a property right, granting authors exclusive, unlimited, and transmissible rights to their work. Secondly, he emphasized the rights of authors and criticized their treatment by US society and law. Authors, he argued, play a central role in society. Literary production is their individual act of participation in the production of shared meaning, within and between nations. Literary property was, to Lieber, an individual and a common good. Authors are champions of civilization and through their works they contribute to education, science, civil progress, and the cultivation of a national identity – these efforts should be rewarded. Lastly, he outlined the conduct he considered appropriate for an honorable and just nation in its treatment of authors, domestic and foreign; a nation would be judged by how it treats authors of other nations, how it values and protects their contribution. Lieber echoed sentiments from the early US state statutes in these entries and reintroduced them to the US discourse, but he also integrated continental-European notions of authors' rights in his narrative: He proposed an understanding of the author as the "Urheber" of a work, who holds all rights to their own creation, including printing and distribution. As the originator of the text, the author expresses their individuality and subjectivity through the act of writing and shares it with the world. Therefore, the integrity of the resulting work must be protected by the state.

In his *Manual of Political Ethics* and the adjunct work *Legal and Political Hermeneutics* Lieber developed his ideas further and built bridges to other issues, highlighting the legal, political, and cultural dimensions of literary property. He also reached out to other issue entrepreneurs who would be interested in his elaborations on the subject. As the analysis confirmed, Lieber's understanding of literary property, author protection, and the value of texts was interwoven with his notions of proper legal and political conduct and informed these works. He frames authorship as a tool for political participation for the individual: Individual articulation is the realization of personhood and citizenship for the author as a subject with rights, which the government has a duty to protect. Structured and good-faith interpretation of the texts resulting from this act of individual articulation is also a way to protect the author. The aim of legal and political hermeneutics is to reconstruct the original meaning of a text and the intention of the author, who expressed their individuality by writing it. This is only possible if the integrity of texts is legally protected, even across national boundaries. In these works, Lieber shaped his narrative of literary property and copyright and again included a transnational perspective by comparing the existing legal framework to the – in his opinion – superior Prussian copyright system. He called for copyright extension but his fully-formed demands of absolute, exclusive, and perpetual property rights to literature for domestic and foreign authors he laid down in his next work, *On International Copyright.*

While it was not his only work on the issues, *On International Copyright* remains Lieber's most comprehensive one. He presented his elaborate narrative of literary property, authors' rights, and international copyright, which he cultivated over more than a decade. He was certainly inspired by the recent passage of the *Prussian Copyright Act* of 1837, which he studied eagerly and translated for a US audience. In his understanding, copyright as a legal instrument was an inadequate attempt to outline an author's fundamental rights to control the printing, distribution, and integrity of their work. On principle Lieber rejected the basic premise of US copyright as an author's exclusive but temporary monopoly on printing and distribution rights, an approach which defines authors' rights in terms of economic benefits. Instead, Lieber framed an author's work as their literary property. He thus referenced the central right of an author to their written work in terms of a property right. Property rights applied to literature go far beyond the benefits granted by a copyright – if framed as a form of property, an author's work assumes the legal characteristics of a property right. An author's literary property is permanent, rather than temporary. It encompasses complete control over the printing and distribution of the work, while being alienable at the same time. After an author's death, the property passes to their relatives or legal successors. At its core, Lieber's understanding of authors' rights emanated from a fundamental perception of literature as a property. He conceptualized property as a naturally occurring social institution which precedes the state and necessitates (rather than results from) the law.

In his narrative Lieber employed property as a nexus between different important categories within a civil society: Through property one can express one's individuality within a group of people. Individuation through the act of possession distinguishes one from the mass of others. By owning property, one qualifies as a citizen. Property structures the relationship between the individual and the state, which exists to protect citizens' property. It allows the accumulation of influence and wealth and thus, political participation. To Lieber, literature was the purest form of property as he believed it resulted entirely from a person's mind, requiring no external resources. He framed writing as an act of individuation and publishing a work as an act of political participation – the work aids in the shared process of meaning-making within a nation, furthers education, and promotes scientific advancements and civil progress. Through printed copies the physical manifestation of a work becomes accessible to everyone, even across national boundaries and geographical distance. Authors can be inspired by knowledge from other national contexts; they combine their knowledge in increasingly transnational works exchanged within international communities and the Republic of Letters. Many cultures benefited from the exchange and production of new knowledge and consequently, the protection of the resulting works did not concern one jurisdiction only, but all. International cooperation became necessary because the mistreatment of authors in one jurisdiction might cause them to stop writing altogether, to everyone's detriment. Literary property, Lieber argued, is an author's most personal creation, an expression and assertion of their individuality. As an inherent and natural right, literature necessarily becomes a transnational form of property. This applies to all authors everywhere in the world, wherefore they must necessarily retain the full rights to their work in all countries. Consequently, Lieber's central narrative framed literature as transnational property.

On International Copyright goes beyond a mere formulation of his theory, his sources and justifications, and even beyond communication with other issue entrepreneurs. This work was clearly directed both at the public at large and at legislators. In the short pamphlet Lieber presented an appealing narrative with an accessible and affective storyline, in which he identified good and bad actors and integrated his demands within the narrative. His aim was to educate and convince those who might not be aware of the issue. With the work Lieber moved beyond criticism and towards effecting actual legal change. To reach that goal he tried to mobilize public support and appeal directly to legislators, such as the addressee William C. Preston, to influence Congressional debates. *On International Copyright* stands in connection with other issue entrepreneurs' efforts from the previous years: Lieber certainly witnessed Henry Clay's and British authors' futile attempts to petition Congress and wanted to support them. Clay and other politicians even addressed the network of issue entrepreneurs and Clay urged Lieber directly to become active. The resulting work *On International Copyright* was part of a broader and coordinated effort by politicians, authors, and publishers to mobilize the public and bring about legal change.

The issue of literary property and its protection through international copyright continued to inform Lieber's later work: He elaborated on his theory in *Essays on Property and Labor* and connected it to his criticisms of communism and commonly-held property. Thus, he integrated his understanding of literary property within the broader property discourse at the time. He illustrated the connections between property as a natural right and inherent human institution and the government's duty to refrain from interfering with it. Literary property constituted an exception, as Lieber argued in his other works: As it is the result of the individual expression of the author as a subject of rights within the state, the government has to protect this vulnerable form of property – even beyond national boundaries. He increasingly emphasized the aspect of international law and cooperation in his narrative, framing international copyright as a necessary step to improve the US relationship with other nations and to live up to the nation's claim of a fair, just, and honorable character – especially in an increasingly connected world, in which knowledge was continuously exchanged across national boundaries.

Privately, Lieber also worked on translating his narrative of literary property, authors' rights, and international copyright into actual legislation. As public opinion slowly changed Lieber focused more on legal change and continued to appeal directly to politicians and legislators. His *Draught of a New Copyright Law for the United States* highlights transnational and especially Prussian influences on Lieber's work, in which he adhered closely to Prussian legislation. While he ultimately did not publish or share this draft with anyone, it reiterates the influence of continental-European notions on the discourse in the US through issue entrepreneurs like Lieber.

In his most successful work *On Civil Liberty and Self-Government* Lieber framed property as a central institution within all societies, which governments must protect to ensure citizens' liberties. While the government should interfere as little as possible with the liberties of its citizens, property is an institution so important that it constitutes an exception and must be protected by law. This includes literary property, which Lieber framed as an articulation of personhood and citizenship. He again built bridges to other central US-American values, such as liberty, political participation, the rights and duties of citizens, and proper government, and continued to integrate his narrative into his general body of thought.

Once Lieber moved to the North, his advocacy changed and he focused on networking and public outreach in person. This change was also prompted by the political upheavals of the time and the consequent Civil War. Lieber applied himself more than ever to political reform. He attended meetings, joined associations, gave public lectures, and his advocacy in other areas continued to be informed by his notions of literary property and international copyright – they had become an integral part of his understanding of culture, law, and politics. He built bridges between his abolitionist stance and his ideas of property, between the importance of knowledge exchange, his opposition to book tariffs, and his advocacy for free trade. Due to his move to the legal faculty at Columbia University, his work on the *Code 100*, and his frequent exchange with jurists in other countries, Lieber also increasingly turned towards international law and cooperation. He connected his demands for international copyright protection to his aspirations for an international community, cross-cultural exchange, and honorable and fair conduct between nations.

Lieber's last speech on international copyright at the meeting of the *International Copyright Association* in 1868 reaffirmed his stance as an issue entrepreneur within a network of advocates in the US. His manner of issue conveyance and his audience had changed but his narrative framing remained the same: While he began early on to reach out to other issue entrepreneurs through published works, he became increasingly organized and connected. After he addressed the public to mobilize support, his focus shifted towards lobbying politicians and in New York City he coordinated his efforts with other issue entrepreneurs, petitioning Congress directly. Lieber's speech sums up his narrative on literary property, authors' rights and international copyright and demonstrates that while the essence of his narrative remained unchanged, its presentation and its integration into his general body of thought evolved; his understanding of literature, authorship, property, labor, legal interpretation, political participation, national identity, and the rights and duties of citizens and the state converged. Lieber still presented authors' rights to their works as a natural right to property which the government has a duty to protect. International copyright was still the legal tool to protect literary property and to value *all* authors' contribution to public education, scientific progress, and civilization. He also explicitly connected present efforts in the US with earlier efforts in Europe – and especially in the German states – and situated them within the transnational movement for the recognition and protection of authors' rights. This transnational movement also aimed for the reform of international law according to the principles of respectful conduct, reciprocity, and cooperation between nations.

The publication of Lieber's speech in the conference proceedings of the *International Copyright Association*, alongside other notable speeches and the petition to Congress, locates his advocacy within the broader continued efforts for international copyright by issue entrepreneurs and legislators in the US. While he did not live to see the *International Copyright Act of 1891* become law, Lieber was certainly an important advocate for the issue, who contributed a unique narrative to the efforts of bringing about normative and legal change. The direct lobbying of members of Congress through his correspondence definitely informed the political debates and resulting legal reform in the US. Within the network of issue entrepreneurs, he was an important figure because he added a valuable transnational and comparative perspective, resulting from his bi-cultural background as a citizen of two countries. By positioning literature as transnational property, Lieber provided a hybrid framework that combined German and US-American cultural and legal notions, expanded the existing discourse in the US, and inspired other issue entrepreneurs.

While the *International Copyright Act of 1891* codified normative change in legal form, it was merely a stopover on the journey towards the transnational protection of literature. Even after its passage, the US only gradually proclaimed reciprocal copyright relations with other countries and refused to join the international *Berne Convention for the Protection of Literary and Artistic Works*. In the wake of technological progress, copyright also needed to change to incorporate new forms of mass media, such as musical recordings and movies. Over time the US became an exporter rather than an importer of copyrighted material and the nation's stance on international copyright protection changed accordingly. In many ways the comprehensiveness, time span, and global reach of current US copyright law resembles Lieber's expectations much more closely than its limited scope during the nineteenth century. While critics in the past condemned limited protection for domestic and foreign authors' works in the US, commentators today denounce the expansiveness of the all-encompassing US copyright system. Some argue that copyright terms are too long and its scope too wide-ranging, inhibiting scientific progress and shared creative processes. Others see copyright law as an outdated measure in today's globalized and digitized age, where immediate access to information and instantaneous sharing of content has become the new normal.

We live in an age of rapid technological progress where new digital mass media accelerate political, economic, cultural, and digital globalization. Via the internet knowledge is more available than ever. Social media opens a window into the lives of people anywhere in the world. Video on-demand, music streaming services, and e-books offer immediate access to cultural products. Through videotelephony services and digital platforms eLearning becomes possible. Worldwide broadcasting enables us to directly witness historic events and participate in global movements using a smartphone. Recent international discussions focus not only on the opportunities, but also on the risks of social media, artificial intelligence, and technological progress for mental health, labor conditions, political stability, and global safety. They demonstrate that these rapid changes need to be carefully scrutinized and integrated into social, philosophical, and political discussions to identify issues and initiate legal reform where necessary.

But social upheavals of similar magnitude have happened before: Francis Lieber's advocacy for comprehensive copyright protection was also a reaction to a changing reality, characterized by technological progress, increased international exchange, and resulting challenges to existing law. The analysis of his narrative within its national and international context illuminates a process of adaptation, from technological changes to the identification of issues, from avid discussions to changes in public opinion, and from normative change over political debate to legal reform. It shows the importance of cultural discourse, of joint examination and discussion of an issue within society, not just in political institutions, and demonstrates the interplay and synergy between society and politics, between culture and law. While it predates today's globalized and digitized world, Lieber's advocacy for literary property, authors' rights, and international copyright nevertheless emphasizes the importance of an international perspective in approaching literature and its protection and promotion. Circumstances change and society evolves, and many of Lieber's demands are no longer seasonable. Nevertheless, his calls for transnational knowledge exchange and international collaboration in the service of the preservation of knowledge, the advancement of education, the progress of science, and the promotion of artistic creativity stand the test of time, especially with regard to literature, a central cultural value and pillar of progress in all societies.

Appendix

Draught of a New Copyright Law for the United States

A draught of a new copyright law for the United States.

[Section 8 of the Const. of the U.S. provides that "Congress shall have power to promote the progress of science and useful arts, by securing for limited times to authors and inventors the exclusive right to their respective writings and discoveries."]

The author of a literary work or composition, his heirs or assignees, or those who derive their authority in writing of reprinting such work or composition already published, or of causing it to be multiplied in any mechanical way or by representing it on the stage from him or them, are the only persons lawfully entitled of doing so.

Every such new multiplication or representation on the stage, without written consent of him who is exclusively ~~entitled~~ authorized to give it, is unlawful and a punishable offence.

It is an equally punishable offence to publish or represent on the stage without authority derived from the author or his legal successors, manuscripts of all works, including letters, whether single or collections of them, ~~of~~ sermons, lectures, orations or discourses, written down while delivering, whether they are published with or without the names of the authors, or abridgements made without authority of the author of the original.

The lawful possession of a manuscript, whether it be an original or a copy, or of sermons, lectures, orations ~~or~~ discourses or plays, written down while they were delivering or performing, does not entitle to their publication or performance.

Nevertheless it is lawful to publish speeches, delivered in any official capacity, or before political meetings, whether they are called together for immediate political action or preparatory for the same, and of all official documents, unless their publication be especially prohibited, and or reports of general interest, and not strictly scientific.

It is likewise lawful to ~~republish~~ reprint any composition first ~~lawfully~~ lawfully published in a newspaper, while in a periodical publication, issuing at least once a week.

It is lawful verbally to quote single passages of a work already printed; to receive single emendations, made by others, into new and lawful editions, but not notes of others, unless permission has been obtained; to embody single

 | HTTPS://DOI.ORG/10.1515/9783112239407-009

essays, poems and other compositions of a similar Kind, in critical and literary-historical works, or in collections for the use of schools; to publish original translations of works already printed or to publish a lawfully possessed manuscript~~s~~, without farther authority, if no legal representative of the author exists, or one hundred years after said manuscript was written.

Nevertheless it is not lawful to ~~mak~~ publish an English translation of a work, issued by its author in a dead language; nor to publish without lawful authority a translation of a work, first published in several living languages, if said translation is made in one of these same living languages nor is it lawful to ~~ma~~ publish an unauthorized translation in a dead language, of a work or manuscript written in a living one.

It is not necessary to state in any part of a publication, that the copyright has been secured, or to quote this present Act, or any other words for that purpose, in order to secure for the said publication all the rights acknowledged and granted by this Act. But the author or his legal representative may cause the words "Copyright waived" to be put on the title page or its reverse, in which case it is lawful for anyone to reprint or multiply the work or composition by whatever means.

Nor is it necessary that the name of the author be mentioned on the title page or under the dedication or preface to secure protection for it.

The protection afforded by the present law against unlawful publication or republication shall be enjoyed by the author during his life, and by his legal heirs and successors for thirty successive years ~~after~~ from the day of his death, provided always that the time of the author's life after the publication of his work, and the thirty years, after his death, be not less than sixty years. The protection shall always be enjoyed for sixty years at least.

If a composition is published without the name of the author, or under an assumed name, the lawful publisher shall stand in place of the author for the claims upon his right of protection, and this protection for such works shall last for fifteen years only, from the ~~day~~ time of publication.

Nevertheless, if within these fifteen years the true name of the author is published by himself or his heirs, by means of a new edition or the issuing of a new title page for the remaining copies, the work acquires thereby the protection in its fullest extent, of other works, to date from the time of the first publication of ~~a~~ the work.

Every lawful new edition of a work, issued within the time during which the preceding edition was entitled to protection, according to the present Act, is considered ~~an origin~~ a new work and entitled to all its protection. Academies, universities, public institutions for instruction, learned and other lawful societies shall enjoy the exclusive right for the new publication of their works for

____ [blank] years. This term is to be counted respecting works which treat of a single subject in one or more volumes, and, consequently may be considered as forming a connected whole, to which class, especially, lexicographical are to be counted – from the time of their completion; respecting works however, which can be considered as continuous collections only, of essays and transactions on various subjects of learned inquiry – from the publication of each separate volume. If, however, the respective authors issues separate editions of such essays and transactions, they shall enjoy the rights guaranteed to original public-cations. Maps and charts enjoy the same protection; but the publication of copies on a reduced or enlarged scale shall be lawful.

Original engravings or woodcuts whether they beorig. compositions first published in these engravings or copies of pictures or ~~statues~~ sculptures, shall be entitled to ~~the same~~ protection; nor shall it be lawful to inne [?] unauthorized copy-engravings on a reduced or enlarged scale.

It shall be lawful to issue engravings or wood-cuts of pictures or sculpture, if the original artist or his heirs has not done so, or authorized ~~to~~ anyone else to do so, ten years after the completion of his work. The lawful possession alone of a picture or sculpture does entitle to the right of making or causing to be made, engravings representing the same.

The present Act extends the same protection to works which have first been published in foreign states, provided their respective governments grant all the rights secured by them for works first published there, likewise to works first published in the U. States.

All the rights or preveleges [sic] granted on this Act shall be equally in force for all authors resident in the U. States, whether they are ~~authors~~ citizens or not. If ~~any~~ No person can acquire the right of making an abridgement of a work, except through the consent of the author or his heirs although the author may have sold (the right?) of multiplying the original work, or it may have been sold to satisfy debts, in due course of Laws.

The exclusive right of publication and distribution of writings belonging to the author and his heirs, may be transferred by them, wholly or in part, for a limited space or time, or not, according to legal agreement.

No on is permitted to issue a ~~work~~ composition under the assumed name of a living author, if not his. It is punishable with ________________ [blank].[1]

1 Lieber, Francis. A Draught of a new copyright law for the United States. Approx. 1840–1850. Francis Lieber papers. mssLI. Box 92, no. 14. LI475. The Huntington. San Marino, CA.

Uncle Tom: A Review of Mrs. Stowe's Book

Uncle Tom
1853

The immense success of this book is owing to the author's talent of writing, the novelty of the scenes; the pathos and evident sincerity as well as sorrow of the writer; the universal sympathy of men with the weak; the pious fervor throughout and appeal to the inmost heart; and, in Europe, to the fact that people can exclaim: Oh, if that is Your American liberty! especially in Germany & France where many are ashamed that their attempts at liberty have so [?] and so paltrily failed.

I know all the facts in the book to be true; I could give many additional facts – painful in the last degree; still Mrs Stowe was bound I think to give more opposite facts, too, to make the picture truthful – the immense sacrifices which this System requires, and the enormous tax it is all the time upon the good (for instance the wasteful numbers of house servants, born in the [?], and whom people will not send to the field or sell, and thousand other things). This does not make slavery better, but it would have made the picture truthfuller [sic].

Is a saint like Uncle Tom possible? That Christianity has produced such saints – so pure, lovely, forbearing so ignorant except in the knowledge of Christ, so lamb-like, we know from the first centuries, and it only remains a question whether Christianity may not present itself to the soul of a peculiarly favored negro with all the freshness, fervor, singleness and [?] of the first centuries? I believe it may – it certainly may. The saying of the London Spectator that a system which could produce such a saint would not be so bad, is utterly fallacious. Was paganism or the Roman empire under Nero and Diocletian an acceptable thing because under its sway the hosts of testifying saints appeared? It is the old gross fallacy of mistaking the occasion for the cause or contemporaneousness as coincidence for causality.

It is striking that although religion is the main thread of this book, the minister does not appear once. It is the gospel per se which floats in it as the burning (?) [?] in the oil of the nightlamp. For that serpent a quakeress (?) might have written it.

It is also striking and truthful that all the Christianity which appears in it as [?] in a [?] is methodism: Methodism has a por[?]eness united with a soulfulness, which admirably [?] its pioneering character. I mean pioneering with reference to locality and classes and some individuals.

The only thing the book obtains in a practical point of view (taking practical still in a literary sense) is the showing of the dread action of the fugitive slave law. Otherwise she nowhere raises the constraint as to what ought to be done towards extinction of slavery.

She judges Northern merchants accidentally (?) come in possession of slavers, for selling them again. The question is: is every such man unworthy to her bound to take them to the North and free them? Suppose a whole plantation falls to his possession by the bankruptcy of some debtors? We do not settle things by taking hold of the outermost fringes of the garment. We must battle with the whole man. And constantly carried out, do we not again reach the point at which Quakers once arrived (now: wholly abandoned) of not using slave sugar, cotton &c?

Miss "Vermont" (that good woman) resolves to love Topsy and gets over her disgust at the black skin. Well and good. But the philosophers must ask at once, would she have married a black, or if she had had a son, see him married to Topsy? There is the eternal rule [?] – one of the fundamental difficulties.

There can be no doubt that slavery appears frequently doubly hideous because brought into such close contact with Christianity, civilization – because opposed in the whole tenor of the modern spirit. Where slaves do not partake of our civilisation, of the bread of Christ &c, as in some parts of the W. Indies, no uncle Tom, no almost white mother born from her children, no learned black minister sold for a price can appear. Where the Whites are not free republicans, the contract (?) and all the fugitive baroness (?) cannot appear so staggering to our souls. It is always so when an institution draws nigh its end, when it is in a transition period. Paganism of the time of Socrates and in Socrates was not so hideous as in Islean the Apostale (?) nor said Socrates such nonsense about it as Julian. Absolute monarchy is never so hideous as when on the eve of paning over into constitutional monarchy. An old style of art is never so caricaturelike [sic] as on the eveof a new style; so styles of [?] thing &c &c

The character of Sanclair [sic] seems to me psychologically false from the moment of Evangeline's death or rather from the moment of her last long conversation with her. His going on reading the paper as before is unnatural with all those conversations with Tom. And, then, why the "at last! at last! Does such a character become converted by a slab and at that moment?

The argument that such things happen with apprentices, in marriage, or that paupers starve in other countries is merelyad absurdum. It is silly. Pauperism is no institution. Frightful [?] crimes happen every where. The question is: Are they punished, is there a system set against it?

Facts

The point is not whether this or that happens, e.g. whether a master kills a slave, for murder happen everywhere, but: Whether the thing can only happenwhere slavery exists; Whether a thing is an unavoidable consequence of it; Whether it be punished or cannot well be punished as things go; Whether the effects are natural, considering the majority of men.

———

Rev. Palmer married a few days ago Cruesa's (?) mother to a man, yet her two previous husbands are living, and to one at least, I believe to both she was solemnly married by the church.

Day before yester-day I saw, at 10 oclock [sic] A M in main street, Columbia S.C. a man on horseback. He held a rope, which was around the neck of a negro, whose hands were tied behind. The rope which tied his hands also passed round the neck of a little boy behind him – perhaps 12 years old. The hands of the latter were also lashed behind. And thus they proceeded (the negro bare footed, in the middle of the street in the mud. Were they runaways? Perhaps they were taken from their families, and fear that their yearning haste would make them run-aways, led to the lashing. Oh God of mercy!

Some years ago a fellow came here who erected a pen, as it were, some few miles from Columbia, into which he put all the children he could pick up, for a southern market. Preston told me of it, with utmost indignation. But then, there the matter stops, I mean the indignation. A black man in Columbia married a black girl. They loved each other much. The man was most gayed. His master owed, besides, a debt to Dr. Toland, and wished to pay it. So, with the consent of the master, Bellinger told the negro to come to him for a task. The moment he appeared he was hand-cuffed & and run off to Alabama, with leave taking &c, where Bellinger sold him. The negro has occasionally written to his wife. Lately he wrotethat he despairs of ever coming backand advises her to marry again. The woman is in consequence so ill that serious doubts about her health are entertained.

I bought Gzaesa [?] at the greatest inconvenience to myself, that she might not be carried off from her husband Titus [?], by traders to the South. Mr G –, who has long lived herewith a black woman, and had a number of children by her, failed [?]. All his property was sold and he was present when his children went off by auction, one here, one there. One of the greatest evils of slavery is that it keeps the whole South in a permanent state of hypocricy [sic]. Could I mount the scaffold for the abolition of slavery I would do it tomorrow.

Not only millions of copies but even adapted to church [?]. The following is from Bent's (English) Literary Advertiser

[Newspaper clipping inserted, dated February 1853, reading: Price 1s, beautifully illustrated with 9 Engravings, and half-bound in cloth, a New Edition of UNCLE TOM'S CABIN, by Mrs. H. B. STOWE.

Adapted expressly for Sabbath Schools, comprising nearly 400 pages, 12mo; with an Address to the Sabbath-School Children of Britain, by Rev. FLETCHER, D.D.; to which is added a beautiful Poem on "The Murdered Slave."]

The theatres have it. It will enter largely into exhibitions of paintings and probably statuary. It will have its music. Every letter I receive from Europe – fr. Germany, France, England – is full of it.

This book is a historic event – I mean certain important public acts and actions and certain trains of thought – either new or old ones invigorated – will date from the appearance of this book. The papers here have the term Uncle-Tomitude, by way of derision.[2]

2 Lieber, Francis. "Uncle Tom: A Review of Mrs. Stowe's Book." No date. Francis Lieber papers. mssLI. Box 4, no. 7. LI496. The Huntington. San Marino, CA.

Bibliography

Primary Literature

A Plea for Authors, and the Rights of Literary Property. By an American (New York: Adlard and Saunders, 1838).

Bluntschli, Johann Casper, "Lieber's Service to Political Science and International Law" in *The Miscellaneous Writings of Francis Lieber. II. Contributions to Political Science*, ed. Daniel C. Gilman (Philadelphia: J. B. Lippincott & Co., 1881), 7–14.

"Buchdruckerzunft" in *Allgemeine deutsche Real-Encyklopädie für die gebildeten Stände* (*Conversations-Lexikon*) (Leipzig: Brockhaus, 1827), 263–267.

"Büchernachdruck" in *Allgemeine deutsche Real-Encyklopädie für die gebildeten Stände* (*Conversations-Lexikon*) (Leipzig: Brockhaus, 1827), 271–273.

Carey, Henry Charles, *Letters on International Copyright* (Philadelphia: Hart, Carey and Hart, 1853).

"Copie" in *Allgemeine deutsche Real-Encyklopädie für die gebildeten Stände* (*Conversations-Lexikon*) (Leipzig: Brockhaus, 1827), 869.

"Copirmaschinen" in *Allgemeine deutsche Real-Encyklopädie für die gebildeten Stände* (*Conversations-Lexikon*) (Leipzig: Brockhaus, 1827), 869–870.

Curtis, George Ticknor, *A Treatise on the Law of Copyright in Books, Dramatic and Musical Compositions, Letters and Other Manuscripts, Engravings and Sculpture, as Enacted and Administered in England and America; with Some Notices of the History of Literary Property* (Boston: Charles C. Little and James Brown, 1847).

Cushing, Luther S, "French Works on Copyright and Patents," *American Jurist and Law Magazine from April 1838 to January 1843*, 22.42 (1839): 225–26.

"Dr. Francis Lieber," *The College Courant*, 11.14 (1872): 160–61.

Drone, Eaton S, *A Treatise on the Law of Property in Intellectual Productions in Great Britain and the United States* (Boston: Little, Brown, and Company, 1879).

"Eigenthum" in *Allgemeine deutsche Real-Encyklopädie für die gebildeten Stände* (*Conversations-Lexikon*) (Leipzig: Brockhaus, 1827), 454.

"Gesetz zum Schutze des Eigenthums an Werken der Wissenschaft und Kunst gegen Nachdruck und Nachbildung. Vom 11. Juni 1837" in *Gesetz-Sammlung für die königlichen preußischen Staaten 1837* (Berlin: Gesetz-Sammlungs-Debits- und Zeitungs-Kontoir, 1838), 165–171.

"Francis Lieber," *The Cap and Gown* 5.1 (1872): 1–3.

Gilman, Daniel C. "Francis Lieber," *The Yale Law Journal* 10.7 (1901): 271–274.

Hitzig, Julius Eduard, *Das königl. preußische Gesetz vom 11. Juni 1837. Zum Schutze des Eigenthums an Werken der Wissenschaft und Kunst gegen Nachdruck und Nachbil-*

 | HTTPS://DOI.ORG/10.1515/9783112239407-010

dung dargestellt in seinem Entstehen und erläutert durch Dr. Julius Eduard Hitzig (Berlin: Ferdinand Dümmler, 1838).

Hurlbut, E. P., *Essays on Human Rights and Their Political Guaranties* (Edinburgh: MacLachlan, Stewart, & Co., 1847).

International Copyright. Meeting of Authors and Publishers (New York: International Copyright Association, 1868).

Journals of the Continental Congress 1774–1789 24.180 (1922).

Lieber, Francis, "Art. I On Political Hermeneutics–Precedents," *The American Jurist and Law Magazine* 18.38 (1838): 282–294.

Lieber, Francis, "Art. III On Political Hermeneutics, or on Political Interpretation and Construction, and Also on Precedents," *The American Jurist and Law Magazine* 18.35 (1837): 37–101.

Lieber, Francis, "Copyright" in *Encyclopædia Americana. A Popular Dictionary of Arts, Sciences, Literature, History, Politics and Biography. Vol. III.*, ed. Francis Lieber et al. (Cornhill: B. B. Mussey & Co., 1830), 527–529.

Lieber, Francis, *Essays on Property and Labor as Connected with Natural Law and the Constitution of Society* (New York: Harper & Brothers, 1841).

Lieber, Francis, *Instructions for the Government of Armies of the United States in the Field, prepared by Francis Lieber, LL.D., Originally Issued As General Orders No. 100, Adjudant General's Office, 1863* (Washington: Government Printing Office, 1898).

Lieber, Francis, *Legal and Political Hermeneutics, Or of Principles of Interpretation and Construction in Law and Politics, with Remarks on Precedents and Authorities* (Boston: Charles C. Little and James Brown, 1839).

Lieber, Francis, "Literary Property" in *Encyclopædia Americana. A Popular Dictionary of Arts, Sciences, Literature, History, Politics and Biography. Vol. VIII.*, ed. Francis Lieber et al. (Philadelphia: Carey and Lea, 1831), 14–16.

Lieber, Francis, *Manual of Political Ethics, Designed Chiefly for the Use of Colleges and Students at Law. Part I* (Boston: Charles C. Little and James Brown, 1838).

Lieber, Francis, *Manual of Political Ethics, Designed Chiefly for the Use of Colleges and Students at Law. Part II* (Boston: Charles C. Little and James Brown, 1839).

Lieber, Francis, *On Civil Liberty and Self-Government. Vol. I.* (Philadelphia: Lippincott, Grambo and Co., 1853).

Lieber, Francis, *On Civil Liberty and Self-Government. Vol. II.* (Philadelphia: Lippincott, Grambo and Co., 1853).

Lieber, Francis, *On International Copyright, In a Letter to the Hon. William C. Preston, Senator of the United States.* (New York: Wiley and Putnam, 1840).

Lieber, Francis, "Property" in *Encyclopædia Americana. A Popular Dictionary of Arts, Sciences, Literature, History, Politics and Biography. Vol. X*, ed. Francis Lieber et al. (Philadelphia: Carey and Lea, 1832), 373.

Lieber, Francis, "Prussian Law of Copyright of 1837." *The Law Reporter* 2.5 (1839): 129–133.

Lieber, Francis, "Speech of Francis Lieber" in *International Copyright. Meeting of Authors and Publishers, at the Rooms of the New York Historical Society, April 9, 1868 and Organization of the International Copyright Association* (New York: International Copyright Association, 1868), 20–24.

Lieber, Francis, *The Life and Letters of Francis Lieber*, ed. Thomas Sergeant Perry (Boston: James R. Osgood and Company, 1882).

Lieber, Francis, *The Miscellaneous Writings of Francis Lieber. I. Reminiscences, Addresses, and Essays*, ed. Daniel C. Gilman (Philadelphia: J. B. Lippincott & Co., 1881).

Lieber, Francis, *The Miscellaneous Writings of Francis Lieber. II. Contributions to Political Science, Including Lectures on the Constitution of the United States and Other Papers*, ed. Daniel C. Gilman (Philadelphia: J. B. Lippincott & Co., 1881).

Lieber, Francis, *The Stranger in America: Comprising Sketches of the Manners, Society, and National Peculiarities of the United States, In a Series of Letters to a Friend in Europe* (London: Richard Bentley, 1835).

"Literatur" in *Allgemeine deutsche Real-Encyklopädie für die gebildeten Stände* (*Conversations-Lexikon*) (Leipzig: Brockhaus, 1827), 615.

Parton, James, "International Copyright," *The Atlantic Monthly* 20 (1867): 430–451.

"Publikations-Patent über den, von der deutschen Bundesversammlung unter dem 9. November d. J. gefaßten Beschluß wegen gleichförmiger Grundsätze zum Schutze des schriftstellerischen und künstlerischen Eigenthums gegen Nachdruck und unbefugte Nachbildung" in *Gesetz-Sammlung für die königlichen preußischen Staaten. 1837* (Berlin: Vereinigtes Gesetz-Sammlungs-Debits- und Zeitungskontoir, 1838), 161–164.

Root, Elihu, and George B. Davis, "Francis Lieber," *Proceedings of the American Society of International Law at Its Annual Meeting* (*1907–1917*) 7 (1913): 8–30.

Thayer, M. R., "Biographical Discourse by Hon. M. R. Thayer" in *The Miscellaneous Writings of Francis Lieber. I. Reminiscences, Addresses, and Essays*, ed. Daniel C. Gilman (Philadelphia: J. B. Lippincott & Co., 1881), 13–44.

Thayer, M. R. *The Life, Character, and Writings of Francis Lieber. A Discourse Delivered before the Historical Society of Pennsylvania, January 13, 1873* (Philadelphia: Collins, 1873).

Van Dyke, Henry, *The National Sin of Literary Piracy* (New York: Charles Scribner's Sons, 1888).

"Verlag, Verlagsrecht, Verleger" in *Allgemeine deutsche Real-Encyklopädie für die gebildeten Stände* (*Conversations-Lexikon*) (Leipzig: Brockhaus, 1827), 668–671.

Secondary Literature

Alexander, Gregory S., and Eduardo M. Peñalver, *An Introduction to Property Theory* (Cambridge: Cambridge UP, 2012).

Andersch, Ulrike, *Die Diskussion über den Büchernachdruck in Deutschland um 1700 bis 1815* (Tübingen: Mohr Siebeck, 2018).

Auderset, Juri, *Transatlantischer Förderalismus* (Berlin/Boston: De Gruyter, 2016).

Baker, Betsy, *Johann Caspar Bluntschli, Francis Lieber und das Modern Völkerrecht 1861–1881* (Baden-Baden: Nomos, 2003).

Baldwin, Peter, *The Copyright Wars. Three Centuries of Trans-Atlantic Battle* (Princeton: Princeton UP, 2014).

Barnes, James J., *Authors, Publishers, and Politicians. The Quest for an Anglo-American Copyright Agreement 1815–1854* (Columbus: Ohio State UP, 1974).

Becker, Peter, "Francis Liebers wissenschaftliche Leistungen in den USA" in *Franz Lieber und die deutsch-amerikanischen Beziehungen im 19. Jahrhundert*, ed. Peter Schäfer and Karl Schmitt (Weimar/Cologne: Böhlau, 1993), 31–44.

Becker, Peter, "Prologue: Lieber's Place in History" in *Francis Lieber and the Culture of the Mind*, ed. Charles R. Mack and Henry H. Lesesne (Columbia: University of South Carolina Press, 2005), 1–10.

Binder, Guyora, "Institutions and Linguistic Conventions: The Pragmatism of Lieber's Legal Hermeneutics," *Cardozo Law Review*, 16.6 (1995): 2169–2189.

Bochner, Stephen, "Introduction" in *The Mediating Person: Bridges between Cultures*, ed. Stephen Bochner (Cambridge: Schenkman Publishing Company, 1981), 3–5.

Bowker, R. R., *Copyright. Its Law and Its Literature* (New York: Sampson Low, Marston, Searle & Rivington, 1886).

Bracha, Oren, "Commentary on George Ticknor Curtis's Treatise on the Law of Copyright (1847)" in *Primary Sources on Copyright (1450–1900)*, ed. Lionel Bently and Martin Kretschmer (Copyrighthistory.org, 2008).

Bracha, Oren, "Commentary on the Copyright Act 1790" in *Primary Sources on Copyright (1450–1900)*, ed. Lionel Bently and Martin Kretschmer (Copyrighthistory.org, 2008).

Bracha, Oren, "Early American Printing Privileges. The Ambivalent Origins of Authors' Copyright in America" in *Privilege and Property. Essays on the History of Copyright*, ed. Ronan Deazley et al. (Cambridge: OpenBook Publishers, 2010), 89–114.

Bracha, Oren, *Owning Ideas. Intellectual Origins of American Intellectual Property, 1790–1909* (Cambridge: Cambridge UP, 2016).

Bracha, Oren, "United States Copyright, 1672–1909" in *Research Handbook on the History of Copyright Law*, ed. Isabella Alexander and H. Tomas Gomez-Arostegui (Cheltenham: Edward Elgar Publishing, 2016), 335–371.

Buinicki, Martin, *Negotiating Copyright: Authorship and the Discourse of Literary Property Rights in Nineteenth-Century America* (London: Routledge, 2006).

Burke, Peter, *A Social History of Knowledge. From Gutenberg to Diderot* (Cambridge: Polity Press, 2000).

Carpenter, R. Charli, "Setting the Advocacy Agenda: Theorizing Issue Emergence and Nonemergence in Transnational Advocacy Networks," *International Studies Quarterly*, 51.1 (2007): 99–120.

Carrington, Paul D., "The Theme of Early American Law Teaching: The Political Ethics of Francis Lieber," *Journal of Legal Education*, 42.3 (1992): 339–398.

Childress, James, "Francis Lieber's Interpretation of the Laws of War: General Orders No. 100 in the Context of His Life and Thought," *The American Journal of Jurisprudence*, 21 (1976): 34–70.

Clair, Colin, *A History of European Printing* (London/New York: Academic Press, 1976).

Cohen, Lara Langer, and Meredith L. McGill, "The Perils of Authorship, Literary Property and Nineteenth-Century American Fiction" in *Oxford History of the Novel in English, Vol 5: The American Novel to 1870*, ed. J. Gerald Kennedy and Leland S. Person (Oxford: Oxford UP, 2014), 195–212.

Curti, Merle, "Francis Lieber and Nationalism," *Huntington Library Quarterly*, 4.3 (1941): 263–292.

Deazley, Ronan, "Commentary on Copyright Amendment Act 1842" in *Primary Sources on Copyright (1450–1900)*, ed. Lionel Bently and Martin Kretschmer (www.copyrighthistory.org, 2008).

Deazley, Ronan, "Commentary on the Statute of Anne," *Primary Sources on Copyright (1450–1900)*, ed. Lionel Bently and Martin Kretschmer (www.copyrighthistory.org, 2008).

Dyer, Brainerd, "Francis Lieber and the American Civil War," *Huntington Library Quarterly*, 2.4 (1939): 449–465.

Eaton, Andrew J., "The American Movement for International Copyright, 1837–60," *The Library Quarterly: Information, Community, Policy*, 15.2 (1945): 95–122.

Eisenstein, Elizabeth, *The Printing Revolution in Early Modern Europe* (Cambridge: Cambridge UP, 2005).

Eskridge, William N. Jr, "Fetch Some Soupmeat," *Cardozo Law Review* 16.6 (1995): 2209–2224.

Farr, James, "Francis Lieber and the Interpretation of American Political Science," *The Journal of Politics*, 52.4 (1990): 1027–49.

Farr, James, "From Moral Philosophy to Political Science: Lieber and the Innovations of Antebellum Political Thought" in *Francis Lieber and the Culture of the Mind*, ed. Charles R. Mack and Henry H. Lesesne (Columbia: University of South Carolina Press, 2005), 113–128.

Farr, James, "The Americanization of Hermeneutics: Francis Lieber's Legal and Political Hermeneutics" in *Legal Hermeneutics: History, Theory, and Practice*, ed. Gregory Leyh (Oakland: University of California Press, 1992), 83–102.

Feather, John, *Publishing, Piracy, and Politics: An Historical Study of Copyright in Britain* (London: Mansell, 1994).

Febvre, Lucien and Henri-Jean Martin, *The Coming of the Book. The Impact of Printing 1450–1800* (London/New York: Verso, 1997).

Finnemore, Martha, and Kathryn Sikkink, "International Norm Dynamics and Political Change," *International Organization* 52.4 (1998): 887–917.

Freidel, Frank, "Francis Lieber, Charles Sumner, and Slavery," *The Journal of Southern History* 9.1 (1943): 75–93.

Freidel, Frank, "Francis Lieber: Transmitter of European Ideas to America," *Bulletin of the John Rylands Library* 38.2 (1956): 342–59.

Freidel, Frank, *Francis Lieber. Nineteenth-Century Liberal* (Baton Rouge: Louisiana State UP, 1948).

Freidel, Frank, "Lieber's Contribution to the International Copyright Movement," *Huntington Library Quarterly* 8.2 (1945): 200–06.

Gadd, Ian, "The Stationers' Company in England before 1710" in *Research Handbook on the History of Copyright Law*, ed. Isabella Alexander and H. Tomás Gómez-Arostegui (Cheltenham: Edward Elgar Publishing, 2016), 81–95.

Gieseke, Ludwig, *Vom Privileg zum Urheberrecht: Die Entwicklung des Urheberrechts in Deutschland bis 1845* (Baden-Baden: Nomos, 1995).

Ginsburg, Jane C., "A Tale of Two Copyrights. Literary Property in Revolutionary France and America," *Tulane Law Review*, 64.5 (1990): 991–1031.

Gross, Robert A., "Building a National Literature: The United States 1800–1890" in *A Companion to the History of the Book*, ed. Simon Eliot and Jonathan Rose (Oxford: Blackwell Publishing, 2008), 315–328.

Haimbaugh, George, "Liebers Bedeutung für die heutige Rechtswissenschaft in den USA" in *Franz Lieber und die deutsch-amerikanischen Beziehungen im 19. Jahrhundert*, ed. Peter Schäfer and Karl Schmitt (Weimar/Cologne: Böhlau, 1993), 73–80.

Harley, Lewis R, *Francis Lieber. His Life and Political Philosophy* (New York: Columbia UP, 1899).

Hartigan, R. S., *Military Rules, Regulations and the Code of War: Francis Lieber and the Certification of Conflict* (London/New York: Routledge, 1983).

Herz, Michael, "Rediscovering Francis Lieber: An Afterword and Introduction," *Cardozo Law Review* 16.6 (1995): 2107–2134.

Hoeflich, M. H., "Transatlantic Friendships & the German Influence on American Law in the First Half of the Nineteenth Century," *The American Journal of Comparative Law* 35.3 (1987): 599–611.

Homestead, Melissa J., *American Women Authors and Literary Property* (Cambridge: Cambridge UP, 2005).

Horenstein, Mike Robert, "The Virtues of Interpretation in a Jural Sociey," *Cardozo Law Review* 16.6 (1995): 2273–2304.

Houtchens, Lawrence, "Charles Dickens and International Copyright," *American Literature*, 13.1 (1941): 18–28.

Hsieh, Wayne Wei-siang, "Francis Lieber, the Laws of War, and the Origins of the Liberal International Order" in *The New Makers of Modern Strategy: From the Ancient World to the Digital Age*, ed. Hal Brans (Princeton: Princeton UP, 2023), 391–414.

Hughes, Justin, "Copyright and Incomplete Historiographies: Of Piracy, Propertization, and Thomas Jefferson," *Southern California Law Review*, 79.5 (2006): 993–1084.

Johns, Adrian, *Piracy. The Intellectual Property Wars from Gutenberg to Gates* (Chicago: University of Chicago Press, 2009).

Joyce, Craig, "Intellectual Property in the United States," *Oxford International Encyclopedia of Legal History* 265 (2009): 1–17.

Kawohl, Friedemann, "Commentary on the Bilateral Treaty between Austria and Sardinia (1840)" in *Primary Sources on Copyright (1450–1900)*, ed. Lionel Bently and Martin Kretschmer (Copyrighthistory.org, 2008).

Keck, Margaret, and Kathryn Sikkink, *Activists Beyond Borders. Advocacy Networks in International Politics* (Ithaca: Cornell UP, 1998).

Keil, Hartmut, "Francis Lieber's Attitudes on Race, Slavery, and Abolition," *Journal of American Ethnic History* 28.1 (2008): 13–33.

Keil, Hartmut, "'That Species of Property': Francis Lieber's Encounter with Slavery and Race" in *Paths Crossing. Essays in German-American Studies*, ed. Cora Lee Kluge (Oxford: Peter Lang, 2011), 55–83.

Kingston, Lindsey M., *Fully Human. Personhood, Citizenship, and Rights* (Oxford: Oxford UP, 2019).

Klippel, Diethelm, "Das Privileg im deutschen Naturrecht des 18. und 19. Jahrhunderts" in *Das Privileg im europäischen Vergleich. Band 1*, ed. Barbara Dölemeyer and Heinz Mohnhaupt (Frankfurt a.M: Klostermann, 1997), 329–346.

Klippel, Diethelm, "Das Privileg in der deutschen Staatsrechtslehre des 19. Jahrhunderts" in *Das Privileg im europäischen Vergleich. Band 2*, ed. Barbara Dölemeyer and Heinz Mohnhaupt (Frankfurt a.M: Klostermann, 1999), 285–308.

Knewitz, Simone, *The Politics of Private Property. Contested Claims to Ownership in U.S. Cultural Discourse* (Lanham: Lexington Books, 2021).

Lessig, Lawrence, "The Limits of Lieber," *Cardozo Law Review*, 16.6 (1995): 2249–2272.

Lokke, Carl L. "The Captured Confederate Records under Francis Lieber," *The American Archivist*, 9.4 (1946): 277–319.

McGill, Meredith L., *American Literature and the Culture of Reprinting, 1834–1853* (Philadelphia: University of Pennsylvania Press, 2003).

McGill, Meredith L., "Copyright and Intellectual Property: The State of the Discipline," *Book History* 16 (2017): 387–427.

Meder, Stephan, "Interpretation und Konstruktion. Zur juristischen Hermeneutik von Francis Lieber (1800–1872)," *JuristenZeitung* 67.11 (2012): 529–38.

Moscati, Laura, "Intellectual Property in the European Legal Context: Tools and Perspectives," *European Business Law Review* 22 (2011): 79–92.

Mueller-Vollmer, Kurt, "German-American Cultural Interaction in the Jacksonian Era: Six Unpublished Letters by Francis Lieber and John Pickering to Wilhelm von Humboldt," *Die Unterrichtspraxis/Teaching German* 31.1 (1998): 1–11.

Nys, Ernest, "Francis Lieber – His Life and His Work: Part I," *The American Journal of International Law* 5.1 (1911): 84–117.

Oliar, Dotan, *The Origins and Meaning of the Intellectual Property Clause* (Cambridge: Berkman Klein Center for Internet and Society at Harvard University, 2005).

Patterson, Lyman Ray, *Copyright in Historical Perspective* (Nashville: Vanderbilt UP, 1968).

Paust, Jordan, "Dr. Francis Lieber and the Lieber Code," *Proceedings of the Annual Meeting (American Society of International Law)* 95 (2001): 112–115.

Phinney, Chester Squire, *Francis Lieber's Influence on American Thought and Some of His Unpublished Letters* (Philadelphia: International Printing Co., 1918).

Preuß, Hugo, *Franz Lieber. Ein Bürger zweier Welten* (Berlin: Verlag von Carl Habel, 1886).

Augustin-Charles Renouard, *Traité Des Droits D'Auteurs, Dans La Littérature, Les Sciences et Les Beaux-Arts. Vol. I.* (Paris: Chez Jules Renouard &c., 1838).

Augustin-Charles Renouard, *Traité Des Droits D'Auteurs, Dans La Littérature, Les Sciences et Les Beaux-Arts. Vol. II.* (Paris: Chez Jules Renouard &c., 1839).

Ricketson, Sam, "The Public International Law of Copyright and Related Rights" in *Research Handbook on the History of Copyright Law*, ed. Isabella Alexander and H. Tomás Gómez-Arostegui (Cheltenham: Edward Elgar Publishing, 2016), 288–312.

Rideau, Frédéric, "Aspects of French Literary Property Developments in the Eighteenth (and Nineteenth) Centuries" in *Research Handbook on the History of Copyright Law*, ed. Isabella Alexander and H. Tomás Gómez-Arostegui (Cheltenham: Edward Elgar Publishing, 2016), 391–422.

Robson, Charles B., "Francis Lieber's Nationalism," *The Journal of Politics* 8.1 (1946): 57–73.

Robson, Charles B., "Francis Lieber's Theories of Society, Government, and Liberty," *The Journal of Politics* 4.2 (1942): 227–249.

Robson, Charles B., "Papers of Francis Lieber," *The Huntington Library Bulletin* 3 (1933): 135–155.

Rose, Mark, *Authors and Owners. The Invention of Copyright* (Cambridge: Harvard UP, 1993).

Rose, Mark, "The Author as Proprietor. Donaldson v. Becket and the Genealogy of Modern Authorship," *Representations* 23 (1988): 51–85.

Rudd, Benjamin W., "Notable Dates in American Copyright 1783–1969," *The Quarterly Journal of the Library of Congress* 28.2 (1971): 137–143.

Rupieper, Hermann J., "Epilogue: The United States and Germany in the Time of Francis Lieber, 1798–1872" in *Francis Lieber and the Culture of the Mind*, ed. Charles R. Mack and Henry H. Lesesne (Columbia: University of South Carolina Press, 2005), 149–163.

Saint-Amour, Paul K., *The Copywrights. Intellectual Property and the Literary Imagination.* (Ithaca, NY: Cornell UP, 2003).

Sallet, Richard, "On Francis Lieber and His Contribution to the Law of Nations Today" in *Recht Im Dienste Der Menschenwürde*, ed. Herbert Kraus (Würzburg: Holzner, 1964), 279–306.

Samson, Steven Alan. "Francis Lieber: Transatlantic Cultural Missionary" in *Francis Lieber and the Culture of the Mind*, ed. Charles R. Mack and Henry H. Lesesne (Columbia: University of South Carolina Press, 2005), 129–142.

Saunders, David. *Authorship and Copyright* (London: Routledge, 1992).

Karl Schmitt, and Peter Schäfer, *Franz Lieber und die deutsch-amerikanischen Beziehungen im 19. Jahrhundert* (Weimar: Böhlau, 1994).

Schmidt-Radefeldt, Roman, *Die Wurzeln des modernen Kriegsvölkerrechts als transatlantisches Erbe. Leben und Werken von Francis Lieber (1798–1872)* (Bremen: Edition Temmen, 2009).

Schneck, Peter, "Narrative Claims: Literary Ownership and the Question of Property" in *Narrative and Law*, ed. Monika Fludernik and Frank L. Schäfer (Würzburg: Ergon Verlag, 2022), 71–92.

Schneck, Peter, "The Hermeneutics of Property: Francis Lieber on Copyright, Labor and Textual Interpretation." *YouTube*, uploaded by rechtalskultur, March 12, 2019, https://www.youtube.com/watch?v=VSeTqYeWF24 (Accessed 11 June 2024).

Schneck, Peter, "Who Owns Uncle Tom's Cabin? Literature as Cultural Property" in *Copyrighting Creativity: Creative Values, Cultural Heritage Institutions and Systems of Intellectual Property*, ed. Helle Porsdam (London: Routledge, 2015), 129–150.

Schnurmann, Claudia, *A Sea of Love. The Atlantic Correspondence of Francis and Mathilde Lieber, 1839–1845* (Leiden: Brill, 2018).

Schnurmann, Claudia, *Brücken aus Papier. Atlantischer Wissenstransfer in dem Briefnetzwerk des deutsch-amerikanischen Ehepaars Francis und Mathilde Lieber, 1827–1872* (Berlin: LIT, 2014).

Schreyer, Alice D., "Copyright and Books in Nineteenth-Century America" in *Getting the Books Out. Papers of the Chicago Conference on the Book in 19th-Century America*, ed. Michael Hackenberg (Washington, DC: Library of Congress, 1987), 121–136.

Seifert, Siegfried, "Der Weimarer Verleger Carl Bertuch und der Wiener Kongreß. Mit einem Anhang bisher ungedruckter Dokumente aus dem Weimarer Goethe- und Schiller-Archiv" in *Beiträge zur Geschichte des Buchwesens im frühen 19. Jahrhundert: Ausgewählte Referate der Tagung des Leipziger Arbeitskreises zur Geschichte des Buchwesens vom 25. bis 27. September 1992*, ed. Mark Lehmstedt (Wiesbaden: Harrassowitz, 1993), 25–52.

Seville, Catherine, *Literary Copyright Reform in Early Victorian England. The Framing of the 1842 Copyright Act* (Cambridge: Cambridge UP, 1999).

Seville, Catherine, "Nineteenth-Century Anglo-US Copyright Relations: The Language of Piracy versus the Moral High Ground" in *Copyright and Piracy: An Interdisciplinary Critique*, ed. Lionel Bently et al. (Cambridge: Cambridge UP, 2010), 19–43.

Siegrist, Hannes, "Geschichte des geistigen Eigentums und der Urheberrechte. Kulturelle Handlungsrechte in der Moderne" in *Wissen und Eigentum. Geschichte, Recht und Ökonomie stoffloser Güter*, ed. Jeanette Hoffmann (Bonn: Bundeszentrale für politische Bildung, 2006), 64–80.

Silbey, Jessica, *Against Progress. Intellectual Property and Fundamental Values in the Internet Age* (Stanford: Stanford UP, 2022).

Slonimsky, Nora, "'To Save the Benefit of the Act of Parliament': Mapping an Early American Copyright," *Law and History Review* 40.4 (2022): 1–30.

Smith, Wilson, "Francis Lieber's Moral Philosophy," *Huntington Library Quarterly* 18.4 (1955): 395–408.

Soifer, Aviam, "Facts, Things, and the Orphans of Girard College: Francis Lieber, Protopragmatist," *Cardozo Law Review* 16.6 (1995): 2305–2319.

Solberg, Thorvald, *Copyright Enactments of the United States 1783–1906* (Washington: Government Printing, 1906).

Solberg, Thorvald, *Copyright in Congress 1789–1904* (Washington: Government Printing, 1905).

Solberg, Thorvald, *International Copyright in the Congress of the United States, 1837–1886* (Boston: Press of Rockwell and Churchill, 1886).

Stokes, Claudia, "Copyrighting American History: International Copyright and the Periodization of the Nineteenth Century" in *American Literature*, ed. Susan Manning and Andrew Taylor (Durham: Duke UP, 2005), 290–317.

Strowel, Alain, "Droit D'auteur and Copyright. Between History and Nature" in *Of Authors and Origins. Essays on Copyright Law*, ed. Brad Sherman and Alain Strowel (Oxford: Clarendon Press, 1994), 235–254.

von Holtzendorff, Franz, *Franz Lieber. Aus den Denkwürdigkeiten eines Deutsch-Amerikaners (1800–1872)* (Stuttgart: W. Spemann, 1885).

Wadle, Elmar, "Der Bundesbeschluß vom 9. November 1837 gegen den Nachdruck. Das Ergebnis einer Kontroverse aus preußischer Sicht," *Zeitschrift der Savigny-Stiftung für Rechtsgeschichte: Germanistische Abteilung* 106.1 (1989): 189–238.

Wadle, Elmar, "Der Langsame Abschied vom Privileg. Das Beispiel des Urheberrechts" in *Das Privileg im Europäischen Vergleich. Band 1*, ed. Barbara Dölemeyer and Heinz Mohnhaupt (Frankfurt am Main: Vittorio Klostermann, 1997), 377–399.

Wadle, Elmar, "Entwicklungsschritte des Geistigen Eigentums in Frankreich und Deutschland. Eine vergleichende Studie" in *Eigentum im internationalen Vergleich (18. – 20. Jahrhundert)*, ed. Hannes Siegrist and David Sugarman (Götting: Vandenhoeck & Ruprecht, 1999), 245–263.

Wadle, Elmar, "Privilegienpraxis in Preußen: Privilegien zum Schutz gegen Nachdruck 1815–1837" in *Das Privileg im Europäischen Vergleich. Band 2*, ed. Barbara Dölemeyer and Heinz Mohnhaupt (Frankfurt am Main: Vittorio Klostermann, 1999), 335–362.

Weiss, Gerhard, "The Americanization of Franz Lieber and the Encyclopedia Americana" in *German Culture in Nineteenth-Century America. Reception, Adaptation, Transformation*, ed. Lynne Tatlock and Matt Erlin (Rochester: Camden House, 2005), 273–288.

Wharton, Robin, "The Regulation of Authorship: Literary Property and the Aesthetics of Resistance" in *Law and Literature*, ed. Kieran Dolin (Cambridge: Cambridge UP, 2018), 291–307.

Wilf, Steven, "Copyright and Social Movements in Late Nineteenth-Century America," *Theoretical Inquiries in Law* 12.123 (2011): 123–160.

Witcombe, Christopher, *Copyright in the Renaissance: Prints and the Privilegio in Sixteenth-Century Venice and Rome* (Leiden: Brill, 2004).

Witt, John Fabian, "A Lost Theory of American Emergency Constitutionalism," *Law and History Review* 36.3 (2018): 551–591.

Witt, John Fabian, *Lincoln's Code: The Laws of War in American History* (New York: Free Press, 2013).

Woodmansee, Martha, "The Genius and the Copyright: Economic and Legal Conditions of the Emergence of the 'Author'," *Eighteenth-Century Studies* 17.4 (1984): 425–448.

Index

 | HTTPS://DOI.ORG/10.1515/9783112239407-011